A RELIGIOUS QUEST OF INDIA INDIAN ISLAM

D1882511

Owing to the antiquity and rarity of this book, certain pages are regrettably absent, and readability is compromised due to the blurring of the original text. If you possess any insights regarding the availability of these missing sections, kindly inform us. Your assistance is crucial in ensuring the completion of this significant work for the benefit of future generations.

A RELIGIOUS QUEST OF INDIA INDIAN ISLAM

A RELIGIOUS HISTORY OF ISLAM IN INDIA

MURRAY T. TITUS

GYAN

Published by

Gyan Publishing House
5, Ansari Road
Daryaganj, New Delhi-110002
Phone: 011-47034999, 9811692060
E-mail: books@gyanbooks.com

Distribution Network
gyanbooks.com
India, USA, Canada, UK, Australia

© Publisher
All rights reserved. No part of this work may be reproduced, stored, adapted, or transmitted in any form or by any means, electronic, mechanical, photocopying, micro-filming, recording or otherwise, or translated in any language, without the prior written permission of the copyright owner and the publisher.

ISBN: 978-93-7447-074-9 (PB)

First Published, 1930

2nd Impression 2026

Printed at: Gyan Press, Delhi.

The book is sold subject to the condition that it shall not, by way of trade or otherwise, be lent, resold, hired out, or otherwise circulated without the prior publisher's written consent.

A RELIGIOUS QUEST OF INDIA INDIAN ISLAM
Author: MURRAY T. TITUS

THE RELIGIOUS QUEST OF INDIA

EDITED BY

E. C. DEWICK, M.A. (CANTAB.)

LITERARY SECRETARY
NATIONAL COUNCIL OF YOUNG MEN'S CHRISTIAN ASSOCIATIONS
INDIA, BURMA AND CEYLON

AND

MURRAY T. TITUS, PH.D., D.D.

MEMBER OF THE ASIATIC SOCIETY OF BENGAL;
MISSIONARY OF THE METHODIST EPISCOPAL CHURCH;
PART-TIME SECRETARY, NATIONAL CHRISTIAN COUNCIL,
INDIA, BURMA AND CEYLON

UNIFORM WITH THIS VOLUME

Already Published

INDIAN THEISM ..	By Nicol Macnicol, M.A., D.Litt. Pp. xvi + 292. Price, 7*s*. 6*d*. net.
THE HEART OF JAINISM	By Mrs. Sinclair Stevenson, M.A., Sc.D. Pp. xxiv + 336. Price, 9*s*. net.
THE TREASURE OF THE MAGI	By James Hope Moulton, D.Litt., D.D., D.C.L. Pp. xv + 273. Price, 8*s*. 6*d*. net.
REDEMPTION: HINDU AND CHRISTIAN	By Sydney Cave, D.D. (Lond.). Pp. xii + 263. Price, 10*s*. 6*d*. net.
THE RELIGIOUS LITERATURE OF INDIA	By J. N. Farquhar, M.A., D.Litt. Pp. xxviii + 451. Price, 18*s*. net.
THE RITES OF THE TWICE-BORN	By Mrs. Sinclair Stevenson, M.A., Sc.D. Pp. xxiv + 474. Price, 21*s*. net.
HINDU ETHICS	By John McKenzie, M.A. Pp. xii + 267. Price, 10s. 6*d*. net.
THE RELIGION OF THE RIGVEDA	By H. D. Griswold, M.A., Ph.D. Pp. xxiv + 392. Price, 12*s*. 6*d*. net.
THE VEDANTA AND MODERN THOUGHT	By W. S. Urquhart, M.A., D.Litt. Pp. xvi + 250. Price, 12*s*. 6*d*. net.

EDITORIAL PREFACE

THE writers of this series of volumes on the variant forms of religious life in India are governed in their work by two impelling motives.

1. They endeavour to work in the sincere and sympathetic spirit of science. They desire to understand the perplexingly involved developments of thought and life in India and dispassionately to estimate their value. They recognize the futility of any such attempt to understand and evaluate, unless it is grounded in a thorough historical study of the phenomena investigated. In recognizing the fact they do no more than share what is common ground among all modern students of religion of any repute. But they also believe that it is necessary to set the practical side of each system in living relation to the beliefs and the literature and that, in this regard, the close and direct contact which they have each had with Indian religious life ought to prove a source of valuable light. For, until a clear understanding has been gained of the practical influence exerted by the habits of worship, by the practice of the ascetic, devotional, or occult discipline, by the social organization and by the family system, the real impact of the faith upon the life of the individual and the community cannot be estimated: and, without the advantage of extended personal intercourse, a trustworthy account of the religious experience of a community can scarcely be achieved by even the most careful student.

2. They seek to set each form of Indian religion by the side of Christianity in such a way that the relationship may stand out clear. Jesus Christ has become to them the light of their seeing and they believe Him destined to be the light of the world. They are persuaded that sooner or later the age-long quest of the Indian spirit of religious truth and power will find in Him at once its goal and a new starting-point, and they will be content if the preparation of this series contributes in the smallest degree to hasten this consummation. If there be readers to whom this motive is unwelcome, they may be reminded that no man

approaches the study of a religion without religious convictions, either positive or negative: for both reader and writer, therefore, it is better that these should be explicitly stated at the outset. Moreover, even a complete lack of sympathy with the motive here acknowledged need not diminish a reader's interest in following an honest and careful attempt to bring the religions of India into comparison with the religion which to-day is their only possible rival, and to which they largely owe their present noticeable and significant revival.

It is possible that to some minds there may seem to be a measure of incompatibility between these two motives. The writers, however, feel otherwise. For them the second motive reinforces the first: for they have found that he who would lead others into a new faith must first of all understand the faith that is theirs already—understand it, moreover, sympathetically, with a mind quick to know not its weakness alone but that in it which has enabled it to survive and has given it its power over the hearts of those who profess it.

The duty of the Editors of the series is limited to seeing that the volumes are in general harmony with the principles here described. Each writer is alone responsible for the opinions expressed in his volume, whether in regard to Indian religions or to Christianity.

THE RELIGIOUS QUEST OF INDIA

INDIAN ISLAM

A RELIGIOUS HISTORY OF ISLAM IN INDIA

BY

MURRAY T. TITUS

PH.D. (HARTFORD, K.S.M.), D.D. (OHIO WESLEYAN)

HUMPHREY MILFORD
OXFORD UNIVERSITY PRESS
LONDON EDINBURGH GLASGOW NEW YORK
TORONTO MELBOURNE CAPETOWN BOMBAY
1930

To

Duncan Black Macdonald

Guide, Counsellor

Friend

PREFACE

Nothing is so fascinating as the study of people. The Muslims of India are particularly interesting, but, strange to say, little has ever been written about them. True, political histories deal with their conquests and political life, but the people themselves and their religion have had scant attention.

The first attempt to write of the Muslims of India was made in 1832, when G. A. Herklots, M.D., surgeon in the Madras Establishment, induced a Deccanī Muslim, Ja'far Sharīf, to write an account of 'The Customs of the Musalmans of India', under the title *Qānūn-i-Islām*, which he translated from the Deccanī Urdū into English, adding some comments of his own. In the same year there appeared *Observations on the Mussulmauns of India*, which were the 'home letters' of an English woman, Mrs. Mīr Ḥasan 'Alī. As the wife of a Shī'ah Muslim of good family, she had long lived in Lucknow, and she intimately describes the life of the high class Muslims of that city. A few years ago both these books were revised and republished by the Oxford University Press.

W. W. Hunter in 1871 published *The Indian Musulmans*, but this deals mostly with the political aspects of the Wahhābī activities. In 1896 Sir T. W. Arnold published *The Preaching of Islam*, in which he devoted a chapter to the peaceful spread of Islam in India. Many scattered articles, too, have appeared from time to time, dealing with various aspects of Islam in India, but nowhere is there to be found any comprehensive treatment of Indian Islam from the standpoint of religious history.

It is with the greatest diffidence, therefore, that this book has been attempted. The ground is so unbroken, the field is so vast, the resources, though often hidden, are so varied and extensive, and one's lack of knowledge in such an enormous field is such a handicap, that it has been difficult to make progress. The manners and customs, as well as the main theological outlines of Islam, have been excluded. The former have been omitted because they may be found in great detail in the revised edition of Herklots' *Islam in India*, so ably prepared by W. Crooke; the latter because there was no need to repeat what had been done before, and so well, by Margoliouth, Sell, and many others. I have, therefore, confined myself to a discussion of the religious history of Islam in India: how it came, how it spread, how it divided and subdivided, how it has been affected by its environment, and how it has reacted to modern conditions.

While it has been my constant aim to treat this subject without bias and prejudice, and I hope not without some measure of success, yet it has been difficult at times to know just what testimony was the most reliable, and what conclusions would be the most just and fair. In all cases the attempt has been made to seek out the facts from purely Islamic sources, or from actual personal experience. If there has been failure to do justice to Indian Islam it has not been because of lack of desire.

Conscious as I am of the inadequate treatment that has been given to many subjects, I earnestly solicit the criticism of readers who are in a better position to correct the deficiencies, which only patient and scholarly investigation can remove.

In the main, the system adopted for the transliteration of Arabic and Persian words is that of the Transliteration Committee of the Tenth International Congress of Orientalists (Geneva, 1894). The chief exception is in the case of the assimilation of the article to the *solar* letters. This was done to guide those who are not familiar with the pronunciation of Arabic; and, as for those who do know, it will be no hindrance to their perceiving what the original was. Some few words, such as current proper names, are spelled according to usage. Usage, likewise, has governed the spelling of others, as *maulvī* rather than *mawlawī*, which would hardly be recognized.

A word of explanation is needed regarding the Appendix. An attempt has been made to make it, in a sense, the focus of the book. I would scarcely have thought of preparing it in its present form but for the fact that the idea occurred to me after seeing the 1925 *Annuaire* of the *Revue du Monde Musulman*, which contains such excellently arranged reference material. Accordingly, I am greatly indebted to M. Louis Massignon, editor of the *Revue*, who has graciously given me permission to translate, use and adapt this material for the Appendix. The statistical tables have been compiled from the *Census of India Report for 1921.*

This book was written as a thesis for the Faculty of the Kennedy School of Missions, of the Hartford Seminary Foundation, Hartford, Conn., U.S.A., in partial fulfilment of the requirement for the degree of Doctor of Philosophy. It is the product of nineteen years' residence in India, but was started only ten years ago, at the request of the late Dr. J. N. Farquhar, without whose constant encouragement, as well as that of my valued friend and teacher, Dr. D. B. Macdonald, it would never have seen the light of day. I am deeply indebted for helpful suggestions to Dr. S. M. Zwemer, Dr. W. G. Shellabear, Sir Thos. W. Arnold, Mr. J. A. Subhan, Miss Marjorie Dimmitt and Mr. Z. A. Hashmie, Deputy Collector. My thanks are due, also, to many others, who have kindly assisted me with their information and criticisms. Last of all thanks are due to my wife, for her tireless patience and labour in assisting in the revision of the manuscript for the press, as well as for her inspiring confidence, which has kept me at the task.

Budaun, India M.T.T.
November, 1929

CONTENTS

TABLE OF ABBREVIATIONS

A.R. ... *Asiatic Researches.*
A.S.B. ... *Asiatic Society of Bengal.*
B.G. ... *The Bombay Gazetteer.*
C.I.R. ... *The Census of India Report.*
E.D. ... Elliot, Sir H. M., and Dowson, J.: *The History of India as Told by Its Own Historians*, 8 vols., London, 1867–77.
G.T.C.P. Rose, H. A.: *A Glossary of the Tribes and Castes of the Punjab and North-West Frontier Province.*
I.G. ... *The Imperial Gazetteer of India.*
J.A.S.B. *The Journal of the Asiatic Society of Bengal.*
J.R.A.S. *The Journal of the Royal Asiatic Society.*
M.W. ... *The Moslem World.*
P.R.F.L. Crooke, W.: *Popular Religion and Folklore of Northern India.*
R.M.M. *Revue du Monde Musulman.*
T.C.B. ... *Tribes and Castes of Bengal.*
T.R.A.S. *Transactions of the Royal Asiatic Society.*

CHAPTER I

THE RELIGIOUS OBJECTIVE OF THE MUSLIM CONQUERORS

INDIA, so commonly described as the land of the Vedas and the home of the Hindus, is also the Motherland of the largest Muslim population found in any single country. Of the total of two hundred and forty million Muslims in the world, nearly seventy millions, or every fourth one, belongs to India. Only by comparison with other nations can these enormous figures be appreciated. In Bengal, for example, where every second person is a Muslim, this single province has a larger population of Muslims than all Arabia, Turkey, and Persia combined. The Punjab has almost as many Muslims as the land of Egypt; and, besides these two outstanding examples, there are at least eight other provinces and states that have Muslim populations ranging anywhere from a million to six and a half millions.

Another feature of the Indian Muslim population which attracts attention is its *diaspora*, or dispersion far beyond the borders of the Indian peninsula. This situation, which is a matter of far-reaching importance, has arisen almost entirely since the close of the eighteenth century. Indian Muslims are to be found in East Africa, South Africa, Madagascar, Mauritius, Argentina, Brazil, Guiana, Trinidad, the West Indies, the United States, Australia, Berlin, London, and Paris. In each country or centre that has been mentioned, there are important groups actively engaged in nationalistic, communal, and religious propaganda. Indian Muslims to-day lead the Muslims of the world in their zeal and practical endeavour for the spread of their faith.

As we contemplate this great community of people, large enough in itself to be a nation with independent existence, and consider its wide distribution, stretching across more than two thousand miles from Baluchistan to Assam, and from Kashmir to the very southern tip of the peninsula, there arises before us a multitude of questions which press for an answer. How did Islam enter India? What were the motives of the conquerors? Was Islam always spread by the sword? Why are there so many sects and divisions among the Muslims of India? How are they organized, and what contribution have they made to the social and religious life of the country? What has been the effect of the Hindu environment? What movements have arisen to modify the religious and social life under the pressure of modern conditions, and what effect does the tumult in the Muslim world have upon these Indian masses? In short, what is the history of the religious quest of the Muslim people of India?

Others have told of the military and political achievements, and the glories of the Mughul Empire. Still others have described the genius of the Muslim poets, artists, and builders. The manners and customs and, to some extent, the religious beliefs of the various sects have already been described. The object of this book is different. It is an attempt to consider Islam in India from the standpoint of its religious mission, the manner of its spread, the means by which its teachings were disseminated, and its institutions established. The conquests of armies, the courts of kings and emperors, arts and commerce will be touched upon only as they are laid under tribute to serve the end in view. The task is an enormous one, and the writer is conscious of its exacting requirements, but he may at least be able to blaze a trail, which can be followed by other investigators, or suggest an outline that will stimulate further research in a field of unbounded interest.

India's Open Doors

India, with its heart-shaped peninsula stretching south into the Indian Ocean, is compassed by two great natural barriers, the mountains and the sea. But these could not serve to keep her completely isolated from the rest of the world, even in ancient times. There were gateways through the towering Himalayas, and the 'Black Water' could be crossed. Long before the coming of the Muḥammadan invader, Aryan hordes from Central Asia had poured through the Khyber Pass and conquered the country, and in turn had been assimilated by it. When the Muslim armies of 'Umar and 'Uthmān were spreading Islam in the seventh century A.D. toward the north, west, and east, and were pressing ever nearer and nearer to the borders of Sind, they would, no doubt, have made good their entrance into India at that time, had it not been for these difficult barriers.

There are three doors by which an invader can enter India. First, there is the sea. But in these early times kings did not venture to send their armies across the waters. The only Muslim invaders who did come by this open door were of the peaceful sort, Arab merchants from Ḥaḍramawt and Iraq.

Secondly, there is the land entrance, which leads from Mesopotamia and South Persia through Baluchistan, south of the mountains of Makrān into Sind. The dry and desert character of this route prevented its being used, and only once did the Arab armies succeed in effecting a successful entry by it into India.

The third entrance is through the Khyber Pass on the north-west frontier, through which, from the earliest times, wave upon wave of humanity has passed down out of the mountain heights and fastnesses of Central Asia to the ever-alluring plains of Hindustan. This door has always been open to any invader who has had the genius and daring to lead his army through it. By this route the Turk, Mongol, and Afg͟han forces of Islam were led into India. These were destined to found an empire not only of kings and rulers, who dwelt in crumbling forts and palaces, but, more important still for the history of India, an empire of the heart reared upon the foundations of a new religious faith, whose ruler dwells in temples not made with hands. Through all three of these doors the Muslims entered: the warrior and trader, the learned and the pious, the Arab, Persian, Turk, and Mongol—all of them missionaries of the Crescent for the establishment of the faith of Islam in the ancient country of the Hindu.

Early Attempts at Invasion

The western coast of India had been the object of plunder by piratical Arab expeditions from earliest times. Although the historians tell us that in the caliphate of 'Umar (A.D. 634–644) expeditions were sent to the towns on this coast, yet there is nothing to indicate that they had any religious significance.[1]

[1] Al-Balād͟hurī, *Futūḥ-ul-Buldān*, tr. F. C. Murgotten, 432.

The first recorded appearance of Muslim arms in India beyond the coast seems to have been in the year A.D. 664, within thirty-two years of the Prophet's death. This was immediately following the invasion of Afghānistān, the capture of Kābul, and the reported conversion of twelve thousand persons in that region. Though the forces led by General al-Muḥallab at that time evidently penetrated as far as Multan, east of the Indus River, and although he carried away many captives to become slaves of Arab masters, it does not appear that he made any attempt either to subdue the country he entered, or to establish the new religion of the conquering Arabian nation.[1]

THE ARAB CONQUEST OF SIND

The history of Islam in India properly begins in the year A.D. 711, when it was introduced into Sind by the Arabian general, 'Imād-ud-dīn Muḥammad bin Qāsim. He led thither an expedition, which was sent by Ḥajjāj bin Yūsuf, governor of Baṣrah.[2] From that time Sind was never without Muslim influence; and the fact that its ancient faith has been so largely supplanted by the faith of Islam that seventy-three per cent of the population is Muslim, is ample testimony to the unremitting zeal of the peaceful as well as the militant missionaries of the Crescent. But this widespread transformation was not the work of a short time. There was a period of suspended military operations for more than two and a half centuries, during which time Muslim conquerors did not trouble themselves about India. When at last a new commander of the armies of the Faithful appeared in India in A.D. 1001, it was not an Arab successor to Muḥammad bin Qāsim, but a Turk, Maḥmūd of Ghaznī, who once more entered upon the task of the Muslim conquest of India.

The interesting thing at this point is the failure of the Arab conquest. Why did the expansionist Umayyad government at Damascus fail to follow up this advance, and carry it into the heart of the country, as had been done in the case of Persia and Afghānistān? Further, why was Sind ultimately abandoned as an Arabian province after the fall of the Umayyad dynasty? This seems very extraordinary considering the zeal and indomitable

[1] *Ibid.*, 432. [2] *Ibid.*, 436.

energy which characterized the spread of Islam throughout so many countries in the period of its early history. There were, however, certain internal developments taking place in the caliphate that undoubtedly affected the policy of expansion and made it all but impossible to continue to hold such a distant and inaccesible province. The historian, Elphinstone, presents these considerations, together with certain local difficulties, with such convincing clearness that I cannot do better than repeat them:

> In India there is a powerful priesthood, closely connected with the government, and deeply revered by their countrymen; and a religion interwoven with the laws and manners of the people, which exercised an irresistible influence over their very thoughts. To this was joined a horror of change and a passive sort of courage, which is perhaps the best suited to allow time for an impetuous attack to spend its force. Even the divisions of the Hindus were in their favour: the downfall of one rājā only removed a rival prince who was next behind; and the invader diminished his numbers, and got further from his resources, without being able to strike a blow which might bring his undertaking to a conclusion.
>
> However these considerations may have weighed with the early invaders, they deserve the greatest attention from the inquirer, for it is principally to them that we must ascribe the slow progress of the Muḥammadan religion in India and the comparatively mild and tolerant form which it assumed in that country.
>
> . . . there were other causes which tended to delay the progress of the Muḥammadans. The spirit of their government was gradually altered. Their chiefs, from fanatical missionaries, became politic sovereigns, more intent on the aggrandizement of their families than the propagation of their faith; and by the same degrees they altered from rude soldiers to magnificent and luxurious princes, who had other occupations besides war, and other pleasures as attractive as those of victory. Omar set out to his army at Jerusalem with his arms and provisions on the same camel with himself; and Othman extinguished his lamp when he had finished the labours of the day, that the public oil might not be expended on his enjoyments. Al-Mahdī, within a century from the last named caliph, loaded 500 camels with ice and snow; and the profusion of one day of the 'Abbāsides would have defrayed all the expenses of the first four caliphs. The translation of the Greek philosophers by al-Ma'mūn was an equally wide departure from the spirit which led to the story of the destruction of the library at Alexandria by Omar.[1]

These are the reasons assigned for the sudden termination of the Arab conquests in the east. It was left for other nations to

[1] Elphinstone, *History of India*, 313.

secure for Islam a permanent foothold in India, which has resulted in giving it the largest Muslim population of any country in the world.

Limited Success of All Conquests

From the time that Maḥmūd of G͟haznī led his hosts out of the mountain fastnesses of Afg͟hānistān down to the plains of India for trading, plunder, and slaughter of infidels, there was a rapid succession of invasions, conquests, and dynasties down to the middle of the nineteenth century. These all contributed to the widespread establishment of Islam in India. Maḥmūd in twelve or more successive raids between A.D. 1001 and 1027 ravaged and plundered the country as far as Gujarāt in western India, and as far as Kanauj to the east. But his only permanent settlement was at Lahore, where he left a governor, who administered the outlying province as best he could.

After Maḥmūd and his dynasty, the political power of Islam was extended far and wide. Following the occupation of Sind, Hindustan, Rajputana, Gujarāt, and Bundelkhand, the territories of Bihar and Bengal were the next to come under the influence of Islam, in the year A.D. 1202. This new conquest was made by the Muslim army under Muḥammad Bak͟htyār K͟haljī. By the beginning of the fourteenth century the Deccan had been invaded by 'Alā-ud-Dīn; and during the reigns of the Mug͟hul emperors (A.D. 1556–1707), from Akbar to Aurangzīb, the Muslim empire and influence attained its greatest extent and importance in the history of India.

When Maḥmūd entered the country, at the beginning of the eleventh century, Islam had scarcely been heard of beyond the confines of Sind, or beyond the western coast, where Muslim traders were wont to go. But during the seven centuries that elapsed between his coming and the death of Aurangzīb, the Muslim empire had been flung across India from Quetta to the mouths of the Hughlī, and from Ceylon to the snows of Kashmir, while the hearts of men had been so seeded down with the faith of Islam that India was henceforth destined to occupy a position of unique importance among the Muslim countries of the world.

Nevertheless, so far as the conversion of India as a whole is concerned, Islam signally failed. In no other country save China where her arms and missionaries have gone has she accomplished so little in proportion to the total population. India may have more Muslims than any other country, but India is not a Muslim country. In other countries, Egypt, North Africa, Asia Minor, Persia, Central Asia, which were overrun so completely in the early centuries of Muslim conquest, the victory of the Muslim faith was complete. Not so in India. In those countries, too, the conquest was made complete in a comparatively short space of time; but India put up a stubborn resistance to the Muslim propaganda even at the point of the sword, and all but successfully withstood the storm.

Even in the palmiest days of the Mughul emperors, and during the time of the empire's greatest extent under Aurangzīb, the south of India never owed any but the most nominal allegiance to Muslim political control; and but few of the people in central and south India ever became converted to the Muslim faith. The largest Muslim state in India, Hyderābād, in the Deccan, has only ten per cent of its population made up of Muslims, while these are found chiefly in the cities, and are largely of foreign origin. In central India only four per cent of the population is Muslim; and in the Madras Presidency only six per cent. Even in Rajputana we find a Muslim population of only nine per cent, although it is so near the imperial city of Delhi and the largely Muslim areas of Sind and the Punjab, while its chief city, Ajmīr, has been for centuries a renowned centre of Muslim activity, and the home and burial place of one of the most honoured of Muslim saints.[1] The United Provinces, Bihar and Orissa tell a similar tale of failure to overcome the solid opposition of the Hindu ranks. In the former only fourteen per cent of the inhabitants are of the Muslim faith, and in the latter province they number only ten per cent. Islam predominates only in the North-Western Provinces, in Sind and in eastern Bengal. By far the greater part of India is solidly Hindu, in spite of the centuries of Muslim rule and invasion. The only conclusion, therefore, that one can reach as to why the attempt to Islamize India was thus only partially successful is that the Hindus were so well organized in their social and religious life under the domination of

[1] See p. 118.

priests and caste that comparatively little could be effected toward the overthrow of their religion. Had they been as well organized in their political affairs, and had there been no outcaste groups to welcome Islam as a release from social bondage, it is safe to say that even a partial victory for Islam would not have been so easily won in the land of the Hindu.

ATTITUDE OF THE CALIPHS TO THE INVASION OF INDIA

That the early caliphs had their eyes fixed on India as a legitimate object of invasion, there can be no doubt. In fact, they considered such an invasion a solemn religious duty. The land, they knew, was under the sway of Hinduism and Buddhism, and war with such infidels and polytheists seemed a peculiarly urgent matter.

Apparently the only thing that kept the Caliph 'Umar from making such an invasion was the fact that the one feasible route for conveying troops to India was by sea, and 'Umar, having great dread of naval expeditions, forbade such an attempt being made. It is said that when ath-Thaqafī was governor of Oman he sent an army to Thāna, near Bombay, in the year A.D. 637. When the army returned safely, he wrote to the Caliph 'Umar informing him of this expedition. The caliph sent back the following reply, expressing his great disapproval of this conduct: 'O brother Thaqīf, thou hast put a worm on the wood. By Allāh, I swear that if they (the army) had been smitten, I would exact from thy tribe a like number.'[1] According to al-Balādhurī, 'Uthmān was the first caliph who planned to invade India. He went so far as to order an explorer to be sent to the frontiers of Sind by the southern land-route across the desert, in order to spy out the land and bring back information. Ḥākim bin Jabala al-'Abdī was sent. On his return the caliph asked him about the country. He replied: 'Water is scarce, the fruits are poor, and the robbers are bold; if few troops are sent they will be slain, if many, they will starve.' So we are told that because of this unfavourable report the caliph 'abstained from sending any expedition there'.[2]

It was not until the caliphate of the Umayyad Walīd that these early designs for the extension of Muslim power to India

[1] Al-Balādhurī, op. cit., 432. [2] *Ibid.*, 432.

were seriously considered. In the early part of the eighth century,[1] and only seventy-nine years after the Prophet's death, Ḥajjāj bin Yūsuf, the governor of Baṣrah, at the head of the Persian Gulf, was able, through the successful generalship of his nephew, Muḥammad b. Qāsim, to effect an occupation of Sind by the armies of Islam. This was the first step in the long series of Muslim conquests, which resulted in giving the Muslim religion a place second only to Hinduism in importance among the religions of India.

In considering the invasions of India it is well to have in mind the Muslim canon law in respect to invasions of non-Muslim countries. Behind them all was a religious as well as a political motive. Early in the development of Islam, *jihād* (holy war) was regarded as a religious duty of Muslim rulers. If practicable, they should fight until the whole world was under the rule of Islam. But if such continual conquest against infidels should be an impossibility, then the requirement of the law would be fulfilled if the sovereign made, or prepared to make, an expedition once a year. This was the canonical position of the early centuries, and one that strictly orthodox Muslims hold even to this day. In addition to the fanatical hatred of idolaters and polytheists which such doctrine so successfully produced, there was the desire for booty: gold, silver, precious gems, and slaves. All these the invaders knew such conquests would yield, since the princes of India were known to be fabulously rich.

With these considerations in mind, let us examine the invasion of Sind in order to discover and set clearly before us the religious motives underlying the undertaking.

Ḥajjāj's Object in Invading Sind

One historian informs us that the reason Ḥajjāj invaded Sind was because an Arab ship had been seized at Debul, one of the seaport towns of that country, and on Rājā Dāhir's refusing to make restitution the governor of Baṣrah decided to send a punitive expedition to bring him to terms.[2] However, judging from the correspondence that took place between Ḥajjāj and Muḥammad, after the latter had reached Sind, it would appear that there had all

[1] See p. 4. [2] Al-Balāḏhurī, op. cit., 436.

along been other reasons as well that induced the invasion; and that the presumptuous act of Rājā Dāhir, in refusing to make amends for the captured Arab ship, was only one among other considerations in the mind of the Baṣrah governor.

In an exchange of dispatches between the leader of the expeditionary force and the governor of Baṣrah, quoted by the author of the Chach-nāmah,[1] it becomes clear that there had been an understanding between Ḥajjāj and Muḥammad relative to the use of the expedition for the purpose of striking a blow at idolatry and polytheism, and of establishing Islam. In one of his dispatches Muḥammad is quoted as saying:

> The nephew of Rājā Dāhir, his warriors and principal officers have been dispatched, and the infidels converted to Islam or destroyed. Instead of idol-temples, mosques and other places of worship have been erected, the *k͟hutbah*[2] is read, the call to prayers is raised, so that devotions are performed at stated hours. The *takbīr* and praise to the Almighty God are offered every morning and evening.[3]

After receiving the above dispatch, which had been forwarded *with the head of the Rājā*, Ḥajjāj sent the following reply to his general:

> Except that you give protection to all, great and small alike, make no difference between enemy and friend. God says, 'Give no quarter to infidels, but cut their throats. Then know that this is the command of the great God. You should not be too ready to grant protection, because it will prolong your work. After this give no quarter to any enemy except those who are of rank.'[4]

Religious Objectives of Later Conquerors and Rulers

At the later periods, too, the religious motive of the invasions was well marked, at any rate up to the time of Bābur's coming in A.D. 1526. And even though, as in the case of Maḥmūd of G͟haznī, the desire for acquisition of some of the fabulous wealth of Hind seems to have amounted almost to a passion, yet the desire to establish Muslim rule in India was seldom if ever dissociated in the mind of the invader from the necessity of establishing the

[1] A history of Sind written in the early part of the eighth century A.D.
[2] The *k͟hutbah* is the Friday sermon preached in the mosque.
[3] *Chach-nāmah*, E.D., I, 164. [4] *Ibid.*, 173.

religion of Islam, and warring against the infidels. Of course this was to be expected, since, from the earliest times, religious domination was regarded as a function of the Muslim State, or conversely, political domination as one of the functions of the 'Church'.

Even Maḥmūd looked upon his numerous invasions of India as the waging of a holy war, though he did not seem to be as anxious to set up a Muslim government in the land as to harass the 'infidels', and secure as much booty from them as possible. Al-'Utbī, the historian of Maḥmūd, makes clear the religious objects of these raids in India.

> 'He demolished idol temples and established Islam. He captured . . . cities, killed the polluted wretches, destroying the idolatrous, and gratifying Muslims.' He then returned home and 'promulgated accounts of the victories obtained for Islam . . . and vowed that every year he would undertake a holy war against Hind'.[1]

Al-'Utbī shows also, in the remarks he makes on the success of the battle of Waihind, how Maḥmūd's contemporaries viewed his expeditions and how they rejoiced because of the glorious victories that were won for Islam. He writes:

> The face of Islam was made resplendent by his exertions, the teeth of the true faith displayed themselves in their laughter, the breasts of religion were expanded, and the back of idolatry was broken.[2]

Muḥammad Gh̲ūrī in his conquests, almost two centuries after the famous Maḥmūd, still shows the same holy zeal in propagating his religion. Ḥasan Niẓāmī says, 'He purged by his sword the land of Hind from the filth of infidelity and vice, and freed the whole of that country from the thorn of God-plurality and the impurity of idol-worship, and by his royal vigour and intrepidity left not one temple standing'.[3]

Iltutmish (A.D. 1210–1236) was likewise enthusiastic in his attempts to put Islam on a firm basis in his domain. Contemporary testimony to this fact is still found over the main arch leading into the Arhāī-Din-kā-Jhoṇprā at Ajmīr.[4] This clearly sets forth the conception of the early sultans of Delhi as to their mission to defend and spread the religion of Islam. The

[1] *Ta'rīkh̲-i-Yamīnī*, E.D., II, 22. [2] *Ibid.*, 28.

[3] *Tāj-ul-Ma'āt̲hir*, E.D., II, 217.

[4] A mosque built from the spoils of ornate Hindu and Jain temples.

inscription carved in imperishable stone in Arabic as translated by Horovitz reads as follows:

This building was ordered by the Sultan, the high, the just, the great, the most exalted Shahanshah, the Lord of the necks of the people, the master of the kings of the Turks and Persians, the Shadow of God in the world, Shams al-Dunya wa al-Din, the help of Islam, and the Muslims, the crown of the kings and Sultans, the subduer of the unbelievers and the heretics, the subjugator of the evil-doers and the polytheists, the defender of Islam, the grandeur of the victorious government and the shining religion . . . Abu al-Muzaffar Iltutmish, the helper of the Caliph of God, the defender of the Prince of the Faithful.[1]

During the reign of 'Alā-ud-Dīn (1296–1316), Amīr Khusrū records in his *Ta'rīkh-i-'Alā'ī* that Mālik Kāfūr, during his invasion of south India, explained to the Hindu Rai of Dhur Samund 'that he was sent with the object of converting him to Islam, or of making him a *dhimmī*[2] and subject to the poll-tax, or of slaying him if neither of these terms were assented to'. But, we are told, 'later (the Rai) prostrated himself to the earth and rubbed the forehead of subjection on the ground when he saw resistance to the splendour of the sword of Islām over his head was useless.'[3]

Amīr Khusrū, recognized still as the foremost Muslim poet that India has ever produced, thus sings the praises of his contemporary 'Alā-ud-Dīn, and such tributes, even at the beginning of the fourteenth century, show no variation whatever from those bestowed on the earliest leaders of Muslim armies: ''Alā-ud-Dīn . . . who has been honoured by the chief of the 'Abbāsids, has destroyed the country of the sun-worshippers. When the arm of his fortune was raised, he became ruler of Hindustan. When he advanced from the capital of Karrā[4] the Hindus in alarm descended into the earth like ants. He departed towards the garden of Bihar to dye that soil with blood red as a tulip. He cleared the road to Ujjain of vile wretches, and created consternation in Bhilsan. When he effected his conquests in that country he drew out of the river the idols which had been concealed in it;' and at Deogīr, 'he destroyed the temples and erected pulpits and arches for mosques'.[5]

[1] J. Horovitz, *Epigraphia Indo-Moslemica*, 30. [2] See p. 27 f.
[3] Amīr Khusrū, E.D., III, 89.
[4] A town on the Jumnā River near Allahabad.
[5] Amīr Khusrū, E.D., III, 543.

The sultans were no doubt actuated by what they believed to be the highest motives. They were under a divine commission to establish good government, and put down practices that were contrary to the religion of Islam. In the *Futūḥāt-i-Fīrūz Shāhī*[1] we see the picture of a ruler who believed he was obeying the dictates of his conscience and the commands of God, and was living up to the highest ideals he knew. The pious Sultan himself writes:

> Thanks be to the merciful creator who gave His impulse for the maintenance of the laws of His religion, for the repression of heresy, the prevention of crime, and the prohibition of things forbidden. . . . First, I would praise Him because when irreligion and sins opposed to the Law prevailed in Hindustan, and men's habits and dispositions were inclined towards them and were averse to the restraints of religion, He inspired me, His humble servant, with an earnest desire to repress irreligion and wickedness, so that I was able to labour diligently until with His blessing the vanities of the world and the things repugnant to religion were set aside and the true was distinguished from the false.[2]

But the ruler was not alone in feeling the need for carrying out the obligations of the faith, and waging war against the 'infidels' and 'polytheists', he was faithfully supported by the religious leaders of his time. In fact, it may be assumed that the Muslim people were all of one mind in respect to the aims and methods employed in the propagation of their faith. This is shown with utter frankness, even as late as the time of the reign of Sher Shah. Although he was constructive and liberal in his governmental policies to a degree before unknown among the Muslim rulers of India, yet we are told that one of his learned associates, Shay<u>kh</u> Niẓām, boldly recommended a *jihād*. 'For', said he, 'there is nothing equal to a religious war against infidels. If you be slain you become a martyr, and if you live you become a *<u>gh</u>āzī* (hero).'[3]

However, times had begun to change, and, although the learned might declare that a holy war was desirable on religious grounds, yet the emperors of Hindustan were more and more coming to realize that it could no longer be defended on political grounds. In place of the policy of antagonism, there was steadily growing up in the government a conviction that Muslims and Hindus must

[1] *Memoirs*, Fīrūz Shāh Tu<u>gh</u>luq, A.D. 1351–1388.

[2] Fīrūz Shāh, E.D., III, 374 f.

[3] 'Abbās <u>Kh</u>āṇ, E.D., IV, 408.

come into closer co-operation, and that there should be less bitterness and arrogance shown by the Muslim rulers to their Hindu subjects. During the later period of Muslim domination in India, between the years A.D. 1526 and 1800, only once, and then for a period of only half a century, was there any marked recurrence of the fanatical religious enthusiasm that characterized the early centuries of Muslim invasion and occupation. This was during the reign of Aurangzīb, from A.D. 1659 to 1707.[1]

[1] It should be pointed out that the views expressed in this chapter do not find favour with some Muslims. There is a liberal school of thought which repudiates the usual interpretation placed upon the term *jihād*. It maintains that Islam is a religion of peace, that the word *jihād* has been perverted from its true meaning by interpreting it as 'holy war', whereas it means only 'striving' or 'making an effort' to spread the faith. Further, those who hold this view insist that the real objectives of the conquerors of India were not religious at all, but political. However, it must not be forgotten that the very essence of Islam is that it is both a religion and a system of government —a church-state. In Islam politics is not *merely* politics, and religion is not *merely* religion. Consequently, if one is to seek for an adequate interpretation of the political activities and military conquests of Muslim rulers, attention must always be paid to this fundamental conception of the Islamic State. While the religious motives and objectives of the conquerors and rulers should not be over-emphasized, on the other hand they must not be ignored altogether, nor lightly set aside by the judgment that such men were inspired by considerations of conquest and political power alone. While realizing the difficulties involved, I have nevertheless sought to hold the balance as evenly as possible between these two points of view.

CHAPTER II

THE METHODS OF THE CONQUERORS

It is beyond dispute that one of the characteristics of the Muslim conquest of India was that of a militant propaganda, with the purpose of establishing not only Muslim government over the people, but the Muslim faith as well. This was all a part of the system and policy of that day. It never occurred to the invaders that Islam could be established as a religion independent of the existence of the Muslim State, which is being proclaimed as a possibility in the more advanced circles of Muslim leadership to-day. Nevertheless, there were traders, religious devotees and preachers who came to realize the necessity, if not the ultimate desirability, of establishing the religion of Islam in India entirely apart from the assistance of the Islamic State. It will be necessary, therefore, to consider the religious history of Islam in India from these two points of view. However, it must always be remembered, that whatever may have been the successes of the peaceful penetration methods of preachers and traders in adding to the Muslim population, yet the prestige and political influence and real power that exists in Indian Islam to-day is due rather to the influence and control of the ruling races that invaded the land. They gave protection to the learned men from Persia and Arabia; they were the patrons of Muslim sciences and arts, and it was they who gave Islam a place of importance in the land. Even to-day the descendants of these ancient ruling chiefs and their associates at the royal court and in the army are among the leaders of the Muslim community of India. Bābur, Akbar, Aurangzīb, and their courtiers are gone, and the Muslim no longer rules in the land; but through their descendants they largely direct the destinies of the nearly seventy million Muslims in India.

Intolerance

Throughout the whole period of Muslim contact with India the attitude of Muslim rulers to their Hindu subjects and their religion has been very largely one of intolerance or indifference. True there was a period of conciliation and appreciation under Akbar, but this period was short-lived and Akbar was generally regarded by Muslims as a heretic. Periods of tolerance seem to have been associated in the minds of the Hindus with weakness and inability to rule. As a result, whenever the opportunity came they rose in rebellion, and upset what had been accomplished by a former strict and capable ruler. The early Muslim conquerors and rulers seldom took a sympathetic interest in their Hindu subjects from a purely humanitarian or cultural point of view. Their whole object, apparently, was the religious one of either converting the infidels, or of 'sending them to hell with the sword'. If they submitted at all, they were subjected to looting and the imposition of the *jizyah* (poll-tax). In order, therefore, that we may understand what the conditions were which the conquering Muslim armies imposed on the conquered, we shall take only the testimony of Muslim historians, who deal with the events and policies of those who sought to establish the Muslim religion in India, through the agency of political and military power.

It will clarify the issue somewhat if we consider the ruling ideas of the leaders of Islam in their broadest aspects. The whole period of Muslim contact with India falls into two divisions. The first ends roughly with the close of the fifteenth century; the second begins with the founding of the Mughul Empire by Bābur at the beginning of the sixteenth century. During the first period, covering eight centuries, there seems to have existed in the minds of the invaders, their resident viceroys, and the independent kings the hope that they would be able as thoroughly to Islamize the country as the armies of the caliphs had been able to do in Persia and western lands.

With the coming of Bābur and the founding of the Mughul Empire this hope seems to have been very largely set aside for the more practical and reasonable policy of government for the good of all the people. The intolerant spirit, begotten of the older Arab influence, gave place to a more kindly spirit of tolerance and appreciation of the indomitable Hindus, the people of the country. In this period even the Afghan, Sher Shāh (A.D. 1539–1545), in his interregnum, showed that a new spirit had been awakened; and Akbar carried it to the fullest extent of realization. Aurangzīb alone, of all the rulers of this second period, showed any determination to revive the hope of the earlier period for the Islamization of India, but even he was forced to recognize the limitations of the task.

MILITANT METHODS

A spirit of intolerance and wild fanatical zeal marked the conquerors who came bearing the message of Islam during the first eight centuries of Muslim contact with India (A.D. 711–1526). The Arab invasion under Muḥammad bin Qāsim, in the year A.D. 711, was ostensibly a punitive expedition only.[1] It was entirely successful from the military point of view, and, having defeated the forces of the Rājā and taken possession of the citadel of Debul,[2] he next turned his attention to the religious problem that confronted him.

Muḥammad was the product of his age. He was filled with the zeal and enthusiasm that marked the early missionaries of the Muslim 'church militant'. Scarce twenty years of age, he had been born while the conquests of the Crescent were moving steadily east, west and north. All through the world in which he moved men talked of these brilliant victories for Allāh. Muslim dominion had been extended from the heart of Arabia to the Atlantic shores of North Africa on the west and to the Hindu Kush on the east. Behind this mighty sweep of armies lay the inspiring magic of the word *jihād*. The underlying philosophy of it, the divine sanction for it, and rules for the treatment of infidels all seem cruelly intolerant to us to-day; but they were considered just and reasonable by those who made them their philosophy and way of life.

As we saw in the last chapter, canon law in Islam holds that it is incumbent on a Muslim ruler to fight to extend the rule of Islam until the whole world shall have been brought under its sway. The world is divided into two camps, *dār-ul-Islām* (abode of Islam), and *dār-ul-Ḥarb* (abode of War). All countries come under one category or the other. Technically, it is the duty of the Muslim ruler, who is capable of doing so, to transform *dār-ul-*

[1] See p. 9. [2] An ancient seaport of Sind at the mouth of the Indus.

Ḥarb into *dār-ul-Islām*. There are, however, certain principles for the waging of *jihād* which must be kept in mind, for it must not be assumed that either Muḥammad or his successors were acting toward their Hindu antagonists other than in accordance with Muslim canon law. When these rules are stated, the actions of the Muslim conquerors become intelligible, however regrettable they may seem.

The rule is that the people against whom the *jihād* is directed must first be invited to embrace Islam. If they refuse they have two alternatives: (1) to submit to Muslim rule, become *dhimmīs*, and pay the *jizyah* (poll-tax) and *kharāj* (land-tax), or (2) fight. If they embrace Islam they forthwith become citizens of the Muslim State, with all the rights and privileges pertaining thereto. If they submit and become *dhimmīs*, though their lives, families, property, and religious practices are assured them, yet they occupy a definitely inferior status. They are not really citizens, and are regarded only as wards of the State. On the other hand, if they fight, they and their families may be led into slavery, and all their property taken as booty, one-fifth of which goes to the sovereign and four-fifths to the army.[1] Further it must be remembered that the status of *dhimmī* may be offered only to those people who have a Scripture (*ahl-ul-Kitāb*). These are understood to be Jews, Christians, Magians, and Sabeans. In the case of pagans, idolaters, polytheists, who are not regarded as *ahl-ul-Kitāb* and have no Scriptures, it is held that for them there is a choice only between Islam or death. All of which is based on the verse, Qur'ān, ix. 29: '. . . Fight them, who have been given a Scripture, that believe not in God and the last day, and who hold not as forbidden what God and His apostle have forbidden, and do not profess the true religion, until they pay the *jizyah* in person in subjection.'[2]

It should be noted, as we proceed, the extent to which the Muslim conquerors deviated from the strict application of the law of *jihād* in dealing with the Hindus who were not *ahl-ul-Kitāb*, and were clearly beyond the rule permitting them to occupy the status of *dhimmīs*. The alternative for them would have been Islam or death. But the application of this rule was of necessity

[1] *E.I.*, art. 'Jihād'. [2] *E.I.*, art. 'Jizyah'.

relaxed. The Muslim armies were too small to enforce the rule extensively. They were far from the base of reinforcements, the numbers of the people opposing them were too vast; and, lastly, it would have been fatal to the welfare of the troops themselves, who were dependent on the services of the agriculturists, artisans and menials of the country to provide them with the necessary means of existence. There was no alternative left to the invaders, therefore, but to make an exception to the rule. It will be noted, however, that, in general, the early conquerors usually went as far as possible in applying the law of *jihād*, and only stopped when it was not practicable to do more. In later times, of course, extreme tolerance toward Hindus became a policy of state.

Muḥammad b. Qāsim's first act of religious zeal was forcibly to circumcise the Brāhmans of the captured city of Debul; but, on discovering that they objected to this sort of conversion, he then proceeded to put all above the age of seventeen to death, and to order all others, with women and children, to be led into slavery. The temple of the Hindus was looted, and the rich booty was divided equally among the soldiers, after one-fifth, the legal portion for the government, had been set aside. But Muḥammad did not continue to inflict the same acts of cruelty on every city he conquered. After the first flush of victory was over, he seems to have proceeded with more care and caution in the treatment of the inhabitants. Henceforth on approaching a city of the infidels he offered them the alternative of embracing Islam or of becoming *d̲h̲immīs* and paying *jizyah*, which was established by the Caliph 'Umar as a head tax for the protection offered by the Muslim State to those of other religions. Those who neither became Muslims nor submitted to the *jizyah* Muḥammad regarded as enemies (*ḥarbīs*), against whom it was lawful to wage war until they were killed or conquered. It is said that in two of the cities of Sind during this invasion no less than six thousand soldiers in each were put to the sword, while the families of the soldiers were taken as slaves. The usual practice seems to have been to exempt the merchants and artisans, farmers and menials from violence of any sort, and from slavery, though of course they were obliged to accept the inferior status of *d̲h̲immīs* and pay the *jizyah*.

While these were the principles of action, let us examine further some of the concrete examples of the intolerant spirit that marked the early centuries, for, painful as such reading is, it is none the less necessary to enable us to understand many subsequent events. Al-Balādhurī tells us that at the capture of Multan, after the surrender of the place, the soldiers were massacred, 'but the children and priests to the number of six thousand were made prisoners.'[1] At Kiraj after the surrender Muḥammad slew some and the rest he reduced to slavery.[2] Another authority says that after the people of Brāhmanābād had held out for six months they finally surrendered to him. He then put all the soldiers to death and took their dependents prisoners. All captives up to thirty years of age were made slaves, and a price put on them, but 'every one who bowed down his head and sued for protection was released'.[3]

Though the early Arab invasion was marked by great cruelty and intolerance, yet there were some acts of clemency that are deserving of notice. The city of Alrūr, which Muḥammad besieged for several months, finally surrendered to him on condition that he should spare the lives of the inhabitants and not touch the temples. This he conceded, saying, 'The idol temples shall be unto us like as the churches of the Christians, the synagogues of the Jews, and the temples of the Magians.'[4] On one occasion he seems to have been in a quandary as to what to do, for, after he had destroyed the temples, the people submitted and requested that they should be allowed to build them and carry on their former worship. Accordingly he referred the matter to the governor at Baṣrah, and received the reply, that:

> As the people of the towns in question had paid tribute, they were entitled to all the privileges of subjects; that they should be allowed to rebuild their temples and perform their rites; that the land and money of the Brāhmans should be restored; and that the three per cent on the revenue, which had been allowed to them by the Hindu government, should be continued by the Mussulman.[5]

At a later date we learn that the Caliph 'Umar bin 'Abd-ul-'Azīz sent letters to the princes of Hind, inviting them to become

[1] Al-Balādhurī, op. cit., 440.
[2] *Ibid.*, 440.
[3] *Chach-nāmah*, E.D., I, 179.
[4] Al-Balādhurī, op. cit., 439.
[5] *Chach-nāmah*, E.D., I, 186.

Muslims, and using his powers of persuasion upon them. It is recorded that, as they had already heard of his promises, character, and creed, so Jaishiya and other princes turned Muslims and took Arab names.[1]

While the Muslim invasion of Sind did not result in a permanent occupation, it did clearly foreshadow the militant methods of the Muslim conquerors, which were to be prosecuted with such unrelenting vigour from the time of the coming of Maḥmūd of G͟haznī in A.D. 1001 down to the appearance of the Mug͟huls in A.D. 1526. Though the caliphate was forced to withdraw its direct control from the distant province of Sind by the middle of the ninth century, Islam did not depart. The history of the intervening centuries is obscure. It seems probable, however, that members of the original army of occupation, and colonists who had been given land and had married women of the country, continued to keep the embers of the faith glowing. Added to these were some of the original converts, who had been given positions in the army and government. These also did their part to keep the new faith alive until the coming of another conqueror, who with his successors saw the practical accomplishment of the conversion of the Hindus of the Indus valley. To-day there are scarcely more than twenty-five per cent of the inhabitants of Sind who have not accepted the faith of Islam.

Systematic Slaughter, Destruction, and Looting

Maḥmūd of G͟haznī from the first adopted those plans that would strike terror to the hearts of the people of India. Al-'Utbī illustrates this with the graphic picture which he draws of the treatment meted out to Rājā Jaipāl after his defeat in A.D. 1001. 'Jaipāl was ordered to be paraded about so that his sons and chieftains might see him in that condition of shame, bonds and disgrace; and that the fear of Islam might fly abroad through the country of the infidels.'[2]

The effect of such attempts to produce fear is shown in the abject surrender of Hardat and his men in the Doāb, and their voluntary acceptance of Islam, concerning which the author of *Ta'rīk͟h-i-Yamīnī* writes thus:

[1] *Chach-nāmah*, E.D., I, 124; al-Balād͟hurī, op. cit., 441.

[2] Al-'Utbī, E.D., II, 27.

When Hardat heard of this invasion by the protected warriors of God who advanced like the waves of the sea, with angels around them on all sides, he became greatly agitated, his steps trembled, and he feared for his life, which was forfeited under the law of God. So he reflected that his safety would best be secured by conforming to the religion of Islam, since God's sword was drawn from the scabbard, and the whip of punishment was uplifted. He came forth, therefore, with ten thousand men, who all proclaimed their anxiety for conversion, and their rejection of idols.[1]

At Muttra we are told that Maḥmūd was greatly impressed by the beauty and size of the buildings; but in spite of this fact Al-'Utbī says that he 'gave orders that all the temples should be burnt with naphtha and fire, and levelled to the ground'.[2]

The slaughtering of 'infidels' seemed to be one thing that gave Maḥmūd particular pleasure. In one attack on Chand Rai, in A.D. 1019, 'many infidels were slain or taken prisoners, and the Muslims paid no regard to booty until they had satiated themselves with the slaughter of the infidels and worshippers of sun and fire'. The historian naïvely adds that the elephants of the Hindu armies 'came to Maḥmūd of their own accord, leaving idols, preferring the service of the religion of Islam!'[3]

Not infrequently the slaughter of the enemy gave a great backset to the indigenous culture of the Hindus, as in the conquest of Bihar by Muḥammad Bakhtyār Khaljī. When he took a certain place, the *Ṭabaqāt-i-Nāṣirī* informs us that 'great plunder fell into the hands of the victors. Most of the inhabitants were Brāhmans with shaven heads. They were put to death. Large numbers of books were found . . . but no one could explain their contents, as all the men had been killed. The whole fort and city being a place of study.'[4]

Of the destruction of temples and the desecration of idols we have an abundance of evidence. Muḥammad b. Qāsim carried out his plan of destruction systematically in Sind, as we have seen; but he made an exception of the famous temple at Multan for purposes of revenue, as this temple was a place of resort for pilgrims, who made large gifts to the idol. Nevertheless, while he thus satisfied his avarice by letting the temple stand, he gave vent to his malignity by having a piece of cow's flesh tied around the neck of the idol.[5]

[1] Al-'Utbī, E.D., II, 42. [2] *Ibid.*, 45. [3] *Ibid.*, 49.

[4] Minhāj-as-Sirāj, *Ṭabaqāt-i-Nāṣirī*, E.D., II, 306.

[5] *History of India*, E.D., I, 470.

Minhāj-as-Sirāj[1] further tells how Maḥmūd became widely known for having destroyed as many as a thousand temples, and of his great feat in destroying the temple of Somnāth and carrying off its idol, which he asserts was broken into four parts. 'One part he deposited in the Jāmi' Masjid of Ghaznī, one he placed at the entrance of the royal palace, the third he sent to Mecca, and the fourth to Medina.'[2]

Muḥammad Ghūrī, one of the enthusiastic successors of Maḥmūd, in his conquest of Ajmīr 'destroyed pillars and foundations of the idol temples, and built in their stead mosques and colleges, and the precepts of Islam and the customs of the law were divulged and established'.[3] At Delhi, 'the city and its vicinity were freed from idols and idol worship, and in the sanctuaries of the images of the gods mosques were raised by the worshippers of the one God'.[4]

Quṭb-ud-Dīn Aybak also is said to have destroyed nearly a thousand temples, and then raised mosques on their foundations. The same author states that he built the Jāmi' Masjid, at Delhi, 'and adorned it with the stones and gold obtained from the temples which had been demolished by elephants, and covered it with inscriptions (from the Qur'ān) containing the divine commands'.[5] We have further evidence of this borrowing process having been systematically employed from the inscription extant over the eastern gateway of this same mosque at Delhi, which relates that the materials of twenty-seven idol temples were used in its construction.[6]

'Alā-ud-Dīn, in his zeal to build a second *minār* to the Jāmi' Masjid, to rival the one built by Quṭb-ud-Dīn, is said by Amīr Khusrū not only to have dug stones out of the hills, but to have demolished temples of the infidels to furnish a supply.[7] In his conquests of south India the destruction of temples was carried out by 'Alā-ud-Dīn as systematically as it had been in the north by his predecessors.

The Sultan Fīrūz Shāh, in his *Futūḥāt*, graphically relates how

[1] A *qāḍī* and historian of Delhi. He died about A.D. 1260.
[2] Minhāj-as-Sirāj, E.D., II, 270. [3] Ḥasan Niẓāmī, E.D., II, 215.
[4] *Ibid.*, 217. [5] *Ibid.* [6] J. Horovitz, op. cit., 13.
[7] Amīr Khusrū, E.D., III, 70.

he treated Hindus who had dared to build new temples. When they did this 'in the city (Delhi) and the environs, in opposition to the Law of the Prophet, which declares that such are not to be tolerated, under Divine guidance I destroyed these edifices, I killed those leaders of infidelity and punished the others with stripes, until this abuse was entirely abolished, . . . and where infidels and idolaters worshipped idols, Mussulmans now by God's mercy perform their devotions to the true God'.[1]

With the destruction of the temples also went the destruction of the implements of worship, and no doubt very often the sacred books. Fīrūz Shāh takes special pains to note how he made his destruction complete: 'The new temple was destroyed, and I also ordered that the infidel books, the idols, and the vessels used in their worship should all be burnt'.[2]

Even in the reign of Shāh Jahān we read of the destruction of temples that the Hindus had started to rebuild, and the account of this direct attack on the piety of the Hindus is thus solemnly recorded in the *Bādshāh-nāmah*:

> 'It had been brought to the notice of His Majesty,' says the historian, 'that during the late reign (of Akbar) many idol temples had been begun but remained unfinished at Benares, the great stronghold of infidelity. The infidels were now desirous of completing them. His Majesty, the defender of the faith, gave orders that at Benares and throughout all his dominions in every place all temples that had been begun should be cast down. It was reported from the province of Allahabad that seventy-six temples had been destroyed in the district of Benares.'[3]

It was left to Aurangzīb to make a final attempt to overthrow idolatry. The author of *Ma'āthir-i-'Ālamgīrī*, dilates upon his efforts to put down Hindu teaching, and his destruction of temples as follows. In April, A.D. 1669, Aurangzīb learned:

> that in the provinces of Thatta, Multan and Benares, but especially in the latter, foolish Brāhmans were in the habit of expounding frivolous books in their schools, and that learners, Muslims as well as Hindus, went there from long distances. . . . The 'Director of the Faith' consequently issued orders to all the governors of provinces to destroy with a willing hand the schools and temples of the infidels; and they were enjoined to put an entire stop to the teaching and practising of idolatrous worship. . . .

[1] Fīrūz Shāh, E.D., III, 380. [2] *Ibid.*, 381.

[3] 'Abd-ul-Ḥamīd Lāhorī, E.D., VII, 36.

Later it was reported to his religious Majesty that the government officers had destroyed the temple of Bishnath at Benares.[1]

This was not all. Perhaps the most vigorous attempt made by Aurangzīb, and one that showed his fanatical attitude toward Hinduism more than any other single act, was his treatment of the sacred city of Muttra. The same writer tells how, in December, A.D. 1669, 'this justice-loving monarch' ordered the destruction of the Hindu temple of Muttra, known as Dehra Kesū Rai, and 'soon that stronghold of infidelity was levelled to the ground'. Then follows a glorification of the piety of the emperor, and his mighty works for the cause of Islam, in these words:

> On the same spot was laid at great expense the foundation of a vast mosque. . . . Glory be to God who has given us the faith of Islam, that in this reign of the destroyer of false gods, an undertaking so difficult of accomplishment has been brought to a successful termination! This vigorous support given to the true faith was a severe blow to the arrogance of the Rājās, and like idols they turned their faces awestruck to the wall. The richly jewelled idols taken from the pagan temples were transferred to Agra, and there placed beneath the steps leading to the Nawab Begam Sahib's mosque, in order that they might ever be pressed under foot by the true believers. Muttra changed its name to Islamabad.[2]

Ten years later, we read that Khāṉ Jahān Bahādūr arrived from Jodhpur, bringing several cartloads of idols taken from Hindu temples that had been razed, and that His Majesty proceeded to Chitor on the first of the month *Ṣafar* of that year, and 'temples to the number of sixty-three were here demolished'. Abū Turāb, who had been commissioned to effect the destruction of temples at Amber, reported *inter alia* that 'three score and six of these edifices had been levelled with the ground'.[3]

But temples were not always destroyed by the conquerors. In some cases where the buildings were at all suitable they were converted into mosques, and enlarged and modified to such an extent that one would not at the present time easily suspect that such a transformation had been made. Two such mosques I have seen, one at Amroha, where the chain that supported the bell of the original Hindu temple is still to be found hanging from the ceiling. The other, in Sambhal,[4] also plainly reveals some of

[1] Muḥammad Sāqī, E.D., VII, 184. [2] *Ibid.*, 184, 185. [3] *Ibid.*, 187, 188.

[4] Amroha and Sambhal are both in the Moradabad District, U.P.

the original structure of the Hindu temple, so well known as the traditional spot where the tenth or *Nishkalank Avatār* (Spotless Incarnation) of Vishnu will one day appear. Still, the general practice in dealing with temples, if they were touched at all, was to destroy them rather than to convert them into mosques.

Slavery

Not only was slaughter of the infidels and the destruction of their temples resorted to in the earlier period of Islam's contact with India, but, as we have seen, many of the vanquished were led into slavery. The dividing up of booty was one of the special attractions to the leaders as well as to the common soldiers in these expeditions. Maḥmūd seems to have made the slaughter of infidels, the destruction of their temples, the capturing of slaves, and the plundering of the wealth of the people, particularly of the temples and the priests, the main object of his raids. On the occasion of his first raid he is said to have taken much booty; and half a million Hindus, 'beautiful men and women,' were reduced to slavery and taken back to Ghaznī![1]

When he later took Kanauj, in A.D. 1017, he took so much booty and so many prisoners that 'the fingers of those who counted them would have tired'.[2] The same authority describes how common Indian slaves had become in Ghaznī and Central Asia after the campaign of A.D. 1019.

> The number of prisoners may be conceived from the fact that each was sold for from two to ten *dirhams*.[3] These were afterwards taken to Ghaznī, and merchants came from far distant cities to purchase them; . . . and the fair and the dark, the rich and the poor were commingled in one common slavery.[4]

In the year A.D. 1202, when Quṭb-ud-Dīn captured Kalinjar, after the temples had been converted into mosques, and 'the very name of idolatry was annihilated, fifty thousand men came under the collar of slavery and the plain became black as pitch with Hindus'.[5]

Fortunately, after the thirteenth century we find practically no references to the practice of reducing Hindus to slavery; though

[1] Al-'Utbī, E.D., II, 26. [2] *Ibid.*, 45.
[3] A *dirham* was worth about five pence. [4] *Ibid.*, 49.
[5] Ḥasan Niẓāmī, E.D., II, 231.

slavery did not by any means die out, and from Shams-i-Sirāj 'Afīf we learn that there were so many royal slaves in the reign of Fīrūz Shāh (A.D. 1351–1388), that, in the city of Delhi and in the various fiefs, there were estimated to be one hundred and eighty thousand slaves. Slavery thus became an established institution.

> Some of the slaves spent their time in reading and committing to memory the Holy Book, others in religious studies, others in copying books. Some . . . went on pilgrimage to Mecca. Some were placed under tradesmen and were taught mechanical arts, so that about twelve thousand slaves became artisans of various kinds. Forty thousand every day were ready to attend as guards in the Sultan's equipage or at the palace.

There was a separate treasury for the payment of the allowance of the slaves, and a distinct department for administering their affairs.[1]

Dhimmīs

During the long period of Muslim rule in India, the government regarded the people as in three classes with reference to the faith. First of all, of course there were the Muslims, who alone were technically citizens and stood first in all rights, honours, and privileges; secondly, there were the *dhimmīs*, or unbelievers who had submitted to the rule of Islam and had agreed to pay the *jizyah* (poll-tax), that, according to the law of Islam, must be levied on all unbelievers; thirdly, there were the *ḥarbīs*, or those who had not yet submitted to the government and were under the process of subjection. Once a territory had been subjugated, as in the case of Sind, the warriors either forcibly converted to Islam or killed, their wives and children made slaves, and the temples destroyed, it was judged expedient to spare the lives of the non-combatant classes, and to fix a tax upon them. Of course, all who became Muslims were exempt from slavery and the *jizyah*, but, as for the others, it was a religious duty that the *jizyah* be imposed, in addition to the *kharāj*, which was levied on the land and other property.

Muḥammad b. Qāsim, during the first occupation of Sind (A.D. 711), placed those who did not embrace Islam in three grades for the

[1] *Ta'rīkh-i-Fīrūz Shāhī*, E.D., III, 341.

purposes of taxation; in the first grade each was to pay silver equal to forty-eight *dirhams* in weight;[1] the second grade paid twenty-four *dirhams*; and the third, and lowest, grade paid twelve *dirhams*. Those who agreed to pay the tribute and kept their ancestral faith were also permitted to keep their property.[2]

All the successive invaders and rulers of India, after Muḥammad b. Qāsim, until the time of Akbar, thought of nothing else than applying the law of the *jizyah* and all other laws, in respect of the treatment of *d͟himmīs*, which, so far as the records go, must have been anything but conducive to approval and respect for the government and religion of the invaders. Maḥmūd levied such tribute during his invasions, and no doubt collected it as often as he made his frequent raids. There is ample evidence to prove that the Hindus very naturally evaded paying the hated tax as often as they could get out of it. During the earlier invasion we are told that Muḥammad b. Qāsim appointed the Brāhmans to be the collectors of the *jizyah*.[3]

This was a matter of necessity, no doubt, because he had not enough men of his own faith to whom he could entrust this work. One can believe that such Brāhmans would be well hated by their fellow countrymen, as the publicans were despised by the Jews in the days of Christ. The Brāhmans, moreover, early gained a favoured position with the conquerors, possibly because of this practice of appointing them as collectors of the poll-tax. During the reign of Fīrūz Shāh (A.D. 1351–1388) it was decided that, although the *jizyah* had never been levied on the Brāhmans of Delhi in the former reigns, it was unwise to continue this liberal policy. After consultation with his counsellors, it was agreed that they should no longer be excused, since, it was pointed out, they 'were the very keys of the chamber of idolatry, and the infidels were dependent on them'. The Brāhmans, in turn, objected, but finally they were compelled to pay, though they gained something for their trouble, as the amount was reduced below the rates commonly applied.[4]

The imposition of such a special tax, based on the idea of

[1] A *dirham* weight was equal to about 3 grammes.

[2] *Chach-nāmah*, E.D., I, 182. [3] *Ibid.*, E.D., I, 184.

[4] *Ta'rīk͟h-i-Fīrūz Shāhī*, E.D., III, 365.

subjection and inferiority, was sufficient in itself either to make the Hindus the avowed enemies of Islam, or to drive some weaker souls to the point of embracing Islam to escape the tax. However that may have been, we learn from a historian of the reign of 'Alā-ud-Dīn what the orthodox attitude was in those early times with respect to the treatment of *dhimmīs*. Although the interpretation of the law of the *jizyah* as given to the Sultan by the *qāḍī* (judge) may never have been literally carried out, and may only have served, as Sir T. W. Arnold suggests, as a counsel of perfection, yet so much is revealed in this statement of the religious attitude of those times that we cannot lightly pass it by.

The Sultan 'Alā-ud-Dīn on one occasion asked a *qāḍī*, 'How are Hindus designated in the law—as payers of tribute or givers of tribute?' The answer was given:

> They are called payers of tribute, and when the revenue officer demands silver from them, they should without question, and with all humility and respect, tender gold. If the officer throws dirt in their mouths, they must without reluctance open their mouths wide to receive it. . . . The due subordination of the *dhimmī* is exhibited in this humble payment, and by this throwing of dirt into their mouths. The glorification of Islam is a duty, and contempt for religion is vain. God holds them in contempt, for he says, 'Keep them in subjection.' To keep the Hindus in abasement is especially a religious duty, because they are the most inveterate enemies of the Prophet, and because the Prophet has commanded us to slay them, plunder them, and make them captive, saying, 'Convert them to Islam or kill them, enslave them, and spoil their wealth and property.' No doctor but the great doctor (Ḥanīfah), to whose school we belong, has assented to the imposition of *jizyah* on Hindus; doctors of other schools allow no other alternative but 'Death or Islam'.[1]

The amount of tax imposed evidently varied with the circumstances and the necessity of the case, sometimes in utter disregard of the limits of the law of Islam. In the days of 'Alā-ud-Dīn, at the beginning of the fourteenth century, the Hindus had in certain parts given the Sultan much trouble. So he determined to impose such taxes on them that they would be prevented from rising in rebellion. 'The Hindu was to be left unable to keep a horse to ride on, to carry arms, to wear fine clothes, or to enjoy any of the luxuries of life.' These edicts, says the historian of the period, 'were so strictly carried out that

[1] Ḍiyā-ud-Dīn Baranī, E.D., III, 184.

the *chaukidhārs* and *khuts* and *muqaddims* were not able to ride on horseback, to find weapons, to get fine clothes, or to indulge in betel! . . . No Hindu could hold up his head. . . . Blows, confinement in the stocks, imprisonment and chains were all employed to enforce payment.'[1]

The payment of the *jizyah* by the Hindus continued throughout the dominions of the sultans, emperors, and kings in various parts of India with more or less regularity, though often the law was in force in theory only; since it depended entirely on the ability of the sovereign to enforce his demands. But, finally, it was abolished throughout the Mug͟hul Empire in the ninth year of the enlightened Akbar's reign (A.D. 1665), after it had been accepted as a fundamental part of Muslim governmental policy in India for a period of more than eight centuries. It ceased to be a part of the policy of Muslim rule until the reign of Aurangzīb, who, because of his adherence to the tenets of orthodoxy, issued 'royal orders to collect the revenues of each province according to the Moslem law'.[2] This was the last serious effort made to impose the *jizyah* on Hindus, and from the beginning of the eighteenth century, after the death of the Emperor Aurangzīb and the rise of the Maratha power, the tax gradually fell into disuse, until finally the Hindus were completely freed from it.

Forced Conversions

Of all the measures taken by the Muslim rulers in India to establish Islam as the religion of the country, none met with more bitter resentment on the part of the Hindus than the various means that were employed to bring about the conversion of their people to the Muslim faith. The echoes of this policy have not even yet died away, though more than a century has passed since the last forced conversions under royal sanction took place.

As we have already seen, Muḥammad b. Qāsim began his invasion of India in A.D. 711 by forcibly circumcising the Brāhmans of Debul, and when they objected to this treatment he put all of the males over seventeen to death. As he advanced eastward and took other cities, we are told that some of the people embraced

[1] Ḍiyā-ud-Dīn Baranī, E.D., III, 182, 183. [2] Bak͟htāwar K͟hāṇ, E.D VII, 160.

Islam rather than die, and we may be sure that all who were made slaves were compelled to embrace the religion of the masters to whom they were allotted. It was the custom also for the invaders to take wives from the Hindus, and, among many instances, we are told that Muḥammad b. Qāsim sent two daughters of the Rājā Dāhir of Sind to Baṣrah to enter the harem of the governor Ḥajjāj. In fact, these early Arab invaders, who came to India without their families, may be pictured, as Elliot says, 'in several military colonies, seeking solace for their lost homes in the arms of native women of the country, and leaving their lands and plunder to be inherited by their Sindo-Arab descendants'. The point is that these alliances, forced, as they were, resulted in conversion to Islam.[1]

We do not know how successful the early Arab invaders were in bringing about conversions of the Hindus by these methods. It is more than likely that they confined operations of this sort chiefly to the cities and towns they captured; and it was not until a much later period that the bulk of the inhabitants of Sind became Muslim. However, with the first invasion of India began the use of the royal prerogative of Islam, as conceived of by the early propagandists, in bringing about conversion of *ḥarbīs* and *dhimmīs* by the use of force.

Though forced conversions were not the only means of increasing the numbers of the faithful, and although the supposition is wrong that Islam in India was propagated entirely by the sword, even in the early days, yet the fact remains that the use of force in some form or other has always been recognized, by the Muslim rulers of India, and by the orthodox lawyers of Islam, as being a proper and lawful method of propagating the faith of the Prophet. It is impossible, therefore, either to ignore or lightly pass over this phase of the religious history of Islam in India, though we may well rejoice that the day of greater liberality and a more generous interpretation of the precepts of Islam has dawned.

Such invaders as Maḥmūd and Tīmūr seem to have been more concerned with iconoclasm, the collection of booty, the enslaving of captives, and the sending of infidels to hell with the 'proselytizing sword' than they were with the conversion of them even by means of force. But when rulers were permanently established

[1] E.D., *History of India*, I, 464.

the winning of converts became a matter of supreme urgency. It was a part of the State policy to establish Islam as the religion of the whole land.

Quṭb-ud-Dīn, whose reputation for destroying temples was almost as great as that of Maḥmūd, in the latter part of the twelfth century and early years of the thirteenth, must have frequently resorted to force as an incentive to conversion. One instance may be noted: when he approached Koil (Aligarh) in A.D. 1194, 'those of the garrison who were wise and acute were converted to Islam, but the others were slain with the sword'.[1]

Further examples of extreme measures employed to effect a change of faith are all too numerous. One pathetic case is mentioned in the time of the reign of Fīrūz Shāh (A.D. 1351–1388). An old Brāhman of Delhi had been accused of worshipping idols in his house, and of even leading Muslim women to become infidels. He was sent for and his case placed before 'the judges, doctors, elders and lawyers. Their reply was that the provisions of the law were clear. The Brāhman must either become a Muslim or be burned. The true faith was declared to him and the right course pointed out, but he refused to accept it.' Consequently he was burned by the order of the Sultan, and the commentator adds, 'Behold the Sultan's strict adherence to law and rectitude, how he would not deviate in the least from its decrees'.[2]

As late as the middle of the eighteenth century, we learn of a case of forced conversions after the crushing defeat of Hindu arms near Delhi by Aḥmad Shāh Abdālī. 'About ninety thousand persons, male and female, were taken prisoners, and obtained eternal happiness by embracing the Muslim faith. Indeed, never was such a splendid victory achieved from the time of Amīr Maḥmūd Sabuktigīn to the present day by any of the Sultans.'[3]

In his interesting study, *The Preaching of Islam*, Sir T. W. Arnold shows to what lengths rulers could go in their zeal for the Faith even down to modern times. Tīpū Sultan, in south India, engaged in the most systematic endeavours for securing forcible conversions that could be imagined.

[1] Ḥasan Niẓāmī, E.D., II, 222.
[2] Shams-i-Sirāj 'Afīf, E.D., III, 365.
[3] Muḥammad Aslam, E.D., VIII.

In 1788 he issued the following proclamation to the people of Malabar:[1]

> From the period of the conquest until this day, during twenty-four years, you have been a turbulent and refractory people, and, in the wars waged during your rainy season, you have caused numbers of our warriors to taste the draught of martyrdom. Be it so. What is past is past. Hereafter, you must proceed in an opposite manner, dwell quietly and pay your dues like good subjects; and, since it is the practice with you for one woman to associate with ten men, and you leave your mothers and sisters unconstrained in their obscene practices, and are thence all born in adultery, and are more shameless in your connections than the beasts of the field, I hereby require you to forsake these sinful practices and to be like the rest of mankind; and if you are disobedient to these commands, I have made repeated vows to honour the whole of you with Islam and to march all the chief persons to the seat of government. This proclamation stirred up a general revolt in Malabar; and early in 1789 Tīpū Sultan prepared to enforce his proclamation with an army of more than twenty thousand men, and issued general orders that every being in the district without distinction should be honoured with Islam, that the houses of such as fled to avoid that honour should be burned, that they should be traced to their lurking places, and that all means of truth and falsehood, force or fraud should be employed to effect their universal conversion. Thousands of Hindus were accordingly circumcised and made to eat beef; but by the end of 1790 the British army had destroyed the last remnant of Tīpū Sultan's power in Malabar, and this monarch himself perished, early in 1799, at the capture of Seringapatam. Most of the Brāhmans and Nayars who had been forcibly converted subsequently disowned their new religion.[2]

Perhaps the greater number of Hindus who were forced to accept the new faith experienced a milder form of compulsion, such as that referred to earlier, when one of the caliphs sent 'letters to the Princes of Hind, inviting them to submit to his authority and embrace Islam'. The historians all speak of the enthusiasm that the sultans and emperors had for 'promulgating the true faith' and doctrines of Islam, and we may assume that quite often the objects of their persuasion were quietly compelled to become Muslims. Fīrūz Shāh, in his *Futūḥāt*, naïvely writes that he encouraged his infidel subjects to embrace the religion of the Prophet, and proclaimed that every one who repeated the creed and became a Muslim should be exempt from the *jizyah*.

> Information of this came to the ears of the people at large, and great numbers of Hindus presented themselves, and were admitted to the

[1] Arnold, *The Preaching of Islam*, 261 f. [2] *Ibid.*

honour of Islam. Thus they came forward day by day from every quarter, and were exonerated from the *jizyah* and were favoured with presents and honours.[1]

Even the mild Akbar makes a confession to having forced Brāhmans by fear of his power to adopt the religion of his ancestors,[2] and Aurangzīb personally taught 'the sacred *kalimah* to many infidels with success', and invested them with *khil'ats* (royal robes) and other favours.[3]

Aurangzīb is also known to have brought about the forced conversion of certain Rajput tribes in the vicinity of Agra, notably the group known as the *Malkānās*. Sometimes it happened that the head of a tribe or family would accept Islam alone, in order to preserve the ancestral property in the family, and then later others of the family would follow; or leading Hindu families and houses of ruling Hindu princes would be compelled to give some of their women as wives to the kings and emperors and Muslim chiefs.

The latest, and we trust the last example of this extreme type of forced conversion, occurred in the year 1921, during the outbreak known as the Moplah Rebellion.[4] This unfortunate occurrence was the outcome of agitation among this most ignorant and fanatical section of all the Muslims of India on the part of certain '*Khilāfat*' preachers. With more zeal than judgment they sought to impress on the Muslims of this section that their assistance was required to help their brethren throughout India to bring pressure to bear on the Government to assist in restoring to the late Turkish caliphate the part of its empire lost in the Great War, particularly the Hejāz, Palestine, and Syria. The Moplahs proved to be too apt pupils, and their enthusiasm soon got beyond the control of the '*Khilāfat*' preachers. Thinking that the way they could best make a contribution to the cause of loyalty to Islam was to take up arms, they proceeded to start a rebellion, in which many innocent Hindus were made the object of their attacks. Numbers who refused to be forcibly converted to Islam

[1] *Futūḥāt-i-Fīrūz Shāhī*, E.D., III, 386.
[2] Abū'l-Faḍl, *Akbar-nāmah*, E.D., VI, 60.
[3] Bakhtāwar Khān, E.D., VII, 159.
[4] J. J. Banninga, *The Moplah Rebellion of 1921*, M.W., XIII, 379.

were killed, but the numbers that were so converted, in order to save their lives and property, were still greater. This affair reminded people of the south of the days of Haydar 'Alī and Tīpū Sultan, and as soon as the rebellion was put down the Hindus immediately arranged to receive back into caste as many of these unfortunate converts as wished to return.

The day of forced conversions as a policy of religion has passed not only beyond the limits of practical possibility in Indian Islam, but well beyond the pale of respectable opinion. Aurangzīb and Tīpū Sultan would find difficulty in understanding to what lengths the representatives of Islam were willing to go at the Delhi Unity Conference in October, 1924, where they mutually agreed with the Hindus that force should not be used in bringing about conversions, and that people should be free to change their religion without fear of persecution.

CHAPTER III

PEACEFUL PENETRATION

THE story of the spread of Islam by the sword has been told so repeatedly that it is not easy for the casual reader of history to realize that its followers ever employed any other method. While India, in common with other conquered countries, furnishes innumerable examples of the employment of military and political power to secure conversions, as we have observed in the preceding chapter, we are now to consider the evidences of peaceful penetration, and the results of the patient missionary endeavours of itinerant preachers and traders. We shall also need to consider the effect of the democratic social system of Islam, with its strong appeal to the down-trodden millions of the depressed classes of Hindus. In fact, there seems to be ample reason for believing that a relatively larger proportion of the present Muslim population of India can be regarded as the result of methods of peaceful penetration than can be associated with the harsher methods of the Muslim conquerors.

There is an abundance of material available on this subject in the extensive biographies of the Indian Muslim saints, which undoubtedly would yield rich reward to the painstaking student.[1] Up to the present, however, very little has been done to uncover this information beyond the able researches of Sir T. W. Arnold, who has presented the main outlines in his chapter on India in *The Preaching of Islam*. Since there is room for no more than a bare sketch of the extensive operations of Muslim missionary efforts, I hereby acknowledge my indebtedness to Prof. Arnold's investigations in what follows.

THE INFLUENCE OF MUSLIM TRADERS

The reason for mentioning the trader first is not that his was a more potent influence for the dissemination of Islam than that

[1] For extensive bibliography see W. Ivanow, *Descriptive Cat. Pers. MS., A.S.B.*, I, 1924, 78-115 ; and II, 71-90.

of other peaceful missionaries, but because he was the first to arrive. It is known that Arab traders have had long and intimate contacts with the western coast of India, but the earliest record of any settlement appears to belong to the eighth century. We may even suppose that while Muḥammad b. Qāsim was fitting out his military expedition for the occupation of Sind, which was to become the most distant eastern province of the Damascus government, traders from Arabia were fitting out their ships, and preparing to say farewell to the homeland in anticipation of the new trading colonies to be established on the western coast of India. The Arabs were the people who, in these early centuries, maintained the commercial routes between India and Europe, and conducted a thriving trade in spices, ivory, and gems. Many of them, also, landing at the ports of Sind, travelled across western India and up into Central Asia; and, if we may judge from the missionary activities credited to Muslim traders in other parts of the world, it is more than likely that these traders from Arabia were a very real influence for the spread of the faith.

One very important factor in the establishment of Muslim settlements on the western coast of India was the encouragement to trade given by the Hindu rulers. The Balhārā dynasty in the north, and the Zamorin of the Malabar coast, were most partial to Muslims; and many a trader, encouraged by the complacent attitude of the Hindu chieftains, took up his abode in Anhilwāra, Cambay and Sindan, or in Calicut and Quilon. They were treated with great consideration, were allowed to build mosques freely, and were permitted to practise their religion without hindrance. Consequently, these early Arab and Persian settlers established themselves all along the coast, intermarried with the Hindu population, and thus gave rise to the Nawaits or Natiā community of the Konkan, and the Mappillas or Moplahs of the Malabar coast.

The traditional account of the introduction of Islam to the Malabar coast is recorded by Zayn-ud-Dīn, an historian of the sixteenth century.[1] He states that the conversion of Cheruman Perumal occurred during the lifetime of the Prophet. A company of pilgrims from Arabia were making a journey to visit Adam's

[1] See Arnold, op. cit., 264 ff.

footprint in Ceylon. On their arrival at Cranganore they paid a visit to the rājā, and told him of the miracle of Muḥammad's having split the moon. Perumal was captivated by this report of the exhibition of such supernatural power. He was converted ; and when the pilgrims returned from their journey he secretly joined them, and went with them to Arabia to visit the Prophet, who had not yet fled to Medina.

The king remained in Arabia for some time, and was on the point of returning to his country for the purpose of erecting mosques and spreading the faith of Islam when he fell sick and died. On his death-bed he requested his companions not to abandon the proposed missionary visit to Malabar. To further this object he gave them letters of recommendation to his viceroys, and also requested them to conceal the fact of his death. After the king had passed away, Sharaf bin Mālik and his companions set sail for Cranganore. They were kindly received on the presentation of the king's letters, and were given a grant of land, on which they erected a mosque. One of the missionaries, Mālik bin Dīnār, decided to settle there, but Mālik bin Ḥabīb journeyed throughout Malabar for the purpose of building mosques. He first went to Quilon and is said to have built a mosque there; thence to Hili Marawi, where he built another mosque, and so on, until he had caused the erection of mosques in seven other places before finally returning to Cranganore. Later on he is said to have visited all these places again, to pray in the mosque of each, and then came back, praising and giving thanks to God for the manifestation of the faith of Islam in a land filled with unbelievers.[1]

While this is an interesting bit of tradition, it unfortunately lacks the support of any historical evidence; and, so far as actual records are concerned, we are not able to trace the arrival of Arab settlers to the Malabar coast earlier than the eighth century A.D., when some refugees from Iraq came and took up their residence in the country. The narrative is of value, however, in that it shows the extent to which it is believed that Islam had its origin in south India from wholly peaceful methods. The Arab traders enjoyed the

[1] J. Duncan, art. 'The Coast of Malabar', *A.R.*, V, 9; Arnold, op. cit., 264 f.

favour of the Hindu rulers, whose states profited extensively from the mercantile relations thus established; and as a result no hindrances were put in the way of their proselytizing. In fact, the native converts are known to have been treated with the same respect and consideration as foreigners, even though they may have been recruited from the lowest classes of society.

One interesting feature of the spread of Islam on the Malabar coast was the part the zamorin of Calicut took in the coming of the Muslims. He is said to have deliberately encouraged the lower castes to become Muslims, in order to have sufficient sailors to man his warships; and to this end ordered 'that, in every family of fishermen in his dominion, one or more of the male members should be brought up as Muḥammadans'.[1] Thus 'a Hindu political necessity' came to lend a hand to the spread of Islam in south India; and, through intermarriage with the women of the country, along the coast, as well as through converts from the lower castes, who welcomed the coming of Islam as a chance to win a degree of social freedom that Hinduism denied them through its cruel and rigid caste system, the immigrant Arab traders, who were constantly being reinforced by new arrivals, gradually brought about the establishment of their faith. So rapid was the process of conversion that took place during the early centuries of the Muslim era, that, had the Portuguese not arrived on the scene when they did, it is claimed, the whole of the Malabar coast would have become solidly Muḥammadan.

It would be interesting to know something of the individuals who took part in this early work of propagating Islam in the Malabar country, but unfortunately no records exist. We do find, however, that a special mission was sent, in A.D. 1441, to the zamorin of Calicut by the Tīmūrid aspirant to the caliphate, Shāh Rukh. 'Abd-ur-Razzāq, who was himself chosen as the special envoy for this mission, has left an account of this unsuccessful expedition, which runs as follows: 'A Muslim ambassador came to the court of Shāh Rukh from the Hindu zamorin of Calicut and represented to the sultan how excellent and meritorious an action it would be to send a special envoy to the zamorin, to invite him to accept Islam in accordance with the

[1] Arnold, op. cit., 266.

injunction, "Summon thou to the ways of thy Lord with wisdom and with kindly warning,"[1] and open the bolt of darkness and error that locked his benighted heart, and let the splendour of the light of faith and the brightness of the sun of Knowledge shine into the window of his soul'.[2] However, 'Abd-ur-Razzāq found the zamorin unresponsive to this proposed plan, so the project had to be abandoned and the special envoy was forced to return to Khurāsān.

The testimony of travellers is illuminating in the matter of showing the extent to which these Muslim trade settlements had become permanently established in south India. Ibn Baṭūṭah (A.D. 1304–1377), in the early part of the fourteenth century, notes that there were many rich merchants with whom the towns of Malabar were crowded, and that five mosques stood as an ornament to Quilon. In the fifteenth century, 'Abd-ur-Razzāq writes that, on every Friday and solemn feast day, 'the *khuṭbah* was read according to the rules of Islam'.[3]

The Muslim community to-day on the Malabar coast of south India is spoken of as the Mappillas or Moplahs, and it is the direct result of the coming of these early Arab traders of the eighth and succeeding centuries. To-day they number one million, one hundred and eight thousand, and are found in the presidency of Madras and the native state of Coorg. Their language is Mālayālam. They are very bigoted and ignorant as a class, and have given trouble from time to time by their fanatical outbursts, the last and most serious of all being in 1921,[4] when they carried on a real rebellion. They endeavoured to set up a Muslim kingdom, and perpetrated forced conversions among the Hindu community. Even to-day Islam is spreading rapidly among the Hindu low-castes through the active but quiet efforts of the Mappillas. Looking farther afield, there is no doubt that Arab traders not only introduced Islam into Ceylon, but that it was even carried from the Malabar coast to the Maldive and Laccadive Islands, which are now wholly Muslim.

[1] Qur'ān, xvi, 126.

[2] 'Abd-ur-Razzāq, tr. R. H. Major, *India in the Fifteenth Century*, 13 ff.; Arnold, op. cit., 266.

[3] Major, op. cit., 15.

[4] See p. 34.

Another interesting Muslim community of south India, which seems to owe its origin to Muslim traders, is that of the Labbāīs on the east Tamil coast. One account relates that they are the descendants of some Arab traders who were shipwrecked on the Indian coast, and compelled to settle there. Another tradition says that they were Arab refugees, exiled from Iraq in the early part of the eighth century by Ḥajjāj bin Yūsuf of Baṣrah, who first landed on the Konkan. Some of them remained there, but others, after crossing over India, settled on the coast, north-east of Cape Comorin. Like the Arabs of the west coast, they intermarried with the Tamil tribes of the lower castes, and steadily added to their community. At the present time they number three hundred and eighty-two thousand. They use the Tamil language written in the Arabic character, with a large sprinkling of Arabic words.[1]

Lastly, mention should be made of the influence of traders, as recorded by al-Balā͟dhurī, in the north-western part of India, which supports the testimony already given, that the Muslim trader has in his quiet way had no little share in the spread of Islam. This author relates an account of the conversion of a king of 'Usayfān, somewhere between Multan and Kashmir, in the caliphate of Mu'taṣim (A.D. 833–842). This king became disgusted because prayers to an idol could not save his son's life, so he attacked the temple, destroyed the idol, and killed the priests. Then he invited a party of Muslim traders to come to him, 'who made known to him the unity of God'. Whereupon he believed in the Unity and became a Muslim.[2]

The Work of Missionaries

Throughout the history of Islam in India the missionary, or itinerant preacher, has been a relatively important factor. His work has not received anything like the attention that it deserves, from the standpoint of the results accomplished. Most writers have chosen to stress the military and political aspects of Muslim life in the country, and, with the exception of the researches of Sir T. W. Arnold, the Muslim missionary has been hitherto almost entirely neglected. It must not be thought that the Muslim

[1] Thurston, *Castes and Tribes of Southern India*, IV, 199.

[2] Al-Balā͟dhurī, *Futūḥ-ul-Buldān*, E.D., I, 129, 130.

preachers were organized for their propaganda work in any modern way. Nor is there any proof, save in one or two instances, that they were ever brought in by the Muslim conquerors. Usually they have been individuals endowed with piety and religious zeal, frequently men of learning, who, through their own personal interest in the spread of Islam, and inspired with a divine call, have been content to wander from place to place and gather disciples.

The period of this individualistic missionary activity extends from the beginning of the eleventh century right up to the present time, though with considerable irregularity. The records show that there were very few missionaries in the first two centuries beginning with the time of Maḥmūd's invasions. But, in the thirteenth century A.D., well-known names begin to appear, particularly that of K͟hwājah Mu'īn-ud-Dīn Chishtī of Ajmīr. The fourteenth century A.D. seems to have been the time of the greatest display of missionary zeal, since the number of missionaries of whose names and work we find a record exceeds that of any other single century. The fifteenth and sixteenth centuries following showed a tendency to a decline in missionary work, probably because of the marked spirit of toleration in the policy of the Mug͟hul emperors; and in the seventeenth centuries names are all but lacking. However, this may be to a large extent due to the fact that, for want of organization of any sort, no careful records could be kept; and, in the absence of such, we are not justified in assuming that no missionary work was accomplished. In fact, we know that quiet personal work must have gone on all the time, as it does at the present day, resulting in numerous accessions to the Muslim community.

One of the earliest missionaries of whom we have any record was Shayk͟h Ismā'īl, who came to Lahore about the year A.D. 1005. He belonged to the Buk͟hārā Sayyids, and was distinguished both for his secular and religious learning. It is said that crowds 'flocked to listen to his sermons, and that no unbeliever ever came into personal contact with him without being converted to the faith of Islam'.[1]

[1] Arnold, op. cit., 280.

To the eleventh century also belong 'Abd Allāh,[1] a missionary from the Yaman, who began his work of preaching in Gujarāt about the year A.D. 1067. It is said that through the performance of his miracles many Hindus were converted to Islam. The Bohrahs regard him as their first missionary.[2]

In the twelfth century we meet with the name of Nūr-ud-Dīn, another Ismā'īlī missionary, more generally known as Nūr Satāgar, the name which he adopted in deference to the Hindus. He was sent from Alamūt, in Persia, the headquarters of the Grand Master of the Ismā'īlīs, and came to Gujarāt in the reign of Siddhā Rāj (A.D. 1094–1143). It is said that he was instrumental in the conversion of the Kanbīs, Kharwas, and Korīs, all low-caste folk. The Khojahs regard Nūr Satāgar as their first missionary.[3]

In the thirteenth century there are several names of importance. One of these is that of Sayyid Jalāl-ud-Dīn of Bukhārā (A.D. 1190–1291). He settled in Uch, in Sind, in A.D. 1244, and was successful in winning many converts to the faith of Islam. Many of his descendants are still revered as saints, and even to this day his tomb is guarded by members of his family. This remarkable family has been responsible for a widening circle of religious influence.[4] Sayyid Ṣadr-ud-Dīn and his son, Ḥasan Kabīr-ud-Dīn, who laboured in the neighbourhood of Uch, are likewise held to have been the cause of many turning to Islam in the thirteenth century, and the latter is said to have possessed such hypnotic influence that as soon as his glance fell upon any Hindu he would at once accept the faith.[5] Sayyid Aḥmad Kabīr, known as Makhdūm-i-Jahāniyāṉ and grandson of Jalāl-ud-Dīn, is said to have been the means of the conversion of several tribes in the Punjab.

Perhaps the most famous Muslim missionary of India was Khwājah Mu'īn-ud-Dīn Chishtī, who died in Ajmīr in A.D. 1236. A native of Sīstān, in what was then east Persia, he is said to have received his missionary call to India while on a pilgrimage to Medina. The Prophet came to him in a dream and said to him, 'The Almighty has entrusted the country of India to thee. Go thither and settle in Ajmīr. By God's help, the faith of Islam shall, through thy piety and that of thy followers, be spread in

[1] Najm-ul-Ghanī Khāṉ, *Madhābib-ul-Islam*, 272. [2] See also p. 98.

[3] Arnold, op. cit., 275. [4] *Ibid.*, 281. [5] *Ibid.*, 282.

in that land.' According to the account, he obeyed the call and came to Ajmīr, where idolatry prevailed under Hindu rule. One of his first converts was a yogi, the spiritual preceptor of the Rājā himself. Little by little Mu'īn-ud-Dīn attracted to himself a body of disciples, whom he had won over from infidelity by his teachings. His fame as a teacher became so well known abroad that Hindus are said to have come to him in great numbers, and that many were induced to embrace Islam. Even during his short stay in the city of Delhi, when on his way to Ajmīr, he is said to have converted seven hundred persons.[1]

Late in the same century, Bū 'Alī Qalandar, a missionary from Persian Iraq, came to north India and settled at Pānīpat, near Delhi. The Muslim Rajputs of this place declare that they are descendants of one Amīr Singh, who was a convert of this saintly man. Bū 'Alī Qalandar died there in A.D. 1324, and his tomb in still an object of veneration to many pilgrims.[2]

Generally speaking, Muslim missionaries have followed in the wake of conquering armies. This was the case in the north, and in Bengal especially. Muḥammad Bakhtyār Khaljī swept over Bihar and Bengal at the close of the twelfth century A.D., and founded a Muslim kingdom there with headquarters at Gaur. Under the protection of this Muslim sovereignty, missionaries of the faith found freedom for the exercise of their zeal; and, as a result of certain social and religious causes, they were eminently successful. In eastern Bengal, Islam is not confined to the cities and centres of government, as is largely the case in northern India. Here, even under the admittedly severe measures of many of the Muslim rulers to spread the religion of Islam, but few, comparatively, of the village people embraced the religion of their conquerors. But in eastern Bengal we find it mostly in the villages; and, judging from the manners and customs of the followers of the Prophet, their physical appearance, and the caste distinctions which they still retain, it seems clear that these converts were recruited from the original inhabitants of the soil.[3] In this part of India, Hinduism was not nearly so well organized and consolidated as in the northern, western, and southern parts of the

[1] Arnold, op. cit., 281. [2] *Ibid.*, 282.

[3] Sir H. H. Risley, *The Tribes and Castes of Bengal.*

country. The inhabitants were under the influence of a crude form of Buddhism; and, despised as they were by their proud Aryan rulers, who held them in disdain, they apparently welcomed the Muslim missionaries gladly. The following statement of W. W. Hunter would seem to be quite a fair interpretation of the response made by the people of eastern Bengal to the work of the Muslim missionaries:

> To these poor people, fishermen, hunters, pirates, and low-caste tillers of the soil, Islam came as a revelation from on high. It was the creed of the ruling race; its missionaries were men of zeal, who brought the Gospel of the unity of God and the equality of men in His sight to a despised and neglected population.[1]

Missionary efforts in Bengal, as elsewhere, are attested by the graves and shrines of missionaries, who are credited with having been zealous for the spread of their faith. One of the earliest of these belonged to the thirteenth century, Shaykh Jalāl-ud-Dīn Tabrīzī, who died in A.D. 1244. He is said to have visited Bengal and died there, though the place of his tomb is unknown. Yet his memory is revered; and a shrine in his honour has been erected, which is still visited by pilgrims.[2]

During the thirteenth and fourteenth centuries A.D., missionary work was carried on in the Punjab, Kashmir, the Deccan, western India, and eastern India with increasing zeal. In the Punjab we find Bahā-ul-Ḥaqq, Bābā Farīd-ud-Dīn, of Pāk Pattan and Aḥmad Kabīr, known as Makhdūm-i-Jahāniyān, at the height of their endeavour. The first of these is said to have converted many on the plains of the western Punjab, and Bābā Farīd-ud-Dīn is said to have been the means of the conversion of some sixteen tribes.[3] Bulbul Shāh is said to have been the first missionary to Kashmir. In the early part of the fourteenth century he converted the first Muḥammadan king of that country, who took the name Ṣadr-ud-Dīn. Later in this century, in A.D. 1388, the progress of Islam was greatly advanced by the coming of Sayyid 'Alī Hamadānī, who is said to have brought with him seven hundred Sayyids. These men 'established hermitages all over the country,

[1] Arnold, op. cit., 279.

[2] *Ibid.*, 280. See also Ibn Baṭūṭah, tr. Yule, *Cathay and the Way Thither*, IV, 151.

[3] Arnold, op. cit., 281 f.

and by their influence appear to have assured the acceptance of the new religion'.[1] We are told, also, that their arrival seems to have aroused considerable fanaticism, for the Sultan Sikandar (A.D. 1393–1417) was given the name But-shikān (idol-smasher), from his destruction of Hindu idols and temples.[2]

In the Deccan and western India we find the well-known Sayyid Muḥammad Gīsū Darāz and Pīr Mahābīr Khamdāyat at work. The latter was an Arab preacher, who came as a missionary to Bījāpūr about the year A.D. 1304, and began work among the peasants. Among these are to be found Muslims who claim that their ancestors were Jains converted by him. At the close of the same century, Gīsū Darāz was working among the Hindus of the Poona district, where he met with success, and later was similarly successful in Belgaum. He was laid to rest from his labours at Gulbarga.

In the fifteenth and sixteenth centuries, Sind and western India particularly were the scene of the labours of Muslim missionaries. In Sind and Cutch, Sayyid Yūsuf-ud-Dīn and Pīr Ṣadr-ud-Dīn became famous for their work. We are told that Sayyid Yūsuf-ud-Dīn, who was a descendant of 'Abd-ul-Qādir Jīlānī,

> was bidden in a dream to leave Baghdad for India and convert its inhabitants to Islam. He came to Sind in A.D. 1422, and, after labouring there for ten years, he succeeded in winning over to Islam seven hundred families of the Lohānā caste, who followed the example of two of their number, by name Sundarji and Hansraj; these men embraced Islam, after seeing miracles performed by the saint, and on their conversion received the names of Ādamjī and Tāj Moḥammed respectively. Under the leadership of the grandson of the former, these people migrated to Cutch, where their numbers were increased by converts from among the Cutch Lohānās.[3]

Pīr Ṣadr-ud-Dīn began his labours in Sind about the year A.D. 1430. He was an Ismā'īlī missionary who was head of the Khojah sect.[4] He made certain concessions to Hindu beliefs and customs, with the result that he won his first converts in the villages and towns of Upper Sind. He also worked in Cutch 'and from these parts the doctrines of his sect spread southwards through Gujarāt to Bombay'.[5]

[1] Arnold, op. cit., 292. [2] *Ibid.* [3] *Ibid.*, 274.
[4] See p. 101. [5] Arnold, op. cit., 275.

In Gujarāt and other parts of western India, missionaries of Islam were actively engaged in spreading their doctrines. Imām Shāh of Pīrānā and Dāwal Shāh Pīr are two whose names are linked together in the latter half of the fifteenth century A.D. The former is said

> to have converted a large body of cultivators by bringing about a fall of rain after two seasons of scarcity. On another occasion, meeting a band of Hindu pilgrims passing through Pīrāna on their way to Benares, he offered to take them there ; they agreed, and in a moment were in the holy city, where they bathed in the Ganges and paid their vows ; they then awoke to find themselves still in Pīrāna, and adopted the faith of the saint who could perform such a miracle.[1]

Mālik 'Abd-ul-Latīf, the real name of Dāwal Shāh Pīr, was the son of one of the nobles of Maḥmūd Begarha (A.D. 1458–1511), of the Muslim kingdom in Gujarāt. Many of the Cutch Muslims hold the Pīr as their spiritual leader, and assert that through his influence many Hindus were converted.[2]

In Nāsik are to be found the descendants of Shāh Muḥammad Ṣādiq, an Arabian missionary, who came from Medina in A.D. 1568, thus following another Arabian missionary, Khwājah Khunmīr Ḥusaynī, who laboured in the same region fifty years before, with considerable success.[3]

To Kashmir, towards the close of the fifteenth century, came a missionary from Tālish, on the Caspian Sea, by the name of Mīr Shams-ud-Dīn. He was a Shī'ah, and with the help of his disciples is said to have soon converted a large number of people.[4]

Arnold tells of another group of people in southern India, the Dudekulas,

> who live by cotton cleaning (as their name denotes) and by weaving coarse fabrics, and attribute their conversion to Bābā Fakhr-ud-Dīn, whose tomb they revere at Penukonda.[5] Legend says that he was originally a king of Sīstān, who abdicated his throne in favour of his brother, became a religious mendicant and set out on a proselytizing mission. The legend goes on to say that he finally settled at Penukonda in the vicinity of a Hindu temple, where his presence was unwelcome to the Rājā of the place. Instead of appealing to force, he applied several tests to discover whether the Muḥammadan saint or his own priest was the better qualified by

[1] Arnold, op. cit., 277.

[2] *Bombay Gazetteer*, V, 89, Bombay, 1877–1904.

[3] *Ibid.*, XVI, 75-76.

[4] Arnold, op. cit., 292.

[5] Eighty-six miles north of Bangalore.

sanctity to possess the temple. As a final test, he had them both tied up in sacks filled with lime, and thrown into tanks. The Hindu priest never reappeared, but Bābā Fakhr-ud-Dīn asserted the superiority of his faith by being miraculously transported to a hill outside the town. The Rājā hereupon became a Mussalman, and his example was followed by a large number of the inhabitants of the neighbourhood, and the temple was turned into a mosque.[1]

Another community, found in south India, that is an excellent example of group conversion by missionaries is that of the Ravuttans, found in the districts of Madura, Tinnevelly, Coimbatore, North Arcot, and the Nilgiris. These people assert that they were converted by the preaching of missionaries, whose tombs they venerate to the present day. Of these the leading one seems to have been Sayyid Nathar Shāh (A.D. 969–1039), variously called also Nādir Shāh and Nathad Valī. This man, who is said to have converted large numbers of Hindus to Islam, made his headquarters at Trichinopoly, after wandering much in Arabia, Persia, and northern India. His tomb is a famous place of pilgrimage in south India.[2]

In considering the work of the earlier Muslim missionaries notice should be taken of the fact that most of the evidence recorded is derived from biographers who undoubtedly have given liberal interpretation to the ability and success of their heroes. Much of their success is attributed to wonder-working powers and the effect of magic on the minds of the credulous, some of the miracles being recorded and others being referred to in the most general terms. Again, others seem to have attracted followers to themselves because of their undoubted piety, which is matter of great consideration among the Hindus. But all seem to have made an impression and won a hearing because of the simple and straightforward religious and social precepts of Islam, which exalt the unity of God, declare the abomination of idolatry, and proclaim the equality of all believers as opposed to the oppressive system of caste, which has been for so many centuries the blight of Hinduism. So, after all due allowance is made for the influence of the miraculous, it remains

[1] Arnold, op. cit., 267.

[2] *Madras District Gazetteers*, Trichinopoly, I, 338, Madras, 1907; Arnold, op. cit., 267.

without question that, as a result of the piety and zeal of the missionaries and the message they had to proclaim, they undoubtedly did win conspicuous success. Just how much may never be measured, and it is a curious thing, to say the least, that in the record of the historians of the kings and emperors of the various dynasties practically no mention is made of the work of the missionaries in spreading the religion of Islam, and thus aiding the rulers who so frequently styled themselves defenders and propagators of the faith. Whether this absence of comment is deliberate or accidental we may never know. Whether it indicates, as some may think, that the success of the missionaries was not nearly so great as is usually attributed to them, is likewise a matter that cannot fully be settled. Nevertheless, the presumption is strong that they were successful, and it is more than likely that the absence of comment is due to the fact that the historians were too interested in royal affairs to busy themselves with the activities of such humble folk as missionaries.

Missionary Work Since 1800

The work of individuals has been going on as before; and, having come under critical review, results can be more accurately evaluated. In the early part of the nineteenth century there was a remarkable revival of the Muḥammadan religion in Bengal, particularly under the inspiration of the Wahhābī reformers,[1] Ḥājī Sharī'at Allāh and his son Dūdhū Miyāṇ, who won many converts from among unbelievers. Nor can the conversions be said to have stopped at the present time.

Since the middle of the nineteenth century there has been a widespread revival of Islam all over India, and the annual conversions are estimated anywhere from ten thousand to six hundred thousand. Some parts of the country report no missionary activity whatever, while in others it is very marked, notably in Bengal and on the Malabar coast. But there are no means of judging the accuracy of any of the statements made. Occasionally gross exaggeration is the only expression that will characterize the work of the preachers, as when in the Punjab a certain Ḥājī Muḥammad is reported to have converted as

[1] See 'Wahhābī Movement', pp. 178 ff.

4

many as two hundred thousand.[1] It is said that between the years 1901 and 1911 conversions frequently took place at the Jāmi' Masjids of Lahore and Delhi. At the former two thousand are said to have accepted Islam and six hundred and forty-six at the latter, while no fewer than forty thousand must have embraced Islam during the decade in the Punjab alone. The converts there were mostly from the lower classes of the *Chuhras* and *Chamārs*.[2]

On the Malabar coast conversions are being made from among the *Tiyans*, *Mukkuvāns*, or fishermen caste, from the *Cheruman*, or agricultural labourers, and other low castes. At Ponānī, under the auspices of the Minnat-ul-Islām Sabhā, there are two schools for new converts, one for boys and another for girls. Here also resides the spiritual head of the majority of the Muslims of Malabar, who directs the work of the Sabhā (Society). It is reported that more than six thousand converts have passed through these schools since they were organized. Those under instruction are not only given free tuition in the tenets of the new faith, but are given material assistance as well. There are sixteen branches of the Sabhā in south Malabar, Travancore, and Cochin; and extensive charities have been organized.[3]

So numerous have the conversions from Hinduism been that there is a decided tendency for the Muḥammadans, of both the west and east coasts of southern India, to retain the aboriginal type from which they are drawn. During the decade ending in 1911, the Mappillas on the west coast increased fourteen per cent, largely through accessions from the lower classes of Hindus. In fact, the increase has been so rapid as to make it possible that, in a few years, the whole of the lower grades of Hindu society of the west coast may become Muḥammadans. This possibility receives support from the evidence of the Census Superintendent of 1881, who wrote concerning the decrease in the number of the Cheruman caste as follows:

> This caste numbered ninety-nine thousand in Malabar at the Census of 1871, and in 1881 only sixty-four thousand, seven hundred and thirty-five. There are forty thousand fewer Cherumans than there would have been but

[1] Garcin de Tassy, *La Langue et la Littêrature Hindoustanies*, Paris, 1874, 343.
[2] *C.I.R.*, 1911, XIV, *Punjab*, pt. I, 170.
[3] *C.I.R.*, Madras, 1911, XII, pt. I, 54.

for some disturbing influence, and this is very well known to be conversion to Muḥammadanism.[1]

There are many zealous Muslim missionaries working at the present time throughout India, with varying results. The most noted of these is undoubtedly Khwājah Ḥasan Niẓāmī, of Delhi, who is himself the living centre of a most active and interesting *tablīgh* (propaganda) movement. He is a Ṣūfī of the Chishtī order, and has followers all over the country. He is the editor-in-chief of several papers, and has developed a considerable amount of literature in the form of tracts, pamphlets and books, which are circulated not only in Urdu but other Muslim languages of India as well. His preachers are instructed to work especially among the untouchables and convert them. He gives the fourfold object of his 'Tablīghī Mission' as follows:

1. To strengthen Muslims through religious teaching.
2. To assist Muslims to improve their economic condition.
3. To inspire Muslims with missionary zeal.
4. To propagate Islam among non-Muslims.

Other important modern missionary agencies are the Jam'īyat-i-Tablīgh-ul-Islām,[2] and the Aḥmadīyah propaganda organizations.[3]

Other Causes of Conversion

When it comes to considering the classes of Hindus from which converts have largely come, it is impossible to account for the size of the numbers wholly through the militant or peaceful zeal of conquerors, traders, and missionaries. There are other elements that enter in from the side of the Hindus themselves, and from the structure of their society, that have been an aid to the spread of Islam. The first of these factors, which have been effective from the earliest times, has been the oppressive social conditions under which the low castes have had to suffer. Consequently any outcaste man, who wished to escape the insults and degradation imposed upon him by his social status, could easily find a welcome freedom by accepting the benefit of a system of religion which has no outcastes, and which permits prince and sweeper to worship together in the house of God.

[1] Thurston, *Castes and Tribes of Southern India*, II, 60.

[2] See p. 201. [3] See pp. 226 ff.

In this way alone can the large number of so-called low-caste Muslims of India, such as the weavers and oil-makers, water-carriers, leather-workers, and even sweepers, be accounted for. Not alone in Bengal, but in the United Provinces, the Punjab, and western India this process of assimilation to a higher form of social life has been going on for centuries. In the middle of the sixteenth century a very remarkable illustration of this sort occurred in the north-eastern part of the province of Bengal. An aboriginal tribe known as the Koch became practically Hinduized ; but the lower classes, on finding themselves regarded as outcastes, all became Muḥammadans.[1]

A very common cause of conversion to Islam arises when a Hindu for any reason loses caste and is ostracized. The door of Islam has always been open to receive all such. Still other causes are found in illicit love affairs, where a Muslim man falls in love with a Hindu woman, or vice versa. In either case, the Hindu must become a Muslim, for there can be no union of Muslim women with unbelievers, and the Hindu women who enter into such alliances perforce become Muslims, and assume Muslim names.

Still another factor which has not been without its influence on Hindus of the lower castes, in leading them into the fold of Islam, is to be found in the fact that enormous numbers of them worship at the shrines of Muslim saints. I have again and again observed Hindus paying their devotions to such shrines, on the principle that they should seek help from all spiritual powers possible; and it is recorded that families have been known to become Muslims from a vow having been made to some saint, if he would grant a son to an imploring father. One such instance is forthcoming from Ghātampur, in the district of Cawnpore, where there is one branch of a large family that is now Muslim as the result of a vow of their ancestor, Ghātam Deo Bais, 'who, while praying for a son at the shrine of a Muḥammadan saint, Madār Shāh, promised that if his prayer was granted half his descendants should be brought up as Moslems'.[2] That this process has gone on for centuries, and is still proceeding, is indicated by the

[1] E. T. Dalton, *Descriptive Ethnology of Bengal*, Calcutta, 1872, 89.
[2] Arnold, op. cit., 289; *Gazetteer of the N.W.P.*, VI, 64, 238.

fact that in northern India in the Census of 1891 there were two million, three hundred and thirty-three thousand, six hundred and forty-three Hindus of the lower castes who were classed as worshippers of Muḥammadan saints.[1]

There can be no doubt that, during all the centuries of Islam in India, one of the very strongest assets has been the privilege of brotherhood, which it has held out freely to all who would come within the pale. True it is that certain aspects of the caste-system are to be found among Indian Muslims to-day; but even so, these disabilities are nothing compared with those of the Hinduism from which these inherited caste-features have emerged; and Islam, even in its Hindu environment, knows no outcastes. What Arnold says is no doubt true. 'It is this absence of class prejudices which constitutes the real strength of Islam in India, and enables it to win so many converts from Hinduism.'[2]

[1] *C.I.R.*, 1891, XVI, 1, 217, 244. [2] Arnold, op. cit., 291.

CHAPTER IV

ORGANIZATION OF THE SUNNĪ COMMUNITY

ISLAM in India has never functioned as an organic unity. It has never developed a thorough-going organization, which through its recognized representatives and hierarchy could exercise a far-reaching and effective control over the whole Muslim community, so that in matters of religion it could act as a unit. However, some earnest efforts have been made during the last half-century to achieve such organization, with promising results. During the period of Muslim domination, the unity of the faithful was brought about, to a certain extent, by the ruler, who was regarded as the chief custodian of Islamic law as well as the defender of religion.

While, in the beginning, this dependence on the power of the ruler was an undoubted help in the establishment of Islam in the country, there can be no doubt that this reliance on the strong arm of the government and on the leadership of a ruler to bring glory to the faith has, in the long run, resulted in producing weakness in the community rather than strength. The same has been true in the case of Christianity whenever it has leaned too hard on temporal power for strength and protection. Yet there is this difference, that the Christian Church has always maintained a spiritual or ecclesiastical organization independent of the temporal; whereas, in theory at least, in Islam there should be no distinction between the temporal and the spiritual. The two organizations merge into one. The Caliph is not only the head of the State, but is also the head of the Church ; for Islam, under ideal conditions, is not a State Religion but a Religious State.

Likewise, the king or emperor in an independent Muslim country is regarded as the viceroy of the Caliph, and as such is the recognized head of the religion of Islam in his dominions. Therefore, so long as Muslim rule could be maintained in India the people looked to the ruler, whether petty chief, king, or emperor, as the visible centre of religious as well as temporal power. Keeping in mind, then, this relationship existing between the sovereign and his people in matters of religion, it is very interesting to observe the development of Islam in India as a religious community, along with all the ecclesiastical, legal, and educational institutions that were set up. We shall devote our attention particularly to the evolution of organization in the Sunnī community, leaving the Shīʿahs for consideration in the following chapter.

Early Relations to the Caliphate

We shall begin by tracing the relation of Indian Islam to the caliphate from the earliest times. We have already noted at the beginning how the Caliph ʿUmar had his eyes fixed on India as a field for the extension of Islam, and was only deterred therefrom because he disliked sending naval expeditions. We have similarly noted how his successor, ʿU̲th̲mān, desired to send an expedition into India, but was kept from it because the only land route then open was through southern Persia and Baluchistan, a desert country which it was exceedingly difficult to cross. But finally, in the reign of the Umayyad Caliph Walīd, when Muḥammad b. Qāsim invaded Sind (A.D. 711), the colonial government which was set up was under the Umayyad caliphate. We learn that Ḥajjāj, the governor of Baṣrah, wrote to Muḥammad b. Qāsim that throughout the cities and towns captured 'the *k̲h̲uṭbah* should be read and the coin struck in the name of this government'.[1] And throughout the period in which the Arab governors held sway over Sind, the *k̲h̲uṭbah* continued to be read in the name of the *K̲h̲alīfah*.[2] Even in the distribution of the booty taken by the early Arab invaders, the *K̲h̲alīfah* was remembered in the portion of one-fifth that was reserved for him, as directed by the Qur'ān.[3]

Maḥmūd of G̲h̲aznī, as ruler of his Indian possessions, recognized the supreme authority of 'the successor of the Prophet of God'. But Iltutmish was the first independent ruler of India (A.D. 1210–1235) to receive the investiture of a diploma and title, which came from al-Mustanṣir, the ʿAbbāsid Caliph of Bagh-

[1] *Chach-nāmah*, E.D., I, 206.

[2] Al-Balād̲h̲urī, *Futūḥ-ul-Buldān*, E.D., I, 210.

[3] E.D., *History of India*, I, 462.

dad in the year A.D. 1229. That he appreciated the honour and his heavy religious responsibility to the full, is indicated in the inscription found over the archway of the main entrance to the Arhāī-Din-kā-Jhoṇprā, at Ajmīr, where he speaks of himself as 'the defender of Islam' and 'the helper of the Caliph of God'. Iltutmish had the document from the caliph read before a great assembly at Delhi, and from that date put the name of the caliph on his coins, and had his name read in the *khuṭbah*.

Iltutmish had made a good beginning in acknowledging the overlordship of the caliph, but the story of what followed has been the subject of extensive research by Prof. T. W. Arnold, so we shall let him continue the recital of matters which are pertinent to the subject in hand. Referring to Iltutmish and later rulers he says:

> His successors followed this pious example. The name of the last 'Abbāsid Khalīfah of Baghdad, Musta'ṣim (1242–1258), first appears on the coins of 'Alā-ud-Dīn Mas'ūd-Shāh (1241–1246); and, though Musta'ṣim was put to death by the Mongols in 1258, his name still appears on the coins of successive kings of Delhi, e.g. Maḥmūd Shāh Nāṣir ad-Dīn (1246–1265), Ghiyāth ad-Dīn Balban (1265–1287), and Mu'izz ad-Dīn Kayqūbād (1287–1290), the last monarch of the so-called 'Slave' dynasty; and the first of these continued to have the name of Musta'ṣim mentioned in the khuṭbah.
>
> A new dynasty arose, that of the Khaljī; the same need for legitimization was apparently still felt, and the coins of Jalāl-ad-Dīn Fīrūz Shāh II (1290-1295) continued to bear the name of Musta'ṣim, though this caliph had been trampled to death by the Mongols more than thirty years before.
>
> What was an unfortunate Muslim monarch to do who felt that his title was insecure? He knew that it was only his sword that had set him on the throne, that his own dynasty might at any time be displaced, as he had himself displaced the dynasty that had preceded him, while his legal advisers and religious guides told him that the only legitimate source of authority was the Khalīfah, the Imām, and he realized that all his devout Muslim subjects shared their opinion. So he went on putting the name of the dead Musta'ṣim on his coins, because he could find no other, and the Muslim theory of the state had not succeeded in adjusting itself to the fact that there was no Khalīfah or Imām in existence. His successor, 'Alā-ad-Dīn Mohammed Shāh I (1295–1315), got out of the difficulty by ceasing to insert Musta'ṣim's name and by describing himself merely as Yamīn al-Khilāfat Nāṣir Amīr al-Mu'minīn, 'The right hand of the Caliphate, the helper of the Commander of the Faithful'; and this was sufficient for the satisfaction of tender consciences; though in reality he was giving no help at all to any caliph, any more than either of his predecessors had done.

who had seen the unhappy Musta'ṣim trampled to death without moving a finger, though they had gone on making use of his name for their own selfish political purposes.[1]

In common with efforts made by other independent Muslim princes, some of the earlier Indian monarchs aspired to assume the dignity of the caliphate of the Muslim world. One of these, Sultan 'Alā-ud-Dīn Khaljī (1296–1316) of Delhi,

> was styled by his biographer, the great poet, Amīr Khusrū, 'the Caliph of the Age', and the 'Shadow of the Merciful on the heads of mankind'. His son, Quṭb ad-Dīn Mubārak Shāh (1316–1320), had inscribed on some of his coins, 'The most exalted Imām, the Khalīfah of the Lord of the worlds, the pole-star of the earth and of the faith, Abū'l-Muẓaffar, Khalīfah of God.'[2]

Whenever a new king came to the throne at Delhi or in any of the independent principalities of India it was the custom to have the *khuṭbah* read in the name of the ruling sovereign, thus recognizing his religious as well as his governmental authority, and the fact that he caused it to be done indicated that he accepted the usual Muslim ruler's responsibility for defending and extending the faith within his dominions.

But the kings at Delhi were not always as fortunate as Iltutmish in obtaining the investiture of authority as Muslim rulers from the caliphate; nor, if we read history aright, did they always regard it as important or necessary. Hence it became the custom for the king to have his own name only read in the *khuṭbah*; for we read that when Muḥammad Shāh Tughluq came to the throne in A.D. 1324, he found this practice prevailing and felt much concerned about it. After making diligent inquiry, he finally decided that the *Khalīfah* of Egypt was the rightful successor of the 'Abbāsid dynasty, and so 'he had his own name and style removed from his coins, and that of the *Khalīfah* (of Egypt) substituted', and, in A.D. 1343, his ambassador to Egypt, Ḥājī Sa'īd Sarsarī, returned to the sultan, bringing 'honours and a robe from the *Khalīfah*'. The reason for the above was that he had come to the conclusion

> that no king or prince could exercise regal power without confirmation by the *Khalīfah* of the race of 'Abbās, and that every king who had

[1] Arnold, *The Caliphate*, 86 ff. [2] *Ibid.*, 116.

or should hereafter reign without such confirmation had been or would be overpowered . . . From that date permission was given that out of respect the *Khalīfah's* name should be repeated in the prayers for Sabbaths and holy days . . . and it was also ordered that in mentioning the names of the kings in the *khuṭbah*, they should be declared to have reigned under the authority and confirmation of the 'Abbāsī Khalīfahs. And the name of the *Khalīfah* was ordered to be inscribed on lofty buildings, and no other name besides.[1]

Likewise, when the pious Fīrūz Shāh III came to the throne, in A.D. 1351, he counted it a great honour to have the recognition of the caliph; for he tells us that

> the greatest and best of honours that I obtained through God's mercy was that by my obedience and piety and friendliness and submission to the *Khalīfah*, the representative of the holy Prophet, my authority was confirmed. . . . A diploma was sent me confirming my authority as deputy of the Khilāfat, and the leader of the faithful was graciously pleased to honour me with the title Sayyid as-Salāṭīn. He also bestowed on me robes, a banner, a sword, a ring, and a footprint as badges of honour and distinction.[2]

Nowhere do we find a better illustration of the Sultan in India being regarded as the national head of the religion of Islam than in these two instances cited above. He was held by all to be the one person in whom the executive function and glory of Islam were centred in the land. If he was strong and able as a ruler, great was the power and glory of Islam. If he was weak and incapable, Islam suffered in proportion.

It is said also that Khiḍr Khāṇ, of the so-called Sayyid dynasty of Delhi (A.D. 1414–1421), had the *khuṭbah* read in the name of Shāh Rukh, son of Tīmūr, who made great efforts to get himself recognized as Caliph, and even provided the text of the *khuṭbah* that Khiḍr Khāṇ was to have read:

> O God, cause the foundations of the kingdom and of the religion to abide forever, uplift the banner of Islam and strengthen the pillars of the incontestible Sharī'at, by maintaining the kingdom of the exalted Sultan, the just Khāqāṇ, the noble overlord of the necks of the nations, the ruler of the sultans of the Arabs and the non-Arabs, the shadow of God upon the earth, the ruler over land and sea, who enlarges the foundations of peace and security, who uplifts the banner of justice and benevolence, who protects the territories of God, who gives help to the servants of God, and to whom

[1] Ḍiyā-ud-Dīn Baranī, *Ta'rīkh-i-Fīrūz Shāhī*, E.D., III, 249, 250.

[2] *Futūhāt-i-Fīrūz Shāhī*, E.D., III, 387.

the help of God has been given, to whom has been granted victory over his enemies, the supporter of truth, the world and religion, Shāh Rukh Bahādūr Khān may Almighty God make his rule and sultanate abide for ever in the Caliphate over the world, and grant increase of His goodness and blessings for the inhabitants of the earth.[1]

The Caliphate Pretensions of the Mughul Emperors

One of the interesting developments in India in respect to the relation to the caliphate came about during the flourishing rule of the Mughul emperors. The very glory, wealth, and power of their court brought about a decidedly independent attitude in respect to the overlordship of the Ottoman Caliph, the significance of which is well pointed out by Arnold, who graphically describes the situation as follows:

> During the sixteenth and seventeenth centuries the only Sunnī monarchs who could rival the Ottoman Sultans in wealth and extent of territory were the Mughal emperors of India. After the manner of their ancestors in Transoxiana,[2] they commonly assumed the title of Khalīfah, and from the reign of Akbar onwards they called their capital *dār al-khilāfat* (the abode of the Caliphate). Akbar's famous gold coin bore the inscription 'The great Sultan, the exalted Khalīfah'. It certainly never formed any part of the policy of the Mughals to acknowledge the over-lordship of the Ottoman Sultan; their own wealth and power made them independent of outside assistance, even if any could have been rendered by an empire so far removed from their own, nor did the current theory of the Caliphate suggest submission to some central Muslim authority. . . . Correspondence was opened in the name of Akbar in 1557 with (the Ottoman) Sultan Sulaiman, when Akbar was only a boy, fourteen years of age; advantage was taken of the presence in India of the Turkish admiral, Sīdī 'Alī Katibī, to establish relations with the Ottoman court, and 'string the kingly pearls of confidence on the thread of affection', and 'bind together the chains of union and love'.

Accordingly, Sulaymān is addressed as 'he who has attained the exalted rank of the caliphate', the familiar verse (Qur'ān, xxxv, 37) is quoted; and prayers are offered that his caliphate may abide for ever. At the same time the Ottoman Sultan is reminded that there is now installed on 'the seat of the Sultanate and the throne of the Khilāfat of the realms of Hind and Sind', a monarch whose magnificence is equal to that of Solomon.

[1] Arnold, *The Caliphate*, 113-14.

[2] The country lying north of Afghanistan and east of the river Amū Darya or Oxus.

'The same claim was repeated in the reign of Shāh Jahān', in a letter to the Sultan Ibrāhīm, but at the same time the letter adds a word of praise and congratulation for the victories of the 'Khalīfah of the (four) rightly Directed Khalīfahs . . .' As the title Khalīfah had been adopted officially by the imperial house, of course historians and men of letters had no hesitation in making use of it, and numerous examples might be given, down to the reign of Shāh 'Ālam II (1759–1806), whose authority for a considerable part of his life was not even effective within the walls of his own palace. Yet his biographer lauds him as Khalīfah and Shadow of God.[1] Nevertheless, in a country like India, in which the study of the Traditions was prosecuted with so much zeal, there was always a considerable body of learned men who remained faithful to the earlier doctrine that the caliphate could belong only to the Quraysh.[2]

Relations to the Caliphate Since 1800

The question of the Indian Muslim community's relation to the caliphate in more recent times has been provocative of intense agitation, throwing the whole country into turmoil, and a state of excitement which has not entirely died down even in the present day. In the absence of a ruler who could act as its immediate temporal and religious head, the Sunnī Muslim community of India has for many years past taken especial interest in the affairs of the Ottoman caliphate; and had been in the habit for many decades of mentioning the name of the Ottoman Caliph in the *khuṭbah*. To him they looked as the defender of the faith, since the only hope of the abiding glory and prestige of Islam was centred in him. In fact, more than once during the last hundred years, the question has arisen whether India, without a Muslim ruler, was technically *dār-ul-Islām*, or if it was not actually *dār-ul-Ḥarb*. Accustomed as they had been for so many centuries to lean on an emperor, sultan, or local king as the support of the faith, to consider him as the leader around which they

[1] Arnold, *The Caliphate*, 159-62. Joseph de Hammer, 'Memoir on the Diplomatic Relations between the Courts of Delhi and Constantinople', *T.R.A.S.*, ii, 462-486.

[2] The Quraysh was the name of the Arab tribe to which Muḥammad belonged.

could rally, the large Muslim community of India was without a leader, and without a voice that could speak with any degree of authority. It found itself floundering among the unaccustomed vicissitudes of a new age, like a ship without a rudder. It was lost, and was trying to find itself, and in the process it began to clutch at the caliphate; for the Caliph symbolized the unity and strength of Islam.

The story of how the Muslims of India have valiantly struggled during the last half century to create a certain amount of organization, unity and internal strength without the aid of any resident ruling authority will be told in a later chapter. But for the present we must note certain aspects of the 'Khilāfat Agitation' which bear upon the subject.

It is well known that, as long as there was even a nominal ruler on the Mughul throne of Delhi, Muslim opinion of India was more or less indifferent to the fate of the Caliph of Constantinople. When, however, in 1853 Bahādur Shāh II reversed the practice of his predecessors, in maintaining a complete independence of the Mughul throne by making a secret avowal of allegiance to Persia, the first step was taken toward disturbing Indian Muslim complacency in regard to the caliphate. Finally, when this last of the Mughul rulers was overthrown in 1857, and the *dār-ul-Khilāfat* of India was empty, then Indian Sunnites, realizing the critical position of their community, were forced to direct their religious loyalty to the Ottoman Caliph.[1]

During the years 1877–1908 the relation of Indian Sunnīs to the Ottoman caliphate began to assume something of form and substance. The Sultan, 'Abd-ul-Ḥamīd II, was developing his doctrine of Pan-Islamism, and under the leadership of such agents as Jamāl-ud-Dīn Afghānī, who made his headquarters at Hyderabad and Calcutta during his enforced stay in India (1879–1881?), an extensive propaganda was developed.[2] When the Damascus-Medina railway project was being promoted by the Caliph, Indian subscriptions were sent forward from Lahore. In 1912, during the war between Italy and Tripoli, Muslim support in India was aroused on behalf of the Caliph with no little success. In 1914,

[1] F. W Buckler, 'A New Interpretation of Akbar's Infallibility Decree', *J.R.A.S.*, 1924, 608. [2] See *E.I.*, art. 'Djamāl-al-Dīn Afghānī'.

however, when the Great War broke like a storm over the heads of the nations of the world, the Caliph sought to play upon the sympathies of the Muslims of India and elsewhere by declaring a *jihād*. It was assumed that, by thus arousing the loyalty of the Muslims of India, sufficient trouble would be created for the Allies to make an easy victory for the Germans and the Islamic hosts possible. But at this critical juncture there was a great dashing of hopes; for Muslim India, contrary to expectations in some quarters, turned a deaf ear to the Caliph's proclamation of a holy war.

However, it was not long until a reaction began to set in. The leaders of the Indian Muslims began to be fearful of the judgment that would be meted out to Turkey in case she was defeated, and they suddenly became anxious to preserve as much of the dignity of the Caliph and of Islam as possible. Here was a problem in loyalties. They honestly desired to be loyal to the Government of India, and at the same time felt their loyalty to the Caliph, as the symbol of Islamic power and prestige, growing stronger and stronger. This second loyalty soon gave birth to the now well-known 'Khilāfat Agitation', which had as its object to help to secure as good terms as possible for a defeated Caliph in the interests of Islam and the Muslim world. The first visible result of this movement was the promise, made by the British Premier in August, 1917, that the Allies would seek to preserve the best interests of Islam in the final settlement with Turkey.

Finally, a permanent 'Khilāfat' organization was effected and a Central Committee was established in Bombay (1920), with provincial and district committees all over India. During the agitation that followed, lasting with varying fortunes even up to the present time, large funds were collected, delegations were sent to Paris and London to seek to secure the best possible terms for the Caliph, while feeling in India grew intense. In their growing interest in the Caliph and the waning fortunes of the caliphate, enthusiasm ran high. Certain leaders preached the doctrine of *ḥijrat*, and declared that India was no longer a suitable place where Muslims could live and exercise the functions of their religion. Hence no less than eighteen thousand people sold their property and fled away to Afghanistan and Central Asia, all because of their devotion to the Caliph.[1] In Malabar, in 1921, a serious rebellion of the fanatical Mappillas[2] against the Government was started; a 'Khilāfat Kingdom' was temporarily set up, and more than a thousand cases of the forcible conversion of Hindus were reported.

The agitation continued in full force from one end of India to the other, and even won the support of the Hindus under the leadership of Mr. M. K. Gandhi, who gave the whole force of his political power and personal endeavour to the movement. Thus matters stood, up to March, 1924, when Kemal Pasha pricked the khilāfat bubble, and rudely shattered the hopes of the Indian Muslims for the maintenance of the dignity and prestige of not only the Caliph but the Muslim world, by summarily deposing the Caliph 'Abd-ul-Majīd, and by banishing him and his family from the Turkish nation.

Even this did not silence the agitation or the agitators. Out of sympathy for the Caliph, telegrams were sent to him from India protesting the loyalty of the Indian Muslims, and even two well-known Shī'ah leaders, the Rt. Hon. Syed Amīr 'Alī and His Highness the Āghā Khān, attempted to criticize the action of Angora and to remonstrate with Kemal Pasha by sending letters, which were published in a certain Constantinople journal. But the Turkish Government paid no attention to these protests from India, and when at last the supporters of the Caliph in India saw there was no more to be expected from that quarter, they turned their attention to attempting to support the call from Cairo for a Khilāfat Conference, with delegates from all over the Muslim world, who should confer and endeavour to agree on the election of a Caliph to act as the head of a 'League of Muslim Nations'. When this conference was finally held in Cairo, during 1926, Indian delegates were present, thus clearly indicating that the Indian Muslim belief in the caliphate as an institution still persists; and that there is a hearty desire that there should be a visible head for Islam in whom Muslims may centre their loyalty, and give expression to their belief in the possibility of maintaining Islam as a united world force.

[1] L. F. Rushbrook Williams, *India in 1920*, Calcutta, 1921, 51-53.

[2] See p. 34 f.

MOSQUES AND CONGREGATIONS

The Muslim religious organization is not congregational in system. It resembles the Church in certain of its episcopal forms, in that it is organized from the top down, rather than from the bottom up. Thus one of the first duties devolving upon a conqueror, such as Muḥammad b. Qāsim in Sind, was to arrange for the organization of the local congregation, made up of converts and the garrison. In fact, he was armed with a mandate to see that, wherever there was an ancient place or famous city or town, 'mosques and pulpits should be erected there'.[1] So, after the capture of Debul, the first city taken in Sind, he marked out a place for the Muslims to dwell in and built a mosque.[2] Likewise at Nīrūn he built a mosque on the site of the temple of Budh, and ordered prayers to be proclaimed in the Muslim fashion, and appointed an *imām*.[3]

Wherever these early Arab armies went they established small colonies or abodes in cities of their own construction, or in cantonments adjacent to the original cities, as in the case of Multan. Some one of the camp followers who was qualified was appointed as an *imām* of the mosque, and placed in charge of the instruction of converts. Much of the conquered land, also, was bestowed on sacred buildings and institutions. Such religious foundations are to be found to-day all over the country. The oldest of them are of course in Sind, where at one time they were so numerous that they consumed one-third of the entire revenue of the State under the Tālpūr kings.[4]

One of the duties of the kings and emperors was to build mosques within their dominions. The largest and most beautiful mosques of India have been built with the funds of the public treasuries of such monarchs as Quṭb-ud-Dīn, who started the mosque at old Delhi, famous for its minār, and who also built the Arhāī-Din-kā-Jhoṇprā, Ajmīr; Shāh Jahān, who built the Jāmi' Masjid, Delhi, and the Motī Masjid at Agra. Likewise the Imāmbārah Masjid of the Shī'ahs, at Lucknow, was built by the King

[1] *Chach-nāmah*, E.D., I, 206.
[2] Al-Balādhurī, *Futūh-ul-Buldān*, E.D., I, 120.
[3] *Chach-nāmah*, E.D., I, 159.
[4] E.D., *History of India*, I, 462.

of Oudh, Āṣaf-ud-Daulah, and the Makka Masjid, at Hyderabad, Deccan, was started by Qulī Quṭb Shāh and finished by Aurangzīb.

Such mosques were endowed with lands or given other income by the State; and to-day the problem of handling these pious foundations for the benefit and best good of the Muslim community has become a matter for the legislation of the various Provincial Councils. Mosques also have been built by individuals for their own private use. Such private chapels are to be found everywhere; and often connected with such a mosque is a private cemetery. Private endowments were assigned to such mosques, and thus their upkeep was provided for.

The first mosques were built, as has been observed, in connexion with military camps and occupation. But, as settlers from the Afghan hills began to increase in number, and as the Muslim chiefs were given grants of land for meritorious service in the government or army where they went to take up their residence, private and community mosques began to spring up. Wherever the governors resided there were mosques, and thus Muslim religious centres began to increase as the government gradually spread over the land and colonies were established. Community effort for the erection of mosques is the practice everywhere to-day. Mosque erection and repair funds are created, and some very large and fine mosques in recent times have been built in this way. Others, scattered through the villages, are poor, mud structures costing but little more than twenty-five or thirty rupees to build. In the case of some of the larger community mosques, years pass before sufficient money is raised to finish the structure; so the process of construction goes on little by little as the funds come in.[1]

[1] In this connexion it is highly interesting to note that a movement is being started by Khwājah Ḥasan Niẓāmī, of Delhi, called the *Tanẓīm-i-Masjid* (Organization of Mosques Movement). It has for its object the taking of a census of all the mosques in India, securing better organization of the congregations, improved arrangements for the appointment and pay of the *imāms* (pastors), and the erection of new mosques where they are needed. See the monthly magazine edited by Ḥasan Niẓāmī, *Niẓām-ul-Mashā'ikh*, March, 1928, 35.

The Ecclesiastical and Civil Organization

Great as the importance of the ruler was in the matter of his relation to the Muslims as a religious community, he was not a wholly independent executive. Islam, it is true, has no state clergy; nevertheless, we find a counterpart to our Christian hierarchies in the 'ulamā[1] who were associated with the court. Islam being a Religious State, these graduates in divinity were also graduates in law. Thus it was from them that the various officers of government as well as religion were chosen, since the civil and religious functions of the State were one and inseparable. It was through these men, whose presence was indispensable to a ruler to assist in the interpretation and execution of the law, that the functions of the religious and social life of the Muslim community were carried on from the beginning. Following the invading armies, traders and adventurers from Muslim lands, came those learned in the law as well as the scriptures.

While the number of such learned men was undoubtedly small at first, as in the case of the Arab invasion of Sind, yet, as time went on, the number increased. Ultimately, through this group, Islam in India came to have a 'permanent establishment' of religious and law officers, who were able to perform the religious and civil functions required by the community. This 'permanent establishment' was largely independent of the existence of a Muslim ruler to whom the community would ordinarily look to perfect the organization, and make the necessary appointments. In a small state, it would be possible for the ruler to be personally responsible for appointments, even of *imāms*[2] for the mosques; as we find Muḥammad b. Qāsim was in the early days of the establishment of Islam in Sind. But when the business of State increased, and the community became great in numbers and was widely spread, the duties of government became more and more complex, so that it would naturally be impossible for the ruler at Delhi to take cognizance of such minor appointments. In fact, the ruler was often entirely in the hands of the learned, and how great their influence was may be judged, as Blochmann points out, from the fact that, 'of all the Muslim emperors at Delhi and

[1] Men learned in Islamic 'sciences'. [2] Prayer leaders or 'ministers'.

Agra, only Akbar, and perhaps 'Alā ad-Dīn Khiljī, succeeded in putting down this haughty set.'[1]

The growth of the ecclesiastical organization has been one of gradual development, and it is possible to indicate only in the merest outline just what has occurred in the past centuries. In the first place it should be noted that the responsible religious leaders, for a considerable period of the history of Islam, were either foreigners, chiefly Arabs or Persians or their descendants.

So far as the invasions of Maḥmūd are concerned, we may assume that they left behind as little in the way of permanent ecclesiastical organization as of political. Lahore was the only place permanently occupied; and, since we hear of one Shaykh Ismā'īl beginning his work as a Muslim missionary there as early as A.D. 1005, it is reasonable to suppose that here also a permanent ecclesiastical organization was effected. Quṭb-ud-Dīn Aybak, who was the first independent king of Delhi, must have found in his time plenty of learned men on whom to draw as suitable appointees for the administration of the religious functions of the mosques as well as the regular affairs of State, for we are told that he built nearly a thousand mosques on the sites of as many temples which he had destroyed.[2]

Another event of great significance for Muslim India was the Mongol invasion, which swept over Central Asia in the thirteenth century and overturned the governments of the countries to which it extended. As a result of this invasion, with its attendant horrors, men of eminence and learning were forced to leave their native lands; and during the reign of Ghiyāth-ud-Dīn Balban (A.D. 1266–1286) they came to India in large numbers, as his was the only Muslim government that was not subverted.[3] 'He used to boast that no less than fifteen sovereign princes had been dependent on his hospitality.' But we are told that the number of literary fugitives was, naturally, still more considerable, including many famous authors of that age. Among these men there were many who occupied positions in the civil and ecclesiastical

[1] H. Blochmann, *Introduction to the Ā'īn-i-Akbarī*, vi.

[2] Ḥasan Niẓāmī, *Tāj-ul-Ma'āthir*, E.D., II, 223.

[3] Elphinstone, op. cit., 380.

establishment of the government, and helped to advance the cause of Muslim learning in India, thus adding to the tradition for scholarship that was rapidly becoming part of the heritage of the community.

An excellent illustration of the manner in which learned and capable men from outside India were used in effecting the organization of Islam in the early stages is afforded by the life of Minhāj as-Sirāj, the author of *Ṭabaqāt-i-Nāṣirī*. His father before him had been appointed a *qāḍī* in the army of Hindustan by Muḥammad G͟hūrī in A.D. 1186, and he himself came from G͟hūr to Sind in A.D. 1227. He was a learned man and was placed in charge of the 'Fīrūzī College', at Uch. Later he was made *Qāḍī* (judge) of Delhi and of all Bahrām Shāh's territories. About A.D. 1246 he was appointed Principal of the Nāṣirīyah College, at Delhi. He also served as *Qāḍī* of Gwalior, and *K͟haṭīb* (preacher) in the cathedral mosque at Delhi. Under Iltutmish he was appointed one of the court preachers, law officer, director of preaching, and of all religious, moral, and judicial affairs.[1]

As the business of government increased with the expansion of Muslim rule and the development of a Muslim community, it became necessary for the ruler to enlarge his organization. One of the earliest lists of officers of government on record is that given by Shihāb-ud-Dīn Abū'l-'Abbās Ḥamīd, of Damascus (A.D. 1297–1348), who visited Delhi early in the fourteenth century. He says that there were four main departmental officers in the central government: the *Amrīyah*, in charge of the army and people at large; the *Ṣadr-i-Jahān*, in charge of the lawyers and learned men; the *Shayk͟h-ul-Islam*, in charge of the *darwīshes*; and lastly there was a department in charge of *dābirs* or secretaries, who were over all travellers, ambassadors, and men of letters.[2]

Under the Mug͟huls, the work of organization and administration of the affairs of the Muslim community reached its highest development. The chief officers of government were the *Qāḍī-ul-Quḍāt* (Chief Justice), who was responsible for the appointment of all the *qāḍīs* (canon-law judges), the *'ādils* (common-law judges), and the *muftīs* (subordinate law officers); secondly, there

[1] E.D., *History of India*, II, 259, 260.

[2] *Masālik-ul-Abṣār fī Mamālik-il-Amṣār*, E.D., III, 576.

was the *Dīwān* (Chancellor of the Exchequer); thirdly, the *K͟hāṇ-i-Sāmān* (Lord High Steward of government property); fourthly, there was the *Ṣadr-uṣ-Ṣudūr*, who was in charge of the *waqfs* (religious endowments). The *Shayk͟h-ul-Islam* was the head of the *darwīshes* as before. Lastly, mention should be made of the officer known as the *Muḥtasib* (Censor of Public Morals). His duties were to enforce the commands of the Prophet and put down practices forbidden by him, such as drinking, gambling, and the use of drugs. Besides he was clothed with authority to put down heretical teaching, and to punish Muslims who neglected the five daily prayers and the fast of Ramaḍān. It apparently was not an uncommon sight to see him going through the streets with a band of soldiers demolishing and plundering liquor shops, distilleries, and gambling dens wherever they were to be found, seeking to enforce the strict observance of religious rites on the Muslim populace. Sometimes his soldiers even had pitched battles with the 'bold sinners who showed fight'. During the reign of Aurangzīb one of the duties of this officer was to demolish temples that had been recently built.[1] The Muslim rulers, as a matter of course, levied the *zakāt* (tithes), amounting to one-fortieth of the income, on the Muslims. In theory they were obliged to spend this money for the erection of mosques, the subsidizing of saints and theological teachers, the endowment of saints' tombs and monasteries, the care of Muslim paupers and orphans, and the providing of dowries for Muslim maidens. But in later times, Muslim rulers frequently abused this trust by spending *zakāt* money on their own personal needs and public works.[2]

While the ruler relied on his *'ulamā* for legal interpretation and advice in affairs of state, on some occasions he acted on his own judgment, regardless of the opinion of the wise and learned counsellors. It is said of Sher Shāh that he lived in such close relations with these advisers that he never breakfasted without the company of his *'ulamā* and priests.[3] When a judgment was needed on the punishment to be meted out to an offending Brāhman, who had caused the apostasy of Muslim women, the

[1] Jadunath Sarkar, *Mug͟hal Administration*, 30 ff.

[2] *Ibid.*, 19, 29, 30.

[3] 'Abbās K͟hāṇ, *Ta'rīk͟h-i-Sher Shāh*, E.D., IV, 408.

case was placed before 'the judges, doctors, elders, and lawyers', who rendered their decision to the Sultan.[1]

But rulers were not always so reliant on their *'ulamā*; and sometimes took matters into their own hands. Akbar went so far as virtually to set aside the authority of the *'ulamā* in his reign in matters of religion, by securing from them the following written decision, which it would appear they were forced to sign:

> If there be a variance of opinion among *mujtahids* upon a question of religion, and His Majesty, in his penetrating understanding and unerring judgment should incline to one opinion . . . and give his decree for the benefit of mankind, and for the due regulation of the world, we do hereby agree that such a decree is binding on us, and on the whole nation. Signed by the principal *'ulamā* and lawyers.[2]

Sometimes, when a ruler was determined and careless in his personal habits, which were contrary in many respects to the Muslim law, the learned men felt called upon to take him to task. But their remonstrances sometimes fell on deaf ears, or received only ridicule. An outstanding instance of this was the case of Jahāngīr. The traveller, Catrou, in his *History of the Mughal Dynasty*, gives the following description of this emperor's attitude toward some of the practices of Islam and the troubles his *'ulamā* had with him.

> The fast which the Muslims observe so scrupulously for an entire month was the subject of his derision. He invited to his table the most conscientious observers of the laws of religion and inveigled them into a companionship in his excess of wine and in eating prohibited meats, the *qāḍī* and the *imāms*, who are the doctors of Muslim law, in vain admonishing him that the use of certain meats was forbidden by Al-Coran. Fatigued with their importunities, he inquired in what religion the use of drinks and food of every species without distinction was permitted. The reply was, 'In the case of the Christian religion alone.' 'We must then', he rejoined, 'all turn Christians. Let there be tailors brought to us to convert our robes into close coats, and our turbans into hats.' At these words the doctors trembled for their sect. Fear and interest made them hold a less severe language. They all declared that the sovereign was not bound by the precepts of Al-Coran and that the monarch might, without scruple, use whatever meats and drinks were most agreeable to him.[3]

[1] *Ta'rīkh-i-Fīrūz Shāhī*, E.D., III, 365.

[2] Budāyūnī, *Muntakhab-ut-Tawārīkh*, E.D., V, 532.

[3] E.D., *History of India*, VI, 513, 514.

Beyond the small group of advisers who surrounded the ruler, the circle widened out first to all the provincial government centres, such as Budaun, Lahore, and the cities of the south and east, where the religious officiants would always be found in sufficient numbers to maintain high standards of knowledge and Islamic observance. But, as the circle widened still further to the smaller towns and villages, it became more and more difficult to secure properly educated men to assume the duties of *imām* and *qāḍī*, with the result that even to-day there are great numbers of Muslims in the villages of India who are but poorly instructed in the faith, and who, if they have a mosque at all, have only a poor affair, built of mud walls with a thatched roof, the *imām* of which is barely able to read the Qur'ān, and then with but little idea of what it really means.

Muslim Law as a Unifying Force in the Community

While the conception of the Law (*Sharī'at*) in its details may often be every hazily conceived and imperfectly understood, yet it wields a potent influence over the minds of the vast majority of the millions of Muslims of India even in the villages, and reverence for it is maintained to the best of their ability. All men, from the ruler to the slave, are alike under the Law of Islam. This Law must be obeyed or the believer will suffer not only the punishment of his community, but, what is worse, the punishment of God Himself on the Last Day.

When Islam was first introduced into India, in the eighth century, the *qāḍīs* were guided solely by the Qur'ān, as it was not until a later date that the Traditions and the Four Schools of Law were developed. As time went on, however, legal decisions were not so easily arrived at. A mass of legal literature, decisions, and commentaries on the Islamic Law Books had been collected in India, which formed a perfect maze. Through this it was an impossibility for any but the most learned to find his way. Akbar tried to simplify matters in his reign by issuing circular orders, which obviated the necessity of referring any religious, political, or fiscal matters touched on in the circulars to *qāḍīs* or *muftīs*.[1]

At a later period Aurangzīb went a step further, and at great

[1] Budāyūnī, *Muntakhab-ut-Tawārīkh*, E.D., V, 487.

expense had an enormous work on Hanafite Law decisions compiled. This compilation, which is known as the *Fatāwa-i-'Ālamgīrī*, is described by Bakhtāwar Khāṇ as follows:

> As it is a great object with this Emperor that all Muslims should follow the principles of the religion as expounded by the most competent law officers and the followers of the Hanafī persuasion . . . and as there was no book which embodied them (the principles of the Hanafite sect) all, . . . therefore His Majesty, the protector of the Faith, determined that a body of eminently learned and able men of Hindustan should take up the voluminous and most trustworthy works which were collected in the royal library, and, having made a digest of them (the legal opinions contained in them), compose a book which might form a standard canon of the law, and afford to all an easy and available means of ascertaining the proper and authoritative interpretation. . . . When the work, with God's pleasure, is completed, it will be for all the world the standard exposition of the law, and render everyone independent of Moslem doctors.[1]

Thus matters stood until the complete dissolution of the Mughul Empire. But with the establishment of the British courts, Muḥammadan Law began to enter upon a new and interesting phase in India, which Sir 'Abdur Raḥīm describes in the following words:

> It is no longer the law of the land, and is applicable to the Muḥammadans so far as its administration by the courts is concerned only by the declaration of the sovereign power.
>
> In the early days of the British settlement the Muḥammadan Code was enforced in all its departments, but in the course of time Muḥammadan laws relating to crimes and punishments, revenues, land tenures, procedure, evidence, and in part also transfer of property, have been gradually abandoned and replaced by enactments of the legislature. Questions relating to family relations, and status, namely, marriage, divorce, maintenance and guardianship of minors, succession and inheritance, religious usages and institutions, and dispositions of property by gift (*hibah*), will, and *waqf* (pious endowment) are still governed by the Muḥammadan law, so far as Muḥammadans are concerned, and in some parts of India the Muḥammadan law of pre-emption is also recognized. Further, if any sect of Muḥammadans has its own rule, that rule, generally speaking, should be followed with respect to litigants of the sect.
>
> The administration of the Muḥammadan as well as Hindu laws was for some time carried on with the help of Indian officers who acted as expert advisers to the courts, the Muḥammadan law officers being called Maulavis and the Hindu law officers Pundits. But for a long time the

[1] *Mir'āt-i-'Ālam*, E.D., VII, 159, 160.

employment of such experts, being considered undesirable and unnecessary, has been abandoned.[1]

> It may be observed here that the Friday and 'Īd prayers are regularly held all over India, and recognized to be validly held according to the Muḥammadan Canonical Law. Further, the Muḥammadans of India enjoy absolute proteetion of person and property and religious freedom, and their laws relating to religious institutions and usages, and those governing family relations and succession and certain forms of transfer of property, are enforced by the Anglo-Indian courts. Another convincing test that India under the present form of government must be regarded as *dār-ul-Islām*, is that these Muḥammadans who strictly follow the rules of juristic law regarding *ribā* (usury) do not feel themselves justified in taking interest on money advanced to non-Muslims.[2]

The situation in regard to the application of Muslim law in relation to the courts, which of course has nothing to do with strictly religious observances, presents a situation of peculiar interest. There have been so many accessions to the Muslim community from Hinduism that not infrequently the tribal or customary law of the converts, which obtained in their former Hindu society, has continued to be recognized as the rule by which they shall be governed, even though it may be quite contrary to Muslim law. This matter of 'Muḥammadan Law *vs.* Customary Law' forms the subject of a very interesting investigation by Mr. S. Roy, who makes the following observations:

> The intimate connexion between law and religion in the Muḥammadan faith is very great, and consequently the authority of law is supreme among Muḥammadans. Any variation or modification of that Koranic law—especially in matters of inheritance and succession—by family or local custom is usually not permitted.[3]

In fact, it has even been assumed by some that 'any attempt to repudiate the Law of the Koran would amount to infidelity'; that no such custom 'should be recognized by our (the Anglo-Indian) courts, which are bound by express enactment to administer Muḥammadan law in questions of inheritance among Muḥammadans'; and that 'the law which governs these Provinces (the United Provinces) gives no opening, where parties are Muḥammadans, to a consideration of custom'.[4]

[1] Sir 'Abdur Raḥīm, *The Principles of Muḥammadan Jurisprudence*, 37.
[2] *Ibid.*, 397.
[3] S. Roy, *Customs and Customary Law in British India*, 378.
[4] *Ibid.*

Nevertheless customs and customary law have been followed again and again in certain instances, thus showing that conditions in India are such that strict interpretation of the Qur'ānic law has neither been deemed wise nor absolutely necessary; thus setting aside the technical opinion, that for Muḥammadans the Muḥammadan law must be followed. In dealing with Hindu converts to Islam it has been held that, 'although the Muḥammadan law, pure and simple as found in the Koran, is part of the Muḥammadan religion, it does not of necessity apply to all who embrace that creed'; and that, in dealing with such converts, the principle is recognized that in questions of succession and inheritance Hindu law is applied to those converts who were originally Hindus, provided they so desire it. In fact, in Bombay, the Punjab, Oudh, and the Central Provinces, 'custom takes precedence of Muḥammadan law'.[1]

The courts give distinct recognition 'to the legal validity of the institution of caste, in some form or other, among Muḥammadans', and consequently in certain communal or internal matters, such as marriage and social status, the courts have held that Muslims of a particular caste must be bound by the rules of that caste.[2]

> The Sunnī Bohoras, in Northern Gujarāt, who were originally Rajputs and were converted to Islam centuries ago, in matters of succession are still governed by the Hindu law. The Molesalam Girasias, of Broach, who, originally Rajputs, were converted some centuries ago, are governed by Hindu law in matters of inheritance and succession. The Mappillas, or Moplahs, on the Malabar coast, generally follow the Moslem law except in matters of inheritance.[3]

The Variety of Legal Schools

In respect of the different legal schools that obtain in India, it thus appears that there is a variety scarcely to be found in any other Muslim country. The majority of Indian Muslims follow the legal interpretations of the Ḥanafite school; there are some followers of the legal code of Imām ash-Shāfi'ī in southern India among the Mappillas. The Shī'ahs (Ithnā 'Asharīyah) of course observe their own Imāmī code, while, in addition, there is the

[1] S. Roy, op. cit., 379-80. [2] *Ibid.*, 401. [3] *Ibid.*, 402.

large area among Muslim converts where customary law in civil matters may be applied. Besides, there are other sects, such as the Ahl-i-Ḥadīth and the Ahl-i-Qur'ān, which have definitely set about modifying the religious law to accord with their own conceptions of legal authority in religion.

The Modern Organization of the 'Ulamā

The graduates in theology (*mawlawīs* or *maulvīs*), who are also called *'ulamā*, on whom the conduct of the religious affairs of the community depended, seem to have been devoid of any sort of organization in a formal sense at first, though they undoubtedly maintained an important form of fellowship through the ever increasing number of colleges which served as centres of control and regulation of the religious development over large areas. In fact, it is these colleges which to-day control the thinking and education of the masses through the ministers of religion who pass through them and out into the varied streams of Indian Muslim life. It is only in these modern times that an attempt has been made to organize the *'ulamā* of all India, so that they can meet and consider problems affecting the life of the Muslim community. This organization is known as the Jam'īyat-ul-'Ulamā-i-Hind. It has annual conferences, and central headquarters at Delhi. The body is not infrequently asked for a legal decision (*fatwā*) on some matter of religious duty, as, for instance, as to whether it was permissible to omit the Pilgrimage to Mecca during the struggle between Ibn Sa'ūd and King Ḥusayn for the control of the Hejāz. To-day the *'ulamā* are better organized than has ever been the case before, and consequently it is becoming possible for them to make their influence felt more widely than in the past.

The Traditional Educational System

We have already mentioned the fact that these learned men (*'ulamā*) have always been the backbone of the religious and legal system of Islam in India. We have seen the enormous amount of influence they wield. It now remains to consider the system by which they have been educated and trained, as well as the general system of Muslim education which has obtained from the beginning, and which has been responsible for the shaping of the community on the lines in which it has developed. The traditional system in India does not differ one whit from that found elsewhere in the Muslim world. There is the mosque school (*maktab*), where elementary principles of reading and writing are taught, as well as the reading of the Qur'ān, and the elements of religious law (*fiqh*). The chief aim of these schools has always been, and still is, religious teaching: to make good Muslims rather than to impart knowledge in the broader sense. The number of such schools of religious education in a country like India is enormous. Beyond the *maktab* is the *madrasah* (college), commonly called also *dār-ul-'ulūm* (abode of the sciences), where the student is kept in residence for years, studying the Islamic 'sciences' pertaining chiefly to the Qur'ān with the commentaries, the Traditions, and the Canon Law.

The need for such schools was early recognized, and it is certain that, as mosques were established from the earliest times, they were made centres for the training of converts and their children, and that the *imāms* were expected to employ no small part of their time in this way. *Madrasahs* came later, but provision was made for them quite early in the history of the spread of the religion of Islam. So far as we are able to ascertain, they were usually built by the ruler. The first record we have of a *madrasah* being founded dates from about the year A.D. 1191, when Muḥammad G͟hūrī, during his conquest of Ajmīr, is said to have 'destroyed pillars and foundations of the idol temples, and built in their stead mosques and colleges'.[1] Muḥammad Bak͟htyār K͟haljī in Bengal established *madrasahs* after his invasion, and most of the rulers did the same. The Fīrūzī College, at Uch, founded about A.D. 1227, and the Nāṣirīyah College, founded about A.D. 1237, at Delhi, by Iltutmish, were two of the most important of these early *madrasahs*, of both of which Minhāj as-Sirāj, the author of the *Ṭabaqāt-i-Nāṣirī*, was the principal at different times in the thirteenth century. That even colleges were numerous in the early days there seems to be no doubt, though the testimony of some writers may be open to question, as, for example, that of Shihāb-ud-Dīn Abū'l-'Abbās

[1] Ḥasan Niẓāmī, *Tāj-ul-Ma'āthir*, E.D., II, 215.

Ḥamīd, who visited India in the first half of the fourteenth century, and in describing Delhi declares that he found one thousand colleges, one of which belonged to the Shāfi'īs and the rest to the Ḥanafīs![1] Colleges built by rulers were always heavily endowed, often with lands; and payment for maintenance of the establishment, if not otherwise provided for, was met from the state treasury.

Besides *madrasahs* built by kings and emperors, there are some which have been built by private individuals. Of these, mention should be made of the one built in A.D. 1478–79 in Bīdar, by Maḥmūd Gawan, the ruins of which are still standing, and of another, founded in A.D. 1561, near Delhi, by Māhum Anagah, the nurse of Akbar.

It is an ill wind that blows nobody good, and, as has been already noted, the devastating raids of the Mongols in Central Asia drove many learned men from their homes to find refuge in India, so that, almost from the outset, the *madrasahs* were well supplied with teachers of the highest learning. Here, in their new-found home, they successfully established the tradition of scholarship which had made the Muslim schools of the west, whence they had come, so famous.

The largest and best of these schools were to be found in the chief centres where Muslim rule was established most firmly. At the present time, the most important of all the Indian *madrasahs* is not found, as might be expected, at Delhi, but at the small city of Deoband, in the Saharanpur district of the western United Provinces. The *Dār-ul-'Ulūm* there is to India what the University *al-Azhar*, in Cairo, is to Egypt and the Near East. From these *madrasahs*, found all over the land, teachers now, as formerly, go out to teach in the *maktabs*, or mosque schools, even to the remotest towns and villages.

We are not surprised that, in the middle of the nineteenth century, Sir Syed Aḥmad Khāṇ found it necessary to enter a protest against the Muslim community's continuing to fetter itself with the exclusively oriental curriculum taught in the schools, and proclaimed far and wide his gospel of modernization. What does strike us as being peculiarly interesting is that a Muslim

[1] *Masālik-ul-Abṣār fī Mamālik-il-Amṣār*, E.D., III, 576.

sovereign, as devoted to orthodoxy as Aurangzīb was, should have criticized the classical curriculum of his day. The statements attributed to him by Bernier are so penetrating and discriminating that we shall give them just as Aurangzīb is supposed to have delivered them to his former teacher, who repeatedly sought an appointment from the Emperor.

Pray what is your pleasure with me, Mullah Ji, Monsieur the Doctor? . . . Do you pretend that I ought to exalt you to the first honours of the State? Let us then examine your title to any mark of distinction. I do not deny you would possess such a title if you had filled my young mind with suitable instruction. Show me a well-educated youth, and I will say that it is doubtful who has the stronger claim to his gratitude, his father or his tutor. But what was the knowledge I derived under your tuition? You taught me that the whole of *Franguistan* (i.e. Europe) was no more than some inconsiderable island, of which the most powerful monarch was formerly the King of Portugal, then he of Holland, and afterward the King of England. In regard to the other sovereigns of *Franguistan*, such as the King of France and him of *Andalusia*, you told me they resembled our petty Rājās, and that the potentates of *Hindoustan* eclipsed the glory of all other kings; that they alone were *Humayons*, *Ekbars*, *Jehan-Guyres*, or *Chah-Jehans*; the Happy, the Great, the Conquerors of the World, and the Kings of the World; and *that Persia*, *Usbec*, *Kachguer*, *Tartary*, and *Cathay*, *Pegu*, *Siam*, and *China* trembled at the name of the Kings of the *Indies*. Admirable geographer! Deeply read historian! Was it not incumbent upon my preceptor to make me acquainted with the distinguishing features of every nation of the earth; its resources and strength; its mode of warfare, its manners, religion, form of government, and wherein its interests principally consist; and, by a regular course of historical reading, to render me familiar with the origin of states, their progress and decline; the events, accidents or errors, owing to which such great changes and mighty revolutions have been effected? Far from having imparted to me a profound and comprehensive knowledge of the history of mankind, scarcely did I learn from you the names of my ancestors, the renowned founders of this empire. You kept me in total ignorance of their lives, of the events which preceded, and the extraordinary talents that enabled them to achieve their extensive conquests. A familiarity with the languages of surrounding nations may be indispensable in a King; but you would teach me to read and write *Arabic*, doubtless conceiving that you place me under an everlasting obligation for sacrificing so large a portion of time to the study of a language wherein no one can hope to become proficient without ten or twelve years of close application. Forgetting how many important subjects ought to be embraced in the education of a Prince, you acted as if it were chiefly necessary that he should possess great skill in grammar, and such knowledge as belongs to a Doctor of Law; and thus did you waste the precious hours of my youth in the dry, unprofitable, and never-ending task of learning words! . . . . .

Were you not aware that it is during the period of infancy, when the memory is commonly so retentive, that the mind may receive a thousand wise precepts, and be easily furnished with such valuable instruction as will elevate it with lofty conceptions, and render the individual capable of glorious deeds? Can we repeat our prayers, or acquire a knowledge of law, and of the sciences, only through the medium of *Arabic*? May not our devotions be offered up as acceptably, and solid information be communicated as easily, in our mother tongue? You gave my father, *Chah-Jehan*, to understand that you instructed me in philosophy; and, indeed, I have perfect remembrance of your having, during several years, harassed my brain with idle and foolish propositions that seldom ever enter into the business of life. . . . O yes, you caused me to devote the most valuable years of my life to your favourite hypotheses, or systems, and when I left you, I could boast of no greater attainment in the sciences than the use of many obscure and uncouth terms, calculated to discourage, confound, and appal a youth of the most masculine understanding; terms invented to cover the vanity and ignorance of pretenders to philosophy; of men who, like yourself, would impose the belief that they transcend others of their species in wisdom, and that their dark and ambiguous jargon conceals many profound mysteries known only to themselves. If you had taught me that philosophy which adapts the mind to reason, and will not suffer it to rest satisfied with anything short of the most solid arguments; if you had inculcated lessons which elevate the soul and fortify it against the assaults of fortune, tending to produce that enviable equanimity which is neither insolently elated by prosperity nor basely depressed by adversity; if you had made me acquainted with the nature of man; accustomed me always to refer to first principles, and given me a sublime and adequate conception of the universe, and of the order and regular motion of its parts;—if such, I say, had been the nature of the philosophy imbibed under your tuition, I should be more indebted to you than *Alexander* was to *Aristotle*, and should consider it my duty to bestow a very different reward on you than *Aristotle* received from that Prince. . . .[1]

The Pilgrimage

One factor of vast importance for strengthening the communal religious consciousness of Indian Muslims, and for maintaining contacts with the rest of the Muslim world, has been the annual pilgrimage to Mecca and Medina. There are no records of the earliest pilgrim journeys from India, and it is not known how long it took before the traffic began to assume large proportions.

[1] Bernier, *Travels in the Mogul Empire*, 155 ff.

Sūrat, in Gujarāt, in the Mughul period, was used as the pilgrim port. In fact, traces of the old pilgrim route still exist in the town and harbour, and there is a street in Sūrat called the 'Mecca Road' to this day. The number of ships that set out from here annually must have been considerable, for Sher Shāh (A.D. 1539–1545), who had the welfare of his people at heart, is said to have regretted that he had not been able to 'build two fleets of fifty large vessels each as commodious as *sarāīs* (hotels) for the use of the pilgrims from India to Mecca'.[1]

In Akbar's time the pilgrimage became a matter for further royal concern. So, after Gujarāt was annexed (A.D. 1572), it was decided that the dignity and importance of his government demanded that 'every year one of the officers of his court should be appointed Mīr Ḥājī, or Leader of the Pilgrimage, to conduct a caravan from Hindustan, like the caravans from Egypt and Syria, to the holy places. The design was carried out, and every year (for five or six years) a party of enlightened men of Hind . . . received provision for their journey from the royal treasury, and went under an appointed leader from the ports of Gujarāt to the holy places.'[2]

At the present time the pilgrimage arrangements are under the careful supervision of the Government of India, which endeavours to see that the comforts and requirements of some sixty thousand pilgrims a year are looked after. Most of these sail from the ports of Calcutta, Bombay, and Karachi, particularly from the two latter.

From this it will be seen how important the pilgrimage is, for the returned pilgrims are found in villages, towns, and cities from one end of the country to the other. They are invariably the promoters of orthodoxy, and return to receive the veneration and respect of all good Muslims. The pilgrims are recruited from all classes. They are both men and women, peasants and landlords, editors of papers as well as the illiterate, men with university degrees, and even rulers of Native States, one such in recent years being Her Highness the Begam Ṣāḥibah of Bhopal. But it remained for 1926 to add a touch that may in the future make

[1] Ni'amat Allāh, *Ta'rīkh-i-Khān Jahān Lodī*, E.D., V, 108.
[2] Niẓām-ud-Dīn Aḥmad, *Ṭabaqāt-i-Akbarī*, E.D., V, 391.

the pilgrimage an affair of unusual importance to Indian Muslims. Among the delegates to the Muslim World Congress, held at Mecca, June 7th to July 5th, were a number from India, and this body decided that henceforth representatives from each of thirty-three Muslim countries and areas, including India, should meet there annually at the time of the pilgrimage. But, whether this Congress functions or not, there is not the least doubt that the pilgrimage to-day continues to be one of the foremost agencies for promoting the traditions of Muslim culture and religion among the great majority of the seventy million Muslims of India.

CHAPTER V

SHĪ'AHS AND MAHDAWĪS

THE diversity of Indian Islam constitutes one of its most interesting phases, and offers ample testimony to the multitude of divisive influences that have been at work through the history of its development. In this respect it suffers from the difficulties of sectarian weakness, just as Christianity does. Of course, the vast majority of India's extensive Muslim community belong to the orthodox fold of Sunnī Islam, but, apart from this group, there is found in India the largest community of Shī'ahs outside of Persia, where the peculiar faith of the Shī'ah is the established religion.

The number of Shī'ahs in India cannot be definitely given, owing to the fact that the Census returns are by no means complete, in spite of efforts to secure accurate tabulations.[1] It is, however, variously estimated at from four to six millions, and is certainly less than ten per cent of the whole Muslim population. The undoubted reason for the difficulty of collecting the exact figures through the Census is that Shī'ahs are permitted, by their religious doctrine of *taqīyah* (guarding one's self), to conceal their sectarian affiliation, in order to secure immunity from persecution from their hereditary enemies, the Sunnīs. However, at the present time, it would seem that more cordial relations exist between the two communities than ever before, and we are told that there are numerous signs that Shī'ahs reveal their identity far more readily than used to be the case. One curious fact, however, in connexion with the 1911 Census in Peshawar, was that the Shī'ahs recorded were far in excess of their actual numbers, and the reason assigned for this was that if the Sunnī enumerators had a grudge against anyone residing in the block with which they had to deal they would be likely to record him as a Shī'ah by sect.[2]

[1] *C.I.R.*, 1921, I, pt. I, 119. [2] *C.I.R.*, 1911, N.W.F.P., para. 125.

Muslims of Sh'īah persuasion are to be found in practically all parts of India, though they are less numerous in the regions of Bengal, Assam, Bihar and Orissa than elsewhere in proportion to the Sunnīs. They are found chiefly in south India, where their principal centre is Hyderabad; in western India where the chief centres are Bombay and Surat; in northern India and the Punjab, Lucknow being their most important centre, not alone of this area, but of all India.

Indian Shī'ahs belong to two of the unorthodox groups that have become famous in Muslim history, which are designated as the *Ithnā 'Asharīyah* (followers of *twelve Imāms*) and the *Sab'īyah* (followers of *seven Imāms*). To the former group most of the Shī'ahs of India belong. Each group will be dealt with in its place. It is not our purpose to state the doctrinal differences between the Shī'ahs and the Sunnīs in any detail, for these are available in the various accounts that have been given by numerous writers; we shall therefore confine our remarks to the matters of distinctly Indian importance, and shall endeavour simply to describe the Indian Shī'ahs in their historical settings, and their present relationship to the rest of the Muslims of the country.

The term '*Shī'ah*' connotes 'party', and is used to designate all those Muslims who support the claim of 'Alī, the fourth Caliph, as the first and rightful successor to the Prophet. This 'Alī 'party' came into existence certainly not later than the period of discussion over the caliphate which immediately followed the death of Muḥammad. It held that the right of succession to the Imāmate, or caliphate, of the Muslim community was vested in 'Alī and his lineal descendants, since through his wife, Fāṭimah, a daughter of the Prophet, they were all of the Prophet's family. The ideas and influence of the 'Alī party spread to different parts of the Muslim world in the early centuries, and, as time went on, divisions and subdivisions developed one after another. The leading branch of the *Shī'ah*, as has been stated, is known as the *Ithnā 'Asharīyah* (the Twelvers). They hold that there have been in all twelve successors of Muḥammad, and that the twelfth one, who mysteriously disappeared, did not die but is still living. He is concealed under Divine care, and is called the Hidden *Imām*.

They also expect him to return to earth in the character of the Mahdī, whose coming is prophesied as a sign of the last days. Another important group of the Shī'ahs came into existence after the death of the sixth Imām, Ja'far as-Ṣiddīq. They recognize his son, Ismā'īl, as the seventh Imām, with whose death they regard the Imāmate closed. They likewise assign to him a Mahdī character. This group is known as the *Sab'īyah* (Seveners). These are the two groups which are to be found in India. The whole matter of the development of the Shī'ah in its theological and political aspects is very involved, but perhaps enough has been said to indicate the fundamental lines of cleavage that exist between the two Shī'ah groups in India, and between them and the orthodox Sunnīs. We now turn to consider them both in more detail, whence they came, how they are organized, and their main activities.

The Ithnā 'Asharīyah or Imāmīs

The Muslim conquerors of India were all Sunnīs, as also were the emperors who ruled at Delhi and Agra. Nevertheless, Shī'ah influence from Persia was at times very strong, and many Shī'ahs found their way into India, and established communities throughout the land. The introduction of the sect in different parts of the country came about in a variety of ways, which we shall now attempt to describe.

The armies of the kings and emperors of the north, up to the time of the Mughuls, were largely recruited from foreign countries. These, composed of Mongols, Persians, Turks, Georgians, Circassians, Calmucs, and other Tartars, were mostly Shī'ahs.[1] We hear especially of these troops being employed in southern India, for the establishment of the Bahmanī Kingdom in the Deccan in A.D. 1347, and in connexion with the factional strife that prevailed between the Sunnīs and Shī'ahs until the larger kingdom was disrupted and divided into several rival states, many of whose rulers were ardent Shī'ahs. Thus it happened that the Shī'ah religion became established throughout the Deccan.

[1] Elphinstone, op. cit., 476.

Influence of Persian Rulers and Saints

To what extent Persian rulers may have had a hand in encouraging the establishment or maintenance of these Shīʻah kingdoms of the south we may never know fully, but that direct Persian influence of one sort or another was present there cannot be the slightest doubt. This is brought out very clearly in the case of the conversion of Aḥmad Shāh I, the ninth king of the Bahmanī dynasty, who was the first Shīʻah to rule in India (A.D. 1422–1436). His conversion was apparently only a personal matter, and he made no attempt whatever to establish his adopted religion. He seems to have become a Shīʻah some time before A.D. 1430, and the circumstances of his conversion are so suggestive of the Shīʻah influence from Persia, which must have been very active, that I shall give them somewhat in detail. The king seems to have heard of the Shīʻah saint, Shāh Niʻmat Allāh, of Mahan, near Karmān in south Persia, and sent a mission to him, composed of Shaykh Ḥabīb Allāh Junaydī, Mīr Shams-ud-Dīn of Qūm, and others to act as proxies, and to demand admission for the king to the circle of the saint's disciples. This favour was accorded the king, so he sent a second mission to ask that the Shaykh should send one of his sons to India to act as his spiritual guide. Instead, however, Niʻmat Allāh sent his grandson, Mīr Nūr Allāh; but on the death of the saint, in A.D. 1430, his son, Khalīl Allāh, with two other sons visited India, and the sons seem to have taken up permanent residence in the Deccan.[1]

Following the break-up of the Bahmanī kingdom, as we have seen, the rulers of the rival dynasties took an active interest in laying foundations for the establishment of the Shīʻah religion in south India. The first of these was Yūsuf ʻĀdil Shāh, of Bījāpūr, who is said to have enjoyed living in Persia, where he became a zealous Shīʻah.[2] On his accession to the throne, in A.D. 1490, he declared the Shīʻah faith to be the established religion of the state. Evidently, however, it was not all smooth sailing, for we learn that 'by a proceeding so unexampled in India, he caused much disaffection among his own subjects, and produced a combi-

[1] Sir Wolseley Haig, 'The Religion of Aḥmad Shāh Bahmanī', *J.R.A.S.*, 1924, 73. [2] Najm-ul-Ghanī Khān, *Madhāhib-ul-Islām*, 438 f.

nation of all the other Muḥammadan kings against him '.[1] At Aḥmadnagar, the second ruler of the Niẓām Shāh dynasty, Burhān by name, openly professed the Shī'ah religion, when he ascended the throne in A.D. 1509, and made good its establishment in the state.[2] In A.D. 1512, just three years later, when the Turk, Qulī Quṭb, founded the Quṭb Shāh dynasty at Golkonda, he likewise found no difficulty in introducing the Shī'ah faith into his dominions, which formed the beginning of the present Hyderabad State.

There may be nothing more than a coincidence in the fact that the Shī'ah kingdoms of the Deccan and the Shī'ah Ṣafawid dynasty of Persia were all founded within a comparatively short time of each other, toward the close of the fifteenth and the beginning of the sixteenth centuries. This much is clear, however, that Shāh Ismā'īl, who was the first ruler of the Ṣafawid dynasty, took great interest in India. In the year A.D. 1511, when Muẓaffar II ascended the throne of the petty kingdom of Gujarāt, he was greeted with a splendid embassy from Shāh Ismā'īl, who paid a similar compliment to most of the Indian princes, with the undoubted design of seeking to win favour for the Shī'ah religion, which he was desirous of introducing.[3]

That the Shī'ah rulers of the Deccan had far more than casual relations with the Shī'ahs of Persia is abundantly shown by the fact that frequent embassies arrived at the court of Ṭahmāsp, from the princes of the southern part of the peninsula. These were sent especially from Niẓām Shāh, of Aḥmadnagar; Quṭb Shāh, of Golkonda and Hyderabad; 'Alī 'Ādil Shāh, of Bījāpūr, also sent embassies and presents and assurances of friendship. The latter went so far as to inform the Shāh that he had ordered the *khuṭbah* of the Shī'ahs to be read in all the mosques of his dominion in the illustrious name of His Majesty the King of Persia. The king was so delighted that he expressed his satisfaction by presenting all manner of royal gifts to the ambassadors.[4]

Encouraged, no doubt, by the apparent success of the establishment of the Shī'ah religion in south India, it is not surprising

[1] Elphinstone, op. cit., 757. [2] *Ibid.*, 758.

[3] 'Alī Muḥammad Khān, *Mir'āt-i-Aḥmadī*, 219.

[4] *Ta'rīkh-i-'Ālam-ārā-i-'Abbāsī*, in Jawhar's *Tadhkirat-ul-Wāqi'āt*, 126.

that Shāh Ṭahmāsp should take advantage of the forced visit of the Emperor Humāyūn to his dominions to make a daring effort to compel his royal guest to embrace the Shī'ah religion. This occurred in the year A.D. 1544, when Humāyūn was a refugee in Persia, whither he had fled after being driven from his throne at Delhi by the daring Afghan, Sher Shāh.

Ṭahmāsp was a shrewd and clever ruler, and he entertained no small hopes that, through the good offices of Humāyūn, he might be able to bring about in the north of India what had been accomplished in the southern territories; and thus, with the Shī'ah faith established in India as in Persia, he no doubt anticipated that his country might exercise political dominion over her as well. At any rate, Humāyūn was confronted with no theory but a fact. Ṭahmāsp insisted that Humāyūn must adopt the religion of the country he had entered, or take the consequences. Finally, after persistent refusal on the part of Humāyūn, Ṭahmāsp sent a *qāḍī* to him with three papers, and was told that he might choose which he would sign. Finally, after indignant refusals, he was persuaded to choose one of the papers, which he read out in apparent assent to its contents. It appears that the paper must have contained the Shī'āh confession of faith, together with a promise to introduce it into India, and a clause relating to the cession of the frontier province of Qandahār. Humāyūn is said to have adopted the Shī'ah mode of reciting the public prayers, and to have further indicated his change of faith by making a pilgrimage to the tomb of Shaykh Ṣafī, at Ardabīl, in north-western Persia, near the Caspian Sea.[1] On Humāyūn's return to India it was, of course, impossible to carry out the wishes of Ṭahmāsp, and to all intents and purposes he died a well-regarded Sunnī. To what extent the perfervid Shī'ah enthusiasts among the Persian rulers may have employed missionaries of their own has not, so far as I know, been discovered; but from the above overt acts it is clear that they must have fostered a propaganda of some sort.

Shī'ahs at the Mughul Court

Further Shī'ah influence was to be found also at the Mughul court in the presence of Bairam Khāṇ and other Persians.[2] This

[1] Jawhar, op. cit., 65 ff.

[2] See also Najm-ul-Ghanī Khāṇ, *Madhāhib-ul-Islām*, 441.

worthy gentleman was one of the favourite noblemen of the Persian Shāh Ṭahmāsp, who became one of Humāyūn's officers. To him, also, was entrusted the care of the youthful Akbar, who made him his first minister. It is little wonder that, on Humāyūn's return from Persia, the orthodox *'ulamā* of the court looked first to their own safety, and that they kept at a discreet distance until after the fall of Bairam Khāṇ. No doubt much of the influence that shaped Akbar's religious experience is to be found in his early contact with this ardent Shī'ah, who was his first minister and guardian. But whatever his religious convictions or those of his associates, he would not allow the Shī'ah religion to become supreme. Nevertheless, Shī'ah influence continued to honeycomb the Muslim community, and as late as 1853 we learn that the impotent and nominal ruler, Bahādur Shāh II, actually made a secret avowal of allegiance to Persia and the Shī'ah faith.[1]

Later Developments

The cause of the Shī'ah has been promoted also by the rulers aud nobility of certain Native States, in comparatively recent times. Sa'ādat Khāṇ, originally a merchant from Khurāsān, came to Delhi, and in the first quarter of the eighteenth century rose to a military command. He was made Governor of the province of Oudh, and ultimately was the founder of the dynasty of the kings of Oudh. Under their patronage and influence Lucknow became one of the most renowned centres of the Shī'ah faith in India, and to-day the Mahārājā of Maḥmūdābād may be said in some sense to continue the tradition of royal patronage to the faith that it formerly enjoyed to such an unrestricted extent. In Rampur and Murshidabad such of the Nawabs as have professed the Shī'ah faith have given it protection, and honoured it with their active support.

In fact, the influence of these Shī'ah rulers has been so great that the rise of the Shī'ah community around their courts, and within their sphere of influence, is found to date from their coming to power. This is particularly true of Oudh, where, after repeated investigation and inquiry, it is clear that the Shī'ah

[1] F. W. Buckler, 'A New Interpretation of Akbar's Infallibility Decree', *J.R.A.S.*, 1924, 608.

community has been largely recruited from the original Sunnī Muḥammadans. Shī'ahs were naturally favoured above others in the sight of the rulers, so, for the sake of personal advancement, the change has often been made. One well-informed person, part of whose family is Shī'ah, gives it as his opinion that most of the Shī'ahs of Oudh are the result of conversions from Sunnī Islam which have taken place in the last two hundred years. Additional evidence of this is found in the fact that such of the Rampur rulers as have been of the Shī'ah persuasion have been led to this decision through the influence of the Lucknow Shī'ahs.[1]

Missionaries

That there were Shī'ah missionaries who were zealous in their work, appears from two very striking instances recorded by Muslim historians. In the latter half of the fourteenth century, during the reign of the pious Fīrūz Shāh III, the ruler himself relates the manner in which they carried on their work and the way in which he dealt with them.

> Some Shī'ahs, also called Rawāfiḍ, had endeavoured to make proselytes. They wrote treatises and books, and gave instruction and lectures on the tenets of their sect, and traduced and reviled the first chiefs of our religion. I seized them all and convicted them of their errors and perversions. . . . Their books I burnt in public, and so by the grace of God the sect was entirely suppressed.[2]

Three other missionaries are mentioned as having come to India during the reign of Akbar, in the sixteenth century. They were three brothers from Gīlān, near the Caspian Sea, by name Ḥakīm Abū'l-Fatḥ, Ḥakīm Humāyūn, and Ḥakīm Humān. Besides, there was one Mullā Muḥammad Yazdī. 'All attached themselves,' says Budāyūnī, 'to the Emperor, flattered him, adapted themselves to his changes in religious ideas, spoke derogatorily of the Companions of the Prophet, and tried hard to make a Shī'ah of him.'[3] It would be interesting to know what other efforts they made to spread their faith, and with what success.

Ḥakīm Abū'l-Fatḥ, at any rate, was associated with one of the most learned and clever Shī'ah theologians that ever came to

[1] Najm-ul-Ghanī Khān, *Madhāhib-ul-Islām*, 444.

[2] *Futūḥāt-i-Fīrūz Shāhī*, E.D., III, 377.

[3] *Muntakhab-ut-Tawārīkh*, E.D., V, 524.

India. This was Sayyid Nūr Allāh bin Sharīf al-Husaynī al-Mar'ashī Shūshtarī, who is known as the *Shāhīd Thālith* of the Ithnā 'Asharīyah Shī'ahs. Sayyid Nūr Allāh came to India from Shūshtar, in Persia, about the year A.D. 1587, during the reign of Akbar. He was well received by Ḥakīm Abū'l-Fatḥ Gīlānī, on whose recommendation he was appointed by the Emperor to be the Qāḍī-ul-Quḍāt of Lahore. He accepted the appointment on condition that he would be permitted to give his decisions according to any one of the four legal systems (*madhhab*) of the Sunnīs. As a matter of fact he was suspected from the very first by the orthodox *'ulamā* of Akbar's court as being a dangerous person in matters of doctrine, and he was closely watched. During his leisure hours as Qāḍī he wrote in defence of Shī'ah doctrines, and has left several important treatises. The most important of these in Persian, the *Majālis-ul-Mu'minīn*, he finished while in Lahore in the year A.D. 1604. It is said that this book was copied by a man who had been employed by the *'ulamā* of Jahāngīr's court, to win the confidence of the Qāḍī; and on the basis of the heretical evidence so secured he was condemned to death. He suffered martyrdom by whipping because of activity for his faith in the year A.D. 1610, and was buried at Agra, where his tomb is greatly revered by all Imāmīs.[1]

Refugees and Adventurers

Still another means of the introduction and spread of the Shī'ah religion in India was the shelter which the country afforded to those who were driven from their own lands by the Mongol invasion of the thirteenth century A.D., in the reign of Balban at Delhi; for the horrors of that catastrophe 'drove men of eminence from the countries to which it extended, and, Balban's being the only Muḥammadan government that was not subverted, his court was filled with illustrious exiles of that religion'.[2] Among these were princes and literary fugitives. Knowing how the ferment of Shī'ahism was working throughout the Muslim lands, it cannot but have happened that some of these refugees were followers of that path.

[1] Mīrzā Muḥammad Hādī, Maulvī, *Shahīd Thālith*, 15 ff.

[2] E. G. Browne, *Persian Literature in Modern Times*, 165.

Lastly, mention should be made of the courtiers from Persia, men of literary genius, and adventurers who came to India to try their fortunes. Especially during the sixteenth and seventeenth centuries, thanks to the generous patronage of Humāyūn, Akbar, and their successors, a great number of the most talented Persian poets were attracted to Hindustan. Budāyūnī mentions one hundred and seventy who had mostly been born in Persia. Shiblī says that fifty-one came in Akbar's time, and Sprenger supplies a long list.[1] Most of these, if not all, were undoubtedly Shīʻahs. In many cases the emperors gave grants of land to their government officers, and in this way Shīʻah communities have been established in many places, such as Amroha, in the Moradabad district. It is also interesting to note that practically all of those Shīʻahs belonging to the I<u>th</u>nā ʻAsharīyah group are of Persian and Turkish descent, and they mostly affect the prefix Sayyid, which indicates that they claim lineage in the family of the Prophet.

Minor Peculiarities

The Indian I<u>th</u>nā ʻAsharīyah does not offer any marked peculiarities as compared with people of this sect in other lands. Their chief theologians are known as *mujtahidīn*, which title is conferred on those of sufficient merit, either by a Shīʻah ruling prince or by the people themselves. While the prevailing legal practices among Muslims have been Sunnī, particularly of the Ḥanafite school, yet practices peculiar to Shīʻahs long ago began to grow up in certain localities which were subject to Shīʻah governors in former times. Naturally, as the local ruler became more and more independent of the supreme head at Delhi and the Shīʻah governments became hereditary, the number of adherents to the faith of the ruler increased, and Shīʻah laws and customs would more and more come into force. In some cases it would even happen, as in Lucknow, that the sect of the local ruler finally came to outnumber that of the distant and nominal head at Delhi. In the beginning Sunnī law was administered; but finally, as in the case of the last kings of Oudh, the Shīʻah law supplanted the Sunnī law and was made the law of the state

[1] Browne, op. cit., 165; also, Sprenger, *Catalogue, King of Oudh MSS.*, I, 46, 55 ff.

or province. But since the British occupation, in 1857, the practice has been to apply none but Shī'ah law to Shī'ahs, and this only in respect to such subjects as marriage, divorce, pre-emption, gifts, pious endowments, wills, and inheritance.[1]

Relations Between Sunnīs and Shī'ahs

In India, as elsewhere, the 'Sunnī-Shī'ah' relations have always been more or less strained, and Shī'ahs have been obliged at times to practice their doctrine of *taqīyah* (pious concealment of their true faith) in order to avoid fanatical persecution from the Sunnīs. Even in the time of the liberal Akbar, when Shaykh Mubārak, father of the famous Abū'l-Faḍl and his brother Fayḍī, turned Shī'ah, as a result he was greatly persecuted, and was obliged to fly with his family from Agra.[2] Prince Shujā', the son of Shah Jahan, was a Shī'ah, and so was regarded with aversion by the orthodox. At the same time his brother, Aurangzīb, who became a model for Muslim orthodoxy, is said to have detested the Shī'ahs almost as much as he did the Hindus.[3]

An interesting occasion for difficulties between the two sects arose during the reign of Shāh 'Ālam (A.D. 1759–1806), which caused a widespread disturbance, extending from Lahore to Ahmadabad. An order was given that the word *waṣī* (heir) should be used among the attributes of the Khalīfah 'Alī in the *khuṭbah* (Friday sermon). This was too much of a Shī'ah innovation, as it tended to indicate that 'Alī was the true successor of the Prophet, and it was met with violent opposition in Lahore, Agra, and Ahmadabad. In the latter city 'the crowd killed the *khaṭīb* (preacher) of the chief mosque'. Finally, after much agitation on the part of the religious leaders, the Emperor ordered that they should return to the form used in the reign of Aurangzīb.[4]

The Muḥarram celebrations usually offer an opportunity for a display of fanatical outbursts between the two communities, owing chiefly to the curses which the Shī'ahs call down upon the heads of the Sunnī caliphs who preceded 'Alī; but in recent years the feeling between the two communities has considerably

[1] N. B. E. Baillie, *A Digest of Muḥammadan Law, Imāmīyah.*

[2] Elphinstone, op. cit., 533. [3] *Ibid.*, 672.

[4] *Khāfī Khān*, *Muntakhab-ul-Lubāb*, E.D., VII, 420 ff, 427 ff.

softened, and one seldom hears of riots occurring between them. This has been brought about in part, no doubt, by the efforts of the British Government to have the Muḥarram processions of the Sunnīs and Shī'ahs move at different times and by different routes on the days when the *ta'ziyahs*[1] are to be buried. Modern education, too, is helping to break down the old prejudices, though undoubtedly the old hostility remains among some of the more fanatical sections.

Evidence of the spread of Shī'ah influence among Sunnīs is common, and it is probable that nowhere else in the world of Islam are the Sunnīs so largely imbued with Shī'ah ideas and customs as in India. Although it is a purely Shī'ah custom to observe the Muḥarram celebrations for the first ten days of the sacred month, many Sunnīs in India are found to observe the ceremonies with the same regularity as the Shī'ahs do. Some even go to the extent of cursing the first three caliphs, and then join in the procession of the *ta'ziyahs* on the tenth of Muḥarram in memory of the martyrdom of Ḥusayn with as much enthusiasm as any Shī'ah. Sunnī literature includes popular poems and stories glorifying the martyrdom of Ḥusayn and cursing the inglorious name of Yazīd, which clearly shows how Shī'ah influence has penetrated the length and breadth of the Sunnī community.

Though the Shī'ahs are reported to be on the decrease numerically, they are far from being an unimportant community. One of their best-known leaders was the late Rt. Hon. Syed Amīr 'Alī, of the Calcutta High Court, who was the author of valuable expository and apologetic works on Islam in English, and who was an outstanding rationalist of the reform school among the Shī'ahs. His books, *The Spirit of Islam* and *The Ethics of Islam*, are highly regarded by all the modern Islamic reformers of India. A new effort at propaganda has, within the last few years, been manifested by the establishment of a school or seminary for the training of preachers at Lucknow, called the *Madrasat-ul-Wā'iẓīn*, under the distinguished patronage of the Mahārājā of Maḥmūdābād, a leading Shī'ah nobleman of Lucknow.

To promote the interests of the community throughout India,

[1] The *ta'ziyah* is a representation or model of the tomb of Ḥusayn at Karbala, carried in procession at the Muḥarram time.

the 'All-India Shī'ah Conference' was organized in 1907, and has regard to the social and educational uplift of the sect. Among other developments has been the establishment of the Shī'ah Intermediate College, at Lucknow. Shī'ahs are inclined to deplore the fact that in many respects they are considered outside the pale by Sunnī organizations; and one of them, writing in a recent periodical of north India, expressed his views under the heading, 'Are Shī'ahs not Moslems, that they are forced to have their own separate conference to consider the interests of their community?' In many things, however, they do act together. The Muslim University at Aligarh has special provision made for the religious teaching of its Shī'ah students. One of the curious developments of the caliphate agitation in India was that the late Rt. Hon. Syed Amīr 'Alī joined the Āghā Khān, who is the head of the Ismā'īlī Khojahs, in sending letters of protest to the Kemalist Government at Angora, Turkey, protesting against the abolition of the Turkish Caliphate and the deposition and banishment of the Caliph, though neither of these gentlemen, nor the Shī'ahs whom they represented, owed the slightest religious allegiance to the Sunnī Caliphate, to which, indeed, in theory they are opposed. The reason for their willingness to assist their Sunnī compatriots in this case was that they felt that in the abolition of the Turkish Caliphate, the world of Islam, of which they were a part, would suffer a loss in prestige.[1] For the most part, however, the Ithnā 'Asharīyah, numbering about five millions, finds it necessary to maintain a separate communal existence, which extends to worship, places of worship, certain festivals such as Muḥarram and Nau-roz, and matters pertaining to the civil code as mentioned above.

The Sab'īyah or Ismā'īlīs

The history of the Ismā'īlīs is of great interest, not only because of the variety of plot and counterplot which it presents, and the extremely esoteric nature of its doctrines, but especially because its tenets are a vital force in certain parts of India to-day. We have already shown how this sect arose as an offshoot from the main branch of Shī'ahs after the death of the

[1] *The Muslim Outlook*, Lahore, Jan. 12, 1924.

sixth Imām, Ja'far as-Ṣiddīq (A.D. 765), through his son, Ismā'īl, while the main branch of the Shī'ahs reject Ismā'īl and claim that his brother, Mūsā Kāẓim, was the true seventh Imām. Because of persecution, the sons of Ismā'īl were forced to leave Medina and escaped into Syria. From their foreign retreats their descendants sent out missionaries (*dā'īs*) to preach the esoteric (*bāṭinī*) doctrines, which are based on allegorical interpretation of the Qur'ān. A son of one of these missionaries, 'Abd Allāh by name, became the head of the social-religious movement known as the Qarmaṭians, which was ultimately used to support the Fāṭimid anti-Caliphate in Egypt (A.D. 910–1171). The adherents seem to have remained fairly well united until the death of the Fāṭimid Caliph Mustanṣir, after which they divided into two parties, each supporting a son of the deceased as the rightful head of the Ismā'īlians. One party supported al-Musta'lī and the other Nizār. Representatives of both groups are found in India. The Nizārīs are represented by the Khojahs[1] of Bombay and the Punjab, and the Musta'līs by the Bohrahs of western India.[2]

The Qarmaṭians, or Carmathians, seem to have been the first of the heretical groups to reach India; but eventually they were followed by members of both the other sects. Consequently, in what follows we shall take up the Qarmaṭians first, and then pass on to consider their successors.

THE QARMAṬIANS

The Qarmaṭians were the forerunners of unorthodox Muslim sects in India[3] as early as the latter part of the ninth century A.D. When they were expelled from Iraq and Egypt because of their political rebellions, many of them fled to Sind for refuge and a group of them from al-Aḥsā, in Baḥrain, founded a principality at Multan. There must have been a considerable number of them, for they seem to have made converts, and obtained a certain amount of political control of the old Arab province of Sind. Maḥmūd of Ghaznī finally put an end to the three centuries of

[1] For the Khojahs, see p. 101 f.; and for Bohrahs, see pp. 97 ff.

[2] *E.I.*, arts. 'Ismā'īlīya' and 'Qarmaṭians'.

[3] For an account of their doctrines and history, see *The Encyclopædia of Islam*, II, 768 ff.

Arab influence there by replacing the Qarmaṭian prince, Abū'l-Fatḥ Lodī, of Manṣūrah, with a Sunnī Muḥammadan.[1] In their zeal they destroyed the famous idol at Multan, which Muhammad b. Qāsim had allowed to remain, massacred the priests, and converted the temple into a mosque to take the place of the one built by the Umayyad conquerors, which they closed to show their hatred. After Maḥmūd had subdued the Qarmaṭians in the eleventh century, he re-opened the ancient mosque and abandoned the new one.[2]

This effort on the part of Maḥmūd, however, did not put an end to the activities of the *mulāḥids* (heretics), as the Qarmaṭians were called; for in A.D. 1175 we find that Muḥammad Ghūrī once again had to deliver Multan out of their hands. Still later, in A.D. 1237, during the brief reign of the Sultana Riḍīyah, they come to notice in a riot at Delhi; which outbreak evidently aroused a determined effort to suppress the heresy, for we do not find the Qarmaṭians mentioned, as such, after this date. This last conflict is graphically described by one of the Muslim historians, who relates that 'the Qarmaṭians and heretics of Hindustan, being seduced by a person with some pretensions of learning named Nūr Turk, flocked to him in large numbers from all parts of Hindustan, such as Gujarāt, Sind, the environs of the capital, and the banks of the Jumna and Ganges. They assembled in Delhi, and declared open hostility against the people of Islam, led by Nūr Turk, who used to say that the learned Sunnīs were *Nasībīs* (enemies of 'Alī) and *Murjīs* (that is, those who think faith sufficient and works unnecessary). He endeavoured to inflame the minds of the common people against the followers of the doctrines of Abū Ḥanīfa and Shāfi'ī, but finally, after an attack on the Jāmi' Masjid on a Friday in March, A.D. 1237, when many Muslims were killed, they were routed, and every heretic and Qarmaṭian sent to hell and the riot quelled.'[3]

While the suppression of the riot may have resulted in suppressing the *name* of Qarmaṭians, it is certain that it did not suppress the extreme Shī'ah views which they held, and which have from time to time made their appearance in one form or another. It would appear certain that the Roshanīyah sect,

[1] E.D., *History of India*, I, 459. Ibn Athīr, *Kāmil-ut-Tawārīkh*, E.D., II, 248. [2] *Ibid.*, 470. [3] Minhāj as-Sirāj, E.D., II, 335 f.

which arose in the Punjab and on the north-west frontier during the time of Akbar, was related to these heretical antecedents. Others probably tended to become more moderate in their views, and became absorbed in the regular Shī'ah group. These early 'Alid refugees have left evidences of their flight into Sind in the many Sayyid families found in that province. Also, in the eastern part of India, there are found many Sayyids who trace their ancestral settlements to the Indus valley. One tribe in Baluchistan still shows evidence of its origin in the name Qarmaṭī.[1]

That the Qarmaṭians of India had connexion with their refugee brethren in other lands, and that they were actively engaged in spreading their doctrines and winning Hindu as well as Muslim converts to their faith, is indicated in a very interesting notice by Elliot, who says,

> In the sacred books of the Druzes we find an epistle of Muktāna Bahā-ud-Dīn, the chief apostle of Ḥamzah, and the principal compiler of the Druze writings, addressed in the year A.D. 1032 (?) to the Unitarians of Multan and Hindustan in general and to Shaikh Ibn Sumār Raja Bal in particular. . . . This indicates that some of the Sumera tribe, including the chiefs, had affiliated themselves to the Qarmaṭians . . . and that the Qarmaṭians of the Indus valley were in relation and correspondence not only with those of Persia and Arabia, but with the Druzes, who adored Ḥākim the Fāṭimide Caliph of Egypt as a God.[2]

This also agrees quite well with the relations sustained to-day between the present Ismā'īlians of India and other members of the group in Arabia, Syria, and Central Asia.

The Bohrahs

The name, Bohrah, belongs to a group of Muslims that is found chiefly in Bombay and Baroda, most of whom are Ismā'īlians. They number one hundred and fifty-three thousand, three hundred and sixty-three,[3] and are mostly Hindu converts, though some few claim to be of Arabian lineage. The term, Bohrah, is said to be of Gujarāti origin, from the word *vohorvu*, meaning to trade, hence Bohrah means trader. As such it is not used exclusively for Muslims, as there are a few Hindus, also, who use it as a caste designation.

The Bohrahs constitute that branch of the Indian Ismā'īlians

[1] E.D., *History of India*, I, 481, 492. [2] *Ibid.*, 491. [3] *C.I.R.*, 1921.

7

which supports the succession of al-Musta'lī as successor of al-Mustanṣir in the line of Fāṭimid Caliphs and head of the Ismā'īlī faith. The sect in India had its origin in the work of missionaries who came from Yaman, in Arabia, whither the head of the sect had to flee from Egypt after the fall of the Fāṭimid dynasty. There is disagreement as to who was the first missionary to India. Some claim that it was one 'Abd Allāh, from Yaman, who landed in Cambay in A.D. 1067 and carried on a very active propaganda; others assert that it was Muḥammad 'Alī, who died in A.D. 1137, and whose tomb is still reverenced in Cambay as that of the first missionary. The work of winning converts went on peacefully under the Hindu rājās, who did not seem to object; but the Bohrahs were cruelly persecuted at times during the occupation of the Sunnī kings, who ruled from A.D. 1396 to 1572.[1]

The modern history of the Bohrahs begins with the year A.D. 1539, when the head of the sect, Yūsuf bin Sulaymān, who had long lived in Yaman, Arabia, came to India and took up his residence at Sidhpur, to the north of Pātan, in Baroda. Up to this time it had been necessary for his Indian followers to go to him for the payment of their tithes and the settlement of their difficulties, but since the coming of Yūsuf bin Sulaymān they have had a head of their own, whom they call their *dā'ī*, and whom they venerate as the representative of the Imām-uz-Zamān (Leader of the Age).

There are two main branches of the Bohrahs. This division came about through a schism that occurred in the year A.D. 1588, after the death of Dā'ūd bin 'Ajab Shāh, who was the head of the sect resident in Yaman. The Bohrahs, of Gujarāt, promptly chose Dā'ūd bin Quṭb Shāh as their head, but the Ismā'īlians of the Yaman would not recognize this choice, and set up one Sulaymān, whom they claimed Dā'ūd had nominated before his death. Sulaymān then came to Gujarāt to make good his claims, which were rejected by all but a few. He finally died at Aḥmadabad, where his tomb and that of his rival, Dā'ūd bin Quṭb Shāh, are to be found. The two branches resulting from this schism bear the names of their respective founders, and are called the Dā'ūdī and Sulaymānī Bohrahs. The head of the Dā'ūdī

[1] *R.M.M.*, X, 471.

branch resides at Sūrat, and that of the Sulaymānī in the Yaman. The latter has a representative who lives in Baroda.[1]

There is a small number of Bohrahs known as the Ja'farīs, who are descendants of Dā'ūdīs. They became Sunnīs in the time of Muẓaffar Shāh (A.D. 1396–1411) and succeeding governors of Gujarāt. These Ja'farī Bohrahs take their name from one Sayyid Aḥmad Ja'far Shīrāzī, of the fifteenth century, whose descendants still officiate as spiritual guides. Besides these three groups of Bohrahs which have been mentioned there are two other minor communities, the product of secession. One is known as the 'Alīyahs, which separated in A.D. 1264 from the Dā'ūdīs to follow 'Alī bin Ibrāhīm as their high priest instead of Shaykh Tayyib, who had been chosen previously.

Lastly there are the Nāgoshīs, who dissented from the 'Alīyahs in the eighteenth century. They derive their name from the belief that flesh-eating is a sin, 'nā' meaning 'no', and 'gosh' or 'gosht' meaning 'meat'.[2]

The Dā'ūdī Bohrahs have a well organized community, which has four grades of *mullās* besides the Dā'ī al-Muṭlaq, or Chief Mullā. These are called the *ma'dhūn*, *mukāsir*, *mashā'ikh*, and *mullā*. A college was founded in 1809, at Sūrat, for the training of aspirants to religious leadership, and it is still in a flourishing condition. The Mullājī, at Sūrat, has a large income from the tithes of his followers, as well as from the *waqfs* (pious endowments) which are under his control, and which he is supposed to administer for the benefit of his followers. Recently he was brought to trial by some responsible persons of his community in Bombay, who charged him with mismanagement of the *waqfs*.[3]

The peculiar religious beliefs of the Bohrahs are for the most part very obscure, as a systematic practice of concealment obtains and little has been published. Of the printed books, the *Ṣaḥīfat-uṣ-Ṣalāt* in Arabic and Gujarāti exists; and among the unprinted books there are the *Dā'im-ul-Islām* and *al-Ḥaqā'iq*, both of which set forth the doctrines and rites of Shī'ah Islam, and give accounts of Bohrah *dā'īs* and their sayings.[4] Since most of the

[1] *E.I.*, art. 'Bohorās'; also Muḥammad Najm-ul-Ghanī Khān, *Madhāhib-ul-Islām*, 312 ff. [2] *R.M.M.*, X, 480 ff.

[3] *Indian Daily Mail*, Feb. 25, 1925. [4] *E.I.*, art. 'Bohorās'.

members of the community are Hindu converts, they have clung to their Hindu customs in many matters. They have not yet adopted the Muslim law of inheritance, and so keep their women from inheriting property. They both give and take interest on loans, and at the Diwālī festival they excel the Hindus in their illuminations, and, like them also, change their old account books for new ones at that time. However, they do not associate with Hindus, and will not take sweetmeats from their hands. If a Hindu *dhobī* washes their clothes they purify them by sprinkling holy water on them.

They also keep themselves distinct from other Muslims. They have separate mosques which they call *Jamā'at-k͟hānas*, and their own exclusive cemeteries. Their calendar is two days ahead of the ordinary Muslim calendar. They observe none of the ordinary distinctions of 'caste' such as Sayyid, Shayk͟h, Mug͟hul and Pathān. The Dā'ūdī Bohrahs offer only three prayers a day—morning, noon and night—instead of the usual five, and they do not meet on Fridays for united worship, as other Muslims do. The Bohrahs use the Gujarātī language, with which they have mixed many Arabic words.

Reforms are at work in this community as in others. I am indebted to the Rev. H. J. Lane Smith, of Bombay, for the following account of the reforms that are under way.[1] A recent High Court action was brought against the *Dā'ī al-Muṭlaq*, or head of the Dā'ūdī Bohrahs, by some members 'who desired to dispute his claim to absolute power over his followers, regarding such claims as not in keeping with the spirit of the times. Those who instituted the action were excommunicated from their community.'

> Recently a number of young men have started a 'Young Men's Bohrah Association', the objects of which are 'to benefit their community by progress and reform, which are now rendered necessary consistently with the times'. From conversation with their secretary, I gather that the means by which they hope to achieve this end is by the establishment of hospitals, high schools and other similar institutions.

Some of the representative men of the community have attained to eminence in Indian life, notably Badr-ud-Dīn Ṭayyibjī

[1] *The Indian Witness*, Lucknow, March 7, 1929, 160.

a Sulaymānī Bohrah, who was judge of the High Court of Bombay. Many of them are very wealthy.

The Khojahs

The Khojahs are a small community of Ismā'īlian Shī'ahs, found chiefly in the Punjab, Sind, Cutch, Kathiawar, and other parts of western India, particularly Bombay and Poona. According to the Census of 1921 they numbered one hundred and forty-six thousand, one hundred and nine. They are an important part of the scattered remnants of the adherents of Niẓār, son of al-Mustanṣir, Fāṭimid Caliph of Egypt, and are consequently 'cousins' of the Bohrahs, since the latter are adherents of the sect that supported the succession of al-Musta'lī, brother of Niẓār. The spiritual ancestors of the Khojahs were those Ismā'īlians known as the Assassins, whose headquarters were at Alamūt, in Persia, and whose founder was Ḥasan bin Ṣabbāḥ (d. A.D. 1124). After their overthrow by the Mongol Hūlāgū Khān, in A.D. 1250, they were widely scattered and driven from place to place. Some of the sect survived in Syria, while the remainder migrated to other parts of the world, and are to-day found in Zanzibar, East Africa, Persia, Oman, in the Hindu Kush region of Central Asia, on the north-west frontier of India, and in Afghānistān.

There is a tradition preserved by the Khojahs that their first *dā'ī* who came to India as a missionary was one Nūr Satāgar or Nūr-ud-Dīn. It is *barely* possible, therefore, that the riot at Delhi, in A.D. 1237, which was led by one Nūr Turk and which included certain heretics other than Qarmaṭians, was an expression of the activity of some of the dispersed Ismā'īlians from the region of Alamūt; and indeed that this Nūr Turk was none other than the first Ismā'īlian missionary of the Khojahs mentioned above.[1] This is the view held by D. Menant.[2] Nūr-ud-Dīn carried on a successful propaganda in Gujarāt, and is said to have won many followers from among the Hindus by reason of his miracles, for which he had a great reputation. The second missionary is said to have been Shams-ud-Dīn, who came from Iraq and settled at Uch, about eighty miles south of Multan; while the third,

[1] See pp. 43 and 96. [2] *R.M.M.*, XII, 220.

Ṣadr-ud-Dīn, came to Sind from Khurāsān in the fifteenth century, and finally died at Uch. His tomb, however, built by the Khojahs in the Bahāwalpur State, is at Trinda Gorgej.

Most of the Khojahs are Hindu converts, and their *dā'īs* made special efforts to adapt their *bāṭinī* (esoteric) teachings to the Hindu beliefs. Ṣadr-ud-Dīn (fifteenth century A.D.) wrote the *Das Avatār* (the Ten Incarnations), for the use of his converts in Sind. He endeavoured to demonstrate that 'Alī was in fact the long-expected tenth incarnation (*avatār*) of Vishnū. Even to-day this book is one of the most sacred of the literature of the Khojahs. Another book, written in Persian by Āghā 'Abd-us-Salām toward the end of the sixteenth century, for the use of his Indian disciples, is called *Pandyād-i-Jawān-mardī*. This has been translated into Sindī and Gujarātī, and is also regarded as personifying the twenty-sixth Khojah *pīr* (saint).[1]

The Khojahs are divided into two well defined groups, which, for the sake of convenience, are designated the Punjab Khojahs and the Āghā Khāṇī Khojahs. The latter is by far the larger group, for it includes not only all the others outside the Punjab, but the Āghā Khāṇ is recognized as the head of the other scattered groups outside India as well, which have already been referred to. The present Āghā Khāṇ, Sulṭān Muḥammad Shāh, of Bombay, claims to be a lineal descendant of Rukn-ud-Dīn Khurshāh, last Grand Master of Alamūt, who claimed descent through Niẓār, son of Mustanṣir, from Ismā'īl the seventh Imām, and great-great-great-grandson of the Prophet's cousin and son-in-law 'Alī.[2]

For more than three centuries the head of the Āghā Khāṇīs was a resident of Persia, with whom his scattered followers maintained direct personal touch. To him they sent their offerings, and many even went to visit him. Finally, however, political events forced him to leave that country. Crossing the deserts of Baluchistan in 1840, he came to Sind, where he was well received by the Niẓārite members of the Tālpūr

[1] *R.M.M.*, XII, 224 ff.; *E.I.*, art. 'Khodja'; Najm-ul-Ghanī Khāṇ, *Madhāhib-ul-Islām*, 334 f.

[2] E. G. Browne, *A Literary History of Persia from Firdausī to Sa'adī*, 210.

family. Since 1845, however, Bombay has been the headquarters of the Āghā Khān, with the exception of a couple of years, when he resided at Poona and Bangalore. The present Āghā Khān III, who is a grandson of the one who was a refugee from Persia, lives a luxurious life, and spends much of his time in Europe and England, where he takes great delight in racing his own horses. Having received a modern English education himself, he has been one of the foremost leaders in Muslim reform movements and efforts to improve the condition of the Muslim community. To this end he has co-operated wholeheartedly with the promoters of the Muslim University, Aligarh, to which institution he has made generous donations from time to time. He has been a strong supporter of British rule in India, and has presented his views in a book called *India in Transition*, which appeared in 1918. He was the first president of the All-India Muslim League, which was founded in 1906. It is very difficult indeed to realize that this modern, cultured Indian prince is the spiritual successor of the 'Old Man of the Mountain'[1] who was the terror of the Lebanon; and to believe that he is almost worshipped as an incarnation by hundreds of thousands of devotees in many countries, who support him in luxury by their gifts, and count themselves fortunate if they ever have the opportunity to kiss his hand.

This community is organized, writes A. Yūsuf 'Alī in the article on the Khojahs in the *Encyclopædia of Islam*,

> in the form of a complete fiscal centralization round the sacred person of the Āghā Khān, but of complete congregational independence in administrative matters, including even questions of excommunications. . . . The officers (of the Jamā'at-khānas) are the *mukhī* (headman, treasurer, chairman) and the *kāmaria* (secretary, accountant). They are sometimes appointed by the Āghā Khān, but are frequently elected. Offerings for the Imām (i.e. the Āghā Khān himself) are collected through them; these comprise the fixed *Dasondh* or tithe (the Momnās split from the community in the sixteenth century, and mainly on their refusal to pay this) and various minor dues on special occasions, either recurring (as the festival of the new moon) or occasional (as the rites of birth, marriage, burial, etc.).[2]

Other secessions from the Āghā Khānī community have

[1] This was the title applied to the head of the Assassins.
[2] *E.I.*, II, 961.

taken place, the most important of which occurred in the last century. At that time a considerable section endeavoured to have the whole group turn Sunnī, while in 1901 a small number of modernists seceded and joined the Ithnā ʻAsharīyah, or 'regular' Shīʻahs.[1] More recent evidence of dissatisfaction within the community is apparent in the existence of the 'Khojah Reformers' Society', of Karachi. In August, 1927, it published an 'Open Letter,' addressed to H.H. the Āghā Khān which gives a detailed account of its grievances and the reforms desired. It contains a strong protest against the selfish worldliness of the Āghā Khān himself, and pleads for reforms in the management of the community which will improve its neglected condition. The statement closes with the following summary of the demands made on His Highness:

> That you will disclaim and repudiate all divine honours paid to you which rightly belong only to the True God Almighty.
>
> That you will change commercial Jamāʻat Khānas into mosques where prayer only might be offered.
>
> That you will arrange for Islamic instruction being imparted to one and all of the followers of Your Highness.
>
> That you will absolutely stop and refuse acceptance of all offerings whatsoever, pecuniary or kind ; and lastly,
>
> That you will be good enough to abolish the councils and repeal the rules altogether, for we respectfully point out that this is the indefensible right of the community as an autonomous body, which alone is competent to govern itself and manage its own affairs.[2]

The Punjab Khojahs do not recognize the Āghā Khān as their head, so, curiously enough, they turn to the *pīrs* of the Sunnite Chishtī and Qādirī orders for practical religious leadership. In most other respects their religious beliefs and practices are identical with the other Khojahs.

There is an active Āghā Khān Press in Bombay, which publishes books, tracts and periodicals in Gujarātī and English. The recent *Year Book* of the Khojahs was a beautifully printed edition of five thousand copies, describing the activities of the Āghā Khān and his community.

[1] *E.I.*, II, 961 ; Najm-ul-Ghanī Khān, *Madhāhib-ul-Islām*, 334 ff.

[2] *An Open Letter to H.H. the Āghā Khān*, 26, 27.

The Roshanīyah Sect

About the middle of the sixteenth century there arose a new sect on the north-west frontier, which bore a direct relation to the Ismā'īlians and was evidently an offshoot from them. This was known as the Roshanīyah, because of the title, 'Pīr Roshan', which the founder, Bāyazīd, took for himself. This title means 'Guide of Light', but his enemies in derision called him 'Pīr Tārīk' or 'Guide of Darkness'. Bāyazīd was born about the year A.D. 1525, in the city of Jullundur, in the Punjab, but his father, Shaykh 'Abd Allāh, soon was compelled to fly with his family to his ancestral home at Kanīguram, in Wazīristān. After he was grown he came under the influence of an Ismā'īlī heretic, by the name of Mullā Sulaymān, upon whose teachings he finally came to base his new doctrines.[1]

In common with all Muslims who are the founders of new sects, Bāyazīd felt called to be a divine messenger. He retired to a cave near Kanīguram, and passed through several stages of austerities which he imposed upon himself. He assumed the title, 'Pīr Roshan' or 'Miyāṇ Roshan', and issued a call to the people to join his way of life. He claimed to have received direct revelations from God, and that Gabriel descended to him. Thus he assumed the character of a prophet, and ordered his adherents to practise religious austerities also. His followers rapidly grew in number, and he established his authority in the regions of the Sulaymān hills and the Khyber. This caused trouble for the Mughul government, and Akbar was at last compelled to send a force to bring the Roshanīyahs into submission. This was accomplished in A.D. 1587, and there was no more trouble until A.D. 1611, when there was another revolt at Kābul, which was at last put down with great slaughter.[2]

The doctrines of Pīr Roshan, which are regarded as peculiarly objectionable, and which show an intimate relationship to Ṣūfī and Ismā'īlian doctrines, with special reference to their promulgator as the manifestation of divinity, are set forth by Ākhūnd Darwīzah as follows:

1. God is all in all, and all existing objects are only forms of his deity.

[1] *Dābistān*, tr. J. Leyden, *Asiatic Researches*, XI, 406 ff, London, 1812.

[2] Elphinstone, op. cit., 517; *E.I.*, art. 'Bāyazīd'.

2. The great manifestations of divinity are *Pīrs*, or religious teachers, who are forms of divinity, or rather deity himself. In the spirit of this opinion, Bāyazīd said to his followers, 'I am your *Pīr*, and your God'.

3. The sole test of right and wrong is obedience to the *Pīr* who is the representative of divinity, or rather deity itself; and therefore, right and wrong are not attributes of a *Pīr*, and the greatest of all sins is disobedience to a *Pīr*, which is disobedience to deity himself.

4. Those who will not receive the precepts of a *Pīr* are in the situation of brutes, to kill which it is in some cases meritorious, and in all cases lawful; or in that of dead men whose property naturally devolves to the living, and may therefore be legally plundered at pleasure by all true believers.

5. Human souls transmigrate into other bodies, and reappear in other forms, and such terms as 'resurrection', 'day of judgment', 'paradise' and 'hell', are only metaphors to express mundane things.

6. The Koran and Hadīs (Islamic Traditions) are not to be interpreted literally or according to the apparent sense, but according to the mystic, secret, or interior meaning. The ordinances of the law have therefore a mystical meaning, and are ordained only as a means of acquiring religious perfection.

7. This mystic sense of the law is only attainable by religious exercises and the instructions of a *Pīr*; it is the source of religious perfection; and this perfection being attained, the exterior ordinances of the law cease to be binding, and are virtually annulled.[1]

The Roshanīs have all but ceased to exist; the only remnant being found among the Afrīdīs of the North-West Frontier Province. Descendants of Bāyazīd still live in Jullundur, and it is thought that the doctrines of the sect have greatly influenced Muḥammadan beliefs throughout the north-west. There are a number of songs still sung by *faqīrs* in the Punjab which commemorate the miracles of Shaykh Darwīsh, and other members of Pīr Roshan's family.[2]

THE MAHDAWĪ DOCTRINES IN INDIA

The heretical Mahdawī movements, which have affected India during the past centuries, have been productive of certain sectarian developments which we shall now notice briefly. The doctrine of the expected Mahdī is based on certain alleged prophecies of the Prophet regarding the advent of a *mujaddid*, or restorer of the faith. The movement seems to have had its

[1] J. Leyden, 'The Rosheniah Sect', *Asiatic Researches*, XI, 420 f.

[2] Rose, *G.T.C.P.*, I, 337.

origin in Badakhshān, beyond Afghānistān, and to have spread from there over Persia and India. The doctrine was closely connected with the completion of the first thousand years of the Muslim era, so that in the last century preceding the close of the first millenium the learned everywhere in India were discussing the question.

Finally, the Mahdī movement took on a definite form through the teaching of one, Mīr Sayyid Muḥammad, of Jaunpur, in the latter part of the fifteenth century A.D.[1] He had much in his favour for the initiation of such a movement. He was a descendant of the Prophet, and bore his name, which fulfilled the prophecy that 'Muḥammad Mahdī shall be of my family'. He next saw in the fall of Jaunpur a sign that the latter days had come; he claimed to work miracles, and announced that a voice from heaven had whispered to him, 'Thou art the Mahdī'. His followers increased in number, but he was finally driven to Gujarāt, where he found an adherent in Sultan Maḥmūd I (A.D. 1458–1511). He finally went on a pilgrimage to Mecca with some of his followers, to the great relief of Maḥmūd; but he was driven away from there also. On his return he is said to have announced to his followers that he had received a revelation to forsake his Mahdī doctrines. He wandered from place to place, and finally died at Farāh, in the valley of the Helmand, north of Baluchistan.[2]

The memory of this Mahdī is still revered in the district of Kirmān, Baluchistan, where there is a sect called the *Zikrī* (*Dhikrī*) whose adherents are mostly of the nomad population. They are sometimes spoken of as *Dā'irewāle*, that is, 'people of the circle', because of a peculiarity which characterizes their practice on the night of Laylat-ul-Qadr. On that occasion they erect a circle of stones (*dā'irah*), within which they practise their heretical ritual.[3]

Another person claiming to be a Mahdī, and a forerunner of the Jaunpūrī Mahdī, is mentioned by Fīrūz Shāh III (A.D. 1351–

[1] An excellent account of this Mahdī is given by Najm-ul-Ghanī Khān in his *Madhāhib-ul-Islām*, 695 ff.

[2] H. Blochmann, *Introduction to Ā'īn-i-Akbarī*, iii.

[3] J. Horovitz, *Monograph on the Dā'ire-wāle Sect*; Goldziher, *Vorlesungen*, 284 ff.

1388), who gives a graphic account of the way he regarded him, and the manner in which he dealt with the pretender:

> There was in Delhi a man named Rukn-ud-Dīn who was called Mahdī because he affirmed himself to be the Imām Mahdī, who is to appear in the latter days, and to be possessed of knowledge by inspiration. He said he had not read or studied under anyone, and that he knew the names of all things, a knowledge which no prophet had acquired since Adam. He pretended that the mysteries of the science of letters had been revealed to him in a way never made known to any other man. . . . He led people astray into mystic practices; and perverted ideas by maintaining that he was . . . the Prophet of God. The elders brought the facts of the case to my attention, and he was convicted of heresy and error. The doctors of the Law said he was an infidel, and worthy of death for having spread such vile and pernicious ideas among the people of Islam . . . so they killed him, with some of his supporters and disciples, and the people rushing in tore him to pieces and broke his bones into fragments. Thus was his iniquity prevented.[1]

In the Mysore State also, at Channapatam, is to be found another group known as *Dā'ire-wāle*, who likewise appear to be spiritual descendants of this same Mahdī from Jaunpur. In this case they seem to have originated from the preaching of one Sayyid Aḥmad, who was born in A.D. 1444 in Gujarāt, and who evidently came in contact with Muḥammad Jaunpūrī, but as he went southward to the Niẓām's Dominions he assumed the rôle of Mahdī himself. He is said to have died in A.D. 1504. The watchword of his followers was 'Imām Mahdī came and went away: he who does not believe this is an infidel'. They have had many conflicts with the orthodox Sunnīs. They have no regular mosque, and worship only in a *jamā'at-khānah*, or assembly room.

Another Madhī appeared during the reign of Islām Shāh (A.D. 1545–1552). He was a *darwīsh* known as Shaykh 'Alāī. He was a resident of Bayana, near Agra, and, having been joined by another like-minded person by the name of Miyāṇ 'Abd Allāh, who had been under the influence of Muḥammad, of Jaunpur, openly professed to be a Mahdī. He collected six or seven hundred heads of families and migrated to Khawaspur, near Jodhpur. Finally he was summoned to Agra before Islām Shāh, and expelled to the Deccan. As he did not cease to proclaim his peculiar doctrines he was again summoned to Agra, and ordered to

[1] *Futūḥāt-i-Fīrūz Shāhī*, E.D., III, 379.

renounce his claims to being a Mahdī. As he refused he was finally 'condemned by the *'ulamā* as a heretic, ordered to be scourged, and at the third blow expired'.[1]

These sects are also known as Ghayr-Mahdawī (i.e. without a Mahdī), because of the fact that they regard the Mahdī as having come, and so do not look for another. Some of them have at times been wildly fanatical toward others, and have caused much disturbance.

The Mahdī movements have been characterized by features that are significant. They have been led by men of education, who have possessed great oratorical power as preachers, and could draw multitudes to them. Secondly, they assumed a definitely hostile attitude toward the learned men who held office at the emperor's court. Thirdly, they undertook to be reformers of Islam, being *mujaddids*. In this connexion it should be pointed out that the two Mahdīs of the nineteenth century, Sayyid Aḥmad, of Rae Barelī, and Mīrzā Ghulām Aḥmad, of Qādiān, have much in common with these earlier Mahdī movements; but, as they have left a deposit of a more modern character, with elements which are still active, we have reserved discussion of them until a later chapter.

[1] 'Abd Allāh, *Ta'rīkh-i-Dā'ūdī*, E.D., IV, 501; Blochmann, *Introduction to Ā'īn-i-Akbarī*, iii ff.

CHAPTER VI

RELIGIOUS ORDERS

Ṣūfīism

Islam, like Christianity, has its monastic orders and saints, the underlying basis of which is the mystic interpretation of the religious life known as Ṣūfīism. It is no part of our present plan, however, to make a detailed study of the mystic side of Islam; for this has been done with the greatest care by Professor R. A. Nicholson and others. An attempt will therefore be made to show the place that Ṣūfīism and the religious orders hold in relation to Islam in India, and the influence they have had on its development and spread.

That men imbued with Ṣūfī doctrines early came to India there cannot be the slightest doubt; but who these earliest comers were, or when they arrived, cannot be definitely ascertained. Sind, the first province of India to be invaded by Muslim armies, was also the first to be occupied by Muslim mystics, so that to-day it rightly claims the distinction of being the home of Indian Ṣūfīism. Nevertheless, no matter where one goes in India, one finds Ṣūfī influences powerful and active, fostered, no doubt, by the similar pantheistic doctrines that abound in Indian religious thought, which provide a very congenial atmosphere for their growth. In fact, because of the very widespread dissemination and influence of Ṣūfī doctrines, attempts have been made by some Muslim theologians to find a way of reconciling them to orthodox Islam. An example of such an effort is that of Muḥammad bin Faḍl Allāh, of Burhānpūr (d. A.D. 1620), who prepared a commentary on *at-Tuḥfat-ul-Mursalah ilā an-Nabī*, seeking to show that the doctrines of Muslim mystics were, after all, in harmony with the teachings of the Qur'ān and the Sunnah.[1]

Largely by means of poetry, Ṣūfī ideas have been spread throughout India. One only needs to inquire for such productions

[1] *E.I.*, II, 489, art. 'India'.

at any Muslim bookshop to see how commonly these are read. Or if one is fortunate enough to attend a *mushā'arah*, or assemblage of Urdū poets, he will hear the erotic notions of the Ṣūfī repeated without limit, as each poet seeks to emulate the mystic gift of expression employed by Jalāl-ud-Dīn Rūmī and 'Umar K̲h̲ayyām.

The Religious Orders

Though Ṣūfīism is found so extensively, it is not the religion of a sect. It is rather a natural revolt of the human heart against the cold formalism of a ritualistic religion. It is an attitude of mind and heart toward God and the problems of life which is as different from strictly orthodox Islam as the Quakers are from the Roman Catholics. But while Ṣūfīs have never been regarded as a separate sect of Muslims, they have nevertheless tended to gather themselves around men of piety and spiritual gifts, and form themselves into religious orders. These have taken on special forms of organization, so that to-day there is a great number of such orders, which, curiously enough, belong only to the Sunnīs. New orders may arise at any time, and old olders may be divided and subdivided again and again, as new saints with some special gifts of spiritual power arise. As Abū'l-Faḍl puts it,

> Any chosen soul who, in the mortification of the deceitful spirit, and in the worship of God, introduced some new motive of conduct, and whose spiritual sons in succession continued to keep alight the lamp of doctrine, was acknowledged as the founder of a new line.[1]

Of the many religious orders that have arisen in the world of Sunnī Islam, India has become the hospitable home for a large number. Abū'l-Faḍl mentions fourteen orders or 'families' (*k̲h̲āndān*), which he says were common in his time, and gives their names as follows:

1. Ḥabībīyah
2. Ṭayfūrīyah
3. Kark̲h̲īyah
4. Saqaṭīyah
5. Junaydīyah
6. Kazrūnīyah
7. Ṭūsīyah
8. Firdawsīyah
9. Suhrawardīyah
10. Zaydīyah
11. 'Iyāḍīyah
12. Adhamīyah
13. Hubayrīyah
14. Chishtīyah[2]

[1] *Ā'īn-i-Akbarī*, tr. H. S. Jarrett, III, 357. [2] *Ibid.*, III, 354.

Few of these are among the names commonly employed to-day, though to practically all of them reference will be found in the Urdū and Persian books dealing with the religious orders. Those which are most frequently spoken of at the present, and which enjoy popular favour and influence, are the Chishtī, the Suhrawardī, the Qādirī, the Shaṭṭārī, and the Naqshbandī orders. But before we give an account of their introduction into India, and the extent of their work, the nature and form of their organization will be briefly explained, since in general all the orders are much the same.

The differences consist chiefly in a sense of personal loyalty to the founders of the orders and the peculiar practices which they enjoined on their followers. However, membership is not necessarily limited to one order, and, as often happens, a Muslim may adopt the teachings and practices of several *darwīsh* orders without in any way affecting his original religious and social standing in his community. Nevertheless, since celibacy is not strictly observed even by the *pīrs* themselves (though it is a state which is said to be preferred), as a result there is a strong tendency to form tribal groups. These groups arise because of the close spiritual affiliation among the members of the various orders, and also because of the long lines of natural and spiritual descendants of the *pīrs*.[1] It is from this circumstance, no doubt, that the term *khāndān* (family) is employed for the *darwīsh* fraternity.

Beliefs and Practices

As has already been indicated, the underlying philosophy and theology of the religious orders is Ṣūfiism; however, it does not follow that all Ṣūfīs are necessarily members of a religious order, nor is it proper to assume that all initiates of a *darwīsh* order are Ṣūfīs. Nevertheless, there is a close and fundamental connexion between the views of Ṣūfīs and the religious orders, so much so that the latter could not have come into being without the former. Ṣūfiism, with its warm, mystical yearning after union and fellowship with God, nowhere found a more suitable soil in which to thrive than India, where the very atmosphere was

[1] H. A. Rose, *G.T.C.P.*, I, 528.

charged with a deep religious longing to find God, with the result that to-day it is estimated that fully two-thirds of India's Muslim population are under the influence of some one or other of the *darwīsh* orders. The effort to effect union of man's soul with God, which is deemed the highest bliss, is the chief function of the religious orders. Thus Ṣūfīism has provided the objective or philosophy of life, while it remains for the *darwīsh* orders to apply the philosophy to the everyday needs of the man in the street.

In doing this the religious orders have performed a great service to the natural mystical instincts of the masses. Their message is something like this. God has endowed all His servants with the capacity for union with Him. They have this capacity hidden in their hearts. But it cannot be developed without guidance. Therefore it is necessary that every person should voluntarily seek to attach himself to some illuminated soul, who has become qualified to lead men to God. To perform the function of spiritual leadership there have arisen pious souls, who, because of their peculiar spiritual gifts and diligence in seeking God, have been divinely blessed with the gift of miraculous powers (*karāmāt*). These men, out of their practical experience in the way (*ṭarīqah*) of coming into union (*waṣl*) with God, have defined the stages (*maqāmāt*) of progress and laid down rules for the guidance of all men who desire to live on terms of the closest possible intimacy with God and His saints (*walīs*).

The spiritual guide is known as the *murshid*, *pīr*, or *shaykh*, and his disciple is called a *murīd*. The practice of spiritual preceptorship, therefore, is known as *pīrī-murīdī*, which has its counterpart in the *gurū-chelā* relationship among Hindus, and is very common throughout India. It is for the *pīr* to win the favour of men through his holy living, or manifestation of the favour of God upon him, through some well attested *karāmāt* such as miraculous healing or the revelation of hidden mysteries or secrets. Having won his reputation for piety, he begins to make disciples of men who voluntarily come to him. He then proceeds to initiate them into the religious fraternity by some simple ceremony, which includes the joining of hands and the pledging of devotion on the part of the *murīd* to the *pīr*.

The *murīd* is now designated a traveller (*sālik*) on the way (*ṭarīqah*), and he must carefully observe the rules of the order and the ritualistic practice of *d̲h̲ikr* if he is to make progress on the way to union (*waṣl*) with Allāh. Having become a *traveller* on the *way*, his aim now is to be guided by the *pīr* until he has advanced through the various stages (*maqāmāt*) of divine illumination (*k̲h̲aṭrāt*). Consequently, the problem becomes one of endeavouring to regulate the illumination or the divine ideas that are ready at all times to descend into the heart of man. Various orders of Ṣūfīs have arisen, differing from one another in respect of the rules for meditation (*fikr*) and ritualistic observance (*d̲h̲ikr*), which are prescribed for the regulation of the divine illumination (*k̲h̲aṭrāt*).

The stages through which the *murīd* is to pass are variously described by the different orders in India, but in the main they are as described by Hughes. The first stage is that of our common humanity (*Nāsūt*), for which one has the law (*Sharī'at*) of Islam; perfection in this leads on to the stage of *Malakūt*, where one has the nature of angels, and must walk in the pathway of purity. The third stage is called *Jabarūt* (possession of power), for which there is *Ma'rifah* (knowledge). The fourth is *Lāhūt* (absorption in divinity), where one has *Ḥaqīqah* (absolute truth).[1]

The religious practices by which the *sālik* proceeds along the way are of vital importance. Those which are known as *d̲h̲ikr* (remembering) have for their object the production of spiritual ecstasy (*wajd*), in which state (*ḥāl*) the one who is engaged in the *d̲h̲ikr* may shut out all other thoughts than that of Allāh himself. The term *d̲h̲ikr*, which is so commonly used among Muslims, means remembrance, hence it is the practice of remembering, or bringing Allāh to mind. The methods are various, some of which I have observed myself. There is the *d̲h̲ikr jalī* (perceptible *d̲h̲ikr*) when the exercises are performed *aloud*, when the voice may be raised very high, in order deliberately to shut out any other thoughts. There is the opposite of this, the *d̲h̲ikr k̲h̲afī* (imperceptible *d̲h̲ikr*), where the person practises his repetitions *quietly*. Finally there is a still further advanced *k̲h̲afī* form, in which the *sālik* shuts his eyes, closes his lips, and fixes his atten-

[1] T. P. Hughes, *A Dictionary of Islam*, 609.

tion on his inhalations and exhalations, and 'when the breath goes out he thinks he says '*Lā ilāhah*' (There is no God) . . . he annihilates all external objects; and when it comes in, he thinks he says '*illā Allāh*' (except Allāh).[1] According to a *darwīsh* friend of mine, there is still another and more advanced form of the *dhikr khafī*. His fanciful view is as follows: Every person in his breathing consciously or unconsciously utters the name Allāh, the syllable 'Al' being the natural sound produced by the incoming breath, and 'lāh' being the natural sound of the outgoing breath.

The loud and vociferous form of *dhikr* one not infrequently meets in India. The most prominent example that has come to my notice was at a railway station in northern India. A man was sitting by himself, and finally began to shout his *dhikr* formula aloud. It was the usual 'Lā ilāhah illā Allāh', throwing his head downward toward his right side as he shouted 'Lā ilāhah', and then bringing it back and throwing it downward toward the left side as he shouted 'illā Allāh'. As he proceeded his shouts grew louder, and his actions became more violent, until finally, in utter exhaustion, he sank back in a stupor, which he possibly would describe as a state of ecstasy (*wajd*), apparently having accomplished what he sought for on that particular occasion. To observe people engaging in silent exercises (*dhikr khafī*) is not uncommon, such having frequently come to my notice while travelling on the train. For this purpose the rosary (*tasbīḥ*) is often employed, to enable one to keep account of the number of times one repeats the formula.

In addition to the *dhikrs* that may be classed according to the voice used, we may also consider them from another standpoint. As will have been noted, the *dhikr* may be practised alone, or it may be performed by a congregation or group. The first kind has just been described, and may be performed at any time and any place, as we have seen. For the group, it is necessary to appoint a time and place. Such meetings are held in India usually on Thursday evenings; but there seems to be no such attempt to make public displays of them as is the case in Egypt even at the present time, and as used to be the case in Turkey. As women

[1] Khāja Khān, *Studies in Tasawwuf*, 110.

belong to *darwīsh* fraternities as well as men, it is necessary for them to arrange their meetings for *dhikr* at such times and places as will be convenient for the women who are to gather. One such meeting was reported by my wife, who observed it in a private *zanānah*, in the Bijnor district, some years ago.

Method of Organization

The government of the order or fraternity centres in the *pīr*. He is either an appointed or hereditary successor to the position of authority, and is variously called *khalīfah* or *sajjādah nishīn*. On him devolves the duty of regulating the functions of the members, of passing on the divine knowledge of the order, maintaining its practices, and of initiating new *murīds* as they seek admission to the fraternity. The *pīr* takes up his residence at the headquarters of the fraternity, which usually goes by the name of *khānaqāh* (monastery). The *khānaqāh* is an ancient institution of the *darwīsh* fraternities. Sometimes it is endowed, but sometimes not. It is often built around or over the tomb of the *pīr* who founded it, which forms the inner sanctuary of the building. One which I visited in 1923, at Aishmaqām, near Islamabad, in Kashmir, was an ancient structure, built above the village on the side of the mountain. I was admitted without difficulty, and in due course was escorted through labyrinthine tunnels in the rock to a cave, which formed the sepulchre of the holy man who had been the founder of the *khānaqāh*. On inquiry concerning the rules of the institution and the religious order, it appeared that membership was of two kinds. The lower order consisted of the laity in the villages and towns round about, who carried on their regular occupations of butcher, baker, water-carrier, tailor, mason, schoolmaster, lawyer, practically all classes being represented. The other class was connected with the monastery itself, and this in turn was divided into two classes or parties: the travellers and the dwellers. The travellers were those to whom was assigned the task of going out into the surrounding country and collecting gifts from the lay members of the order. The countryside was divided into circles (*ḥalqahs*), and each of the travellers was assigned his particular circle for visitation and collection. In due course he must return to the *k͟hānaqāh* with the results of his labours, which income was disposed of according to the rules of the institution. The dwellers, or those who constantly stay in the *k͟hānaqāh*, were divided into three classes: the *ahl-i-k͟hidmat* (servants), the *ahl-i-ṣuḥbat* (associates), and the *ahl-i-k͟hilwat* (recluses). The first named, according to Rose, who describes them with precision,[1]

> are novices who do service in order to become acceptable to the men 'of deeds and stages', those who are engaged in practices and have advanced some stages on the path or way. By service they acquire fitness for 'kinship', admission to the next degree in the order, and thus become a 'slipper out of the garment of alienation and farness', or 'put off the garment of separation from the Divine'.

The *k͟hānaqāh* exercises extensive influence for good or ill in the religious life of the Muslims of India who have elected to follow a spiritual guide, for the various *darwīsh* fraternities touch all classes, excepting those who have been influenced by modern education or extreme Wahhābī teachings.

Introduction of the Regular Religious Orders into India

The religious orders, through which Ṣūfī doctrines and practices have been chiefly introduced into India, have a long history. Out of the country from beyond the north-west frontier, and from Iraq, came the missionaries of these orders, the first one arriving toward the close of the twelfth century. They brought with them the fervour, devotion, and piety begotten of long contact and discipleship with spiritual leaders in those lands, and the best that they had learned from a long experience in journeyings, fastings, and pilgrimages to shrines of the saints and to holy Mecca. They easily won the favour of the multitudes, while numbers of their spiritual successors became influential guides of sovereigns, not only in spiritual but in political affairs as well. During life they enjoyed popular and royal favour; and after death their tombs became places of pilgrimage for multitudes of devout Muslims of all classes, and have continued to draw enormous crowds of devotees all through succeeding centuries.

[1] *G.T.C.P.*, I, 518 ff.

An attempt will now be made to give a brief account of each of the various orders found in India, attention being given to the historical order in which they were introduced.

The Chishtī Order

The oldest of the *darwīsh* fraternities in India is the Chishtī order, which traces its origin to Khwājah Abū Abdāl Chishtī, who died A.D. 966. It was introduced into India by Khwājah Mu'īn-ud-Dīn Chishtī, of Sīstān, a southern district of Afghanistan, where he was born A.D. 1142. He later removed with his parents to the region of Khurāsān, and thence to the neighbourhood of Nīshāpūr, near Meshed, where he became the disciple of Khwājah 'Uthmān Chishtī Hārūnī. After more than twenty years' discipleship, he went on a pilgrimage to Mecca and Medina. Then he made a journey through Iraq and Persia, during which he made the acquaintance of many noted Ṣūfīs, such as 'Abd-ul-Qādir Jīlānī and Khwājah Quṭb-ud-Dīn Bakhtyār Kākī, who became one of his disciples. Finally, his travels brought him back to Herat, Balkh and Ghaznī, from whence he came in A.D. 1192 with the army of Shihāb-ud-Dīn Ghūrī to Delhi, where he stayed for a time. At the age of fifty-two, in the year A.D. 1195, he went to Ajmīr, which henceforth became his permanent residence, until his death in A.D. 1236.[1]

His tomb, in the famous *dargāh* of the Khwājah Ṣāḥib, at Ajmīr, is the centre of attraction for tens of thousands of Muslims, and even Hindus, who annually visit the city on the occasion of the '*urs*, or festival, which celebrates the anniversary of the death of the saint. On this occasion two enormous kettles are filled with rice, at the expense of wealthy Muslims who thereby seek to win merit. The contents are distributed in portions to any of the people present who may desire some. In connexion with the *dargāh* mosque, which was built by Akbar, there is a flourishing *madrasah*, which is largely supported by grants from H.E.H. the Niẓām of Hyderābād. The Emperor Akbar was greatly devoted to the Khwājah Ṣāḥib's tomb, and during a part of his reign made annual pilgrimages to it in performance of a vow.

Akbar's connexion with the Chishtī tomb of Ajmīr forms a

[1] *Ā'īn-i-Akbarī*, Blochmann, II, 214.

very important chapter in the history of the life of the Emperor as well as that of the tomb. In fact, it was because of the many pilgrimages he made to the shrine of Khwājah Ṣāḥib that he found it necessary to build a palace there. His tomb-worship seems to have begun as the result of a vow he once made in connexion with his campaign against Chitor. He vowed that, if he took the fort of Chitor, he would walk on foot from Agra to the tomb of the holy man in Ajmīr. The fort was taken in A.D. 1568, and the vow was paid to the letter. He had made a similar vow before the birth of Jahāngīr, in A.D. 1567, and for ten successive years he made an annual pilgrimage to it. His last pilgrimage to Ajmīr seems to have been in A.D. 1579.[1]

The spiritual descendants of Khwājah Mu'īn-ud-Dīn Chishtī have been among the most famous saints of India, and, in order that the reader may have a clearer view of the line of successors of this important order, a list of some of their names in order is given on page 120, and special mention will be made of some of them. Attention should be paid to the tendency of the order to subdivide, a characteristic that is not uncommon in the history of religious orders.

The most noted of the above list of Chishtī saints would include Khwājah Quṭb-ud-Dīn, Bakhtyār Kākī, of Ush, near Baghdad, who is buried near the Quṭb Minār, at Delhi, for whom, it is said, this great column was named. He was a disciple and intimate friend of Mu'īn-ud-Dīn, and died in the same year as his master.

Shaykh Farīd-ud-Dīn Shakarganj, better known as Bābā Farīd, who died in A.D. 1265, and whose tomb is at Pāk Pattan, in the Punjab, is known throughout India. The crowd that each year attends his *'urs*, on the fifth of the month of Muḥarram, is enormous, and includes Hindus as well as Muslims. He was succeeded by two famous disciples, Ḥaḍrat Niẓām-ud-Dīn Awliyā, of Delhi, and Ḥaḍrat Makhdūm 'Alā-ud-Dīn 'Alī Aḥmad Ṣābir.

Niẓām-ud-Dīn Awliyā, whose real name was Muḥammad bin Aḥmad bin Dāniyal al-Bukhārī, was a native of Budaun, U.P., where he was born in A.D. 1238. He soon became a favourite with his master, and was nominated by Bābā Farīd to be his *khalīfah* (successor) when he was only twenty years of age, seven years

[1] Douglas, *Bombay and Western India*, I, 289.

THE CHISHTĪ FAMILY TREE[1]

Khwājah Mu'īn-ud-Dīn Chishtī, the saint of *Ajmīr*

|

Khwājah Quṭb-ud-Dīn, of Delhi, the Quṭb Ṣāḥib

|

Shaykh Farīd-ud-Dīn, Shakarganj, the famous Bābā Farīd, of Pāk Pattan

- *Ḥaḍrat Niẓām-ud-Dīn Awliyā, of Delhi*, whose spiritual descendants are called NIẒĀMĪS
  - and so on
- *Ḥaḍrat Makhdūm 'Alā-ud-Dīn 'Alī Aḥmad Ṣābir*, of Pīrān Kalīr (near Rurkī), His spiritual descendants are called ṢĀBIRĪS
  - *Sh. Shams-ud-Dīn Turk, of Pānīpat*
  - *Shāh-i-Walāyat Sh. Jalāl-ud-Dīn, of Pānīpat*
  - *Sh. 'Abd-ul-Ḥaqq, of Radaulī* (U.P.)
  - *Sh. 'Ārif Ṣāḥib*
  - *Sh. Muḥammad Ṣāḥib*
  - *Sh. 'Abd-ul-Quddūs Ṣāḥib, Quṭb of Gangoh* (U.P.)
  - *Sh. Jalāl-ud-Dīn, of Thanesar*
  - *Sh. Niẓām-ud-Dīn, of Balkh*, Afghanistan
  - *Sh. Abū Sa'īd, of Gangoh*
  - *Sh. Muḥammad Ṣādiq, of Gangoh*
  - *Sh. Dā'ūd Ṣāḥib, of Gangoh*
  - *Shāh 'Abd-ul-Maiālī*
  - *Ḥaḍrat Mīrān Sayyid Shāh Bhīk*, the famous Mīrān Ṣāḥib, whose tomb is at Ghuram, in Patiāla State ; and so on

[1] Rose, *G.T.C.P.*, I, 527.

before the death of Farīd-ud-Dīn. During his life he enjoyed the society of many eminent contemporaries, some of whom became his disciples. The most noted of these were the poets Amīr Khusrū and Amīr Ḥasan Dihlawī, and the historian Ḍiyā-ud-Dīn Baranī. He died in the year A.D. 1325 and his tomb in the suburbs of Delhi, surrounded by the graves of many of his followers, is still visited by devout pilgrims from near and far.

Ḥaḍrat Makhdūm 'Alā-ud-Dīn 'Alī Aḥmad Ṣābir, the second disciple of Farīd-ud-Dīn to become his successor, likewise acquired a great reputation for piety before his death in A.D. 1291. His tomb is just north of Rurkī, at a spot called Pīrān Kalīr, where there is a large gathering every year on the occasion of the saint's *'urs*. His followers are called *Ṣābirīs*.

Niẓām-ud-Dīn Awliyā left as his *khalīfah* Naṣīr-ud-Dīn Muḥammad, the Lamp of Delhi (Chirāgh-i-Dihlī), who died in A.D. 1356. There followed a long line of saints in this order, who became so well known that the Chishtī fraternity spread far and wide. One of the most important of these later saints was Shaykh Salīm Chishtī. He exerted a potent influence in the lives of the Mughul emperors and the royal families of his time. The Emperor Jahāngīr was born in his house, and the saint himself lies buried in a beautiful tomb at Fatḥpūr Sikri. The followers of the saint, Niẓām-ud-Dīn Awliyā, and his successors are called *Niẓāmīs*.

During the two centuries following the death of Shaykh Salīm Chishtī in A.D. 1572, the Chishtī movement experienced a period of decay, which became very marked by the middle of the eighteenth century. Toward the close of that century a revival of the order throughout the Punjab and Sind was led by Khwājah Nūr Muḥammad Qiblah-i-'Ālam, who was by ancestry a Rajput, and not of Sayyid origin, as had been the case of the former great leaders of the fraternity. Therefore, as Rose points out, 'it would seem that in a sense the modern rise of the Chishtī sect marks an indigenous revival of Islam, under religious leaders of local tribes, instead of the older Sayyid families'.[1]

The names or titles given to the holy men of the religious orders, such as Ṣābir and Shakarganj and so on, are very

[1] *G.T.C.P.*, II, 173.

interesting in the matter of their origin. One cannot go into the account of them all, and the explanation commonly given by the followers of Ṣābir Ṣāḥib must suffice as an illustration. It will be noted that the name usually reveals some special spiritual characteristic, or some special ability. The title given to 'Alā-ud-Dīn 'Alī Aḥmad is thus explained in the *Gular Ṣābirī*: 'One day Bābā Farīd, 'Alī Aḥmad's spiritual director and maternal uncle, bade him give food and alms on his behalf to the poor. This he did, and, though stationed at the kitchen (*langar khānah*) night and day, he did not quit it to take his food at his own house. As he got weaker day by day, his mother asked him the reason, and he replied that he had taken no food for several days as his leader's orders bade him to distribute it to others, but did not authorize him to take any himself. Also as he was required to be present at the kitchen, he could not leave it. For this he received the name Ṣābir (the patient one).'[1]

The Suhrawardī Order

Following the appearance of the Chishtī order in India, the next *darwīsh* fraternity to be introduced was the Suhrawardī order, which was sponsored by Bahā'-ud-Dīn Zakarīyā, a native of Multan. He went to Baghdad and attached himself to Shihāb-ud-Dīn Suhrawardī, the founder of the order, who was himself a contemporary of 'Abd-ul-Qādir Jīlānī, founder of the Qādirī order. In A.D. 1266 he died at Multan, where his tomb is greatly revered.

His work was carried on by one of his disciples, Sayyid Jalāl-ud-Dīn Surkh-posh (A.D. 1199–1291), who was born in Bukhārā, and settled in Uch, Sind. That the order has had an extensive influence, particularly in Sind and Gujarāt, can be gathered from the following account given by Arnold. Sayyid Jalāl-ud-Dīn 'is the ancestor of generations of saints, some of whom were active and successful propagandists of Islam. His *khalīfah* was his grandson, Jalāl bin Aḥmad Kabīr, commonly known as Makhdūm-i-Jahāniyān (d. A.D. 1384), who is said to have made the pilgrimage to Mecca thirty-six times and to have performed innumerable miracles. One of Makhdūm-i-Jahāniyān's

[1] *G.T.C.P.*, I, 530; Muḥammad Yāsīn, *Ḥālāt-i-Ṣābir*.

grandsons, Abū Muḥammad 'Abd Allāh, known as Burhān-ud-Dīn Quṭb-i-'Ālam (d. A.D. 1453), went to Gujarāt, where his tomb is still a place of pilgrimage at Batuwa. His son, Sayyid Muḥammad Shāh 'Ālam (d. A.D. 1475), became still more famous and played an important part in the political and religious life of his time; his tomb is at Rasūlābād, near Aḥmadābād.'[1]

The Shaṭṭārī Order

The third of the major orders in India is the Shaṭṭārī. The Emperor Humāyūn received his spiritual instruction from one of the leaders of this order, Muḥammad Ghawth, who was buried in the year A.D. 1562 at Gwalior, where Akbar raised a magnificent tomb in his honour.[2] One of his leading disciples, Wajīh-ud-Dīn Gujarātī (d. 1589), is buried at Aḥmadābād.[3] At Meerut we find a tomb built by the Empress Nūr Jahān to the memory of Shāh Pīr, who died in A.D. 1632. This order was introduced into India from Persia by 'Abd Allāh Shaṭṭārī, who passed away in Mālwa in A.D. 1406.[4]

The Qādirī Order

The fourth religious order to find entrance into the religious life of Indian Islam was the well-known Qādirī order, so named from its founder, 'Abd-ul-Qādir al-Jīlī or Jīlānī, whose tomb is at Baghdad. This famous saint is highly regarded throughout India, and frequently goes by the titles, Pīr Dastgīr, or Pīr-i-Pīrān, as well as other honorific names. Shrines are erected to secure his beneficent assistance. His festival, or *'urs*, is widely celebrated on the eleventh of the month, *Rabī ath-Thānī*. Though the founder died in A.D. 1166, the order was not introduced into India until more than three hundred years later. In A.D. 1482 Sayyid Bandagī Muḥammad Ghawth, one of his descendants, took up his residence in Sind, at Uch, already made famous in the annals of Muslim saints by the Suhrawardī order. Muḥammad Ghawth died in Uch in A.D. 1517, but his sanctity has been handed down through a long line of descendants, some of whom were saints and miracle workers, and to this day representatives of the

[1] *E.I.*, II, 488. [2] Budāyūnī, *Muntakhab-ut-Tawārīkh*, III, 4-6.
[3] *Ibid.*, III, 43, 44.
[4] *E.I.*, art. 'Shaṭṭārīya'; Herklots, *Islam in India*, 289.

family can be found there.[1] There are numerous tombs of the saints of this order all over northern India, and the Punjab in particular. One of the most important of those was Shaykh Mīr Muḥammad, or Miyāṇ Mīr, especially distinguished because of the fact that he was the religious teacher of Prince Dārā Shikūh, son of Shāh Jahān. The biography of this saint, under the title, *Sakīnat-ul-Awliyā'*, was written by his royal disciple. Miyāṇ Mīr passed away in Lahore in the year A.D. 1635, where his tomb is still a well preserved object of veneration.

Some of the descendants of Pīr Dastgīr, through their ancestor, Muḥammad Ghawth, have been canonized as patron saints of certain industrial castes or guilds in the Punjab and Kashmir, to which we shall refer later on. This point is emphasized here to indicate the direct relationship that Indian Islam holds to some of the ancient founders of these orders that are spread so widely throughout the Muslim world.

The Naqshbandī Order

The fifth, and last, of the great religious orders to be introduced into India is known as the Naqshbandīyah, which was founded by Khwājah Bahā'ud-Dīn Naqshband of Turkestan, who died in A.D. 1389, and was buried near Bukhārā. According to Rose,[2] this order was introduced into India by Khwājah Muḥammad Bāqī Bi'llāh Berang, who died in A.D. 1603, and whose tomb is at Delhi. But according to Arnold,[3] who refers to his letters,[4] it was introduced by Shaykh Aḥmad al-Farūqī as-Sirhindī, who died in A.D. 1625. In the list of Naqshbandī *pīrs* given by Rose, Shaykh Aḥmad is mentioned as the *khalīfah* of Muḥammad Bāqī; but he is apparently regarded as something more than an ordinary *pīr*, for his full title is given as 'Imām Rabbānī Mujaddid Alif ath-thānī Shaykh Aḥmad Farūqī Sirhindī', which indicates that he was considered to be the reformer at the beginning of the second thousand years after the Prophet. His tomb is at Sirhind, in Patiāla.

This order does not seem to have been as much favoured with success as the earlier orders. Perhaps this is due to the fact

[1] *E.I.*, II, 489. [2] *G.T.C.P.*, I, 548. [3] *E.I.*, II, 489.
[4] Ethe, *Cat. Pers. MSS, India Office*, No. 1891.

of its late entry on the scene, as it came to India about four centuries after Khwājah Mu'īn-ud-Dīn Chishtī made his appearance with his order, which has the largest following of all the fraternities. However, in recent times there has been a Naqshbandī revival in the Punjab and Kashmir. It is specially favoured by the educated.

The Irregular or Be-shar' Orders

The religious orders that have just been discussed are known as *ba-shar'* (with the law) orders, because of the fact that their followers observe the customary Islamic practices of fasting, prayer, and the like, and consequently are in better standing with the world of Islam than are the *be-shar'* (without the law) orders, whose followers in many cases are but Muslims in name. Nevertheless, this second group, which is without the law, influences a very large multitude in India. It is because of the fact that representatives of these free (*āzād*) orders are so widely found throughout the country that attention must be paid to them, though, as far as real Islam is concerned, they are deserving of but scant respect and consideration.

In reality, these groups cannot be styled religious orders in the same sense as those of the *ba-shar'* type, even though some of them appear to be offshoots of the original respectable orders. First of all, there is not the same attention given to the organization and control of the order as we find among the Ṣābirīs, for example. There is not the same regard for learning, and so the *pīrs* of these groups are not among the society of the learned and the great, as we found to be the case with Shaykh Mu'īn-ud-Dīn Chishtī, and men of his type. The *pīrs* of these orders are as often as not ignorant and even scoundrels; and since it is a case of 'like priest like people', those who associate themselves with these orders are apt to be of a similar nature.

The ordinary Muslim *faqīrs* of the bazaar or village belong to this sort of mendicant order. As they go about begging, singing, giving demonstrations of their ability in magic and sleight of hand, telling fortunes, writing amulets, and making charms, the uninitiated observer is likely to assume that all *darwīshes* are like these charlatans. Nothing could be farther from the truth. Between the

Qalandar[1] and the devout follower of one of the regular orders is a vast difference. I think of one *faqīr*, especially, who was a frequent visitor at our home. He happened to be a member of the Qādirī order, and often went about in a patchwork robe of many colours. By occupation he was a tobacco merchant, and very well-to-do. Nevertheless, he spent much time reading Ṣūfī literature, and engaging in devotions that would lead to religious ecstasy. He was a plain, unobtrusive citizen of the business world, but his sincerity showed that he was a man who had really achieved a measure of the religious experience which he sought.

It is exceedingly difficult to give any sort of classification to the *be-shar'* orders which may be made in such a way as to relate them either historically to the orders from which they sprang, or to the peculiar circumstances out of which they may have arisen. Our knowledge has not gone sufficiently far to enable us to do that completely. Furthermore, it is in this field of investigation that it is most difficult to penetrate secrets of this sort, because the members of the orders are very reticent about giving information; and, since the organizations are of a more or less secret nature, the histories and the rituals have not been fully brought to light. Much of the history and ritual of these orders is handed down orally, and there are practically no publications to be found that make reference to them.

There are several of the *be-shar'* orders that seem to be degenerate off-shoots of regular *ba-shar'* fraternities; indeed, possibly all of them might be found to have some such connexion, if we could unravel all the mystery surrounding their origin. Secondly, there is another group that appear to be connected with some historical founder; for the possibility of founding new orders is not limited, as Abū'l-Faḍl reminds us.[2] Thirdly, we find a group whose origin it is very difficult to determine. They certainly have no conscious philosophical basis, such as is found for the regular orders; nor do they seem to have founders whose historicity can be guaranteed. Their principle of cohesion appears to consist of a common desire on the part of the members to secure a living, coupled with a common religious instinct to seek the favour of God through mediation.

[1] See p. 129. [2] *Ā'īn-i-Akbarī*, tr. Jarrett, III, 357.

Offshoots of the Regular Orders

Of the first class, which are mendicant subdivisions or degenerate offshoots from the regular orders, the following which will be described are the more important:

From the Qadirī order has arisen the Benawā order, founded by G͟hulām ʻAlī Shāh, of Delhi.[1] There are also the Qayṣar Shāhī and Naushāhī sub-orders. According to Rose, the founder of the Naushāhī order was Ḥājī Pīr Muḥammad Sachiār, whose tomb is at Naushahra, on the banks of the Chenāb, in the Punjab. He was called Naushāh, or bridegroom, because he became a *faqīr* while still a bridegroom. This author goes on further to describe them as follows:

> Another story has it that Ḥajī Muḥammad Naushāhī Ganjbaksh, who was a year old when his father, ʻAlā-ud-Dīn, a cattle dealer, died, was brought up in a family of potters and followed Sakhī Sarwār; he left four disciples, namely (1) Shāh Raḥmān Pīr, who is buried in Gujranwala, (2) Pīr Muḥammad Sachiār, (3) K͟hwājah K͟hujayl, who is buried at Kabul, and (4) Shāh Fatḥ, who is buried in the Ganjī Bār. However this may be, the followers of this sect differ from the Qādirīs, both in allowing the use of instrumental music at divine service and in the extreme religious excitement permitted on such occasions, during which they shake their heads to and fro (*ḥāl khēlnā*) in a most alarming manner, and are even said to be held up by the back. Their principal shrine in Sialkot is that of Gulū Shāh, near the village of Korake, in the Pasrūr taḥsīl, where there is a large annual fair. They have a branch called the Pākraḥmānīs.[2]

From the Suhrawardī order has arisen the Jalālī order, founded by Sayyid Jalāl Buk͟hārī, of Uch, who lived from A.D. 1307 to 1374. They are also divided into sub-orders, one of which is called the Chihaltan, the 'forty bodies', since they claim origin from a woman 'who, desiring to be a mother, swallowed forty philtres instead of one, and produced forty children'.[3] The Malang *faqīrs* are said to have some connexion with this order, but according to other authorities they are an offshoot of the Madārīs, which to me seems more likely.

From the Naqshbandī order we have two off-shoots, called the Nūrbak͟hshī and Rabbānī sub-orders. They are of slight importance, however.

[1] K͟hāja K͟hāṇ, *Studies in Tasawwuf*, 155.

[2] *G.T.C.P.*, III, 166. [3] Rose, *G.T.C.P.*, I, 552; Herklots, op. cit., 292.

From the Ṭayfūrī order, though by a long line of descent, we have the Madārī faqīrs. Accounts differ as to the manner in which this order was introduced into India. According to one account, the founder's name was Shāh Badī'-ud-Dīn Quṭb-ul-Madār; it is related that he was a disciple of Muḥammad Ṭayfūr Shāmī, who is said to have been a Christian at one time; that he came to India from Syria, and during his travels in north India made many disciples and converts to Islam. This account fixes the date of his death as A.D. 1436. Another account indicates that he was a converted Jew of the eleventh century, from Aleppo. In all probability, the former date is more correct.

His reputation for miracles is great; and among other wonders he is reputed to have exorcised a Hindu demon, by the name of Makan Deo, from the spot where his own tomb is now worshipped in Makanpur, Oudh, near the city of Cawnpore. A great fair assembles here annually, so great and widespread is the devotion to Zinda Shāh Madār. His *faqīrs* claim immunity from fire and from snake and scorpion bites.[1]

From the Junaydī order, one of the fourteen mentioned by Abū'l-Faḍl,[2] is the Rafā'ī order. In some parts of India it is known as the Gurzmār order, because the *faqīrs* carry a sort of mace (*gurz*) with which they strike their bodies, or even inflict grievous wounds on themselves with swords, which they claim to heal with saliva. This belief in the therapeutic value of saliva is based on the initiation ceremony. When the *faqīr* is being initiated the *murshid* passes on the healing power of the saliva of the founder of the order, which he has himself received from his *murshid*, by rubbing a little of his own saliva on the tongue of the *murīd*. At the same time he says, 'Wield the mace on yourself without fear, and if you are cut apply your own spittle to the wound, and it will quickly heal by the influence of your *pīr*, Aḥmad Sa'īd'.[3]

Closely allied to the Rafā'īs[4] are other similar orders, such as the Rasūlshāhīs, of Gujarāt, known as Mastān, 'mad-men', and the Chhalapdārs, of Delhi. However, it is doubtful if there is any connexion other than similarity of practice. The former are the

[1] Khāja Khān, op. cit., 155; *E.I.*, II, 489.

[2] *Ā'īn-i-Akbarī*, tr. Jarrett, III, 354. [3] Herklots, op. cit., 291. [4] *Ibid.*

followers of one Rasūl Shāh, of the Alwār State, who founded his order in the eighteenth century, after having received the power to work miracles from a saint in Egypt. *Faqīrs* of this order are found in the Punjab and Gujarāt. In the former province they are said to be men of respectable families, but in Gujarāt they have earned an uneviable reputation for insobriety, and for their ascetic practices, which are said to be 'for appearance' only.

Be-Shar' Orders of Independent Origin

The orders which seem to have arisen independently of the regular orders, and yet have quite well defined historical beginnings, are a large group. It is impossible to describe them all, but an account will be given of the Qalandarī order. In north India the term *Qalandar* connotes one who leads about a bear or a monkey, from the dancing and tricks of which he earns a living; or it is associated with a poor, ragged beggar, obviously a Muslim, who goes from door to door singing and asking alms. If the person in the house responds, divine blessings are prayed for, but should there be a refusal or great delay, then the *faqīr* calls down a curse upon the dwelling. However, so credulous are the common folk of the villages, Hindus and Muslims and Christians alike, that few, if any, would dare risk the danger of a curse coming true, and as a rule the beggar does not have long to wait.

According to Sell[1] the order was introduced into India by its founder, 'Alī Abū Yūsuf Qalandar, known as Bū 'Alī Qalandar, who was a native of Spain. After having been connected with the Baktāshī and Chishtī orders, he finally left them both, and organized an order of his own. In his travels he ultimately came to India, and settled down at Panipat, near Delhi, where he died in A.D. 1323. The tomb of Bū 'Alī Qalandar is the chief shrine of the order, and is greatly venerated by his followers.

Scattered more or less all over India, other similar *be-shar'* independent orders are found, which profit by the credulity and open-hearted generosity of the people. It is the common belief that giving to any poor beggar, who asks in the name of God or some saint, will somehow benefit the giver as well as the one who receives the gift. The following list is fairly complete, and

[1] *The Religious Orders of Islam*, 51.

includes the Mawlāī, the Dafalī, the Alif Shāhī, the Mūsā Sohāgī, the Habshī or Sīdī, the Shamsī, the Malang *faqīrs*, which may be a branch of the Madārī, and the Imām Shāhī. All these independent orders have more or less organization, with initiation ceremonies, and obedience to the head of the order, who can excommunicate a *faqīr* if he deserves it. They have their central headquarters, which receive a share of all that is collected by the *faqīrs*; and they settle their own internal disputes with order and dignity.[1]

The Unorganized Be-shar' Groups

In addition to these, there is a third class of *be-shar' faqīrs* who seem to be without any form of organization whatever. They are usually devotees of some particular saint's shrine, but their only organizing principle seems to be that they go to the keeper of the shrine, and indicate their desire to be initiated as *faqīrs* who shall henceforth be permitted to go about and beg in the name of the saint. After a brief form of initiation, the *faqīr* is permitted to go forth and demand alms wherever he may choose to wander. One particular instance of this is in connexion with the shrine of Dīn Panāh, in the Muẓaffargarh district, in the Punjab, and those who go out to beg are called 'Dīn Panāhīs'.

[1] See Herklots, op. cit., 289-99.

CHAPTER VII

SAINT-WORSHIP

THE religious life of Islam is so intimately connected with saints and their worship, and its history is so intertwined with them, that to think of the one without the other becomes an impossibility. In life they were men of piety, and usually attracted attention because of alleged miraculous powers, which were proofs of Divine favour. Men sought their company for worldly as well as spiritual profit. Their words and deeds were carefully noted, and faithful disciples wrote their biographies. The historians, too, noted the lives and deeds of these men, as did, for instance, Abū'l-Faḍl and Budāyūnī; while even emperors gave heed to their teachings, spent much time in their company, built elaborate tombs over their graves, and made pilgrimages to their shrines.

The belief in saints, and the worship of their shrines and tombs by the Muslims of India is not, however, peculiar to Indian Islam. In fact, this all came largely ready-made to India, through those who introduced the religious orders into the country from Afghanistan, Persia, and Iraq. Further, owing to the ancient *gurū-chelā* practice existing among the Hindus, and the universal belief in the worship of local gods and goddesses, which was the heritage of the majority of the Muslims of India through their Hindu origin, it became all the more easy for saint-worship to become a fixed part of Muslim religious life. In fact, the Muslim masses of India seem to enter into the worship of saints with more enthusiasm than into the regular religious exercises which are obligatory. And in spite of all the influence of modern education and various reform movements, it is doubtful if there is really less saint-worship to-day than there was formerly.

To be sure there are groups, such as the Wahhābī reformers, and the ultra-orthodox, and those of western education who have cast this all aside, but to the masses the belief in saints, and their ability to grant requests, fulfil desires, and perform miracles is still a real, positive, and practical belief. The devotee believes that the spirit of the saint is actually present in the tomb, that he hears the petitioner, and will intercede with God to grant requests, or that the saint may even fulfil them himself. This close, intimate, personal relationship which the individual feels with the saint, and which he somehow believes the saint holds for him, forms one of the most interesting phases in the study of Islam in India. It is a clear indication of the deep personal need which the individual feels for closer contact and fellowship with Allāh; and which somehow he believes he can secure through the mediation of the saint who was both a companion (*walī*) of God on the one hand, and a friend and companion of man on the other.

The belief in the miraculous powers of saints to help and to heal covers almost the whole category of human need. Some saints are supposed to exhibit certain virtues that others do not. At Amroha, in the Moradabad district, is the tomb of a saint who is supposed to heal scorpion stings, and it is asserted that the scorpions around his tomb will not sting. Another saint, in the same place, has the power to produce the flow of milk in cows which have gone dry prematurely, and nursing mothers, who have need, also seek help from him. The graves of saints are visited by litigants seeking victory in law cases; by the farmer who has lost a horse; by the woman who desires a child; by the father who seeks healing for his sick boy; by the merchant who desires prosperity in business; by the hunter who wants a lucky day; by the gambler, and even by the thief.

There are many instances to show the reverence and fear with which the saints were regarded even by the rulers themselves. Their anger once aroused, could, it was believed, bring the most unexpected and terrible disasters; and their favour, when procured, was productive of great blessing. For example, we are told that the sudden death of Ghiyāth-ud-Dīn Tughluq Shāh, in A.D. 1325, was due to a prophecy by Shaykh Niẓām-ud-Dīn Awliyā, who felt insulted at some remarks made by that sovereign. The pious Emperor Fīrūz Shāh was especially careful about his treatment of these holy men. He writes, 'Wherever I heard of a *faqīr* I went to visit him, and ministered to his necessities, so that I might attain the blessing promised to those who befriend the poor'.[1] The same sovereign, before his expedition to Thatta, 'made pilgrimages to the saints and holy men who were buried near Delhi, . . . as the other great kings had done before him, to invoke the assistance of their prayers, . . . to cast himself on their protection, not trusting to his own power and greatness'.[2]

One very striking instance of the supposed effect of arousing divine displeasure by the ill-treatment of a *darwīsh* was the case of Sīdī Mawlā, in the reign of Fīrūz Shāh Khaljī, about the year A.D. 1295. The *darwīsh* was believed to have been plotting against the emperor. So he was ordered to be put to death; and Amīr Khusrū, in his *Ta'rīkh-i-'Alā'ī*, relates that 'the divine displeasure was manifest at the killing of such a holy man. I, the author, well remember that on the day of the Sīdī's death a black storm arose which made the world dark. Troubles afterwards arose in the State. . . . In the same year there was a scarcity of rain, there was dearth in Delhi, and grain rose to a *jital* (about half a penny) per *sīr* (three-quarters of a pound, then).[3] In the Siwalik also the dearth was greatly felt. The Hindus of that country came into Delhi with their families, twenty or thirty of them together, and in the extremity of their hunger drowned themselves in the Jumna.'[4]

Shrines

The shrine where a saint is worshipped and at which his favours are sought, is not always his tomb. It may be presumed, however, that tombs receive more regard than the memorial shrines, which are not infrequently set up by the saint's devotees. On the part of those who believe in saints, it is conceived that it is possible to erect a memorial to a saint anywhere, to call it by his name, and that, by virtue of this act, prayers and offerings made at this shrine will be quite as effective as a visit to his actual resting-place. The shrine, which has been so dedicated to a saint, may be made of bricks, stone, or mud. Sometimes it is

[1] *Futūḥāt-i-Fīrūz Shāhī*, E.D., III, 387.
[2] Shams-i-Sirāj 'Afīf, E.D., III, 321.
[3] See S. Lane-Poole, *Mediæval India*, 150.
[4] Amīr Khusrū, E.D., III, 146.

made in the form of a tomb, with a head-stone, provided with niches to receive lights placed there by the worshipper. It may be of any size, and I have seen crude piles of earth doing service for shrines. Often there is a flag (*jhandā*) on a long pole attached to the shrine; and not infrequently the neighbouring trees and bushes are considered specially sacred to the saint, and must not be violated. Rags or thread tied on a shrine are in testimony of prayers answered.

The common name which is applied to the saint, living or dead, as well as to his tomb or shrine, is *pīr*. Another name which is often employed for the shrine, especially in Kashmir, is *ziyārat*. The number of such ubiquitous *pīrs* is legion. They are found in every village, town, or city where Muslims live. Even in lonely lanes of the country-side, in the fields and groves, in forests, and in the mountains one may find the grave of a *pīr*, who, though he may have been dead hundreds of years, is still an active source of blessing to all who believe in him. Sometimes, in the course of years, a shrine of a *pīr* will become neglected, then forgotten, and then obliterated. The saint thus forgotten may remain disregarded for generations, and then something will occur to bring him back to active usefulness again. One of the most unusual cases of this sort that has come to my notice was in north India, in the Moradabad district, near the village of Pākbarā. In an open cultivated field near the village was a tree, under which, not long since, it was discovered there were some bricks, which appeared on close examination to form what was believed to be the tomb of a Muslim saint which had fallen into neglect. The elders from the surrounding villages were consulted, and the general conviction was forthcoming that this was indeed the grave of a saint which had been for many years sadly neglected. Additional proof as to the validity of this conviction, moreover, was found, when it was noted that the tree itself, which was adjacent to the tomb, exuded a gummy juice of a reddish colour, which was said to betoken the miracle-working power of the saint. The result was that the tomb, which had been neglected for such a long time, was restored to good and regular standing among the *pīrs* of the country-side. Devotees began to seek favours. Among them was one, in particular, that came to my knowledge. A man was suffering from incipient blindness, and in order to secure relief his wife took him a very long and tiresome journey in an ox-cart, to beseech this newly-found *pīr* for relief.

The tombs and shrines of saints are usually under the care of guardians. If the tomb is that of a very important saint, such as that of Mu'īn-ud-Dīn Chishtī, at Ajmīr, it is well cared for. The guardians of the shrine are usually the direct lineal or spiritual descendants of the saint. In addition to the income that is derived from the collections made by the wandering members of the religious order, there is that which comes from visitors, even including tourists from foreign lands, who go only out of curiosity. Besides this, emperors used to repair certain tombs at public expense, and sometimes the tombs were endowed by them. Even to-day the Government of India is at some pains to keep the tomb of the saint, Salīm Chishtī, at Fatḥpūr Sikri, in repair, because of its undoubted archæological interest.

Worship of the Sainted Dead

The shrines of the humbler saints, however, enjoy a humbler form of care, in accord with their dignity and worth. Here one finds by the roadside a tomb. Once a year or so it receives a coat of whitewash if it is built of brick, or only a coat of clay-wash if it is of raised earth. Either by inheritance, or by appointment from his brotherhood, the caretaker obtains his right to look after the tomb, keep it in repair, and receive part or all of his daily sustenance from the gifts of those who come to pay their vows. So, either daily or weekly on some fixed day, he takes up his duties as officiant of the shrine, and waits for the devotees to arrive.

The worship at the shrines is of a simple character. It consists of two separate divisions. The first is for the benefit of the saint, the second for the benefit of the worshipper. The first may consist of offerings of money or anything of value, the offering of flowers or the lighting of a lamp (*chirāgh*), or merely the repetition of the *Fātiḥah* (the first chapter of the Qur'ān) for the benefit of the saint himself. For the second part of the worship the individual stands or sits somewhere near the shrine, facing it. Here he communes in his heart with the saint, telling him his troubles, difficulties, desires, or aspirations, and vowing that, if the saint will be gracious enough to fulfil this desire, he will return and make an offering and oblation, which he there and then determines upon and promises to the saint. I happened to be present once at a shrine when the offerings were being brought in, and people were paying their vows. An inquiry elicited the following information: Nearly every one who came to pay his vows brought a *chirāgh* (a small cup containing oil and a wick) to be lighted. In addition, each worshipper brought some other thing which the guardian of the shrine could make use of. One brought money, a few *pice*; another brought a couple of yards of green cloth, which was spread over the tomb; another brought cooked rice; another some sugar; another some sweets, and so on. This was placed first of all on the shrine, and then some of it was taken off, and small portions of the sweets, sugar, or rice were distributed to those who were present. Such distributed portions are known as *tabarruk*, portions that have received the saint's special blessing. I have received such 'blessed portions' on several occasions. Of the persons questioned, one said that he had come to the shrine because he had vowed to the saint a week ago that if his pony, which had been lost, were found he would make such and such an offering, and he had come to keep his vow. Another said her child had been sick and was well again. Thus the story goes, and this was but one shrine out of thousands in India which Muslims venerate, and to which they pay a large part of their most fervent religious devotion.

While there are usually special days each week on which the saints' tombs are regularly visited, the great day of the year for each saint is the time of the celebration of his *'urs*. This is an Arabic term which means 'wedding', and is used to refer to the saint's death, because of the Ṣūfī idea that at his death there occurs the union (*waṣl*) or 'wedding' of his soul to Allāh. Sometimes the *'urs* lasts several days, but the great day of the feast is always the anniversary of the saint's death. Such an occasion is made a time of great rejoicing, meeting of friends, and feasting, as well as the observance of religious exercises in memory of the saint. Shop-keepers come and set up their rows of shops.

Amusement makers are present with their merry-go-rounds and swinging chairs. Books, containing the biography of the saint, accounts of his miracles and marvellous deeds, and elegies written in his praise, are sold to the throngs that gather from a wide circuit. People go dressed in their best and gayest attire. It is a time of outing, and people of all classes will be found in such gatherings, whether they have any particular belief in saints or not. Sometimes a gathering of this sort will be made an occasion for the display of certain alleged relics of the Prophet himself. At one such *'urs*, I saw an exhibition of a hair of the Prophet's beard, one of his garments, and a stone bearing an imprint of the Prophet's foot, this relic being called the noble foot-print (*qadam sharīf*), of which there are numerous examples in India.

The solemn part of the *'urs*, of course, has to do with the rites in connexion with the saint's tomb. Every comer is permitted to enter the enclosure of the shrine, if there be one, after having carefully removed his shoes. *Fātiḥahs* are said for the saint, offerings of money and sweets and the like are made, and the worshippers pass out. When night comes on, the readers of the Holy Qur'ān take their position near the shrine, and the most serious part of the ceremony begins. The programme calls for the reading of the whole of the Qur'ān through at one sitting, which ceremony is called a *k͟hatm*. In order to do this the thirty divisions, or *juz*, of the Qur'ān are allotted to thirty readers. These *juz* are approximately of equal length, and so by this method the whole of the Qur'ān is read for the benefit of the saint's soul. The *'urs* is a very important factor in the religious life of Indian Muslims, and takes its place along with the other religious festivals. While some *'urses* are of only local importance, others, such as that of Bābā Farīd-ud-Dīn, at Pāk Pattan, Mu'īn-ud-Dīn Chishtī, at Ajmīr, and Zinda Shāh Madār, at Makanpur, Oudh, have a most extended influence, and many thousands visit them annually from great distances.

The manner in which the tomb of a saint may become the centre of the religious activity of a place is well illustrated in the case of the well-known *dargāh* of K͟hwājah Mu'īn-ud-Dīn Chishtī Ṣāḥib, at Ajmīr, to which reference has been made again and again. There is in connexion with this shrine a mosque built by the Emperor Akbar, in which is a mosque school, or *madrasah*, for the training of religious leaders, and also a *takyah*, or hostelry, for *darwīshes*. In other places the shrine becomes the centre for a monastery (*k͟hānaqāh*).

VARIOUS KINDS OF TOMBS: MARTYRS

The tombs and shrines of saints or *pīrs* may be also considered from the standpoint of their origin. Some have a historical connexion with some religious order; and these we have already considered in their relation to the religious life of Indian Muslims. These have come into the calendar of saints in a perfectly regular manner, but there are others whose legitimacy is not so well attested, and the records of whose lives are so overlaid with legend that it is really impossible to give an accurate account of their origin. Some of these come in the class of *shahīds*, or martyrs, who died fighting the battles of Islam in the early days of Muslim conquest. Two of the most important of these semi-legendary characters are known as G͟hāzī Miyāṇ Sālār Mas'ūd and Sakhī Sarwār Sulṭān, of whom some notice will now be taken. The former was a nephew of Maḥmūd of G͟haznī. While still a youth of only nineteen, he is said to have invaded Oudh, where he met his death in a battle in the year A.D. 1033, near Bahraich. His tomb is venerated by Muslims, who regard him as a martyr (*shahīd*). Sakhī Sarwār Sulṭān belongs to the Punjab, and though little is historically certain about his origin he has many devotees. Shrines raised to his honour are found in almost every village of the central Punjab.[1] At Dhonkal, we are told, Sulṭān had taken up his abode, and produced a well with a marvellous stream of water, which is now regarded as sacred. There is a fair held here every year, which lasts for a month in June and July, to which come as many as two hundred thousand people, 'who drink the sacred water and take away fans and sprigs of *menhdī* (henna) as mementos of their visit'.[2]

HINDU-MUSLIM SAINTS

Other well-known saints, of more or less legendary character, that have a certain amount of standing with certain classes are

[1] Rose, *G.T.C.P.*, I, 570. [2] *Ibid.*

numerous. Some of them, while having Muslim names to-day, seem to have little connexion with the Muslim community or faith. Mere mention will be made of them here, as they have more of a bearing on the influence of Islam on the indigenous faiths of the country than with Islam itself. However, they should be mentioned, as showing the manner in which saint-worship among Muslims gradually shades off until it is scarcely distinguishable from some of the animistic phases of primitive religious life. One such 'saint' is Gūgā Pīr, or Ẓāhir Pīr, who is thought to have been a Hindu convert to Islam, and is said to have flourished toward the middle of the twelfth century. He is particularly associated with Rajputana; but his devotees, mainly low-caste people, are found throughout large areas of northern India and the north-west, where his shrines are built even in the houses. Lāl Beg is another such 'saint', who is particularly patronized by the sweeper community of north India. There is also a following of a group of saints known as the Panj Pīr (five *pīrs*). Worshippers of this group erect shrines to all five of the saints and worship at them. The lists, however, do not agree. Lucknow, for instance, has one list, Benares another, Bihar another, the Punjab another. One list includes G͟hāzī Miyāṇ, Pīr Hathīlī sister's son of G͟hāzī Miyān, Parihar, Sahjā Māī, and ʻAjab Sālār. According to Crooke, Benares has no less than five lists that are current. They, too, are worshipped by the low-caste Hindus. A more respectable list is the following: Bahā'-ul-Ḥaqq, of Multan; Shāh Ruqʻah-i-ʻĀlam Ḥaḍrat, of Lucknow; Shāh Shams Tabrīz, of Multan; Mak͟hdūm-i-Jahāniyān, of Uch; and Bābā Farīd-ud-Dīn, of Pāk Pattan.[1]

Legendary Saints

Attention must be paid, also, to the wholly legendary saints of Islam. One of these, K͟hwājah K͟hiḍr, enjoys a reputation that is as wide as the Muslim world itself, but the remainder appear to be of purely local origin. K͟hwājah K͟hiḍr goes by various names in different parts of India, such as Rājā Kidar, where Hindu influence is strong. In Bengal his name is Kāwaj, or Pīr Badr.[2] There may also be other local corruptions of the name, which one must always be prepared to meet. K͟hwājah

[1] Crooke, *P.R.F.L.*, I, 203. [2] *Ibid.*, I, 47.

Khiḍr is a legendary saint of Muslim lore, who is said to trace his connexion to Noah, and throughout the Muslim world he is associated with water. Thus he comes to be a saint of the sea. His special vehicle is a fish, on which he is often pictured as riding. His garments are green, whence his name Khiḍr is derived, and he is thought to have life-giving powers. In fact, he is considered to be alive in the world still, though unseen. So far as I am aware, shrines are not built to this saint, but he is worshipped in connexion with such ceremonies as the *'aqīqah*, or shaving of the head of a child for the first time. Offerings are also made to him at wells; and persons who are travelling by sea, or who are descending into a well, will seek his favour. He is also propitiated when the water in a river is low or there is danger of a flood.[1] His worship naturally becomes a prominent part in the life of those who believe in him, since water is identified so closely with all that concerns the maintenance of life itself. Little wonder that he is looked upon as the giver of life and the restorer of life, when one remembers to what an extent the Indians depend on the rivers and the wells for irrigation, and the quenching of thirst during the long seasons of no rainfall, when all is parched and dry under a burning sun.

In addition to the occasional or special worship of Khwājah Khiḍr, Indian Muḥammadans make much of what is called his *Berā*. This is a festival which takes its name from the *berā*, or raft, on which the worshippers place burning lamps (*chirāgh*), bouquets of flowers, fruits, sweetmeats, and other eatables. These are then set afloat on the stream in the name of Khiḍr, whose blessing they seek.[2]

Another saint of the very opposite character to the beneficent Khiḍr is Shaykh Saddū, who has votaries throughout India, particularly among women. The legend goes that he was an Arabic scholar, with occult powers, who used certain verses of the Qur'ān for magical purposes, by which he is popularly supposed to have been able to bring the Jinn under his control. It is related that, at one time, he fell in love with a beautiful princess; and,

[1] Rose, *G.T.C.P.*, I, 564.

[2] Abū'l-Anwār, *Moslem Festivals*, 55 ff; Herklots, op. cit., 135, 136; *E.I.*, art. 'Khiḍr'.

finding it impossible to secure her hand in marriage, he invoked the help of his friends, the Jinn, to bring her by night to his residence. This became a regular performance, and she was always returned to the palace before dawn. All this appeared to the princess as a dream; but, being at last overcome by the performance, she reported the matter to the king, who had the Shaykh executed.[1] Another account says that he was ultimately torn to pieces at Amroha, near Mordabad, by the Jinn he was supposed to control.[2] In any case, many ignorant Muslims still believe that he haunts and worries their women, and he is also supposed to harm children. Women become 'possessed', as they believe, by Shaykh Saddū through the performance known as *baithak*, where, dressed in men's clothes, they gather and sit the whole night listening to the music that is supposed to induce the possession of the Shaykh's spirit. In this state of ecstasy they are supposed to be able to reveal the Shaykh's advice as to how to attain their desires, or those of their friends.

There is another ceremony similar to the *zār*,[3] or 'black mass', so common in Egypt, which is known as the *Bakrā-i-Shaykh Saddū*. This is celebrated in order to drive out his spirit, and to keep him away from women and children. This ceremony of exorcism is observed by the slaughter of kids and goats. Then there is a feast, which is sometimes accompanied with music and dancing, and by the recital of poems composed in commendation of the virtues and excellences of the Shaykh. Oftentimes women 'possessed' by the Shaykh are taken to the place of the performance, which, they imagine, will instantaneously cure their sufferings.[4] At his tomb or place of worship, at Amroha, it is said that there is much noise and disturbance always going on.[5]

In addition to the legendary saints above mentioned, there are many others, such as Pīr Shitāb, Pīr Milao, Pīr Dīdār, Kath Bāwā Ṣāḥib, Pīr Imām Zāmin, and the like. It is always of interest to try to ascertain the names of the saints who are being worshipped by the Muslims of a given locality, in order to discover how many of them are more or less universally venerated, and how many enjoy only a local or provincial celebrity.[6]

[1] Abū'l-Anwār, *Moslem Festivals*, 59 f. [2] Herklots, op. cit., 139.
[3] Cf. S. M. Zwemer, *Animism in Islam*, 227 ff.
[4] Abū'l-Anwār, *Moslem Festivals*, 59. [5] Herklots, op. cit., 139.
[6] *Ibid.*, 134 ff.

Nau-gazā Pīrs

The *nau-gazā pīrs* form a curious class of shrine which deserves closer study than it has yet received. The term refers to the length of the tomb, *nau-gazā* meaning nine yards, and merely indicates that the saint was a personage of great stature. One such tomb is at Multan, where Shadma Shahīd is said to be buried, but as a rule *nau-gazās* are not connected with *shahīds*.[1] For the most part they are associated with giants of former days. Possibly they are only shrines of the ancient prophets, who are thought by some to have attained enormous height. The following statement, given by Crooke, is all I have been able to find on the subject. 'There is one of these tombs at Nagaur, in Rajputana, and several others have been discovered in the course of the Archæological Survey. Five of them at Vijhi measure respectively twenty-nine, thirty-one, thirty, and thirty-eight feet. . . . Adam himself is supposed to have been sixty yards in height, and there was a monster called 'Uj in the days of Adam, and the flood of Noah reached only to his waist. There is a tomb of Noah at Faizabad which is said to have been built by Alexander the Great, and not far off are those of Seth and Job. The latter, curiously enough, are gradually growing in size. They are now seventeen and twelve feet long respectively, but when Abū'l-Fazl wrote they were only ten and a half and nine feet long.'[2] I have seen one such tomb in the fields lying between Moradabad and Rampur, which was said to be a *nau-gazā pīr*, and it measured between twelve and fifteen feet in length.

There are other shrines worshipped by Muslims, which seem to be of Hindu or Buddhist origin, but attention will be given to them when we come to consider the influence of Hinduism on Islam in India.

Patron Saints

Patron saints deserve special study, because of their close relationship to certain classes of work and particular classes of individuals. First of all, the patron saint may be considered from the standpoint of the immediate vicinity or village, or quarter of

[1] Crooke, *Introduction to P.R.F.L.*, 140.
[2] Crooke, *P.R.F.L.*, I, 223 f.

a city, with which he may be connected. In Lucknow, in the quarter known as Golaganj, there is the tomb of a saint of little known reputation, who is specially worshipped by the people of the locality, over whose welfare he is supposed to preside. On one occasion, when new buildings of the Lucknow Christian College were being erected, some very heavy steel girders had to be raised, which placed many lives in jeopardy. After they had all been safely raised, the Muslim workmen proceeded to procure some sweetmeats, and forthwith went to the tomb to make the offering and express their gratitude for the protecting care of the saint who lies buried in the same compound.

As we have already seen, Khwājah Khiḍr is intimately connected with water, and so naturally becomes the patron saint of sailors, and also of *dhobīs* and *bihishtīs* (washermen and water-carriers). The local descendants of the famous 'Abd-ul-Qādir-i-Jīlānī, known as the *Pīr Dastgīr*, have given some patron saints to India especially associated with industrial castes or local guilds in the Punjab. At Lahore, Fīrūz Shāh Jīlānī, a disciple of Shāh 'Ālam, is the saint of the *dandigars* or *kheradīs* (turners). Ḥassan Telī is the patron saint of the oilmen (*telīs*), while the dyers of Lahore look to Pīṛ 'Alī Rangrez.[1] Ma'lūm-i-yār is another patron saint of boatmen and sailors, while Sher Shāh, of Multan, cares for the interests of persecuted lovers. Shāh Dawlah takes care of 'microcephalic children', called Shāh Dawlah's rats! [2]

New Saints

As we have seen, there are all kinds of saints in India, who are in one way or another connected with the life-history of Islam. There are good saints, whose lives were lived on a high plane; there are also some not so good. There are historical saints and legendary saints; real saints and fantastic saints; universal saints and local saints; and, lastly, old saints and new saints. Canonization still continues. Various writers have mentioned instances which are on record, such as Patūkī Sā'īn, of Motihari, Bihar, whose grave is said to be visited chiefly by litigants. His death occurred as late as the decade between 1860 and 1870.

[1] Rose, *G.T.C.P.*, I, 543. [2] *E.I.*, II, 489.

One of the newest saints to be placed in the calendar is the one commonly spoken of as the 'New Market Saint' of Calcutta. This is one of the most remarkable examples of its kind on record. For a long time there had been sitting in the public market in Calcutta a beggar, who was regarded as being above the ordinary in sanctity because he did not talk and was supposed to have taken a vow of silence. Day after day he sat in the market, and lived on the alms of passers-by. One day, while sitting in his regular place in a small alley between two rows of shops, he died. The Muslims at once claimed the body, and declared that, since he was regarded as a very holy man, his body should be buried on the spot where he died. The grave was dug, and the burial was performed. The alley, which had formerly been a regular passage for the public, was closed up, and when I saw it in the month of November, 1924, the newly canonized 'saint' was being carefully looked after by the duly appointed guardians of the tomb. They received the cash offerings, which must have been considerable, since, from the standpoint of drawing crowds, the spot was the best location for saints in all Calcutta. A saint's tomb in a public market, however, was not an unmixed blessing, and the city authorities endeavoured to have the body removed. This aroused great opposition, so finally the matter was compromised by completely enclosing the passage-way to prevent access to the tomb, which remains there to this day.

Persistence of the Belief in Saint Worship

Bernier relates, in his most interesting account of his travels in the Mughul Empire, the following description of a visit to a saint's tomb in Kashmir, which at once reveals the fact that the Muslim masses of India have changed but little through hundreds of years in respect to their credulity and reverence for the sainted dead. The author says that he was importuned by one Dānishmand Khāṇ to visit Bāramūla, where he would see a mosque containing the tomb of a celebrated *pīr*, who, though dead, miraculously cures the sick and infirm.

> 'Perhaps', said Dānishmand Khāṇ, 'you may deny the reality either of the disease or of the cure; but another miracle is wrought by the power of the holy man, which no person can see without acknowledging. There is a large round stone that the strongest man can scarcely raise from the ground,

but which eleven men, after a prayer made to the saint, lift up with the tips of their eleven fingers with the same ease as they would move a piece of straw.'

Bernier describes his experience in his usual vivid fashion :

'I found,' he writes, 'the *Mosque* to be a tolerable building and the *Saint's* tomb is richly adorned. It was surrounded with a great number of people, engaged in acts of devotion, who said they were ill. Adjoining the *Mosque* is a kitchen, wherein I observed large boilers filled with meat and rice, which I conceived at once to be the magnet that draws the sick and the miracle that cures them. On the other side of the mosque are the apartments and garden of the *Mullahs*, who pursue the even tenor of their way under the shadow of the *Pīr's* miraculous sanctity. They are sufficiently zealous in celebrating his praises, but as I am always unhappy on similar occasions, he performed no miracle upon the sick while I remained there. As to the round and heavy stone that was to convert me, I noticed that eleven *Mullahs* formed themselves into a circle round it, but what with their long *cabayes*, or vests, and the studied compactness of the circle, I had great difficulty to see the mode in which they held the stone. I watched narrowly, however, the whole of this cheating process, and, although the *Mullahs* stoutly maintained that each person used only the tip of one finger, and that the stone felt as light as a feather, yet I could clearly discover that it was not raised from the ground without a great effort, and it seemed to me that the *Mullahs* made use of the thumb as well as of the forefinger. Still I mixed my voice with the cries of these impostors and bystanders, exclaiming *Karamet! Karamet!* A miracle! a miracle! I then presented them with a *roupie*, and, assuming a look of deepest devotion, entreated that I might have for once the distinguished honour of being among the eleven who lifted the stone. The *Mullahs* were reluctant to comply with my request, but, having presented them with a second *roupie*, and expressed my belief in the truth of the miracle, one of them gave up his place to me. No doubt they hoped that ten would be able, by an extraordinary effort, to lift the stone, although I contributed no other aid than the tip of my finger, and they expected to manage so adroitly that I should not discover the imposture. But they were much mortified to find that the stone, to which I persevered in applying the end of my finger only, was constantly inclining and falling towards me. I considered it prudent at last to hold it firmly with both by finger and thumb, when we succeeded, but with great difficulty, in raising it to the usual height. Observing that every person looked at me with an evil eye, not knowing what to think of me, and that I incurred the danger of being stoned, I continued to join in the cry of *Karamet!* and, throwing down a third *roupie*, stole away from the crowd. Though I had taken no refreshment since my arrival, I did not hesitate to mount my horse directly, and to quit forever the *Dervishe* and his miracles.'[1]

[1] Bernier, op. cit., 414 ff.

There is no other phase of the life of Muslims in India that is so full of interest as this which has to do with the religious orders and saints. It may not be orthodox; it may be condemned by the *maulvis*, the Wahhābīs, and the modern reformers of the day, but nevertheless it does not die. It persists, lives, and functions in the lives of those who believe, because for them there is something intimately personal and satisfying in this form of worship which they do not find in the more rigid and respectable forms. They seem to long for a mediator and intercessor with God, just as they find an intercessor so valuable in dealing with the Collector, the Judge, the Governor, or any others of the great ones with whom they have to deal. The Muslim masses move on as always with the same devotion to their *pīrs*, living or dead; and until the time arrives when general enlightenment shall come through widespread modern education, it is not likely that there will be much lessening of the hold that the *pīrs* have on the minds, hearts, and purses of the people.

CHAPTER VIII

ISLAM IN ITS HINDU ENVIRONMENT

In order the better to understand and appreciate the effect of Indian surroundings on Islam, it will be useful to know the extent to which Indian religious thought reached Muslim countries and affected the religion of Muḥammad before the Muslim conquest of India took place. Much scholarly investigation has been done in this field, so by way of introduction a summary of the results of this work will be presented.

The contacts of the Muslim world with India were definite and well-established even before the tenth century.[1]

As we have already seen, there had been a partially successful attempt, early in the eighth century, on the part of the Umayyad caliphate to annex Sind to its rapidly expanding empire. Unfortunately, we do not know to what extent this connexion with India may have influenced later developments in religious thought; but such contacts as this, which brought Indian thought well within the horizon of Islam, could not but help to produce an influence, as Goldziher aptly points out.[2]

Secondly, there was the presence of wandering Indian monks, who 'did not appear on the Moslem horizon in any theoretical way alone,' for, as early as the time of the 'Abbāsid caliphate at Baghdad, these monks 'were a factor of practical importance to the adherents of Islam, just as in earlier times the wandering Christian monks had attracted attention in Syria. Jāḥiẓ (d. A.D. 866) pictures very graphically the wandering monks, who could have belonged neither to Christianity nor to Islam. He calls them 'Zindiq monks. . . . One of the anecdotes told of the beggar lives of these monks goes so far as to say that one of them preferred to bring suspicion of theft upon himself, and endure maltreatment, rather than betray a thieving bird, because he did

[1] For Arabian connexion with India before Islam see De Lacy O'Leary's *Arabia Before Muḥammad*, 59-83.

[2] *Vorlesungen über den Islam*, 161, 162.

not wish to be the cause of the death of a living being. If these people were not actually Indian *sādhūs* or Buddhist monks, they were at least men who were following the example and method of the latter.'[1]

Thirdly, mention should be made of Buddhist works, which were translated in the second century of the Islamic era, largely under the 'Abbāsid Caliphs, Manṣūr (A.D. 754–775) and Hārūn (A.D. 786–809). These were rendered into Arabic partly from the Persian or Pahlavī translations, while others were translated direct from the Sanskrit.[2]

Among these translations of Indian books that became embodied in Arabic literature 'we find an Arabic version of the *Balauhar wa Būdāsāf*' (Barlaam and Josaphat),[3] and also a Budd-book.[4-5]

Fourthly, we may mention the direct contact of Buddhist monasteries in Eastern Persia and Transoxiana, which were in existence and flourishing in Balkh long before the eleventh century, when the extended Muslim conquest of India began.[6]

These points of contact with Indian life and thought may be traced to three lines of influence in Islam. First is the influence in secular or popular literature. 'Many a deliverance of ethical and political wisdom, in the dress of proverbs, was taken over from the fables and tales of India, such as the Tales of the Panchatantra.'[7]

Secondly, in the realm of science. Through the translations of Indian works on mathematics and astrology, 'the latter in combination with practical medicine and magic,' secular wisdom in Islam was largely indebted to the East; and 'the astrology of the Siddhānta of Brāhma Gupta, which was translated from the Sanskrit under Manṣūr by Fazārī, assisted by Indian scholars, was known even before Ptolemy's *Almagest*. A wide world and future was thereby opened up.'[8]

The third line of influence comes within the distinctly religious sphere. But it is not by any means the whole of Islamic thought

[1] Goldziher, *Vorlesungen*, tr. Seelye, 172, 173.

[2] T. J. de Boer, *History of the Philosophy of Islam*, 9.

[3] The story of the conversion of an Indian prince, Josaphat (Buddha), by the ascetic Barlaam. [4] A book teaching the doctrines of Buddha.

[5] Goldziher, op. cit., 161. [6] R. A. Nicholson, *The Mystics of Islam*, 16.

[7] de Boer, op. cit., 9. [8] *Ibid.*

that has been affected; and apparently it is only in the development of Islamic mysticism, or Ṣūfīism, that any well-defined traces can be found, but these are all important. Here the contribution seems to be made in thought, religious imagery of expression, and pious practices, which come from both Buddhist and Vedantic sources. I shall now give the conclusions arrived at in respect of these factors.

One of the earliest evidences of the influence of contact with Indian ideals of life appears to have manifested itself in the religious view 'which arose in opposition to legal Islam, known as *zuhd*, or asceticism', but which in itself is not identical with Ṣūfīism. Goldziher further points out how one of the advocates of the *zuhd* doctrine, Abū'l-'Atāhiyah (A.D. 748–825), was set up as 'an example of a highly honoured man: "the king in the garments of a beggar . . . it is he whose reverence is great among men"'. And then he goes on to suggest his own views as to whence this ideal was drawn, by asking, 'Is this not the Buddha?'[1]

When we come to the more advanced philosophic conceptions of Ṣūfīism there is likewise general agreement in the following points. First, that, escaping beyond the logical confines and implications of the neo-Platonic theory of pantheism, which first laid its hold on Islamic thought, the idea of absorption (*fanā*) of the personality in God (*fī Allāh*) comes to hold a definite place among the Ṣūfī conceptions of the possible relations between the Soul of the Universe and the human soul. While this idea of *fanā*, as understood by the Ṣūfī, carries with it a concomitant theory of *baqā*, or continuance of the personality somehow in or with Allāh, which notion is excluded from Hindu ideas of absorption, yet Professor Nicholson states his conviction that the idea of 'passing away (*fanā*) into Universal Being is certainly of Indian origin'. He further goes on to say that, while its first great exponent was the Persian mystic, Bāyazīd of Bistām (d. A.D. 875), yet he is inclined to believe that he may have received it from his teacher, Abū 'Alī, of Sind, who may have himself become indoctrinated with Vedantic teachings.[2]

[1] Goldziher, op. cit., 172.

[2] Nicholson, *The Mystics of Islam*, 16 ff.; see also Horten, *Indische Strömungen*, etc., 4, note; 17 ff.

The Ṣūfī doctrine of *tawḥīd*, or the unity of God, appears to Goldziher to be dependent on Indian philosophy, and he goes on to show how the Ṣūfī idea is 'fundamentally different from the usual Muslim monotheistic conception of God'. A Ṣūfī goes so far as to say it is *shirk* (giving associates to God) to assert that 'I KNOW GOD': for in this sentence duality between perceiving subject and object of knowledge is involved; and this is also the current Indian view.[1]

The religious practices in Ṣūfī communities connected with the following of the mystic path are clearly traced in some of their aspects to Buddhism. This would include 'ethical self-culture, ascetic meditation, and intellectual abstraction', through the well-known *yoga* practices of Indian asceticism.[2] Goldziher, likewise, on the authority of Kremer, agrees when he says that 'many of the forms of the religious practice of *dhikr* in the Ṣūfī communities, as well as the means for bringing about the *kenosis* and ecstasy, the discipline of breathing', are clearly traced to Indian origin. One of the most common of these means of devotion is the rosary, or *tasbīh*, 'which soon spread beyond the Ṣūfī circle, the Indian origin of which . . . is beyond question. It began in Eastern Islam, which is the hearth of Indian influence exerted on Ṣūfī society.'[3]

The First Concession to the Indian Environment

During the early centuries of its residence in India, Islam made a determined struggle to maintain its purity and to extend the faith to the last man of the land. Both proved to be unsuccessful. The Qur'ān never really began to supplant the Vedas, but, on the contrary, the very faith (*imān*) and practice (*dīn*) of Islam became modified to a serious extent among large sections of the ever-growing community. The first change to be noted began to show itself very early. The Muslim armies of Muḥammad b. Qāsim, in the eighth century, were forced to realize that the fundamental law of no quarter for idolaters could not possibly be carried out to the letter. The people would not accept Islam by any such forceful methods as were offered to them, even though

[1] Goldziher, op. cit., 176.
[2] Nicholson, op. cit., 16.
[3] Goldziher, op. cit., 176, 177.

their temples were destroyed, many of their priests slain, and their fighting men put to the sword. To be sure, there were cases here and there of mass-conversion through fear or hope of reward; but the hold of the Brāhmanic religion on the people was too strong and subtle to be shaken entirely by fear or favour. Further, the forces that could be brought from a foreign country at any one time were not sufficient to police such a large country and such an enormous population, and bring them to accept Islam through fear of superior power.

It therefore became necessary to yield to the force of circumstances, and accord to the polytheistic and idolatrous Hindus the status of *dhimmīs*, or those under protection of the Muslim State, as was permitted by the law in the case of people to whom a Scripture had been given, such as Jews, Christians, and Magians. This was in itself a marked concession, and marks the first change in Muslim practice, on a large scale, that of necessity came to be adopted in India as a regular policy.

Following this decision, it became necessary to make as much special provision as possible for the maintenance of the purity of Islamic faith and customs. Idolaters and idolatrous practices were regarded with horror and contempt. All the vocabulary of abuse that could be summoned for their description was commonly used by zealots, even down to the close of Aurangzīb's reign. Thus it was always in good form to use such epithets and phrases as 'the filth of infidelity', the 'thorn of god-plurality', 'the impurity of idol-worship', of which many historians make all too frequent use.[1] Since this was the attitude of the Muslims toward the inhabitants of the land whither they had come, it is little wonder that a policy of separation was adopted in order to preserve purity of faith. Consequently, we find the early invaders like Muḥammad b. Qāsim, in Sind, building cantonments for the Muslims, apart from the cities they captured.

Hindu Influence in Government and Army

Gradually, however, Hindu influence began to creep in and to make itself felt within the camp. Brāhmans, we are told, were appointed to be the collectors of the poll-tax (*jizyah*).[2] After the

[1] Ḥasan Niẓāmī, E.D., II, 217. [2] *Chach-nāmah*, E.D., 184.

Ghaznawid conquests and the establishment of a settled Muslim rule in Delhi, the emperors not only began to make use of Hindus to an increasing extent in the government of the country, but Hindu princes, who had come into favour with the Muslim rulers, became useful allies, and employed their Hindu troops in the service of the Muslim authority. In fact, the wars with the Hindus in different parts of the country undoubtedly did much to increase the respect of the Muslim for the inhabitants of India, and to break down the overbearing and unreasonable attitude of intolerance which he had adopted at first. Thus we not only read of Hindu troops being employed by Muslim rulers, but that men of both religions freely began to enter each other's service. Elphinstone relates how the flower of the Muslim king of Malwa's army, during an invasion of the Bahmanī territories, was said to have consisted of twelve thousand Afghāns and Rājputs; while Deo Rāj, Rājā of Bijaynagar, recruited Muslims, assigned lands to their chiefs, and built a mosque at his capital expressly for their encouragement.[1] Furthermore, when 'Alā-ud-Dīn, at the close of the thirteenth century, made his unauthorized expedition to south India, he seems to have excited no comment when he asserted, by way of a pretext, on his advance, that he was on his way to enter the service of the Hindu Rājā of Rajamandri.[2]

While Hindus thus came to be used for certain minor posts in the work of administration at a very early date, it was not until the time of Akbar that they were employed even in the highest offices. Among the officials whom he employed to be intimately associated with himself in the government of his empire were Rājā Todar Mal and Rājā Birbal. The former was a Kayasth by caste, from the Punjab. He showed such skill in revenue work that Akbar made him his minister of finance. He was also one of the emperor's trusted military commanders.[3] Birbal, though a Hindu, was elevated to the rank of prime minister, and became the emperor's greatest personal favourite. Birbal's name has become a household word in north India, and many are the amusing anecdotes that are told concerning Akbar and his close personal Hindu friend. That these two Hindu officials had a great influence on the government appointments cannot for a moment be doubted;

[1] Elphinstone, op. cit., 475. [2] *Ibid.*, 388. [3] *Ibid.*, 510 f.

and the selection of Hindus, who had become very proficient in Persian, was so increased and extended that when Aurangzīb came to the throne we find him confronted with an awkward problem when he endeavoured to exclude Hindus entirely from holding public office.[1]

Effect of Social Contacts

Not alone in the matter of military and administrative affairs do we find a gradual 'letting down of the bars' and association with Hindus on equal terms. More important still, for its effect on Islam, was the gradual encroachment of social contacts, that could not by any artificial process for long be avoided. I refer particularly to contacts through marriage. Though the Muslim invader may have regarded the religion of the idolaters with disgust, this feeling did not extend to their women, and Muḥammad b. Qāsim had no hesitancy whatever in sending the two daughters of the Hindu Rājā Dāhir to Baṣrah, to become harem inmates of his superior, Ḥajjāj; nor was there any aversion shown to keeping the Hindu women of the conquered warriors of the cities and towns as slaves. Jahāngīr gives a characteristic expression to this feeling which existed in connexion with some practices among certain imperfect Muslim brethren, whom he encountered at Pampur, in Kashmir. He found them marrying their daughters to the Hindus and taking daughters from them, so he comments by saying, 'As for taking, it does not so much matter; but as for giving their own daughters—heaven protect us!'[2]

One of the earliest and most famous of the Hindu-Muslim alliances was that which occurred in A.D. 1306 between 'Alā-ud-Dīn Khaljī and the beautiful Kaulā Devī, wife of the Rājā of Gujarāt. But such mixed marriages were not confined to royalty. In fact, they appear to have formed a part of the policy of absorption and domination by which it was hoped Hinduism would be overthrown. Consequently, the practice became well established, and it has contributed largely to the increase in the Muslim population.

It was, however, a doubtful advantage, for the Hindu wives

[1] Bakhtāwar Khān, E.D., VII, 159.
[2] *Wāqi'āt-i-Jahāngīrī*, E.D., VI, 376.

have brought with them many strange customs and practices, which have had a profound effect on succeeding generations of Indian Muslims. What this effect has been may be inferred, to a certain extent, from the practices in which the women indulged in the Imperial Zanānah of Akbar. This is no doubt an extreme case, due to the unwonted liberality of the emperor; but just because of that liberality we are permitted to see all the more easily what must have taken place, more or less secretly perhaps, in every home throughout the land where a Muslim husband had taken a Hindu wife. This would sometimes react on the husband's views towards Hindus and their religion, to say nothing of the influence of the Hindu mother on her Hindu-Muslim children. It is recorded that Akbar, 'from his earliest youth, in compliment to his wives, the daughters of the Rājās of Hind, had within the female apartments continued to burn the *hom* (sacred fire)'.[1] Even the austere and fanatical Aurangzīb had two Hindu wives, but apparently their faith made no difference to him.[2] The practice of making such unions still goes on; for I know personally of more than one prominent family of northern India where the relationship with certain Hindu families is not only clearly traced, but inter-marriages still take place. Among the lower classes the practice is said to be very extended, usually growing out of illicit relations.

MUSLIM PĪRS AND HINDU DISCIPLES

Another very curious relationship with the Hindus, which has not been without its effect on Islam in India, has been the fact that many Muslim *pīrs* had Hindu disciples; and, similarly, some Hindu *yogīs* have had Muslim *chelās*. Sir T. W. Arnold tells us that 'instances are not unknown of friendship between saints of the rival creeds. At Girot, in the Punjab, the tombs of two ascetics, Jamālī Sultan and Diyāl Bhāwan, who lived in close amity during the early part of the nineteenth century, stand close to one another, and are reverenced by Hindus and Muḥammadans alike. Bāwā Fattū (1700), a Muslim saint, whose tomb is at Ranital, in the Kangra district, received the gift of prophecy by the blessing of a Hindu saint, Sodhī

[1] Budāyūnī, E.D., V, 530. [2] Bernier, op. cit., 126.

Gurū Gulāb Singh. On the other hand, Bābā Shāhānā, a Hindu saint whose cult is observed in the Jang district, is said to have been the *chelā*, or spiritual disciple, of a Muslim *faqīr*, who changed the original name, Mihra, of his Hindu follower, into Mīr Shāh.'[1]

The Changing Attitude to Indian Culture

Before proceeding to trace the effect of the foregoing contacts on the development of Islam in India, attention must be paid to the influence of Hindu thought and culture on the Muslim mind. The antipathy of the Muslim invaders and many of the rulers to things Indian appears as one of the outstanding characteristics of of those unpleasant times. Although Islam under the 'Abbāsids had been the patron of letters and culture, even to the extent of welcoming translations of books on Buddhist and Indian philosophy and science within the ever-growing circle of their literature ; and although al-Bīrūnī, a contemporary of Maḥmūd of Ghaznī in the eleventh century, showed a profound interest in, and clear understanding of, Indian sciences, philosophies, and religions ; yet there was a period of more than five centuries before Akbar arose to take al-Bīrūnī's place with an attempt to turn the tide in favour of Indian culture.

Al-Bīrūnī was an altogether exceptional man, not only for his own time but for any time. He certainly was not the product of his age. He had no praise for the expeditions of Maḥmūd of Ghaznī, but spoke of him as having 'utterly ruined the prosperity of the country, and performed there wonderful exploits, by which Hindus became like atoms of dust scattered in all directions. . . . Their scattered remains cherish, of course, the most inveterate aversion towards all Muslims. This is the reason, too, why Hindu sciences have retired away from those parts of the country conquered by us, and have fled to places which our hand cannot reach—to Kashmir, Benares, and other places.'[2] He was not much interested in the holy wars of Maḥmūd, but preferred to engage himself in making diligent inquiry into the manners, customs, and beliefs of the Hindus. To this end he had to acquire Sanskrit, and he clearly recognized that he stood alone in his inquiries regarding

[1] *E.I.*, II, 490. [2] Al-Bīrūnī, *India*, Sachau, I, 22

the Indians. The marvellous extent of his researches, and his interest in Hindu thought, may be roughly indicated by reference to the sources which he used. In his account of theology and philosophy he made use of the *Sānkhya*, by Kapila and Patañjali, the *Bhagavad Gītā*, and the *Purānas*. His sources for his chapters on astronomy, geography, and astrology include twenty-two different Sanskrit titles.[1] Unfortunately, however, al-Bīrūnī's work produced no effect on the Muslim attitude toward Hindus, and it apparently went entirely unnoticed by them.[2]

More than five hundred years after al-Bīrūnī, who left India in A.D. 1030, Akbar came to the throne, and set about to cultivate, in an entirely new and unheard-of manner, associations with his Hindu subjects. It was a part of his governmental policy to effect a fusion of the two great elements of Indian religious and social life, and he did everything in his power to conciliate the Hindus, to affect their manners and customs, and to encourage the obliteration of difference between the two communities. Consequently, there was scarcely a department of his own private life in which some modification of the Islamic rule was not introduced. Although he was a man of the most meagre sort of education, yet he evinced the profoundest interest in Hindu religion and philosophy, and in his time had translations made from the Sanskrit into Persian of the *Atharva Veda*, the *Mahābhārata*, and the *Rāmāyaṇa*.[3]

All of these contacts with the Hindu environment gradually tended to produce an attitude of tolerance among the Muslims of India, which has given to Indian Islam some peculiar characteristics. Further proofs of this are found in the terms of a confidential will which Bābur left to his son Humāyūn, the original

[1] Cf. Sachau, Preface to al-Bīrūnī's *India*, I, xxxix.

[2] However, it must not be overlooked that certain evidences of the effect of the Indian environment on Muslim life early became apparent. This is noticeable in literature especially. For instance, in the poetry of Amīr Khusrū, of the Tughluq period, adaptation to the Indian mode is found ; and to him, it is said, the origin of the modern Urdū language can be traced. The greatest influence of environment is found, of course, in the Mughul period. The metaphors are changed, the similes are taken from Indian birds and seasons, and in fact from the whole of Indian life.

[3] 'Abd-ul-Qādir Budāyūnī, E.D., V, 483.

copy of which is preserved in the State Library at Bhopal. The document, as translated, runs as follows:

O my son: People of diverse religions inhabit India; and it is a matter of thanksgiving to God that the King of kings has entrusted the government of this country to you. It therefore behoves you that:

1. You should not allow religious prejudices to influence your mind, and administer impartial justice, having due regard to the religious susceptibilities and religious customs of all sections of the people.

2. In particular refrain from the slaughter of cows, which will help you to obtain a hold on the hearts of the people of India. Thus you will bind the people of the land to yourself by ties of gratitude.

3. You should never destroy the places of worship of any community and always be justice-loving, so that relations between the king and his subjects may remain cordial and there be peace and contentment in the land.

4. The propagation of Islam will be better carried on with the sword of love and obligation than with the sword of oppression.

5. Always ignore the mutual dissension of Shī'ahs and Sunnīs, otherwise they will lead to the weakness of Islam.

6. Treat the different peculiarities of your subjects as the different seasons of the year, so that the body politic may remain free from disease.[1]

Akbar's Adoption of Hindu Beliefs and Practices

Akbar not only put an end to the killing of cows, but did more than Bābur suggests, and abolished the hated *jizyah.*[2] He went still further. Under the influence of his Hindu wives and his beloved *wazīr*, Rājā Birbal, he began to worship the sun; he wore clothes that in colour corresponded to the ruling planet of the day; he began at midnight to mutter spells which the Hindus taught him, in an endeavour to make the sun serve his wishes; he was even known to appear in public with his forehead marked as a Hindu, and celebrated the festivals of *Rakhsha Bandhan* and *Diwālī*. He even refrained from eating meat on certain days. These observances were also followed to some extent by Jahāngīr; but Shāh Jahān began to make changes; and with Aurangzīb the pendulum swung entirely in the opposite direction.[3]

Akbar's leanings, and the practices which he actually adopted,

[1] Dr. Syed Maḥmud, *The Indian Review*, Aug. 1923, 499. [2] See p. 27.

[3] 'Abd-ul-Qādir Budāyūnī, E.D., V, 530 ff.; *E.I.*, II, 490.

and sought to bring his Muslim subjects to follow in their relations to Hindus, ultimately produced a profound effect on his own religious thought. During the course of his reign, too, he was greatly influenced in his religious thinking by two men, Abū'l-Faḍl and his brother Fayḍī, sons of the heretically-inclined Shay<u>kh</u> Mubārak Nāgorī. They held a liberal attitude toward Hinduism, and religion in general, that led them to be regarded by the orthodox as arch-heretics, who were the cause of the emperor's being led astray.

It is doubtful, however, if the turning of Akbar from orthodoxy can be laid to the blame of these two favourites of his. Rather, it may be said they were the two congenial friends, whose minds ran along with his, who furthered the ends he had in mind. Akbar's tolerant spirit found frequent opportunity for displeasure with the 'Pharaoh-like pride' of the *'ulamā* at court, which ran counter to his personal feelings and the government policy which he desired should prevail in the empire. Blochmann, who has carefully studied the relations between Akbar and Abū'l-Faḍl, says that he was affected most deeply by the religious persecutions and sentences of death passed by his chief justice, Ma<u>kh</u>dūm-ul-Mulk, on Shī'ahs and other heretics. He began to realize that the 'Scribes and Pharisees formed a power of their own in his kingdom, at the construction of which he had for twenty years been working'. During this time he had resolved upon ruling, 'with an even hand, men of every creed in his dominion'. He was, however, being continually urged by the learned lawyers to 'persecute instead of heal', and as a result he instituted the Thursday evening discussions in the audience hall, or *'ibādat <u>kh</u>ānah*, at Fatḥpūr Sikri, which he had erected especially for this purpose.[1]

It is thought that these discussions were inaugurated by Akbar solely for the purpose of trying to discover whether or not he was in error in his policy, and because he felt it his duty as a ruler to inquire. If this be so, the results went even farther than Akbar probably anticipated, to the dismay and consternation of the orthodox party, who no doubt from the very first feared the outcome. And little wonder that they should fear the effect of such an open forum, where night after night the emperor listened

[1] H. Blochmann, Introduction to *Ā'īn-i-Akbarī*, viii.

to the views of the theologians of various religions, including Hindu *pandits*, Parsees, Roman Catholic priests from Goa, as well as the learned *maulvīs* of the different schools.

The first obvious result of the discussions was that the outward unity of the learned Muslim *'ulamā* at once began to disappear. Akbar's doubts, therefore, increased instead of being cleared up. In certain points of law the Hanafite school seemed to lag behind that of the other three schools of Muslim jurisprudence; while even 'the moral character of the Prophet was scrutinized and found wanting'.[1] Thus the discussions led to Akbar's disillusionment, and the great discomfiture of the orthodox party, who were in constant opposition. Finally, it is said that Abū'l-Faḍl, pointing out the divisions among the *'ulamā*, persuaded the emperor that a subject ought to look upon the king not alone as the temporal but also as the only spiritual guide.

This, however, was a new doctrine, in direct opposition to the received opinion in Islam, where the law stands above every king, and makes the promulgation of a national constitution impossible. In cases where kings such as 'Alā-ud-Dīn Khaljī had before tried to assert the law of expediency above the Qur'ānic law, they never actually managed to bring about the separation of religion and law, and make the administration of the civil government independent of the *mullā*. The seeds of division had, however, been sown; and so, when Abū'l-Faḍl forced the issue at one of the Thursday evening meetings, after four years of unrest and discussion, he 'raised a perfect storm'. Up to this point the disputations had been confined to the life of Muḥammad or the differences between the sects; they now began to turn on the very principles of Islam itself.[2]

The outcome was a complete personal triumph for Akbar. The *'ulamā* were put down, and, much to their disgust, were forced to sign Akbar's famous 'decree of infallibility',[3] which, as

[1] *Ibid.* [2] *Ibid.*

[3] 'If there be a variance of opinion among *mujtahids* (divines) upon a question of religion, and His Majesty, in his penetrating understanding and unerring judgment should incline to one opinion . . . and give his decree for the benefit of mankind, and for the due regulation of the world, we do hereby agree that such a decree is binding on us, and on the whole nation.' Signed by the principal *'ulamā* of the court. Budāyūnī, *Muntakhab-ut-Tawārīkh*, E.D., V, 532; see p. 70.

a state document, 'stands unique in the whole history of Islam'. There followed the banishment of Makhdūm-ul-Mulk and his associate 'Abd-un-Nabī, and the disputations were brought to an end, and Akbar was now free to proceed to develop his religious notions as he pleased.[1]

Budāyūnī describes the events of this period in vivid detail, and assigns still another reason for Akbar's innovation in religion. He had become convinced that a period of one thousand years was to be the duration of the religion of Islam; and, as that period was all but completed, no obstacle prevented his making the innovation, as he was now independent of the *shaykhs* and *'ulamā*. He had even come to the place where he was ready to make public use of the formula, 'There is no God but God, and Akbar is God's apostle', but was too fearful of the consequences actually to do so. However, he did proclaim the establishment of his new religion, which he called *Tawḥīd-i-Ilāhī*, or Divine Monotheism. While it is Islamic in an external sense it is in fact a complete denial of Islam, for it substituted an entirely different ceremonial law, as well as new theological doctrines. In the latter the Ṣūfī idea of absorption of the soul in the Divine Being is prominent, while in the former the Zoroastrian contribution is quite apparent in the central position occupied by the worship of the sacred fire, which was made over to the charge of Abū'l-Faḍl, the high-priest, who was instructed to take care that it was never extinguished.[2]

Akbar's governmental policy of seeking a closer identification of Muslims with Hindus in one great commonwealth undoubtedly did produce an effect which was good and wholesome; but, so far as his attempt to bring about the introduction of a new religion was concerned, it may be said that the effort died with him. It was in no sense intended as a reform of Islam, but was an actual denial of it. In closing this study of Akbar, I shall quote the pertinent observations of Goldziher, who says his innovation was a break with the traditions of Islam 'more decided even than that which manifests itself in the doctrine of Ismā'īl. It remained, therefore, without any decided influence on the development of Islam. Limited to the court circles and to the intellectuals, it did

[1] H. Blochmann, op. cit., viii.

[2] 'Abd-ul-Qādir Budāyūnī, E.D., V, 530 ff.

not outlive its founders. . . . Without violent disturbance, orthodox Islam resumed its former control after Akbar's death (A.D. 1605), and it is not until we come to the latest rationalistic movement among Brāhmans and Moslems in Anglo-India that we find Akbar proclaimed as the precursor of the effort to bring Brāhmanism, Parseeism and Islam into closer touch.'[1]

DĀRĀ SHIKŪH AND HINDU-MUSLIM UNITY

The effect of such close associations with Hindus as were practised and advocated by Akbar could not but be passed on to some extent; and, as a matter of fact, the mantle of the liberal-minded emperor fell upon his grandson, Dārā Shikūh. If this prince had not been summarily executed on a charge of heresy, he might have lived to exert still further influence in support of the cause of Hindu-Muslim unity. During his life he gave himself to the acquiring of knowledge about the religion and philosophy of the Hindus, particularly on the mystic side; and to this purpose he not only read and translated Sanskrit books into Persian, but assiduously sought the company of Hindu ascetics. The books that he had translated include the *Rāmāyaṇa* and the *Gītā*, the *Upanishāds*, under the title *Sirr-ul-Asrār*, and the *Yogavashishta*.[2]

Contemporary orthodox opinion about Dārā and his fraternization with Hindus does not do him justice; but it was time for the pendulum to swing, and Dārā had to pay the price for his attempt to pioneer in the realm of religious unity. His conception, after much study and contemplation, was that between Hindu and Muslim mysticism there exists only verbal differences, and he wrote his *Majma'-ul-Baḥrayn*[3] to show 'where' the 'two seas' of mystic thought 'meet'. But the orthodox Muslims, who had regained their control, would have none of it, as may be seen from the following comment by an historian:

> Dārā Shikūh in his later days did not restrict himself to the free-thinking and heretical notions which he had adopted under the name of *tasawwuf* (Ṣūfiism), but showed an inclination for the religion and institutions of the Hindus. He was constantly in the society of Brāhmans, *yogīs*, and *sannyāsīs*, and he used to regard these worthless teachers of delusions as learned and true masters of wisdom. He considered their

[1] Goldziher, op. cit., 328–30. [2] *R.M.M.*, LXIII, 1926, 5.

[3] For text and translation with full account of Dārā Shikūh see *Majma'-ul-Baḥrayn*, ed. and tr. M. Mahfuz-ul-Haq, Asiatic Society of Bengal, 1929.

> books, which they call *Bed* (Vedas), as being the Word of God, and revealed from heaven, and he called them ancient and excellent books, in the translation of which he was much employed. Instead of the sacred name of Allāh he adopted the Hindu name *Prabhū* (lord) . . . and he had this name engraved in Hindi letters upon his rings. . . . Through these perverted opinions he had given up the prayers, fasting, and other obligations imposed by the law, and . . . it became manifest that if Dārā Shikūh obtained the throne, and established his power, the foundations of the faith would be in danger, and the precepts of Islam would be changed for the *rant* of infidelity (Hinduism) and Judaism.[1]

He was finally condemned for heresy, and put to death, in A.D. 1659, by Aurangzīb, his own brother.

Later Developments

While Akbar and Dārā Shikūh made little headway with liberalizing Islamic thought in their day, and incurred naught but displeasure, yet the same influence of contact with Hinduism that led them into strange vagaries of thought, and away from the central conceptions of Islam, has produced a liberality of attitude regarding Hindu gods and scriptures in some modern minds that is truly amazing. There are those who declare that the Hindu gods, Rāma and Kṛishṇa, should be regarded as prophets, and the *Vedas*, the *Rāmāyaṇa*, the *Bhagavad Gītā*, for instance, as gifts of divine revelation, basing their argument on the Qur'ānic texts, which say, 'And every people hath its guide';[2] and, 'To every people we have sent an apostle'.[3] The most modern and persistent exponents of this doctrine are the Aḥmadīyah propagandists, who make frequent reference to it in their publications. The editor of one of their papers, published in Lahore, in answer to a question of a correspondent on this point, gives his position thus:

'The Qur'ān says that every nation has seen its warner; hence India, too, must have received revelation. As the *Vedas* and *Gītā* are held in great reverence as divine books, we assume that these were revealed to the prophets who appeared in this country.'[4] In another place the editor affirms his belief that probably Rāma and Kṛishṇa were prophets, since it is not necessary to know the names of all the prophets.[5] For we cannot assume that they

[1] Muḥammad Kāzim, E.D., VII, 179. [2] Sūrah, XIII, 7.
[3] *Ibid.*, XVI, 36. [4] *The Light*, Lahore, June 1, 1923, 4.
[5] Cp. *Al-Aqā'īd an-Nasafī*.

should be excluded simply because the Qur'ān does not mention them, when at the same time it does enunciate 'the principle that *every nation* has seen its warner or apostle'.[1] It is simply inconceivable that such a large country as India would have been excluded from the manifestation of God's grace.

Other proofs of an amazing unorthodoxy and extreme liberality of attitude toward Hindu polytheists, which would have shocked the strict Aurangzīb beyond measure, may be found in the Muslim poets of Bengal, such as Karam 'Alī and Karīm Allāh, who sang the praises of Rādhā and Kṛishṇa, and composed hymns in honour of the goddess Kālī.[2] On one occasion, in Bijnor, in north India, when trouble was expected between the two communities on a certain Hindu festival, I remember the Muslim secretary of the municipal board told me that he sought to avoid it by having garlands made and sent to all the Hindu temples of the city, to be presented as offerings to the idols. While this was a mere matter of expediency rather than an indication of belief, it nevertheless shows to what length Muslims in the midst of their Hindu environment will sometimes go.

Results of Incomplete Conversion

In a land like India, where the majority of the Muslim population has been recruited from Hindu caste and outcaste groups by mass conversion, whether from fear of military power, or to attain some desirable object, or because of persuasion, complete Islamization of the converts has not been accomplished. There are great sections of the Muslim community, here and there, which reveal their Hindu origin in their religious and social life almost at every turn, constituting a curious mixture of the old and the new. There is little wonder that this should be so. The Muslim armies moved over the country in wave after wave for centuries, from Peshawar to Dacca and beyond, and from the Himalayas to the southern end of the peninsula. It often happened that hastily converted peoples were left behind after the army moved on. These had been given but scant instruction in the new faith, and were left to remember and practise what they could.

[1] *The Light*, July 16, 1923, 4.

[2] D. C. Sen, *History of Bengali Language and Literature*, 798, 799.

The pressure of the old idolatrous surroundings upon them was great. Not only their neighbours, but many of their relatives in other places were still Hindu. Little wonder that the worship of the village godlings went on as before, that animistic beliefs continued, that Brāhman priests were still employed, and Hindu festivals observed. The wonder is, not that these hereditary customs and beliefs were adhered to, but that any belief in Islam remained at all.

One of the earliest records we find of official recognition of the existence of mixed customs and beliefs among village Muslims occurred in the reign of Jahāngīr, when he was visiting Kashmir. Here, near the village of Pampur, on the Jhelum, it is said that he found at Rajaur some Muslims who were originally Hindus, but that their chiefs were still styled Rājās. Hindu customs were still observed, such as the burning of widows, and intermarriage with Hindus was practised. This led to an attempt to mend matters; for the emperor issued orders prohibiting such practices in the future, and suitable 'punishments were enjoined for their infraction'.[1] However, from the evidences that are still found in certain quarters of Muslim India, chiefly in the remote village areas, at a distance from the influence of the *'ulamā*, it is apparent that all the king's horses and all the king's men were not able to bring about the desired reforms. Still, there is no doubt that the situation to-day is far better than it was a century ago, as a result of the reform efforts of Muslim preachers, the more general diffusion of education, and the extensive revival of the Islamic spirit and learning in connexion with the modern reform movements.

Let us now take a glance at a few of these groups that show the results of incomplete conversion, and then pass to a closer consideration of the main religious and social phenomena growing out of it. The *Malkāna* community is the best known of these groups in north India, a description of which I quote from Mr. Blunt, who was the United Provinces census officer for 1911. Concerning them he writes:

> These are converted Hindus of various castes, belonging to Agra and adjoining districts, chiefly Muttra, Etah, and Mainpuri. They are of

[1] *Wāqi'āt-i-Jahāngīrī*, E.D., VI, 376.

Rājput, *Jāt*, and *Baniyā* descent. They are reluctant to describe themselves as Muslims, and generally give their caste name, and scarcely recognize the name *Malkāna*. Their names are mostly Hindu; they mostly worship at Hindu temples; they use the salutation *Rām, Rām*, intermarry mostly among themselves only. On the other hand, they sometimes frequent a mosque, practise circumcision, bury their dead, and they will eat with Muslims if they are particular friends. They prefer to be addressed as *Miyān Thākur*. They admit they are neither Hindus nor Muslims, but a mixture of both.[1]

From Gujarāt, in western India, comes a similar story. The *Momnās*, or *Memons*, of Cutch are Shī'ahs in name, but they do not associate with Muslims, eat no flesh, do not practise circumcision, do not observe the stated prayers (*ṣalāt*) or the fast of *Ramaḍān*. Their salutation is *Rām, Rām*; they worship the Hindu triad—Brahmā, Vishṇū, and Śiva—and consider Imām Shāh, the missionary who originally converted them some three centuries ago, as an incarnation of Brahmā.[2] The same sort of condition is likewise found in the Punjab, Bengal, central and southern India, among certain remote sections of the Muslim community.

In the religious life of the illiterate and partly-converted Muslim masses of the villages of India the remnants of earlier beliefs and practices form a long list, and we shall attempt now to give them in some detail. To begin with, sacred sites have been carried over into the new system, and have been invested with wholly arbitrary Muslim names and legends, just as happened in Palestine, where to-day we find such sacred mounts as Tell Asūr, in northern Judea, venerated by the Muslim population as highly as they were by the Jews and Canaanites, whom they followed. This transformation of sacred Hindu sites, or *tirthas*, is most commonly found in Kashmir, where they go by the name of *ziyārat*. Sometimes it has been discovered that the tomb of a Muslim saint was formerly a Hindu temple. For instance, the tomb of Bāma Dīn Ṣāḥib, in Kashmir, has been shown to have been originally a Hindu temple, built by Bhīma Sāhi, the last Hindu king of Kabul. The current legend, however, is that the saint was a Hindu ascetic, who, before his conversion to Islam, went by the name of Bhūma Sādhī.[3]

[1] *C.I.R.*, 1911, Vol. I, pt. 1, 118. [2] *C.I.R.*, 1911, VII, Bombay, 59.
[3] *E.I.*, II, 491.

Idolatrous Practices

The practices, however, that find greatest disfavour with strict Muslims are the idolatrous practices, and the worship of Hindu gods and godlings, which have prevailed to such an extent in the village life of Islam. While no attempt is made to give a complete list of all the objects or types of this adherence to polytheism, a few of the more prominent cases will be noticed. The *Churihāras* of the United Provinces are said to worship *Kalkā Sahjā Maī*, and observe the *shrādda* ceremony of the Hindus.[1] The *Meos* of the Punjab worship countless godlings, such as *Siansi*, *Magtī*, and *Lalchī*. The *Mirāsīs* of Amritsar take offerings to *Durgā Bhawānī*. While *Lakshmī Devī* is worshipped by the Turk-Nawas of eastern Bengal.[2] Among the *Dudekulas* of the Madras Presidency tools are worshipped, as is done by the Hindus at the *Dasehra* festival. Saint worship is common everywhere, and in some places great reverence is paid to Shaykh Saddū, which is, without doubt, demon worship. Evil spirits are avoided by the use of charms (*ta'wīdh*) bound on the arm or neck, and the use of magic (*siḥr*); while fortune-telling, under the name of geomancy (*'ilm-ur-raml*), astrology, the magic square, opening the Qur'ān for guidance, and the like, are employed by all classes.[3]

The belief in the spirits or godlings that cause disease is probably the most difficult of all to eradicate, and has met with the most stubborn opposition. While many idolatrous practices have been given up, as the census reports and personal observation bear witness, yet in times of sickness and plague we find Muslims in the villages, especially women, going pathetically to the shrines, seeking every known means to secure healing or immunity from disease. When a child is attacked with the dread disease, smallpox, medicine as a rule is not given, for fear of offending the goddess Śītalā. In the eastern Punjab 'the assistance of the female attendant of the Śītalā temple is requisitioned, offerings being given away according to her suggestion, with a view to pleasing the goddess and saving the life of the patient'.[4] The use of the scapegoat for ridding a village of a plague is not altogether uncommon.[5]

[1] *C.I.R.*, 1911, XV, United Provinces, pt. I, 141.

[2] H. H. Risley, *T.C.B.*, I, 309.

[3] Herklots, op. cit., 218 ff.

[4] *C.I.R.*, 1911, Punjab, pt. I, 174.

[5] Crooke, *P.R.F.L.*, I, 91.

Brāhmans are used as family priests, as, for instance, by the Avans of the north-west corner of the Punjab, and their brother Muslim Bhāts of the United Provinces.[1] Special reverence is shown for the cow among the Shīns of the Indus valley, who will not eat beef. The same is true of the Momnās of Cutch.[2] While Bābur and Akbar did not affect any special reverence for the cow as such, yet the former, as we have seen, recommended that his son Humāyūn respect Hindu feelings in this matter, and Akbar went so far as to prohibit the killing of cows altogether by Muslims. Jahāngīr also prohibited their slaughter for a period of years, because of the shortage of cattle.[3]

Ascetics among Muslims are occasionally found who observe tonsure and smearing of the body with ashes, as practised among Hindus. They are also found as the guardians of sacred shrines which are worshipped by both Hindus and Muḥammadans, as in the case of Sakhī Sarwār, in the Punjab.

The sacred fire is also found. At the shrine of Ṣādiq Nihang, in the Jhang district, in the Punjab, the Muslim *faqīrs* keep a fire going night and day, called *dhūni*. Once a year, on the occasion of the *'urs* of the saint, a large loaf of bread, called a *rot*, is cooked with this sacred fire, and is then broken up and distributed to all present.[4] Another example of the sacred fire is at the Imāmbārah in Gorakhpur. According to Crooke, it was first started by a renowed Shī'ah *faqīr*, named Roshan 'Alī, and has been maintained unquenched for more than a hundred years, a special body of attendants and supplies of wood being provided for it. It is respected by Hindus as well as Muḥammadans, and, as in the case of fires kept up by noted *yogīs*, the ashes have a reputation for the cure of fever.[5]

Many Muslims are found to join with their Hindu neighbours in their festivals, as their ancestors did from time immemorial, before they adopted Islam. Among those festivals that one can commonly find observed by village Muslims are the *Holī* and *Diwālī*, and even the Hindu New Year's day, *Baisākhī*, while *Basant-panchamī* was officially adopted by the Shī'ah kings of

[1] Bains, *Ethnography*, 44; *C.I.R.*, United Provinces, 1911, pt. I, 141.
[2] *C.I.R.*, 1911, VII, Bombay, pt. I, 59.
[3] Bernier, op. cit., 326.
[4] *C.I.R.*, Punjab, 1911, pt. I, 175.
[5] Crooke, op. cit., I, 312.

Oudh as the time for their *Nau-roz* celebration.[1] Akbar's and Jahāngīr's adherence to certain Hindu festivals we have already noted.

Hindu Influence in Social Life

The social life of many Muslim groups is honeycombed with Hindu customs and observances. This is clearly revealed in names. The *Avans* of the Punjab, for instance, though they are nearly all Muslims, retain Hindu names and keep their genealogies in the Brāhmanic fashion.[2] Hindu titles are also found; for instance, among the converts from the *Tagā Brāhmans* of the western part of the United Provinces the title *Chaudahrī* is kept in prominent families; and at Lucknow we find important Muslim princes bearing such titles as the Mahārājā of Mahmūdābād, and the Rājā of Jahāngīrābād.

In marriage certain groups, that are Muslim in name only, either use the Hindu ceremony alone, or may perform the ceremony first by Hindu rites and then call in a *qāḍī* to perform the Muslim ceremony. In some sections, for example in Mysore, among Muslims the joint-family system of the Hindus obtains in the rural areas.[3] In fact, the principle has been pretty generally established that in matters of inheritance, dowry, and the like, Muslim converts may adhere legally, as they do in many cases in fact, to the tribal customs or customary law of the group to which they or their ancestors belonged before conversion.

Caste in Muslim Society

In the social sphere the influence of Hinduism on Islam has nowhere left a more definite mark than in the creation of caste distinctions, which indicate social status as clearly as they do in Hindu society. As the existence of numerous sectarian divisions is deplored on the religious side by the modern reformers and leaders of the Muslim community in India, so also are the equally numerous social divisions, which tend to prevent the welding of the Muslims of India into a single brotherhood, according to the Islamic ideal. It is true that one reason for the spread of Islam in India was the elevation in social status that came from the

[1] Herklots, op. cit., 191. [2] Bains, op. cit., 44.
[3] *C.I.R.*, Mysore, 1911, 61.

breaking of the bondage and oppression of the Hindu caste system, and the freedom which Islam had to offer in its social system. But in the working out of the practical difficulties attending adjustment within the social structure of Islam there were in India handicaps to unity and brotherhood which Islam had never before encountered.

First, there were the foreign Muslims, the Arabs, Turks, and Persians, who were at the top of the social scale from the very start because of their position as rulers and the various places they held in the army and government. They had no doubts as to their superiority over the local converts; and in this very attitude we can see the beginnings of the Muslim caste system in India. Secondly, as the converts from various classes and castes of Hindus came in, from Brāhmans and Rājputs to the lowest outcastes, and as the lower caste groups continued to live mostly in their ancestral villages, it was inevitable that there should continue among these Hindu converts the same general feeling of aloofness the one from the other. This was especially true as many of these converts changed their beliefs and customs but little from what they were before. Therefore, to-day it is not astonishing that we should find it the common practice to regard Muslims as belonging to two social groups: the '*Sharīf zāts*' (high castes) and the '*ajlāf zāts*' (low castes).

In fact, to such an extent does the Hindu idea of a fourfold social division prevail, that is: Brāhman, Kshatriya, Vaishya, and Śūdra, that in some parts of the country converts to Islam consider that they are bound to enroll themselves as either Sayyid, Shaykh, Mughul, or Pathān.[1] This is not the place to go into the matter of racial origins, but it may be stated that the present-day social significance that attaches to these names has a definite racial and historical basis. The terms Sayyid and Shaykh imply Arabian origin; the former being used exclusively for descendants of the Prophet's family through his daughter Fāṭimah, and the latter being used to designate any other of Arab origin. The name Mughul ranks next in importance, because the ruling dynasties at Delhi rank next to those of Arabian origin, which was the nation of the Prophet. Inci-

[1] Bains, *Ethnography*, 139.

dentally, the term Mughul includes those of Turkish origin, as the Mughuls of Delhi were not in fact Mughuls or Mongols at all, but Turks, and this term came to be used in order to distinguish these Islamic rulers from the Ottoman rulers in Turkey. The term Pathān is used to apply, broadly speaking, to all who have had their origin in Afghanistan and the neighbourhood of the great North-West Frontier. In addition, these groups have their subdivisions, based on family and tribal origins.

One other fact, too, needs to be mentioned. No one pretends any longer that those who give themselves one of the four above-mentioned designations are all of them necessarily of the origin indicated by the name. There is a strong tendency for the converts from among the Hindus to assume a position in one of the recognized groups of *sharīf zāts* just as soon as practicable. The one that is most affected by such converts is one of the two that imply Arab origin, namely Shaykh. However, there is another explanation for the assumption of this title, which probably gives a more correct interpretation of the reason for its use. The term Shaykh is widely used as a term of respect for an old man, a learned man, or a great man; hence many converts, who had nothing in their origin to boast of, adopted this respectable designation, and so have formed into a separate caste.[1] However, not all converts have assumed one of the fourfold classifications. This is particularly true of the agricultural and high caste converts. The *Rājputs*, *Jāts*, and *Ahirs* for the most part retain their identity on embracing Islam, and one of the important Muslim families of Oudh still keeps the original caste title *Thākur* along with the title of *Nawāb*. Brāhmans may assume the title *Sayyid* on conversion, which course is said to have been approved by the Emperor Akbar.[2] Converts from the lower caste Hindus and outcastes as a rule go by the name of *Nau-Muslims*, or newly converted Muslims, and must remain in this probationary status for a time, their further advance being dependent on conduct or prosperity. Thus an old saying is to the point, 'Last year I was a Julāhā (weaver); this year a Shaykh; and next year, if the harvest be good, I shall be a Sayyid'. This practice of adopting a tribal designation is said to be based on a tradition from the Prophet to the effect: 'All converts to my faith are of me and my tribe'.[3]

[1] *C.I.R.*, Punjab, 1911, 75. [2] Bains, op. cit., 140. [3] *Ibid.*

There is a wide range of caste names found in the second division of Muslims, such as *Julāhā*, *Telī*, *Bhāt*, *Jogīs*, and the like. Most of them indicate occupation, as the *Telī*, who makes oil (*tel*). Most of them are just the old Hindu caste or guild name carried over. Not only do caste names prevail, but many of the original caste prejudices as well, in respect of eating, drinking, and marriage. There is even a caste, called the *Kalāl*, in north India, which engages in liquor dealing, quite contrary to the precepts of the faith; but in spite of this some of the men of this class have become prominent in Indian affairs.

One thing which is very creditable indeed is that, though caste may be recognized in social relations, yet when it comes to worship all the influence of Brāhman exclusiveness disappears, and in the mosque the Islamic ideal of brotherhood is triumphant; the beggar, the sweeper, and the prince worship side by side.

Attempts to Solve the Caste Problem

Caste in Islam in India presents a serious problem. This, together with the religious divisions, which are undoubtedly more numerous here than in any other country of the Muslim world, cause the leaders of the community no little concern. I cannot do better than bring this matter to a conclusion by letting the foremost Muslim philosopher of India, Sir Shaikh Muḥammad Iqbāl, of Lahore, sum up the situation as he presented it to his co-religionists not many years ago, and which, for the most part, still holds good:

> Is the organic unity of Islam intact in this land? Religious adventurers set up different sects and fraternities, ever quarrelling with one another; and there are castes and sub-castes like the Hindus! Surely we have out-Hindued the Hindu himself; we are suffering from a double caste system — the religious caste system, sectarianism, and the social caste system, which we have either learned or inherited from the Hindus. This is one of the quiet ways in which the conquered nations revenge themselves on their conquerors.
>
> Islam is one and indivisible. It brooks no distinctions in it. There are no Wahhābīs, Shī'ahs, Mirzāīs, or Sunnīs in Islam. Fight not for the interpretation of the truth when the truth itself is in danger. Let all come forward and contribute their respective shares in the great toil of the nation. Let the idols of class-distinctions and sectarianism be smashed for ever; let the Musulmans of the country be once more united into a great vital whole. How can we, in the presence of violent internal

disputes, expect to succeed in persuading others to our way of thinking? The work of freeing humanity from superstition—the ultimate ideal of Islam as a community, for the realization of which we have done so little in this great land of myth and superstition—will ever remain undone if the emancipators themselves are becoming gradually enchained in the very fetters from which it is their mission to set others free.[1]

Influence on Hinduism

If the Indian environment has produced a profound effect on Islam during its long residence in the country, it is no less true that Islam has in turn reacted on Hinduism and Indian life. It is impossible to pursue this investigation far; nor is it necessary, for it has already been done by others; but, that the picture may be fairly complete, we should see at any rate in what directions this influence was felt, and observe the present status of relationships between the two communities.

As wave after wave of invasion from the plateaus of central Asia swept over northern India from the year A.D. 1000 to 1400, Hinduism, maimed and bleeding, fled, in the person of its priests and scholars, from before the iconoclastic conquerors, and sought hiding, first in Kashmir and Benares, and later in Bengal, endeavouring by every means possible to preserve itself.[2] Their sacred books were kept hidden with much care, 'lest they should fall into the hands of Moslems and be burnt, as frequently happened'.[3] Not only so, but it is related that, during Muḥammad Bakhtyār's invasion of Bihar, in one place, where he slew all the men, some religious books were discovered, but not a soul could be found who could read them, as all the pandits had been put to the sword.[4] Confronted with such a foe as this, it is no wonder that Hinduism underwent a blight for a period of about four hundred years.

During this time we find large numbers of Muslim Ṣūfīs entering India. Two, at least, of the foremost religious orders, the Chishtī and Suhrawardī, were introduced; and, as we have seen, it was not uncommon for Hindus to become the disciples of Muslim saints and vice versa. In fact, it was through Ṣūfīism that

[1] *Hindustan Review*, quoted in *C.I.R.*, 1911, XIV, Punjab, pt. I, 165.
[2] Al-Bīrūnī, *India*, tr. Sachau, I, 22. [3] Bernier, *Travels*, 336.
[4] Minhāj as-Sirāj, E.D., II, 306.

Islam really found a point of contact with Hinduism and an effective 'entrance to Hindu hearts'. It was not until the latter part of the fifteenth century, however, that any influence of Islam is noticed in Hinduism.[1] Here it begins with the great Hindu reformers of north India, Kabīr and Nānak, who in the fifteenth and early sixteenth centuries began a campaign against polytheism, idolatry, and caste. Kabīr (A.D. 1440–1518) himself is thought by some to have been a Muslim, as he undoubtedly bears a Muslim name ; but in any case he became a disciple of the famous teacher Rāmānanda, and ultimately outran his master. In his life, says Dr. J. N. Farquhar:

> The two religions mingled. The strongest elements of each laid hold of him and formed his thought. . . . He denounces idolatry as foolish, false and wrong, declares divine incarnation impossible, and laughs at the forms of ascetism as silly practices. . . He was a strict theist calling God *Rām*, but recognizing no consort, incarnation, or other divine attendant.'[2]

His tomb or shrine is at Maghar, near Gorakhpur, where, in fact, there are two places kept by his devotees—one by a group of Muslims and another by the Hindus!

The influence of Kabīr, who was the earliest teacher to mingle Islam and Hinduism, may be gathered from the number of sects in Hinduism which trace their origin either directly or indirectly to him. Eleven sects, whose present-day followers probably exceed five millions, are given by Dr. Farquhar. They are found scattered everywhere throughout the Hindi-speaking region of northern and central India, as far north-west as the Punjab, and through Bihar down into Bengal. The list, as Dr. Farquhar gives it, appears at head of page 174.[3]

The Kabīrpanthī community, founded by Kabīr, bears but few of the marks of reform which the founder advocated, and, in

[1] An earlier example, however, of an attempted mingling of Islam and Hinduism is to be found in the woman saint of Kashmir, Lāllā-Vakyānī (latter half of the fourteenth century A.D.), many of whose 'wise sayings' are said to be still popular in that country. See S. G. Grierson and L. Barnett, 'Lalla-Vakyani', 1920, *Royal Asiatic Society Monographs*, XVII.

[2] J. N. Farquhar, *An Outline of the Religious Literature of India*, 332 f.

[3] *Ibid.*, 334.

Name of Sect	Founder	Approx. Date, A.D.	Centre
1. Kabīrpanthīs ...	Kabīr	1470	Benares
2. Sikhs	Nānak	1500	Punjab
3. Dādūpanthīs ...	Dādū	1575	Rajputana
4. Lāl Dāsīs ...	Lāl Dās	1600	Alwar
5. Satnāmīs ...	...	1600	Narnol, south of Delhi
6. Bābā Lālīs ...	Bābā Lāl	1625	Dehanpur, near Sirhind
7. Sādhs	Birbhan	1658	Near Delhi
8. Charan Dāsīs ...	Charan Dās	1703	Delhi
9. Śiva Narayanīs ...	Śiva Narayana	1734	Chandrawar, Ghazipur
10. Garīb Dāsīs ...	Gārīb Dās	1740	Chudani, Rohtak
11. Rām Sanehīs ...	Rām Charan	1750	Shahapur, Rajputana

common with the other sects, has practically reverted to the usual Hindu type.

Nānak (A.D. 1469–1538), who was the founder of the Sikh religion, was also affected to such an extent by the monotheistic principle of Islam and the Hindu revival in his time that he attempted a syncretism or fusion of the two faiths that had come so close in contact. His religious position did not seem to differ greatly from that of Kabīr, at least in the beginning. Ultimately, Hindu ideas and practices crept in, and this, together with the persecution of the Sikhs by Aurangzīb, drove them in religion, as well as association, farther and farther from the Muslims, until to-day they bear few of the traces of Muslim influence, and are regarded as being practically within the pale of Hinduism.

Apart from the Muslim influence found in the life and work of these great Hindu leaders who attempted to form mixed sects, we find others that have arisen from time to time. Some of these are still flourishing, in which a definite mixture of Hindu and Muslim notions and practices prevail, though neither the followers nor their ancestors appear ever to have been converted to Islam. Such attempts in the reconciliation of the two systems go by a variety of names, but they are of no special consequence, either in numbers or influence, and exist rather as interesting curiosities. Among them are the *Pīrzādas*, a sect that had its origin with one Muḥammad Shāh Dulla about the middle of the seventeenth century. In the book which he compiled he arranged selections for the Hindu and Muslim scriptures, and set up Vishnū in his tenth or *nishkalank* (sinless) incarnation, which is to come as his supreme deity.[1] The *Suthras* are a sect in the Punjab in which both Muslims and Hindus are found in fellowship. The Muslim *Suthras* carry a *dandā* (staff), with which they strike their iron bracelets (*churīs*) and keep time to their singing in a most weird fashion. The *Chhajjūpanthī* sect claims to have been founded by *bhagat* Chhajjū, of Lahore, in the time of Aurangzīb, and reveals a curious combination of Hindu and Muslim creeds. It prevails only among the lower castes. The *Ḥusaynī Brāhmans* are Hindus, and are said to derive their name from the fact that they narrate the story of Ḥaḍrat Imām Ḥusayn. They mark their foreheads with the *tilak*, but they beg from Muslims. They have adopted many Muslim beliefs and practices, such as keeping the fast of Ramaḍān, and are special devotees of the shrine of Khwājah Mu'īn-ud-Dīn Chishtī, of Ajmīr.[2] The *Shamsīs* are a sect which outwardly appears to be Hindu, but actually seems to be affiliated with the Ismā'īlī Khojahs. It is said to take its name from the great saint of Multan, Pīr Shams-ud-Dīn Tabrīzī. Their numbers are confined chiefly to the west of the Jhelum river. They worship no idols, but reverence the *Bhagavad Gītā*. It is asserted, however, that they hold secret beliefs, and worship the Āghā Khāṇ, whom they regard as an incarnation of the Hindu triad—Brahmā, Vishnū and Śiva.[3]

Such is the maze of belief that prevails in India. No doubt Islam, with its clear, definite, and simple creed, which stood in contrast to the indigenous vagaries of the imagination and speculation about God, appealed to many Hindus as a satisfying solution of the vexed problem of theology. To others its social democracy granted a welcome release from the bondage of caste. But when all is said, there seems to be little doubt that Hinduism has wrought a far greater change in Islam than Islam has wrought in Hinduism, which still continues to pursue the even tenor of its way with a complacency and confidence that are amazing. For more than twelve long centuries Islam has been in contact with Hinduism in India. For twelve centuries each community has been

[1] *E.I.*, II, 491. [2] Rose, *G.T.C.P.*, I, 141.
[3] *Ibid.*, 402 ; see also Najm-ul-Ghanī Khāṇ, *Madhāhib-ul-Islām.*

confronted by the other. Not always have they been on the best of terms. Their differences of belief, together with communal aspirations on the one hand contending with an instinct for communal preservation on the other, have been the source of much friction, which continues even to the present day. No one dare prophesy what the future holds ; but one of the great desires of all friends of India is that the two great communities, which have so much to share—native land, language, blood relationship, and a common destiny—shall come to live in peaceful relations, doing unto others as they would be done by. Only so can India ever emerge from the present impasse and national unity be established.[1]

Dr. J. N. Sircar,[2] in a recent lecture on 'Islam in India', gives the following list of benefits derived by India from the advent of Islam and Muslim rule :

1. Restoration of touch with the outer world, including the revival of an Indian navy and sea-borne trade, both of which had been lost since the decline of the Cholas.
2. Internal peace over a large part of India, especially north of the Vindhyas.
3. Uniformity secured by the imposition of the same type of administration.
4. Uniformity of social manners and dress among the upper classes, irrespective of creed.
5. Indo-Saracen art, in which the mediæval Hindu and Chinese schools were blended together. Also a new style of architecture, and the promo-

[1] It is sometimes asserted by Muslims, and not without reason, that the Aryā Samāj was formed partly as a result of the contact of Hinduism with Islam. Those who hold this view, point to the reform programme of the Samāj in such matters as widow remarriage and the abolition of caste restrictions of the untouchables.

A further illustration of the social effect of Islam on Hinduism is found among the Kayasthas. This caste is often regarded by orthodox Hindus as half-Muslim, since the members of the group served freely in the Mughul government offices and were greatly influenced in their social activities, dress, religious outlook and education by their Muslim superiors. There are Kayasthas still who dress like Muslims, in their long, flowing *achkans* and *payjāmahs*, skin-tight to the knee. Some even read the Qur'ān, and memorize long passages.

[2] From *The Hindu*, Madras, in *The Indian Social Reformer*, March 31, 1928.

tion of industries of a refined variety (e.g. shawl, muslin, and carpet-making, inlaying, etc.).

6. A common *lingua franca*, called Hindustāni or Rekhta, and an official prose style, mostly the creation of Hindu *munshīs* writing Persian.

7. Rise of our vernacular literature as the fruits of peace and economic prosperity under the empire of Delhi.

8. Monotheistic religious revival and Ṣūfiism.

9. Historical literature.

10. Improvement in the art of war, and in civilization in general.

CHAPTER IX

MODERN MOVEMENTS: REACTIONARY AND PROGRESSIVE

INDIAN Islam has provided abundant incentive to reformers in the last century in two directions. The widespread saint worship, and the masses whose imperfect conversion to Islam left them in possession of customs and beliefs that were far more Hindu than Muslim, led certain ardent souls to inaugurate a puritanical reform, not unlike that carried on by the followers of Muḥammad 'Abd-ul-Wahhāb in Arabia. While the latter movement began with the opening of the nineteenth century, and was wholly reactionary in character, yet it persists even to the present time, and not without beneficial results to the Muslim community. More than fifty years later a reform movement of a wholly different nature was inaugurated, being definitely progressive and modern. Strange to say, the chief characters in each movement bore the name Sayyid Aḥmad. But the one was a violent individual, who pronounced India *Dār-ul-Ḥarb*, declared war on the infidels, and took for his slogan, 'Back to the original Islam'; while the other was a peaceful, loyal British subject, who declared India to be *Dār-ul-Islām*, and sought to justify his progressive policies to his orthodox critics by asserting that he was interpreting the spirit of the real Islam. Each desired to rest his case on the Prophet, the Qur'ān, and Traditions; each sought to sweep away the theological and legal incrustations of the intervening centuries that had covered the true Faith: but there they parted, and moved in completely opposite directions. The one had no use for modernism: Muslims must go back to the original purity of Islam. The other would employ 'Reason' to adapt Islam to modern conditions. We shall now consider these two developments, which may be broadly designated as the Wahhābī Movement and the Aligarh Movement, whose influence has been India-wide.

THE WAHHĀBĪ MOVEMENT

The puritanical sect, founded in Arabia during the eighteenth century by Muḥammad 'Abd-ul-Wahhāb, was destined to have far-reaching influences throughout the Muslim world, and nowhere outside the land of its birth has that influence been more pronounced than in India. Although the sect as such has never been formally organized in India under the name 'Wahhābī', yet the doctrines professed by certain of the Indian reformers have been of that school, and the popular tendency has been to describe their activities as the 'Wahhābī Movement'.

In general, the movement has been marked by renewed emphasis of *tawḥīd* (the unity of God); adherence to the principle of *ijtihād*, or the right of the individual to interpret the Qur'ān and the *Ḥadīth* (Traditions), and rejection of the four orthodox schools of canon law; opposition to the worship of saints, which they hold to be a form of polytheism (*shirk*); and earnest endeavour to remove all traces of the practices of early faiths from the worship of Hindu converts to Islam. In this movement there was a 'right' and a 'left' wing. The former was led by Sharī'at Allāh and Karāmat 'Alī, attempting nothing beyond definite efforts to root out undesirable practices belonging to the earlier faiths, and working peacefully for the purification of Islam in India. The left wing, led by Sayyid Aḥmad, of Rae Bareli, even went so far as to declare a holy war (*jihād*).

The first appearance of Wahhābī ideas in India was about the year 1804, when the *Farā'iḍī* sect was founded in eastern Bengal by Ḥājī Sharī'at Allāh. The account of his life and work, as given by M. Hidayet Hosain,[1] states that he was born of obscure parents in the village of Bahādurpūr, in the district of Farīdpūr, Bengal, and when eighteen years of age he went on a pilgrimage to Mecca. Here he stayed for twenty years as a disciple of Shaykh Ṭāhir as-Sunbul al-Makkī, who at that time was the head of the Shāfi'ī sect at Mecca. On returning to India, about 1802, he began quietly to promulgate his newly-framed doctrines in the villages of his native district. Although he encountered much opposition and abuse, he succeeded in gathering around him a body of devoted followers, and little by little came to be regarded as a holy man.

His major emphasis was the assertion that India under non-Muslim rule was *Dār-ul-Ḥarb*, and, therefore, it was not

[1] *The Encyclopædia of Islam*, II, 57 ff.

lawful to observe Friday prayers or the two great festivals, 'Īd-ul-Fiṭr and 'Īd-ul-Aḍḥā. He also discontinued the use of the term *pīr* (priest) and *murīd* (disciple), and substituted in their place the titles *ustādh* (teacher) and *shāgird* (pupil), because they did not imply complete submission of the pupil to the religious preceptor, as the other terms did. For the same reason he prohibited the ceremony of joining hands, which was customary at the initiation of a disciple, but instead he required from every one of his disciples repentance (*tawbah*) for past sins, and declaration of intention to lead a more righteous and godly life in the future.

The extent of the influence of the work of this remarkable character is further described by M. Hidayet Hosain as follows:

> That he came of obscure parentage amid the swamps of eastern Bengal, and should be the first preacher to denounce the superstitions and corrupt beliefs, which long contact with Hindu polytheism had developed, is remarkable enough; but that the apathetic and careless Bengali peasant should be roused into enthusiam is still more so. To effect this required a sincere and sympathetic preacher; and no one ever appealed more strongly to the sympathies of a people than Sharī'at Allāh, whose blameless and exemplary life was admired by his countrymen, who venerated him as a father able to advise them in times of adversity, and give consolation in cases of affliction.[1]

The sect was further developed by the son of the founder, Dūdhū Miyān, who was born in 1819. Early in his career he made the pilgrimage to Mecca, and on his return devoted his time and talents to the spread of his father's doctrines, besides adding some new ones of his own. Among other things, we are told that he insisted upon his disciples eating the common grasshopper (*phanga*), which they detested, because the locust (*tiddī*) was used as food in Arabia! He had a genius for organization, and, making his headquarters at Bahadurpur, he divided eastern Bengal into circles (*ḥalqah*), appointing a deputy, or *khalīfah*, over each to collect contributions from the members for furthering the ends of the central association. He also established an espionage system, and used his agents to secure information throughout their areas for the purpose of protecting members of the sect against landlords. He even tried to make all Muḥammadan peasants join his sect, 'and on refusal caused them to be beaten and excommuni-

[1] *Ibid.*

cated from the society of the faithful, and destroyed their crops'. His success was won chiefly among the cultivators and village workmen, because he took up the cudgels on their behalf. 'He asserted the equality of mankind, and taught that the welfare of the lowly and poor was as much an object of interest as that of the high and rich. When a brother fell into distress it was, he taught, the duty of his neighbours to assist him, and nothing, he affirmed, was criminal, or unjustifiable, which might be used to that end. He also taught that there was no sin in persecuting those who refused to embrace his doctrines, or who appealed to government courts against the orders of the society and its acknowledged leaders.'[1]

The sect as such seems to be slowly dying out; but its chief doctrines of reform still live in what is known as the Ahl-i-Ḥadīth sect, which has served in these later times as the organization into which most of the reforming tendencies of the early so-called 'Wahhābī reformers' of India have been absorbed.

The Ṭarīqah-i-Muḥammadīyah Sect

Of the various attempts at reform in Indian Islam during the early part of the nineteenth century, none was prosecuted more vigorously or over a wider area than that sponsored by Sayyid Aḥmad, of Rae Bareli. This adventurous spirit was born in the year 1782, and spent a considerable portion of his young manhood as a freebooter and outlaw. Later, however, he abandoned this sort of life, and about 1816 became a religious disciple of the pious and learned Shāh 'Abd-ul-'Azīz, of Delhi, where his spiritual gifts were soon recognized. He became a noted preacher, and, after three years discipleship, went forth to preach against the abuses that had crept into the faith and practice of the Indian Muslims. The first work he attempted was among the Rohillas of north India, where he soon 'obtained a zealous and turbulent following'.[2] Encouraged by this success, he pressed forward, and, according to Dr. W. W. Hunter, his advance assumed the character of a triumphal procession as he journeyed slowly southwards during the year 1820. His disciples rendered him menial service in acknowledgment of his spiritual dignity, and men of

[1] *Ibid.* [2] W. W. Hunter, *The Indian Musalmans*, 12.

rank and learning ran like common servants, with their shoes off, by the side of the palanquin.[1]

After he reached Patna, in Bihar, where he stayed for a considerable time, the number of his followers became so increased that a regular system of government had to be devised.

> He appointed agents to go forth and collect a tax from the profits of trade in all the large towns which had lain on his route. He further nominated four khalīfas, or spiritual vice-regents, and a high priest, by a formal deed, such as the Muḥammadan emperors used in appointing governors of provinces. Having thus formed a permanent centre at Patna, he proceeded towards Calcutta, following the course of the Ganges, making converts and appointing agents in every important town by the way. In Calcutta the masses flocked to him in such numbers that he was unable to go through the ceremony of initiation by the separate laying on of hands. Unrolling his turban, therefore, he declared that all who could touch any part of its ample length became his disciples.[2]

Elated with his remarkable success, he started on a pilgrimage to Mecca from Calcutta in the year 1822. After his travels through Arabia and Syria, where he undoubtedly came into contact with the Wahhābī reformers, he returned to India, more disgusted than ever with the abuses and degradation of Islam which had grown up largely from contact with Hinduism. So, inspired by what he saw in other lands, he began to preach with renewed vigour, centring his attack on these abuses, seeking to free Islam from Hindu corruptions. He also preached the necessity of a holy war (*jihād*), because India, under the domination of a non-Muslim power, was no longer *Dār-ul-Islām*, but *Dār-ul-Ḥarb*. In less than two years the majority of respectable Muslims had adopted his ideas.[3]

From that time the Muslims of India began to be divided into two camps, and the effects of that division have not passed away even yet; for the principles of Wahhābism, which were taught by Sayyid Aḥmad and his associate preachers, were too fundamental, and too closely related to the freedom of the spirit, to die. The party of the reformers did not, however, find its path strewn with roses all the way. There were many adversaries. Sayyid Aḥmad called his sect the *Ṭarīqah-i-Muḥammadīyah*

[1] *Ibid.*, 13. [2] *Ibid.*, 13.

[3] Garcin De Tassy, *Histoire de la littérature hindoue et hindoustanie*, III, 33.

(The Way of Muḥammad), which had a strong 'Back to Muḥammad' slogan in it; but the opponents of the sect, the orthodox *maulvīs* and others, spoke of them derisively as '*Wahhābīs*'. On the other hand, Sayyid Aḥmad and his followers retaliated by calling all who did not accept the principles of reform '*Mushrik*' (Polytheists)!

Sayyid Aḥmad, however, was not to lead his movement for long. Carried to excessive lengths by his zeal for prosecuting a holy war against the Sikhs, he finally met his end in an engagement on the frontier near Peshawar, in the year 1831; and his hosts, without their leader, were speedily dispersed. The 'warlike ramifications' of this Wahhābī leader were indeed of no small character, and were not confined to the Punjab and Bengal. In fact, writes Hunter:

> It seemed as if a Fanatic Confederacy had firmly established itself in the heart of southern India. . . . The Wahhābī organization included a brother of the Nizam, who was to have been raised to the Hyderabad throne; and, had the plan not broken down the leaders would have had a great store of newly-cast cannon and munitions of all sorts, with a formidable body of adherents, both among the semi-independent native chiefs, and in the military courts of the south.[1]

With the passing of the great leader it seemed for a time as though the end of the organization of which he was the centre and inspiration had come. Three things, however, made it possible to carry his work forward. It must be noted first that while the reformers had been forced to give up the prosecution of a holy war as an impracticable part of their programme, for the time being, yet effort was made to keep the smouldering embers of hatred for the infidel rule alive, so that when the time should be ripe, another, and perchance a more successful, effort might be made. Secondly, the desire for the purification and reform of Islam seemed to have taken hold of the preachers of the movement, with a consuming passion. Thirdly, credit must be given to the keen foresight of Sayyid Aḥmad in establishing an organization that could carry on effectively after his death. These three things, then—a passion for the freedom of Islam, a passion for the reform of Islam, and a wellnigh perfect organiza-

[1] Hunter, op. cit., 42.

tion for propaganda—saved the day for the Wahhābīs, and, as Hunter says:

> The missionary zeal of the Patna *khalīfahs*, and the immense pecuniary resources at their command, once more raised the sacred banner from the dust. They covered India with their emissaries, and brought about one of the greatest religious revivals that has ever taken place. The two *khalīfahs* themselves went through Bengal and southern India. The minor missionaries were innumerable, and a skilful organization enabled them to settle in any place where the multitude of converts made it worth their while. In this way almost every one of the fanatic districts had its permanent preacher, whose zeal was sharpened from time to time by visits of the itinerant missionaries, and whose influence was consolidated and rendered permanent by the Central Propaganda at Patna. . . . Everywhere they stirred the Muhammadan population to its depths.[1]

THE THEOLOGICAL IMPLICATIONS OF THE MOVEMENT

The intense zeal and remarkable success that attended the preaching of Sayyid Aḥmad indicate an unusual personality. Combined with this strong personal force were other elements that contributed not a little to the interest that was aroused. He was lineally descended from the Prophet Muḥammad himself. He was subject to trances, or fits of ecstasy, 'during which he communed with God and the Apostles. In dreams, the beloved daughter of Muḥammad and her husband (his lineal ancestors) visited him, saluted him as their son, bathed him in sweet essences, and arrayed him in royal apparel.' Furthermore, his disciples saw in his 'grave, taciturn and gentle demeanour; even in his person' much that reminded them of their Prophet, and attracted them to him.[2]

But that was not all. Behind this strong personality lay the ancient popular belief in the coming of the promised 'Imām Mahdī',[3] who was to come and lead the faithful in a last great crusade against the Anti-Christ, who should rise in the last days. His disciples not only grew to believe that he was the promised Imām Mahdī, but so insistent were they that he himself finally yielded to their arguments, and assumed all the titles, dignities, and authority appertaining to such a distinguished personage. To a certain extent, therefore, this movement had much in common with the *Mahdawī* movements already considered.

[1] *Ibid.*, 49 ff. [2] *Ibid.* [3] See pp. 106 ff.

Having settled the question of the divine mission of the leader, it became necessary to promulgate other more general and less personal doctrines, which should sustain the movement. He found these in asserting that God alone must be worshipped without the 'interposition of humanly devised forms and ceremonies'. From this position he developed his entire body of teaching, which he and his disciples have elaborated in an extensive literature.

In the *Ṣirāṭ-ul-Mustaqīm*,[1] which contains the views of the Sayyid as they were set down by his disciple, Ḥājī Muḥammad Ismā'īl, of Delhi, we read that:

> The law of the Prophet is founded on two things: First, the not attributing to any creature the attribute of God; and second, not inventing forms and practices which were not invented in the days of the Prophet, and his successors, the Khalīfahs. The first consists in disbelieving that angels, spirits, spiritual guides, disciples, teachers, students, prophets or saints remove one's difficulties. In abstaining from having recourse to any of the above creations for the attainment of any wish or desire. In denying that any of them has the power of granting favour or removing evils; in considering them as helpless and ignorant as one's self in respect of the power of God. In never making any offering to any prophet, saint, holy man, or angel, for the obtaining of any object, but merely to consider them as friends of God. To believe that they have power to rule the accidents of life, and that they are acquainted with the sacred knowledge of God, is downright infidelity.
>
> With regard to the second point, true and undefiled religion consists in strongly adhering to all the devotions and practices in the affairs of life which were observed by the Prophet. In avoiding all such innovations as marriage ceremonies, mourning ceremonies, adorning of tombs, erection of large edifices over graves, lavish expenditure on the anniversaries of the dead, street processions, and the like, and in endeavouring as far as may be practicable to put a stop to these practices.[2]

This whole programme, as outlined above, was a direct attempt to secure the reform of practices which had long been a part of the regular Islamic life of the country. But to urge their discontinuance was to immediately divide the Muslims into two camps. Still, there can be no denying that Indian Islam needed, and still needs, reform exactly at the spots where the Sayyid attacked it so vigorously a century and a quarter ago. That he attained as

[1] This book is in Urdū, and is obtainable in the ordinary Indian bazaar.

[2] W. W. Hunter, *The Indian Musalmans*, 54.

much success as he did speaks well for the spirit of earnestness latent in the religious life of Indian Muslims, without which no progress whatever can be made. In fact, it is this part of his propaganda that has lasted the longest. Reform of Muslim practices is a serious matter ; and as it then engaged the attention of some of the best minds of Muslim India, so it still forms a matter of earnest concern for those advanced leaders of Muslim thought who would like to see Indian Islam purged of all the hurtful, degrading, and un-Islamic practices that keep it from being fashioned on more rational and progressive lines.

Since these reforming doctrines went right to the heart of the everyday life of Muslims in the villages of India, the approach of a 'Wahhābī' preacher was as likely to create a storm as to produce a following. That a storm not unfrequently broke is indicated by the following incident, related by Hunter, which occurred in one of the villages of western Bengal. A reformer had come to the village and had delivered himself of the new doctrines,

> and as the group broke up at the close of the harangue, public opinion, though divided, was mainly against the preacher. One said: 'This man would have us let the lamp go out at the tomb of our father.' Another : 'He forbids the drums and dancing girls at the marriage of our daughters.' A third was more favourable; . . . but a Mullā ended the discussion. 'This fellow', he said, 'is a follower of the false Imām who took the holy cities by the sword, closed up the path of pilgrimage, and wrote on the door of the pure house, There is no God but God, and Saud is His Prophet.'

The Peaceful Reforms of Karāmat 'Alī

The reform propaganda initiated by Sayyid Aḥmad was still further developed by Maulvī Karāmat 'Alī, whose work largely paved the way for the establishment of the organization which has more recently developed under the name of Ahl-i-Ḥadīth. Karāmat 'Alī was born at Jaunpur, U.P., in the early part of the nineteenth century. Some time between the years 1820 and 1824, during one of the tours of Sayyid Aḥmad in northern India, Karāmat 'Alī became one of the most ardent and devoted of his younger disciples. However, as A. Yūsuf 'Alī remarks, 'He does not appear to have taken part in the *jihād* which Sayyid Aḥmad waged against the Sikhs, or to have ever been in the Afg͟hān borderland, where Sayyid Aḥmad was slain in battle in 1831'.[1]

In fact, he not only identified himself with the peaceful propaganda for the reform of Islam in Bihar and Bengal, but he even seems to have refused to go to extremes in many matters advocated by the reformers. He was, after all, very moderate in his ideas, for he gave himself with unreserved zeal to the double task of combating the Hindu customs and superstitions which had crept into the practice of Islam in eastern Bengal, and of trying to bring back into the fold of orthodoxy the new heterodox schools, which had grown up as a result of the work of Sharī'at Allāh and his son Dūdhū Miyān. In some particulars he was far separated from the reform principles of Sayyid Aḥmad, for he boldly accepted the doctrine of 'spiritual preceptorship' (*pīrī-murīdī*), which the former vigorously denounced, and even went so far as to write tracts against Sharī'at Allāh, Dūdhū Miyān, and the Wahhābīs. He was thus only an orthodox reformer, who adhered to the tradition that in every century a teacher is born to renew the faith. He regarded Sayyid Aḥmad as such a renewer (*mujaddid*) for the thirteenth century of the Hegira, and held that he should be followed until another renewer arise for the fourteenth.[2]

Karāmat 'Alī exhibited remarkable power for the regeneration of Islam all his life, so that at the time of his death, in 1873, there was scarcely a village in Bengal that did not contain some of his disciples. His work has been carried on by his son, Maulvī Ḥāfiẓ Aḥmad, who died in 1898, and by his nephew, Muḥammad Muḥsin; and there are certain districts of the province where his influence is still a living force.

The Ahl-i-Ḥadī͟th

The influence of the so-called Wahhābī Movement still continues in two directions: one is in the organizations that it has left behind and the other in the effects on the development of the larger orthodox group. Traces of the original community left by Sayyid Aḥmad are still to be found on the North-West Frontier, as are also similar traces of the schools of Sharī'at

[1] *E.I.*, II, 752. [2] *Ibid.*, 753.

Allāh and Karāmat 'Alī found in Bengal; but the most vigorous line of descent goes by the name of the Ahl-i-Ḥadīth (People of Tradition). While the numbers of this sect are not extremely numerous, yet it receives regular mention in the Census of India. It has an organization known as the 'All-India Ahl-i-Ḥadīth Conference', which holds annual sessions; while district organizations are found in a large part of India, particularly the Punjab, north India, Bihar, and Bengal. Religious journals, books, and tracts are published; theological schools (*madrasahs*) for the training of preachers are maintained, and separate mosques are built.

The leaders of the Ahl-i-Ḥadīth sect declare that it is in no way related to the founder of the Wahhābī Movement of Arabia; but, however vigorously they may deny any connexion, the spirit and the aims of this group appear to be identical with those of the Najdī reformer. Their creed and aim are concisely stated thus: 'Whatever the Prophet Muḥammad taught in the Qur'ān and the authoritative Traditions (*Aḥādīth Saḥīḥ*), that alone is the basis of the religion known as the Ahl-i-Ḥadīth'.[1] The tenets of the sect give clear expression to the zeal which seeks to go back to first principles and to restore the original simplicity and sincerity of faith and practice. Emphasis is put upon the following:

1. The reassertion of the unity (*tawḥīd*) of Allāh, and a denial of occult powers, and knowledge of the hidden things (*'ilm-ul-ghayb*) to any of his creatures. This is a direct attack on the belief in saints, which has been so commonly adopted throughout India.

2. The rejection of the four recognized schools of canon law, and the assertion that the Qur'ān and Traditions, as accepted by the Companions of the Prophet, are the only worthy guide for true Muslims. By thus casting aside the legal opinions, decisions, and judgments of the four orthodox schools of law, they reject the common notion that *ijtihād* (legal conclusions) of the founders of these four schools are of final authority, and rather contend that every believer is free to follow his own interpretations of the

[1] Maulana Abū'l-Wafā Thanā Allāh, *Risālah Ahl-i-Ḥadīth ka Madhhab*, 82, 83.

Qur'ān and the Traditions, provided he has sufficient learning to enable him to give a valid interpretation. Consequently, they do not accept the *ijmā'* (agreement) of the people of Islam as final, but are inclined to the view that it is incumbent on the learned people of each succeeding age to seek for their generation their own interpretation of the Qur'ān and Traditions, rather than to rely on *taqlīd* (blind acceptance) of the teaching and imitation of predecessors. This is a far-reaching principle, and the application and spirit of it have gone far beyond the confines of the Ahl-i-Ḥadīth organization in influencing reform in India.

3. As a corollary to the preceding positions, every effort is made to eradicate customs that may be traced either to innovation or to Hindu or other un-Islamic origin. India is a land where formal adherence to the Qur'ān and precepts of Islam sits lightly upon the masses, the real religious life being overlaid with practices and beliefs that belong to a contrary system. In the address of the chairman of the All-India Ahl-i-Ḥadīth Conference, held in Gujranwala, in the Punjab, in 1924, we are given a vivid picture of the need for this work. This gentleman wrote as follows: 'Up to sixty years ago in this district and city the name of Ahl-i-Ḥadīth was not known to anyone. Polytheism, innovations, and the customs of the infidels were so common among Muslims that it was impossible to distinguish them from non-Muslims, except in the very special matters of religious observance. Islamic duties were performed, but in a wholly perfunctory manner, and very little attention indeed was paid to their inner truth and meaning.'[1] To correct this situation the Ahl-i-Ḥadīth earnestly labours throughout India, and thus proves itself the spiritual offspring of 'Abd-ul-Wahhāb, Sharī'at Allāh, Sayyid Aḥmad, and Karāmat 'Alī.

The Ahl-i-Qur'ān

The spirit of reform that gave birth to the Ahl-i-Ḥadīth was productive of still another sect, known as the Ahl-i-Qur'ān, founded in 1902, which rejects not only all traditional theology, and all the legal requirements of the four schools of canon law, but even the

[1] Translated from the *Khuṭbah-i-Ṣadārat* (presidential address), published by the All-India Ahl-i-Ḥadīth Conference.

ijmā' (agreement) of the Companions of the Prophet, as expressed in the authoritative Traditions, and insists that the Qur'ān alone is sufficient for guidance. The founder of this sect was Maulvī 'Abd Allāh Chakrālawī, who had his headquarters in Lahore. He preached and wrote with great zeal during the early part of the present century, and, in addition to preparing a special form of creed and pledge to be signed by his followers (*'Ahdnāmah-i-Aqā'id-i-Ahl-i-Dhikr wa al-Qur'ān*), prepared also a special prayer ritual for their use. He likewise had his own mosque for the adherents of his sect. Although this new group does not seem to have attained to any great importance or influence outside the Punjab, and the numbers seem to be on the decrease, yet it still continues to defend its position, and issues a monthly magazine, called the *Ishā 'at-ul-Qur'ān.*

In addition to the above peculiarities are the following: They consider the call to prayer (*adhān*) unnecessary; the *takbīr* (repetition of the phrase 'God is great') is not said aloud; in prayer only the obligatory (*farḍ*) portions are binding, while the *sunnah* (traditional) and *nafl* (optional) *rak'āts* (sections of ritual prayer) are rejected altogether. While other Muḥammadans bend both knees in prayer, the Ahl-i-Qur'ān kneel on one knee only. Funeral and 'Īd prayers are considered unnecessary, and they assert that offering of prayers and alms for the dead are of no avail.

Reforms under the Influences of Western Civilization

During the first eleven centuries of the history of Islam in India (A.D. 711–1800) the influence of Muslim states and centres of learning had been paramount. As we have seen, there was a constant and varied stream of immigrants moving towards India, from the time of Maḥmūd of Ghaznī: Arabs, Persians, Afghāns, Turks, and Mongols. They were recruits for the armies and government posts; poets and artists from Persia; saints, preachers, and men of learning; merchants and adventurers. All these, coming with new life and fresh vigour, acted as a tremendous force for the continual regeneration and reinforcement of the constantly growing indigenous Muslim population, and served not only as a reminder of the dependence of Indian Islam upon the older countries of the Faith towards the west, but also became the models and examples after which the native Muslims of India sought to pattern their lives and culture. At the beginning Arabic was the language of Indian Muslims, but this gave way to Persian, which was the dominant court and literary language for more than eight centuries.

Beginning, however, with the early part of the nineteenth century, marked changes set in. For more than a hundred years, after the death of Aurangzīb, the last of the powerful Mughuls, disintegration had been going on, not only in Muslim political power, but in Muslim life and culture as well, owing to the lack of a strong central government and leadership. Furthermore, the influence of western civilization, which was slowly but surely creeping closer and closer to Muslim India, was destined to invade the innermost precincts of its life, and begin a transformation the end of which cannot yet be determined. This close contact of Indian Islam with the west began with the commercial and political ascendancy which Britain gained over the Indian peninsula, and which in 1857 removed the last vestige of Mughul imperial authority. For many years before this date, and continuously since, the influence of western civilization has been the dominant factor in moulding the higher life of Islam in India, no escape from it being possible.

Immediate Effects of British Occupation

The effects of British occupation, and the consolidation of political authority which followed the complete disintegration and overthrow of Muslim power, soon became apparent. Muslims were withdrawn from government positions which it had been their privilege to enjoy for centuries under the patronage of their own rulers. Persian as the official language was discarded in 1837, and English and the vernaculars of India put in its place. From that date, in every school and court, this change of language served as a constant reminder to the Muslim of the distinct loss that had come to his community, and of the fact that he was now among the subject races of mankind. It is true that in the distinctly 'Muslimized' sections of the country, such as the United Provinces and the Punjab, the newly-developed Indian Muslim language, Urdū, was accepted rather than Hindī as the vernacular preferred in the courts. But this offered little consolation to the wounded feelings of Muslims in the early days, though at the present time it has come to be one of the elements of Muslim culture in India that is most dearly prized by the community. Another effect of British control which wounded the susceptibilities of Muslims was the abolition of the government posts of *Qāḍī* and *Qāḍī-ul-Quḍāt*, and the consequent effect upon the administration of Muslim law. All of this secularization of the life of Muslims by a non-Muslim power came to be viewed with great apprehension, with consequences of the most reactionary character.

The first result to be noted was a feeling of 'sullen discontent', which spread over the Muslim community, and even before all of the above changes had taken place Sharī'at Allāh and Sayyid Aḥmad, of Rae Bareli, in the spirit of the Arabian Wahhābīs, had begun to raise the question whether India was any longer a suitable place of residence for Muslims. Thus a discussion was started in the Muslim community which lasted for half a century, as to whether India was *Dār-ul-Ḥarb* or *Dār-ul-Islām*. Some of the more zealous elements, as we have seen, under the leadership of Sayyid Aḥmad, actually did declare a holy war, preached the necessity of emigration (*ḥijrat*) to lands under Muslim rule, and carried their agitation all over India. In fact, it is believed that the Mutiny of 1857 was partly due, at least, to a recrudescence of this spirit, which sought to re-establish the Mughul power, but which resulted rather in the ruin of many old Muslim families, whose estates were confiscated because of complicity in the rebellion.

Along with the processes of direct action which were aimed at the overthrow of alien domination and the re-establishment of Muslim power in all its ancient glory and influence with truly religious significance for the protection of Islam, there arose an effective conspiracy on the part of Muslims everywhere. Led by their conservative *maulvīs*, they determined to boycott the western institutions which were rapidly taking root and flourishing everywhere. This prohibition had a particular reference to western education, which included the teaching of English and modern science in the Government and Mission schools, everywhere springing up. With vehement language the reactionary *maulvīs* inveighed against the institutions of the infidels. The faithful were warned that the end of such education was sure and certain infidelity, and that those who attended such schools, or permitted their sons to do so, would be accounted apostates. Even life itself was threatened in order to prevent the introduction of such a serious innovation, with all its implications for the religion of Islam, as viewed by the conservatives. The result of this attitude on the part of the learned leaders of the community was that for many decades Muslims in India fell farther and farther behind their Hindu compatriots in the matter of education ; for the latter were not at all slow to avail themselves of the new educational facilities, and to adapt themselves to changing circumstances and the requirements of the new Government. With a stubborn but fruitless resistance, the Muslim community pursued its disastrous policy of isolation and self-sufficiency, until well past the middle of the nineteenth century, when there arose that daring apostle of reconciliation, Sir Syed Aḥmad Khāṇ, whose name will ever be associated with all that is progressive and forward-looking in the annals of Islam in India.

The Dawn of a New Day

With Sir Syed we arrive at the dawn of a new day, the beginning of a new era. No other figure in Indian Islam deserves such reverent consideration and respect as this sturdy pioneer and beloved leader, who, through endless opposition, but with dauntless courage and faith, blazed a new trail for succeeding generations of his Muslim brethren to follow.

Syed Aḥmad Khāṇ (1817–1898), born of a noble Delhi family, received the usual orthodox education, and qualified for a subordinate position in the British Government. He early came to realize the value of the newly-established government for the country, and at the same time saw with painful clearness the hopelessness of the attitude toward modern life which his people had adopted. While he was still a young man, the Mutiny of 1857 burst with all its fury of racial and religious hate upon his country. During this time he remained loyal to the established rule, as did many other Muslims in those difficult days, in spite of injured pride. But he became increasingly certain that his people could be rescued from their condition of ruin and utter despair only by adopting a wholly new policy of action toward the revolutionizing influences from the west. On the one hand he sought to win the sympathy of the ruling power toward his people by showing that they were essentially loyal to the British Government.[1] At the same time he diligently set about seeking to convert his community to the new attitude toward life which he was convinced would alone save it from complete destruction.

First, he insisted that there must be a change of political outlook. Instead of regarding India under British rule as *Dār-ul-Ḥarb*, he insisted that, even though it was not under Muslim rule, it was to be regarded as *Dār-ul-Islām*, because Muslims were perfectly free to exercise all the essential rites and ceremonies of their religion.

Secondly, he declared that there must be a change in the religious outlook. He considered that Muslims were suffering from the effects of a religious and theological straight-jacket, which had been imposed on them by well-meaning but irrational custom. While he guarded as jealously as any the prophetic office of Muḥammad, the Qur'ān as the final revelation of God, and well-attested Tradition as the 'pillars of the faith', he insisted that the individual should assert his natural right to interpret these matters for himself in the light of reason. Religion rests on a natural basis and must conform to the laws of Nature, not on the deductions of man. At this point he took issue with conservatives, who insist on blind acceptance and observance (*taqlīd*) of the religious ordinances as handed down from ancient religious authorities, for he wrote, 'I hope every lover of truth will candidly and impartially investigate the truth of Islam, and make a just and accurate distinction between its real principles and those which have been laid down for the perpetual and firm maintenance and observance of the same, as well as between those that are solely the productions of those persons whom we designate as learned men, divines, doctors, and lawyers'.[2]

[1] A pamphlet, entitled *The Causes of the Indian Mutiny*.

[2] Syed Aḥmad Khāṇ, *Essays on the Life of Mohammed*, I, xi.

While he was endeavouring to introduce a new spirit of inquiry into his people, and set up for them a new norm of interpretation of Islam through rationalizing processes of investigation, at the same time he was led to make a study of Christianity. This led to an effort on his part to try to reconcile the two religions. He pleaded for more sympathy from both sides. He asserted that he believed that the gospel writers were inspired, that the Christians and Jews did not corrupt their scriptures, and that the books spoken of in the holy Qur'ān were the same books as exist to-day among Jews and Christians.[1] In furtherance of his desire to bring about a better understanding between Christians and Muslims, he attempted to bring out a *Mohammedan Commentary on the Holy Bible*, the first volume of which was published in 1862 at Ghazipur, and the second volume at Aligarh in 1865. As one turns the pages of these two volumes, one is struck with the daring purpose of the author, and is not surprised that the second volume is finished without getting any further than the close of the eleventh chapter of Genesis. The marvel is that he had the courage to make the attempt at all! The method, too, is unique. Most of the space is taken up with essays about religion in general and Islam in particular, but when the commentary does begin he places the Hebrew text, with interlinear translation in Urdū, followed by the English version just below, and in a parallel column on the same page are placed corresponding portions of the Qur'ān and the Traditions in Arabic, with similar translations, all of which is followed by elaborate notes.

Thirdly, he stated that there must be a change in the method and purpose of education. He held that the old ideas of education were wholly inadequate; that modern science and oriental learning were not mutually exclusive, and that Muslims must make an effort to combine them. He held that, since the world of Nature about us, which is God's work, and Revelation, which is His word, both proceed from the same source, there can be no ultimate conflict between Science and Religion. He insisted that it was only as his community came to know and share the benefits of

[1] Syed Aḥmad Kẖāṇ, *The Mohammedan Commentary on the Holy Bible* I, 23.

western science that they could also come truly to understand and appreciate their own religion. With this end in view, in 1869 he paid a long visit to England, where he spent much time studying the educational system and facilities of the country. On his return to India he determined to establish an institution which should embody his ideas. He was denounced, and execrated, and even his life was threatened, yet he stuck to his one high purpose, and, through the aid of certain kindred spirits whom he had won as disciples to his cause, the Muḥammadan Anglo-Oriental College was finally opened at Aligarh in 1875.

Syed Aḥmad had a vision of an Indian Muslim Oxford, which should train young men of character and capacity in all that is best in Occidental and Oriental learning. He wisely sought to lay the foundation of this education on a religious basis, and not only arranged for systematic religious worship and instruction, but appointed a *maulvī*, who was noted both for his orthodoxy and his piety, to conduct worship in the college mosque. At the same time differences in religion were recognized, so that Sunnī students should be given their religious instruction by a Sunnī, and Shī'ah students by a Shī'ah. To-day the work of Sir Syed Aḥmad ranks as one of the great pioneering achievements in the realm of Muslim education, not only in India but in the world. In 1920 the college became by charter the Muslim University, yet, in spite of this rise and development, it still retains the impress of its founder. Science has not driven out religion, as some feared it might; and the newly-organized Department of Religion had for its first 'Dean' one of the original appointees of Sir Syed Aḥmad himself. It is safe to say that, in spite of all that the reactionary *maulvīs* thought of him, Sir Syed never considered himself as anything but a man of genuinely Muslim outlook. One of his chief passions was that the young men who passed through his college should have a vital knowledge and appreciation of their faith, but without that bigotry and fanaticism which he found so frequently associated with a training which was narrowly Islamic in character.

Fourthly, he laid emphasis on the need for social reform, and carried on a vigorous and fearless campaign in its behalf, particularly through his magazine, *Tahdhīb-ul-Akhlāq* (Reform of Morals). He especially challenged the ideas that inter-dining with

Christians was unlawful, that the *purdah* was a necessity for women, and that it was not necessary to educate them. How far the community has advanced in following the lead he gave may be judged from the fact that there is a girls' intermediate college at Aligarh in connexion with the university, and the highly-cultured and refined wives of many of the professors enjoy social functions in the company of their husbands with as much ease and grace as any of their European sisters.

The Aligarh Movement

Since the time of Sir Syed Aḥmad Khāṇ, who himself formed the turning-point in the history of Indian Islam from the old to the new, there have been two lines of development—one ever tending to more liberal and progressive aims, the other remaining conservative and reactionary. The liberal wing is represented in a copious literature by such exponents as Maulvī Chirāgh 'Alī, the Right Hon. Syed Amīr 'Alī, and a host of others. The work of all these writers is largely in defence of Islam, with two-well defined aims in view. One is a desire to defend Islam from what are held to be unjustifiable attacks by Christian critics. The reforms which are taking place in Muslim society, under the pressure of Christian teaching, western education, and economic changes are not at all at variance with the real Islam, but are rather in complete harmony with it.

With rare skill, advocates of the New Islam, like Sir Shaikh Muḥammad Iqbāl, of Lahore, Prof. S. Khudā Bakhsh, of Calcutta, and Prof. A. M. Maulvī, present the case for the reforms. They are well versed in the findings of Orientalists like Goldziher and Hurgronje, and consequently do not attempt to gloss over admitted difficulties in legal matters. Rather they would sweep away the whole legalistic structure of Islam, if necessary, and go back to 'the pristine beauty of the matchless Book and matchless Prophet'. However, as Sir Muḥammad Iqbāl candidly remarks, in an unpublished essay on *Ijtihād*, it is doubtful if India is yet far enough advanced for many to take such an advanced position. Nevertheless, it may be safely said that steady advance is being made in the improvement of the community through the growing volume of enlightened public opinion with regard to the outstanding evils of the seclusion of women, the practice of polygamy, divorce, child-marriage, fatalism, and religious formalism. For the light of progress thus shed on the path of Indian Muslims, credit is undoubtedly due to the peerless Sir Syed Aḥmad of Aligarh.

One of the fruitful sources for the enrichment of Islamic culture which Sir Syed Aḥmad early discovered was the vast treasure contained in English literature and scientific books. With an intense desire to unlock this treasure-house of western knowledge, he not only urged that the British Government should provide translations for Indians in their own vernaculars, but he even set about having some of it done through his own private press at Ghazipur, and later at Aligarh. He did not, however, seem to stress the idea that higher education should be through the vernaculars, as some are doing at the present. Nevertheless, it is but fair to assume that the work of Sir Syed, in arousing an interest in western learning and methods of education, did pave the way for the interesting experiment in higher education through the medium of Urdū, the Muslim national language of India, which is being carried out in Hyderabad, Deccan, under the patronage of His Exalted Highness the Niẓām. The Osmānia University, for such is its name, came into being in 1917, in accordance with a *firmān* (order) issued by the Niẓām, which sets forth the purpose of this unique experiment:

> I am pleased to express my approval . . . regarding the inauguration of a university in the state, in which the knowledge and culture of ancient and modern times may be blended so harmoniously as to remove the defects created by the present system of education and full advantage may be taken of all that is best in the ancient and modern systems of physical, intellectual, and spiritual culture. In addition to its primary object to diffuse knowledge, it should aim at the moral training of students and give an impetus to research in all scientific subjects. The fundamental principle in the working of the university should be that Urdū should form the medium of higher education, but that a knowledge of English as a language should at the same time be deemed compulsory for all students. With this object in view I am pleased to order that steps be taken for the inauguration of a university for the Dominions, to be called the Osmānia University of Hyderabad, in commemoration of my accession to the throne.[1]

[1] *Prospectus of the Osmānia University*, 4, 5.

Modern scientific and historical books, suitable for higher education in Urdū, were not, however, available. Hence the first task of the university was to establish a Bureau of Translation, with a modern steam-lithographic press. The work of this bureau is deserving of the highest praise for the manner in which it is performing a most difficult task. The works translated from English include the whole range of university studies, such as history, philosophy, psychology, economics, mathematics, physics, chemistry, biology, and law. It is too early yet to judge of the value of the experiment, but, should it have marked elements of success, it may be fairly assumed that other Muslim institutions of higher learning will be founded on the principle of the Osmānia University; which should make not only for the deepening of a truly national consciousness, but, what is even more important, for the wider diffusion of true international science and culture.

The second result of Sir Syed Aḥmad's attempts at reform in Muslim education was an interesting attempt to conserve the older Muslim learning, while making such adjustments in the curriculum of studies as the more conservative and orthodox elements in the community considered advisable. To meet these requirements, a society was formed in Lucknow, in 1890, known as the Nadwat-ul-'Ulamā. Five years later, this society laid the foundation of a college known as the Dār-ul-'Ulūm, which has for its main purpose the training of religious teachers. The aims of the society, as published thirty-four years ago, clearly show the middle ground that this group of mild reformers sought to occupy.

> To create a feeling of harmony and sympathy in the different sections of the *'ulamās*, and to centralize their strength so that they may be able to keep up religious and social traditions of the community with the help of mutual consultation.
>
> To create good-will between the different sects of the community, with a view to bringing about an end to the everyday quarrels. The only remedy for this is education, specially that offered by the Nadwa.
>
> To bring about such changes in the present Arabic course as would prove beneficial to literature, and to the understanding of the Qur'ān, and which may prove useful according to the needs of the day. In such a way, *'ulamās* will be produced by the institute, who will be able to lead the community rightly in the light of modern requirements.
>
> To propagate the religion by educating the ignorant masses.[1]

[1] Nawāb Hisām-ul-Mulk, in the *Muslim Outlook*, Lahore, April 13, 1924.

Muslim Organization Expressive of the New Life

Sir Syed Aḥmad and his associates did more than establish an institution of learning in Aligarh. They succeeded in rousing to new life the whole of Indian Islam. There are tens of thousands of humble Muslims who, though they are not aware of it, owe their present educational aspirations for their sons and daughters to the indefatigable efforts of one who spent his life in unselfish service for such as they. This newness of life soon began to be expressed in a multitude of associations (*anjumans*), which have sprung up all over the country, to take the place of the former central control over Muslim life which was exercised by the Muslim ruler and his government. In fact, such societies tend to form a new basis for democratic social organization, since they enable men, who never could be leaders under the older forms of society, to rise to places of influence and importance in their community.

Two of the earliest of these were founded in the year 1863, the first being the Muḥammadan Literary Society of Calcutta, organized by Nawāb 'Abd-ul-Laṭīf, and the second, the Scientific Society of Ghazipur, which was founded by Sir Syed Aḥmad Khāṇ for the purpose of translating scientific and historical books from English to Urdū. In 1864 the latter society was transferred from Ghazipur to Aligarh, but ceased to flourish in 1875, after the opening of the Muḥammadan Anglo-Oriental College. Another organization of note is the All-India Muḥammadan Educational Conference, which was founded in 1886, by Sir Syed Aḥmad Khāṇ, and has for its object the promotion of western learning among Muslims. It has its permanent headquarters by the side of the Muslim University at Aligarh; and the conferences are held annually in different cities of India, usually in the north.

The All-India Muslim League was organized in 1906, for the purpose of giving special attention to the political interests of the community, inasmuch as men had come to feel that the policy of Sir Syed, in abstaining from taking an active part in the political life of the country, had caused Muslim interests to suffer. With the exception of a number of years during the period of the Great War and after, when agreement on policies could not be reached, the league has functioned regularly through annual meetings, and through the establishment of provincial leagues, which are affiliated to the central organization.

Besides these, there is a veritable host of other *anjumans*, each seeking in its own way to serve the community, both locally and nationally. The learned theologians are served by the Jam'īyat-ul-'Ulamā-i-Hind, with provincial branches. The Central Jam'īyat-i-Tablīgh-ul-Islām (Society for the Propagation of Islam), with headquarters in Ambala City, Punjab, is a strong, growing organization of India-wide character, with not only provincial but district organizations as well. Its twofold task is said to be (1) to prevent apostasy by seeking to counteract the efforts of the Ārya Samāj Shuddhī Movement, and the work of Christian Missions;[1] and (2) to send missionaries to teach backward Muslims. To accomplish these objects a campaign is being carried on to raise twenty-five lakhs of rupees (Rs. 2,500,000, or about £190,000).[2]

Also in almost every important town there is an Anjuman-i-Islāmīyah, looking after the local Muslim educational interests. One of the strongest of these is the Anjuman-i-Ḥimāyat-i-Islām, of Lahore, which undertakes a variety of duties, such as the refutation of objections to Islam, the care of Muslim orphans, and the employment of preachers. It has established schools and orphanages, and maintains a college affiliated with the Punjab University.

The latest organization of a political character is the Central Khilāfat Committee of Bombay, with an elaborate and extensive network of provincial and local bodies, which have their 'humble signboards in almost every town' where Muslims live. For a time this India-wide organization took over the political interests of the Muslim community from the All-India Muslim League, not only for the purpose of joining the Hindus in an attempt to secure political control of India, but also to guard the extra-national interests of Indian Muslims with regard to the sovereignty of

[1] The Shuddhī Movement seeks to win back to the fold of Hinduism some of those tribes which were formerly converted to Islam. The movement has been most active among the Malkāna Muslims of the Agra district.

[2] *A Plea and an Appeal*, by the General Secretary of the Central Jam'īyat-i-Tablīgh-ul-Islām, Ambala City, Punjab, June, 1926.

Turkey and the dignity of the caliphate. Enormous funds were gathered for the central committee, from rich and poor alike, from every Muslim hamlet in the country. A scheme of 'nationalist' education was initiated. 'National' schools, supported by the local Khilāfat committees, sprang up everywhere, and the whole programme was perfected by the establishment at Aligarh of the National Muslim University, with the redoubtable Maulānā Muḥammad 'Alī as the moving spirit, and 'Abdul Majīd Khwāja as Principal, or *Shaykh-ul-Jāmi'ah*. This institution has since been removed to Delhi, the present Principal being Maulvī Zākir Ḥussain. An Indian Khilāfat delegation was sent to England and Paris, to give full expression to the views of Indian Muslims with reference to the settlement that should be made with Turkey at the close of the War, and to see that the rights of the caliphate, together with the sanctity of the Jazīrat-ul-Arab (the peninsula of Arabia) were not violated. More recently this organization has functioned in connexion with the sending of delegates to the Caliphate Congress, which was held by the *'ulamā* of the Azhar University, in Cairo, in May, 1926, and to the Muslim World Congress, at Mecca, in July of the same year. The work of the Khilāfat Committee would seem to have been finished with the abolition of the Turkish caliphate in 1924, but it still continues to exist, with its main emphasis on the work of *tanẓīm*, or the more effective organization of the Muslims of India for the purpose of improving their educational and economic condition, and of guarding communal interests in every particular.

The Muslim Woman and Modern Movements

The ferment of the modern world is also noticeable behind the *purdah*. Although Indian Muslim women are literate only to the extent of one-half of one per cent of the total female part of the community, yet there is a marked effort for reform among them. In 1914, the All-India Muslim Ladies' Conference was organized, and held its first meeting. Since then meetings have been held annually in various centres. Provincial conferences are also held, and these, together with the All-India Conference, are doing much to educate Muslim public opinion in regard to the improvement of the condition of women.

Though no marked changes in Muslim society as a whole are yet noticeable, advances are certainly being made. The problems of polygamy, divorce and the *purdah* are certainly being faced. At the All-India Conference, in 1924, a resolution was passed which declared against the marriage of girls to men already married. Little by little, also, the *purdah* system is being forced aside. The number of educated Muslim women who are coming out of seclusion, to mix freely yet modestly in general society, is slowly but steadily increasing. There is a vast amount of prejudice to overcome, and, as there is no Mustafa Kemal Pasha to force the pace, no doubt it will require much time yet before any marked difference is apparent.

Strange to say, one of the most pronounced adherents of the *purdah* system (though under protest) is also one of the most vigorous leaders in the cause of women. I refer to Her Highness the Dowager Begam of Bhopal. This remarkable lady's life is a notable example in this respect. She has introduced educational and social reforms for women in her own state; she has served with distinction as Chancellor of the Muslim University, Aligarh; and in the early part of last year (1928), she was the first president of the newly-organized All-India Woman's Conference, where she gave her whole-hearted support to the cause of primary education for girls.

Even with the enormous handicaps placed around them, some Indian Muslim women are beginning to enter different fields of activity. In Lahore the *Tahdhīb-un-Niswān*, a journal for women, and *Phūl*, for children, are both edited by women. Aside from journalism, which claims but a small group, by far the larger number of educated Muslim women are engaged in educational work, a few are engaged in the practice of medicine, and some are nurses. In 1924 a Muslim woman was appointed an honorary magistrate in Bombay.

The Muslim Press

Another direct outcome of the influence of the west on Islam in India is seen in the rapid development of journalism and the Press, mostly within the last fifty years. Journalism was started, in a modern way at least, by an Englishman in Calcutta in the year 1780. However, even as late as 1858, after the close of the Mutiny, there were only 19 Anglo-Indian papers and 25 Indian papers.[1]

As compared with these figures for all India, which applied seventy years ago, the Muslim Press has made astounding progress. To-day the Indian Muslim Press alone publishes no less than 238 periodicals. It employs 10 languages, and has presses in 67 different towns and cities. The languages used in the order of importance may be indicated as follows:

Language	*No. of periodicals*	*Language*	*No. of periodicals*
Urdū	 165	Malayālam	 5
English	 18	Sindhī	 3
Gujarātī	 17	Hindī	 1
Bengālī	 9	Arabic	 1
Tamil	 7	Persian	 1

Besides these there are a number of bi-lingual periodicals, usually combining English with a vernacular. Of the 67 places where presses are at work there are six which can boast of ten or more publications. Lahore leads the list with 56; then follows Bombay with 17; Calcutta, 16; Madras, 11; Amritsar, 10; and Lucknow, 10.[2]

From the above résumé of the statistics it will be readily seen that the Press has been the handmaid of the Muslim awakening in India, of which the Aligarh Movement was the progenitor. No 'movement' or organization can long exist without its 'official organ'. Sir Syed set the example by establishing his own Press at Ghazipur in connexion with his Scientific Society, in 1863, and by issuing from Aligarh, on his return from England in 1870, the well-known *Tahdhīb-ul-Akhlāq* (Social Reformer). Since that time the Muslim Press has developed a ceaseless and ever-increasing activity.

The Press covers every phase of activity and thought among Muslims, and admirably serves their need. The publications may

[1] *The Indian Year Book*, 1928: The Times Press, Bombay, 606.

[2] The above statistics have been furnished me by the Rev. William Paton, formerly secretary of the National Christian Council for India, who secured them from the Indian Government's Public Information Department (see Appendix for complete list).

be classed as follows: the communal or political group, which is by far the largest of all; the religious journals, which serve the different sects, including the purely propaganda publications; the literary group; the social reform group; the women's and children's group; and the scientific group, which is the smallest of all. In the long list found in the Appendix there are dailies, weeklies, monthlies and quarterlies, the foremost daily being the one in English, the *Muslim Outlook* of Lahore.

There are three characteristics of the Muslim Press in India which deserve consideration. On the whole it is progressive and forward-looking. It sees a changing world around it, and the pressure of necessity is developing a more progressive editorial outlook. The *mullā* (priestly) mind is becoming less and less evident. Reform movements in Turkey, intellectual ferment as a result of modern education, a new spiritual awakening, economic pressure, the abolition of the Turkish caliphate, the feminist movement and the nationalist agitation in India have all compelled the editors to look to the future.

Secondly, the Press is frankly communal. It gives hearty support to the policy of communal electorates, without which it feels as a community the Muslims would be greatly handicapped. It is not always innocent, either, of promoting strife, though some sections of the Press are passionate advocates of Hindu-Muslim unity.

Thirdly, the Press is religious. A truly secular paper or magazine can hardly be found. After all, this but reflects the remarkable nature of Islam in that it not only claims to dominate, but succeeds in dominating, all departments of life. In a certain sense, the object which dominates editorial thinking in the Muslim Press is one, and one only. It is Islam. In the words of the *Islamic World*, an English quarterly of Lahore, this object is expressed thus: 'to propagate and defend Islam against its hostile critics, and to study the progress of Islamic thought, art and civilization in the world'.

Conclusion

The last century and a quarter has seen a revolution in Islamic thought and life in India which very faithfully corresponds to the influences which have been at work throughout the Muslim world as a whole. Stirred at first by resentment at non-Muslim rule and the puritanical influence of Wahhābism, there was a strong reactionary movement which threatened permanently to block all progress and keep the Muslim community locked behind doors of ignorance and an effete mediævalism. Then came the awakening, brought about by the leadership of men who had the prophetic vision for the new day which modern science had ushered into the world. It is safe to say that the Muslim community of India owes a debt of gratitude to its 'apostle of reconciliation', Sir Syed Aḥmad Khāṇ, which it will never be able fully to repay. What the future holds no one knows, but there can be no doubt that it should express its gratitude by seeking to realize as completely as possible all the benefits he sought to secure for his people by laying the foundations of the University at Aligarh.

It can hardly be said that any have exceeded him in his broad sympathies for all his fellow-countrymen and their religions; and it is to be seriously doubted if any have equalled him in his attempts at a scientific, historical investigation of the basis of Islam. The hopes that Sir Syed raised in this direction have been sadly disappointed, for Aligarh to-day seems to rest content with the accepted orthodoxy of the time. Nevertheless, however much the Muslim University may fail to realize the hopes that were raised of advancing the cause of research in religion, it is, without doubt, the greatest single influence that exists for progress and the enlightenment of Muslim India.

CHAPTER X

THE NEW MUSLIM APOLOGETIC AND POLEMIC

In no phase of Indian Muslim life has contact with the west produced a more marked change than in the realm of religious thought. Some attention has already been paid to this; but we have still to consider it in detail, and to show what the new Muslim apologetic and polemic are. In the first place, it may be said that the change consists in a new attitude of mind rather than in a new system of thought. This changed attitude has been conditioned entirely by modern scientific, social, and economic influences. It has arisen out of the force of circumstances which were clearly threatening Islam not only from without but from within. The prophets of the movement have all along seen that Islam could not be modernized in any secular fashion without serious danger that its modernized adherents would abandon the faith, unless it could likewise be rationalized in keeping with the discoveries of modern scientific truth and modern social requirements. They had come to see that Islam, as understood and expounded by the orthodox formalists, would not long continue to have an appeal for a Muslim with a university degree. The time had arrived for a break, not with Islam itself, but with its traditionalist exponents, 'who have degraded the religion by paying undue attention to formulas and forms, to the exclusion and neglect of its living spirit and reality'.[1] In addition, two other reasons may be mentioned which have stirred men to produce a new apologetic—one being the need to defend Islam against the criticisms of modern Hindu and Christian writers, and the other a desire to make Islam attractive to non-Muslims, particularly to Christians of western countries.

Attempts at a Rationalistic Interpretation of Islam

The 'modernists', who have laboured with great pains to give what they call a scientific interpretation of Islam, belong to a school

[1] Sir Aḥmad Ḥussain, *Notes on Islam*, 12.

of thought that has been variously designated as *Necharī* (i.e. according to Nature) and *neo-Mu'tazilite.* The first name was given because of the extensive use made of the term 'nature' by Sir Syed Aḥmad Kh̲āṇ and his successors, in their attempt to show that Islam, rightly understood, is, of all the religions of the world, the most in accord with the nature of man, and Nature in the scientific sense. The second term is used by certain persons to describe the followers of the movement, as they resemble a group of rationalistic Islamic theologians of the eighth century A.D., called Mu'tazilites, who revolted against the current orthodox teachings of their day.

The problem that confronted the pioneers in this modernist movement was a perplexing one indeed. Sir Syed Aḥmad Kh̲āṇ, who was the first to move in this, as in all other directions of reform, was a stout defender of the faith as it had been delivered to Muḥammad and his companions. All his reading and contacts with the west had never for a moment shaken his belief in the fundamental truth of Islam. Nevertheless, he was convinced that a radical reform in theology was as necessary as in education and society. So he began by preaching and writing in favour of a return to Muḥammad and the Qur'ān for a new interpretation, and setting forth the first principles of the religion of Islam. This, in fact, is the plea of all the modernists. They all agree that the 'Islam of Muḥammad', the 'Islam of the Qur'ān', is without blemish and without spot, and that 'its genuine and chief principles are in perfect harmony' with Nature and reason.

Further, they maintain that Islam is not only the most rational religion, but it is the universal religion that was proclaimed by all the prophets of mankind, and, as such, is offered to all men everywhere. In fact, the belief is often expressed that, in accordance with the Qur'ānic text, all nations have had their prophets and have been given divine revelations in sacred books; and, on this assumption, it is not considered improper to speak of the Hindu incarnations, Rām and Kṛishṇa, as among the prophets, and to pray for God's peace upon them when mentioning them.[1]

Others are inclined to go still further, and say that Islam is but

[1] 'Ināyat Allāh Kh̲āṇ, *Tadh̲kirah,* I, Dībāchah, 63.

one of *many* true religions in the world, and 'observe that most Muḥammadans of to-day have forgotten this principle, and have therefore become intolerant fanatics'.[1] This writer goes on to say that he would not object to calling all who believe in one God *Muslims*, whether they be Jews, Christians or theistic Hindus, but only those are *Mu'mins* (believers in the Islamic sense) who believe that Muḥammad is the messenger of God.[2] Finally, he insists that there is:

> No inherent antagonism between Christianity and Islam, if and when the sayings and doings of the founders of each are rightly viewed and understood in a simple and natural manner. Muḥammad never ceased saying that he had come to attest and complete the mission of Jesus and His predecessors, who were God's messengers like himself. The greatest and the best rule of human conduct which Jesus laid down was, 'Love thy neighbour as thyself'. This is quite consistent with human nature, and is the most comprehensive rule of conduct which has ever been laid down for the guidance of mankind. To my mind, there is no better proof of the identity in spirit of Christianity and Islam than the confirmation of Christ's command by Muḥammad himself. 'No one will be a faithful Muslim until he loves his neighbour as he loves himself.' For this reason, I believe that there is no difference between the two religions, if the metaphysical doctrines engrafted on both be eliminated. Thus Islam is but true Christianity writ short. Both recognize that the source of virtue is love.[3]

The Rt. Hon. Syed Amīr 'Alī also sums up his position by saying that, except for the conception of the divine sonship of Jesus, no fundamental difference exists between Christianity and Islam.[4]

The New Emphasis on Muḥammad

A new emphasis is being placed to-day on the character of the Prophet of Islam, and a process of idealization is going on which represents him as the perfect model for mankind (*insān-ul-kāmil*). This is not only at variance with the historical 'lives', such as that of Ibn Hishām, but even to the express statements of Muḥammad himself, as set forth in the Qur'ān, where he asks forgiveness for his own sins. The whole purpose of this new effort would seem to be to offset the character of the 'sinless Christ of Christianity', as well as to arouse a new enthusiasm for

[1] Sir Aḥmad Ḥussain, *Notes on Islam*, 30. [2] *Ibid.*, 32. [3] *Ibid.*, 84.

[4] Syed Amīr 'Alī, *The Life and Teachings of Muḥammad*, 282.

Islam by recognizing that religion thrives best when it can lay claim to a person in whom centre all the highest spiritual and moral values, and around whom loyal followers can rally. In the new apologetic it is no longer the Qur'ān and the Sharī'at (*the Law*) to which men are called, but to Muḥammad himself.

The Prophet is pictured as tender-hearted, and as abolishing the atrocities of War. He was gentle and merciful even to his greatest enemies. In him were combined the highest attributes that the human mind can conceive: justice and mercy.[1] Muḥammad was believed in by his wife and nearest relatives, on the other hand, Jesus' brothers never believed in Him, and even His immediate disciples were not firm in their belief;[2] also, his preaching was equal to that of Isaiah or Jesus.[3] If Jesus had a triumphal entry, so did Muḥammad. 'Thus at length', says Syed Amīr 'Alī, 'Muḥammad entered Mecca as a conqueror. He who was a fugitive and persecuted now came to prove his mission by deeds of mercy. The city which had treated him so cruelly, driven him and his faithful band for refuge amongst strangers, which had sworn to take his life and the lives of his devoted disciples, lay at his feet. His old persecutors, relentless and ruthless, who had disgraced humanity by inflicting cruel outrages upon the inoffensive men and women, even upon the lifeless dead, were now completely at his mercy. But in the hour of triumph every evil suffered was forgotten, every injury inflicted was forgiven, and a general amnesty was extended to the population of Mecca. Only four criminals, "whom justice condemned", made up Muḥammad's proscription list when he entered as a conqueror the city of his bitterest enemies. The army followed his example, and entered gently and peaceably; no house was robbed, no woman insulted. Most truly has it been said that, through all the annals of conquest, there has been no triumphant entry like this one.'[4]

Furthermore, Muḥammad is considered superior to Jesus because he offered no materialistic miracles to prove his mission.

> Whereas the disciples of Jesus, with their materialistic sceptism, were always asking for miracles, it must be said to the credit of the disciples of

[1] Syed Amīr 'Alī, *The Spirit of Islam*, 158, 178. [2] *Ibid.*, 96.
[3] *Ibid.*, 254. [4] *Ibid.*, 192, 193.

the Arabian teacher that they never called for a miracle from their Master. They looked rather for the moral evidences of his mission.[1]

Still another proof of this superiority of Muḥammad is found in the fact that he was more practical than Jesus. Jesus' teaching was too visionary and idealistic, and so far above the natural instincts and moral and spiritual possibilities in man that it was doomed to failure; on the other hand, 'in Islam is joined a lofty idealism with the most rationalistic practicality, . . . which does not ignore human nature'.[2] Jesus gave no systematic teaching to the world and did not bring His work to completion. Muḥammad did both. The systematic teachings and ritual in Islam are a mark of superiority, the absence of which in Christianity, as given by Jesus, is a defect. Muḥammad came to finish the work which Jesus left unsystematized. 'Jesus produced no visible effect on the Jews to whom He came; but it was reserved for Muḥammad to fulfil his mission and that of his predecessors.'[3] In this connexion, also, it is alleged that Jesus' mission was national, and only to the 'lost sheep of the house of Israel', while Muḥammad's mission was to all the world.[4] In short, Muḥammad's life is regarded as incomparable in respect of its purity and truth.[5]

A large share of the new apologetic and polemic is concerned, too, with the justification or rationalistic explanation of some of the teachings of Islam, which, in the light of modern developments, seemed to demand a new interpretation. Among these the most important are the following.

The Doctrine of Abrogation

It is commonly held that the doctrine of *Nāsikh* and *Mansūkh* (the abrogator and the abrogated) is applied to the abrogation of former scriptures by the Qur'ān, and to the abrogation of one verse of the Qur'ān by a verse that was revealed later. The modern apologist for Islam takes the position so well expressed by Sir Syed Aḥmad Khāṇ, who says:

[1] *Ibid.*, 102, 103. [2] *Ibid.*, 278. [3] *Ibid.*, 273, 19, 211.

[4] See Muḥammad 'Alī, *Muḥammad or Christ*.

[5] Syed Amīr 'Alī, op. cit., 219, 221.

> It is a religious duty of Muḥammadans to believe that God is omniscient—that is, that He has a perfect knowledge of all that is past, present and to come; therefore were we to understand by *Nāsikh* and *Mansūkh* that God, for some cause or other, cancelled a former Revelation by a later one, we should be implying that, at the time of the first Revelation, God had lost His power of omniscience, which opinion, according to Islam, savours of infidelity . . . (therefore) these expressions are not applied by Muḥammadan divines to the loss of preceding prophets.

Nor do they apply to the Qur'ān in the sense in which they are often taken.

> There are to be found in the Qur'ān, and in the sayings of the Prophet, commandments relating to one and the same matter, but under different circumstances; and when one of those circumstances no longer remains the commandment relating thereto does not remain in force, while the commandment which is intended to meet the altered circumstance then comes into operation; the former commandment being called *Mansūkh* (the cancelled), and the subsequent one *Nāsikh* (the canceller). This, however, by no means implies that the former commandment was in any way defective, but that, the circumstance to which it was applicable has ceased to exist, and consequently that the commandment itself ceases to be in force; but that, should the same circumstance again present itself the same commandment will again come into operation, and that the one which was subsequent to it will then, in its turn, cease.[1]

Islam a Religion of Peace

Islam is presented as the religion of peace, toleration, charity, and brotherhood. The verse most often quoted in support of this position is, 'Let there be no compulsion in religion'.[2] Proselytism by the sword is held by some to be wholly contrary to the instincts of Muḥammad; nor did Islam consecrate slavery, but rather proclaimed the natural equality of all human beings.[3]

Islam and Woman

One of the frequent assertions made by those who seek to justify the position of woman in Islam is that she occupies a place far superior to that in any other religion. It is held, also, that the teaching of the Qur'ān in respect of polygamy is to be justified on

[1] Sir Syed Aḥmad Khāṇ, *Essays on the Life of Muḥammad, On the Qur'ān*, 19 ff.

[2] *Sūrah*, II, 257. [3] Syed Amīr 'Alī, op. cit., 306, 379

the grounds that it is a rational attempt to meet the needs of human society, which outside Islamic circles is met by more or less legalized forms of prostitution. As opposed to this, others with more advanced views frankly admit that 'polygamy in the present day is an adulterous connexion, and is contrary to the Spirit of Islam—an opinion which is shared by a large number of Moslems'.[1] Nevertheless, they are faced with the fact that provision for polygamy occurs in the Qur'ān. But in reference to this it has become common to point out that the essential teaching of the Qur'ān is monogamous, for, while the law permits a man to take four wives, it is strictly on the condition that he can deal justly with all of them. Since it is a practical impossibility to deal fairly with four at one time, it must be assumed that the essential meaning of the Qur'ān is that a man should have but one wife. But there are others who view the position of woman in Islam with considerable concern, and it is through such bold and fearless souls that the way seems to be opening up for extended reforms, and the real improvement of Islamic society. Prof. K͟hudā Bak͟hsh takes contemporary reformers to task, and makes them face the facts. Criticizing the shallowness of the 'moderate' position, he says in all fearlessness:

> The author of *Reforms under Muslim Rule* seeks to make out that polygamy is an institution which Islam does not sanction, but I am not quite sure that he is right. At all events, the unanimity and concensus of opinion is the other way. It may, with growth of education and freedom of women, die out, but the question which we must decide, and that once for all, is whether it is an institution compatible with present-day notions. Is this institution to be retained or done away with? Is it conducive to the interests of society, or otherwise? If the general sense of the Muḥammadan world condemns it as pernicious to the stability, happiness, comfort and peace of the family, let it be expunged from our law. If it approves it, retain it by all means. I do not believe in the argument, constantly put forward, that the conditions which the Qur'ān imposes upon its practice are too difficult of realization, and as such, according to the strict letter of the law, the practice cannot be supported or sustained. But this is no answer to the question raised here. Is the institution *per se* good or bad? Is it beneficial to the interest, or subversive of the well-being, of society? There can be no two opinions on this point. To our mind, the social corruption behind the *zenana* is to a large extent due to this system.[2]

[1] *Ibid.*, 365. S. K͟hudā Bak͟hsh, *Essays, Indian and Islamic*, 253 ff.
[2] *Ibid.* 256.

The above writer deals no less firmly with the problem of Islamic divorce, and joins hands with Sir Muḥammad Iqbāl in demanding a radical change in the treatment of women in this respect. With a sense of inward shame he declares, 'In eastern Bengal divorce is the order of the day, and wives are put away as we cast off our old clothes. . . . No judicial inquiry, no positive proof, not a tittle of evidence of any sort is needed. The lord of creation is invested with the power of divorce, and he makes full and free use of it.'[1] Dr. Iqbāl at the same time asserts that the only way in which a woman can get rid of a scapegrace of a husband is by becoming an apostate.[2]

All of this comes perilously near to throwing away the Qur'ān as a guide for social legislation. Though there may be but few who would follow him all the way, still it is worth while for us to consider again the words of Prof. Khudā Bakhsh on this subject, for he is one of a small but ever-growing group of Muslims who are hopefully trying to find their way out of the present social-religious entanglement of their community. This keen student writes:

> With all our reverence and devotion to our religion, we do not believe that the moral and other laws are to be learned by experience and observation, but solely by the study of the Qur'ān and the practice of the Prophet. This view I hold to be utterly unsupported by our religion. . . . and that it is a wholly unfounded doctrine, without any religious basis or sanction for it.[3]

He goes on to plead for full freedom of thought, and for a modern use of the Qur'ān as a source of inspiration and as a devotional manual.

[1] *Ibid.*, 258.

[2] It should be noted, however, that there is a permissible form of divorce which the wife may take advantage of, known as *khul'*. A Muslim magistrate friend of mine gives his opinion regarding the subject of divorce as follows: 'The defect at present lies in the prevalent code of civil laws, where the provision for *khul'* has not been kept up. Also, if the proper restrictions were imposed, as laid down by the Law of Islam, viz. if the dowry (*mahr*) were really given to the woman, or vice versa, if the responsibility to support a pregnant divorced wife and the issue were enforced, and if the right of the issue to inherit property were recognized, as they should be where true Islamic conditions prevail, then the number of divorces would come down very low.'

[3] S. Khudā Bakhsh, op. cit., 281.

The Idealism of Iqbāl

Perhaps the most inspiring of all the modernists in Indian Islam is the poet-philosopher Sir Muḥammad Iqbāl, who has delivered a message to his co-religionists that has produced a profound impression. In his writings, notably the *Asrār-i-khudī* (Secrets of the Self), he has sought to combine in unique fashion the teaching of the Qur'ān with the philosophies of Bergson and Nietzsche. The key-note of his philosophy is the development of personality, which he asserts can best be realized by going 'back to the Qur'ān'. With bitter scorn he denounces the inactivity and aloofness from the world of the Ṣūfī saints and mystics. His Ideal Man will not be absorbed in God, but will himself overcome the world, and absorb the qualities of God, and so save mankind. The Prophet of Islam was one whose radiance of soul exceeded all poetic fancies, for he it was who succeeded in transforming the whole world by the sublimity of his ideals. By thus setting forth the possibility of individual regeneration, and the development of the highest type of personality, by means of the exercise of will and the fulfilling of man's highest possibilities, as revealed in the Qur'ān and by the Prophet Muḥammad, he has made a powerful appeal to the younger generation of Muslims, who see in him one of the worthiest successors of the revered Sir Syed Aḥmad Khāṇ.

The Modernists and Higher Criticism of the Qur'ān

In the foregoing analysis of the modern apologetic for Islam which has been attempted, it will strike the critical observer as curious that we have made no mention of any disposition on the part of Muslims themselves to undertake the difficult task of higher criticism of the Qur'ān, or to make an inquiry into the vexed question of revelation and the authority of the Prophet Muḥammad. When Sir Syed Aḥmad Khāṇ, with his liberal views on religion, began to make his investigations in Qur'ānic and Biblical studies, it was thought that possibly a new day had dawned, and that Indian Muslims themselves would seriously undertake the historical and scientific criticism of the bases of their religion. But nothing of any consequence seems to have developed. It is true that Prof. Khudā Bakhsh freely admits the debt of Islam to

Christianity, Judaism, and Pre-Islamic Arabia, and he holds that Islam was thus developed by Muḥammad into an eclectic system. Syed Amīr 'Alī makes bold to state that the Qur'ān is the product of the mind of Muḥammad, and reflects the processes of development of his religious consciousness.[1] Another of like mind, in speaking of the Qur'ān, calls it 'a collection of sermons, commands and instructions, delivered and issued from time to time as occasion required . . . and you have to interpret the Qur'ān quite naturally as any other book or historic document.[2] But for the most part the modernists leave the question of revelation (*waḥy*) and the authority of the Prophet strictly alone, and take it that these are beyond the scope or necessity of legitimate criticism and investigation. Sir Syed Aḥmad Khān frankly admits that he considers the orthodox position in regard to the revelation of the Qur'ān and the authority of Muḥammad perfectly sound and according to Nature and Reason. Finally, Maulvī Muḥammad 'Alī, of Lahore, who has brought out such an elaborate commentary on the Qur'ān in English, fails to face these questions squarely, in spite of the fact that he claims to be thoroughly modern and scientific in his scholastic labours.[3]

The truth is that, while the investigators of religious truth among Muslims may be perfectly sincere in their endeavours to make their investigations with an impartial mind, they have as yet been unable wholly to throw off the psychological bias in favour of certain views, and to approach the subject from a purely scientific view-point. The result is that, however much they may try to avoid doing so, they give the impression that their conclusions have been reached before the investigation was made. So, in the end, the writings of all lead to the conclusion expressed by Syed Amīr 'Alī, that

> The Islam of Muḥammad contains nothing which in itself bars the progress of the intellectual development of humanity. The wonderful adaptability of the Islamic precepts to all ages and nations; their entire concordance with the light of reason; the absence of all mysterious doctrines to cast

[1] *The Spirit of Islam*, 398, 399.

[2] Sir Aḥmad Ḥussain, op. cit., 39, 83.

[3] Maulvī Muḥammad 'Ali, *Translation of the Holy Qur'ān*, Lahore, 1920, 940, 941.

a shade of sentimental ignorance round the primal truths implanted in the human breast—all prove that Islam represents the latest development of the religious faculties of our being.[1]

This, then, is the end of the matter, and, since this conclusion represents the sound and reasoned judgment of the learned leaders of Indian Islam, there is nothing more to be said; and for the Muslim doubts and questionings are altogether out of place. One cannot help wondering, however, judging from the intellectual ferment and spiritual unrest which is stirring Christendom, and some parts of the Muslim world, just how long the new wine of intellectual freedom and honest, scientific inquiry can be contained in the old Islamic bottles. One may be pardoned for thinking that, ultimately, either the bottles will burst or the new wine will grow stale.

The Aḥmadīyah Movement

Along with the development of these intellectual and rationalizing tendencies in the Muslim community, a wholly new sect has arisen, which centres around the person and teaching of Mīrzā Ghulām Aḥmad.[2] The 'movement' represents a reaction to the naturalistic interpretations of Islam as set forth by the Aligarh reformers, while at the same time repudiating the authority of the orthodox *mullā*. Over against the claims of both, Mīrzā sets his own personal claims to be the correct interpreter of Islam for the present age, to which he brings a new message. It is this 'message' of Aḥmad and his followers that constitutes a very distinct contribution to the new Muslim apologetic and polemic which we are now considering, since the Aḥmadīs are at present the most active propagandists of Islam in the world.

The founder of the Aḥmadīyah Movement, Mīrzā Ghulām Aḥmad, was born in Qadian, a small town of the Punjab, in the year 1839. He belonged to a respectable Mughul family, which traces its migration into India from the time of Bābur, in the sixteenth century. He received a good education in Muslim languages and sciences, and, some time before the year 1880, he

[1] *The Spirit of Islam*, 639, 275.

[2] For a thorough study of the movement see *The Aḥmadīya Movement*, H. A. Walter. Association Press, Calcutta, 1918.

evidently came to the conclusion that he was called to undertake a special divine mission. However, it was not until 1889 that he announced that he had been the recipient of a divine revelation, which made it lawful for him formally to initiate followers or disciples. From this time onward he began to formulate and declare his new doctrines with a boldness and determination that brooked no opposition.

Aḥmad sought to base his claims on the Muslim prophecies concerning the appearance of the Messiah and the Imām Mahdī, whom Muslims look for at the approach of the last day. The Jews still look for the coming of the Messiah, and Christians and Muslims anticipate His second coming. Further, he maintained that the scriptures of the Zoroastrians, the Hindus, and Buddhists, all prophesied the coming of a great World Teacher. So Aḥmad began to declare himself as the one in whom the hopes of all peoples and nations were to be fulfilled. Further, he insisted that, in keeping with the Islamic tradition that God is supposed to send a special individual to be a 'renewer' (*mujaddid*) to restore the faith of Islam at the beginning of each century, Mīrzā Ghulām Aḥmad had all the divine marks of being the *mujaddid* for the fourteenth century of the Islamic era.

The arguments advanced to support these unique claims, together with the interpretation thereof, are set forth in voluminous writings by the Promised Messiah himself, as well as by certain of his followers. Since his chief emphasis is placed on the fact of his being the Promised Messiah, we shall first consider this aspect of his teaching.

The Promised Messiah

According to his calculations, six millenniums have elapsed since the birth of Adam, and at the beginning of the seventh millennium it has been prophesied God would raise up a man in the likeness of Adam who would be called Messiah. 'The Promises of God, therefore, make it absolutely necessary that the second Adam must have been born already, though not recognized as yet by the world.' Further, he was convinced that he must be the Messiah of prophecy, since this second Adam must appear in the East, and thus he resembled the first in respect of his locality.[1] Also, 'earthquakes, plague, famine, wars, and terrestrial as well as heavenly phenomena, bear witness to the one fact that there is to be no more waiting for the Messiah's advent'.[2] Among these signs which bore witness to his claim were a solar and lunar eclipse, which occurred in the month of Ramaḍān, 1894, corruption of Muslim *mullās*, the neglect of the Qur'ān, and the splitting of Islam into sects.

Having thus satisfied himself that the outward conditions of prophecy were fulfilled for the appearance of the Promised Messiah, it became necessary to explain in what sense he could lay claim to that high distinction. Here he fell back on divine revelation, on which, in fact, he rested his whole claim as a 'messenger of the latter days'. Thus he asserted that he had not come in the person of Jesus, but only in His 'spirit and power'. To make good this assertion, it became necessary to attack the doctrine current among Muslims, as well as Christians, that Jesus Himself would return as the Messiah. This belief must be set aside; otherwise his claim to Messiahship would be presumptuous. The whole question turned on the post-mortem existence of Jesus. Aḥmad set out to prove that Jesus did not die on the cross, though, contrary to the Qur'ānic text, he admitted He was crucified. He held that He merely swooned away, and that His wounds were completely healed, after He was taken down from the cross, by the application of the *marham-i-'Isā* (the Jesus ointment), the ingredients of which were divinely revealed to the disciples; which preparation is being sold to-day by the followers of Aḥmad at Qadian. After forty days' sojourn with the disciples, Jesus came to Afg͟hānistān and Kashmir on a mission to their inhabitants, whom Aḥmad claims are the ten lost tribes of Israel.[3]

Aḥmad sought to prove that Jesus died a natural death and was buried in Kashmir. In support of his contention, he claims to have discovered His grave. The tomb which Aḥmad's followers assert is the grave of Jesus is to be found in K͟hāṇ Yār Street, Srinagar, Kashmir, and bears the inscription of one Yūs

[1] *Review of Religions*, I, 15. [2] *Ibid.*, III, 397.
[3] H. A. Walter, *The Aḥmadīya Movement*, 90 f.

Āṣaf, who is worshipped as a Muslim saint. In fact, it is more than probable that the tomb is not even that of a Muslim, but is only a shrine of Buddhist origin. Nevertheless, from the name alone, he made his deductions to suit his case. Yūs was a corruption of Yasū', the Arabic name of Jesus, and Āṣaf he took to be the same as the Hebrew *asaf*, which signifies gathering, which he insisted referred to Jesus' mission as 'Gatherer' of the ten lost tribes. The ascended Jesus of the Muslims and Christians being thus set aside through the 'proof' of His natural death, and the 'discovery' of His last resting-place, the one great obstacle to the justifying of his new doctrine of the appearance of the Mahdī-Messiah, messenger of the latter days, was cleared away, for it was obvious that a dead Messiah could not possibly come with power from on high.[1]

The Mahdī

The Aḥmadīyah conception of the Mahdī doctrine of Islam is as unique as that of the Messiah; and, like the former, is based on the underlying assumption that all such appearances, prophesied in all religions whatsoever, are but manifestations of God's power to raise up 'Renewers' of religion from age to age, and that He has not left any nation without a prophet. This Aḥmad was constantly asserting. He took the view that the references in the Qur'ān to prophecies to the coming of the Messiah, the Prophet, and the Mahdī all referred to the same person, and that he was the person in whom all converged. As Promised Messiah he claimed to come in the 'spirit and power of Jesus', and that in a spiritual sense he and Jesus were one; so in the capacity of Mahdī he regarded himself as 'the second advent of our Lord Muḥammad', and as 'an image of the Holy Prophet'. But the Mahdī of orthodox Islam is to be a man of war whose path is red with the blood of unbelievers, while Aḥmad was a man of peace. So he declared that 'under existing circumstances' the only *jihād* (holy war) allowable was spiritual, he advocated the utmost loyalty to the British Government, and refused to support the political policies of the All-India Muslim League.

[1] *Ibid.*, 93 ff.

The World Messenger of the Latter Days

To be a messenger for all the world, and to fulfil the prophecy of the coming of a great World Teacher who should unite people of all faiths and countries, it was necessary to seek refuge in further revelation, which he said was given to him as follows:

> He has told me, not on one occasion but repeatedly, that so I am Kṛishṇa for the Hindus and the Promised Messiah for the Muḥammadans and the Christians . . . this is a revelation from God which I cannot but announce, and this is the first day that I announce this claim in such a large gathering, for those who come from God do not fear being blamed or reviled. Now Rājā Kṛishṇa was revealed to me as so great and perfect a man that his equal is not to be found among the Hindu *rishīs* and *avatārs*. . . . Spiritually Kṛishṇa and the Promised Messiah are one and the same person, there being no difference except that which exists in the terminology of the two people, Hindu and Muḥammadan.[1]

To-day his followers regard him as 'the Messenger for all nations', and the fulfilment of all ancient prophecies.[2]

Reformer or Prophet

In addition to the usual terminology employed by Aḥmad to designate his mission as Mahdī-Messiah, further interpretation of his nature and functions are set forth in the fifth and last two articles of the Creed of the Aḥmadī community[3] as follows:

> The door of inspiration has always been, and will always be, open, and no attribute of God ever became useless. As He used to hold communion with His good servants, so He does even now, and will continue to do up to the end of the world.

It is on this belief that Aḥmad rests his claim to having been the recipient of divine revelation, which is clearly understood by him as *ilhām* (inspiration or subjective revelation), for he seems to have made no claim to having received revelation in the Qur'ānic sense of *waḥy*, or objective revelation, such as that by which the Qur'ān was held to have been revealed to Muḥammad. Nevertheless, he regarded the revelations he received through *ilhām* as having real and objective validity, on which he sought to base his whole claim to being the manifestation (*burūz*) of

[1] *Review of Religions*, III, 411.

[2] *The Holy Qur'ān*, English tr., Qadian, 1915, pt. I (B).

[3] *Condition of Bay'at*, a pamphlet published by the Aḥmadī Community, Qadian, setting forth the conditions of membership.

both the spirit and power of Jesus, Muḥammad, Kṛishṇa, and, in short, of the divine spirit.

To continue the quotation:

> We believe among his (Muḥammad's) followers reformers (*mujaddid*) have appeared, and will continue to appear, with spiritual knowledge of a very high order. Not only this, but a man can even gain prophethood by the help of our Lord Muḥammad's spiritual powers. But no prophet with a new book, or having been appointed direct, will ever come; for in this case it would be an insult to the perfect prophethood of our Lord, and this is the meaning of the seal of the prophets, and in this sense the Lord has, on the one hand, said, 'There is no prophet (i.e. an independent prophet or prophet with a new law) after me', and, on the other hand, has called the coming Messiah a prophet (*nabī*) of God.
>
> According to this we believe that a man, the Promised Messiah, has gained prophethood in spite of his being a follower of our Lord. . . .

In the above articles of faith is set forth not only the grounds for accepting Aḥmad as a reformer, but even in some sense as a prophet. He is regarded as standing in the same relation to Muḥammad as Jesus did to Moses, and, as Jesus brought the Mosaic dispensation to a close, 'similarly the Muḥammadan dispensation has been consummated in the person of Mīrzā Ghulām Aḥmad of Qadian'.[1] He not only claimed that God supported his mission with evidentiary miracles, as in the case of former prophets, but he plainly asserted his superiority to Jesus, whom, of course, he regarded as one of the prophets. The claim to prophethood ultimately came to be a cause of division in the ranks after the founder's death, one party regarding him only as a *mujaddid* (reformer), but the other still asserting that his character and mission were in some sense those of a prophet.

Relation of the Movement to Orthodox Islam

The movement initiated by Mīrzā Ghulām Aḥmad occupies a unique position, in relation to both the orthodox party and the rationalistic reformers represented by Sir Syed Aḥmad Khāṇ and his neo-Mu'tazilite followers. Aḥmad himself declaimed bitterly against the professional *mullās* of Islam, who kept the people in darkness, who had allowed Islam to die of formalism, who had not prevented the division into sects. He deplored the popular worship of saints, and set himself as a true reformer to restore

[1] *The Holy Qur'ān*, tr., Qadian, 1915, pt. I, 35.

the true and unpolluted faith of Islam to the followers of the prophet. At the same time, he could not tolerate the rationalizing expositors of Islam, such as Syed Amīr 'Alī and Prof. S. Khudā Bakhsh, who were beginning to throw doubt on the Qur'ān, as a perfect work of divine revelation, in tracing some of the sources of Islam to pre-Islamic Arabia, Judaism, and even to Christianity. In regard to social reform, Aḥmad stood by the conservatives. He repudiated the abolition of *purdah*, and staunchly defended the Islamic law of divorce and polygamy, 'spurning any attempt within Islam to adapt Muḥammad's teaching and practice to present day customs in Christian lands'.[1] He frankly regarded Islam as the only religion 'which not only claims to be free from every error and falsehood, but also offers proof of this freedom from error'.[2]

Aḥmad and his followers earned the bitter enmity of the orthodox party, following such severe denunciation of the very people whom he had come to reform. He was branded a heretic, a blasphemer, and an enemy of the faith, as well as an impostor. Naturally, he was excommunicated, and from that time on he and his followers were forbidden the use of the ordinary mosques. Thenceforth he ordered his followers to pray under the leadership of Aḥmadī Imāms only, and where there were no Aḥmadī Imāms they should offer their prayers alone. No less than four Aḥmadī missionaries have suffered the penalty of death for heresy in the Muslim country of Afghānistān, the last two being in 1924, at which time the uncompromising attitude of the orthodox Muslims of India to the Aḥmadīs was shown by the fact that their leaders sent telegrams to the Amīr at Kabul expressing their approval of the measures he had taken in the interest of the faith.[3]

The Polemic

The Aḥmadī writers and preachers, from the time of Aḥmad down to the present, have distinguished themselves among Muslims by the virulence and vigour of the attack which they have made on the credibility of the Bible, the person of Jesus Christ,

[1] H. A. Walter, *The Aḥmadīya Movement*, 68.

[2] *Review of Religions*, III, 29.

[3] *The Muslim Outlook*, Lahore, September 24, 1914.

and the Christian Church. As this polemic is not only one of the most important, but one of the most interesting parts of the propaganda carried on by the *Anjuman*, it is necessary to give it some attention. In following up this point, it should be noted that extensive use has been made of the works of the 'higher critics' of certain extreme schools of thought in Germany and England; and that, without regard to actual historical values, selection of the authorities has been made solely to suit the purpose in hand, and the conclusions reached are always represented as the concensus of opinion of the best Christian scholarship of the day. This is the method *par excellence* used by Maulvī Muḥammad 'Alī in his book, *Muḥammad or Christ*, and by Khwājah Kamāl-ud-Dīn in his *Sources of Christianity*.

Against the Bible

As over against the Qur'ān, which is asserted to have been preserved from change by the miraculous protection of God, the Bible is held to be full of interpolations; and the Qur'ān, instead of confirming it, offers clear refutations of certain matters contained in the Christian scriptures. As, for instance,

> That the blind and leprous are impure; that Solomon was an idolater; that David became a prey to temptations; that Aaron joined in the worship of the calf out of fear of his people; that Jesus is the Son of God; that one person can bear the sins of others; that the law is a curse; that God feels tired or repentant; that He chose the Israelites for His special favours. In fact, there is quite a large number of beliefs and teachings in the Bible which the holy Qur'ān refutes by giving powerful arguments against them, and declares forcibly as being not revelations from God, but interpolations of man. In the face of such a forcible condemnation of a large number of Biblical doctrines, it is preposterous to think that the holy Qur'ān confirms the Bible, as it is before us to-day.[1]

Against Jesus Christ

The virgin birth is attacked in subtle fashion. No categorical denial is offered, but such statements as these: that Adam had neither father nor mother, that thousands of worms are brought into existence without any father, and that learned physicians of the Greek and Indian schools have shown the possibility of a child being formed in the mother's womb without the seed of man—all

[1] *The Holy Qur'ān*, tr., Qadian, 1915, pt. I, 38.

indicate that the doctrine is a futile one on which to base Christ's claims to divinity.[1]

The miracles of Jesus are denied, belittled, explained away by the 'neurotic theory', and sometimes admitted, apparently for the sake of argument. The verse, 'A wicked and adulterous generation seeketh after a sign, and there shall be no sign given unto it', is thus mutilated and quoted to prove that Jesus Himself denied having performed any miracles.[2] Such miracles as the turning of water into wine, the cursing of the fig tree, and the destruction of the herd of swine are cited as proofs of Jesus' lack of moral judgment.

The character and work of Jesus are challenged again and again by the Aḥmadī protagonists with such allegations as these, based on Bible references:

That He was given to drunkenness.

That He exceeded all bounds in vulgar abuse of the Jews.

That He was a coward and afraid to face death.

That He was disrespectful to His mother.

That He was friendly with women of questionable character.

That His teachings were too idealistic and impracticable.

That He grew angry and lost His temper.

That He was provincial, and that His message was only for the Jews.

That He was weak and helpless.

That His mission was a failure.

That Jesus did not die on the Cross, and that there was no Resurrection.

Against the Church

The attacks on organized Christianity are no less direct. As over against Islam, which is declared to be the only divinely-revealed religion, it is asserted that Christianity is a man-made religion. Paul, not Jesus, was its founder. Its ritual, feasts, and doctrines are but the modified sun-worship of pre-Christian times. The idea of the Book of Common Prayer being subject to alteration by Act of Parliament is held up to ridicule.

Social conditions in Christendom likewise come in for con-

[1] *Review of Religions*, I, 72.

[2] Matt. 12 : 39.

demnation, and the superiority of Islam is pointed out. Legalized prostitution is far worse than polygamy. The condition of woman under Islam is preferable to that under Christianity, the following Qur'ānic and Biblical proofs being cited:[1]

In the Bible.	*In the Qur'ān.*
Made of man's rib. Gen. 2 : 21, 22.	Made of the same essence as man.
Tempter to sin. Gen. 2 : 6.	Satan, not woman, the tempter to sin. II : 36.
The cause of perpetuating sin.	No original sin. XCV : 21.
To be ruled by man. Gen. 3 : 16.	Has equal rights with man. II : 28.
Part and parcel of husband's property. Exod. 20 : 17.	Herself the owner of property. IV : 32.
Meant for sorrow. Gen. 3 : 16.	Islamic marriage based on love. XXX : 21.
Too unclean for a temple. II Chron. 8 : 11.	As clean as men. IV : 129; XXXIII : 35.
Doubly unclean. Lev. 12 : 2-5.	
Used as a snare. 1 Sam. 18 : 21.	

Such writers never grow weary in asserting that the true religion of Jesus was Islam; that Islam is not *one* of the religions of the world, but *the* universal religion of mankind; that Christianity is a failure and the churches of western lands are deserted; and that the final triumph of Islam in the world is imminent under the guidance vouchsafed to mankind in the person of the Promised Messiah, the Reformer and Prophet of the latter days.

The Aḥmadīyah Community and Organization

The activity of the community in the work of propaganda is one of the chief marks of its vitality as well as the cause of its increase. Beginning with a few followers in 1889, the community has grown until it is now claimed that well over half a million adherents of the Promised Messiah are to be found, in all parts of India, Burma, Ceylon, Afghānistān, Arabia, Egypt, Africa, Syria, Mauritius, Australia, China, Hong-Kong, England, France, Germany and America; though in India alone it is doubtful if there are more than 60,000. Mīrzā Ghulām Aḥmad passed away in 1908, and since then the affairs of the community have been directed by a Khalīfah, who has his headquarters in Qadian, where an elaborate organization exists for carrying on the

[1] *The Light*, Lahore, October 6, 1924, 6.

work of education and propaganda, which has spread literally to the ends of the earth. But even before his death, Aḥmad had settled the main outlines of the work to be done. Qadian became the Mecca, so to speak, of the faithful, from which all influences for the spread of the new movement emanated, and where annually, in December, as many as possible assemble for the community gathering. To care for the interests and work of the community, two societies have been formed: one called the Ṣadr-Anjuman-i-Aḥmadīyah, which looks after the executive and educational necessities of the community, and the other, the Anjuman-i-Taraqqī-i-Islam, which has charge of the propaganda efforts of the community. Well-organized offices at the headquarters in Qadian care for this growing work, which entails an enormous amount of labour over details. An English high school is maintained at Qadian, also a *madrasah* for the training of missionaries, and a school for girls; while primary schools have been opened in various districts.

The passion for print is evidenced by the fact that, besides the monthly journal, the *Review of Religions*, which appears in both English and Urdū, the following Urdū papers are published at Qadian: *al-Farūq*, weekly, chiefly against the Ārya Samāj; *al-Faḍl*, bi-weekly, for Aḥmadīs; *Nūr*, bi-monthly, chiefly for Sikhs; *Miṣbāḥ*, bi-monthly, for women; *Aḥmadīyah Gazette*, monthly, official organ. *The Review of Religions* is directed chiefly against Christianity. Besides these periodicals, an extensive literature has been prepared, one of the efforts being a translation of the Qur'ān into English, with elaborate notes directly attacking Christianity, and arguments supporting the claims of Aḥmad to be the Promised Messiah. It is to be published in thirty parts, but only one part, published in 1915, has so far appeared.

The Schism

An event of fundamental importance occurred in the community when a group, headed by K͟hwājah Kamāl-ud-Dīn and Maulvī Muḥammad 'Alī, seceded after the death of the first K͟halīfah, Nūr-ud-Dīn, in 1914, and formed what is known as the Lahore party, the original group being called the Qadian party. This occurred at the time of the election of the second K͟halīfah, or successor to Aḥmad, his son, Mīrzā Bashīr-ud-Dīn Maḥmūd

Aḥmad, being chosen. Though there were some minor differences over the method of control of the community which accentuated the party feeling, yet there was a far more basic difference which came to the surface, and which now definitely distinguishes the one from the other. This had to do with the nature of the claims of the founder. The Qadian party emphasize the fact that he must be regarded as a prophet (*nabī*), while the Lahore party insist that he was only a reformer (*mujaddid*) in Islam. The former insist on pressing the points of difference that exist between their views and those of other Muslims, while the Lahore party would minimize them.

The Lahore party has organized itself under the title of the Aḥmadīya Anjuman-i-Ishā'at-i-Islam, with Maulvī Muḥammad 'Alī as its head. This section of the community likewise has an extensive missionary propaganda throughout India and in foreign countries. Khwājah Kamāl-ud-Dīn is Imām of the mosque at Woking, and head of the Mission to England ; Maulvī Ṣadr-ud-Dīn is head of the Mission to Germany ; and Maulvī Muḥammad 'Alī has distinguished himself not only by the publication of numerous apologetic and polemic works, but especially by a complete translation of the Qur'ān into English, with a critical commentary which purports to present the results of the most modern Muslim scholarship. In the writings and work of these men and their associates, references to Mīrzā Ghulām Aḥmad and his claims are scarcely to be found, though the hostile attitude to Christianity is all too evident.

The Problem Facing Educated Muslims

This attitude, and the reasons lying behind it, together form one of the most difficult problems for the student of Islam in India. To be sure, Muslims are not alone to blame for their attitude toward Christianity. The failure of Christians to reflect the spirit of Christ must not be forgotten. The Crusades, and the spirit of the Crusades that too often in the past has been reflected by Christians in the Muslim controversy, must bear a share of the blame as well. In India, Islam has come more closely into contact with Christianity in recent times than in any other country. One might think that the attitude of Islam toward Christianity here would exhibit a new spirit of toleration and appreciation.[1] But such can hardly be said to be the case, if one is to judge from the attitude of most of the Islamic apologists. On the other hand, here we find the newest and most aggressive forms of propaganda against Christianity which have ever originated, and from here a world-wide programme of Muslim Foreign Missions is being maintained and financed. This, after all, is the logical issue of the spirit and teaching of Islam under the influence of modern conditions. It is one of the forms of adjustment which have been forced upon the Muslims of India, who are struggling for the defence and maintenance of their Faith in the face of the most disturbing and challenging conditions that the world has ever known. The end no one can foresee. But it cannot be that honest, truth-seeking Muslims will continue indefinitely to refuse to face *all* the facts, and pursue a policy of evasion of the real issues of history and life, even though such investigation leads to the questioning and study of the very sources of revelation itself.

There are still some who hold that Christians attempted such investigations at the peril of their faith. But it must be remembered by all lovers of truth, that the truth itself is more important than any current interpretation thereof. God is constantly revealing more and more of His truth to men who *seek* for it. Consequently, after all the critical examination to which it has been subjected, the essential truth of Christianity is better attested and better understood to-day than ever before. The sum of it all is, that the highest revelation of God to man is through a living personality. That the modern Muslim apologist is becoming more and more conscious of the fundamental importance of this truth

[1] A somewhat unique bit of evidence with regard to a new spirit of toleration comes from an altogether unexpected source. K͟hwājah Ḥasan Niẓāmī, of the Tablīg͟hī Mission, Delhi, in the year 1927 published a 'Life of Christ', called *Ta'rīk͟h-i-Masīḥ*, which he based on the four Gospels and the works of leading Christian scholars. The work is free from any sort of controversial comments, and the 'Life' is a remarkably true presentation of the Gospel record. His object in writing such a book is that Muslims may come to know exactly what Christians believe about Christ, and, by the imparting of such knowledge, to soften the attitude of Muslims toward Christians. The same author has prepared a similar book relating to Hinduism, called *Kṛishaṇ Bītī*, which is a 'Life of Kṛishṇa'.

is revealed in the fact that he is emphasizing the personality and character of Muḥammad as the means by which God's grace was shed upon the world, and as the fact of central importance in Islam. The problem, therefore, for the Muslim as for the Christian investigator, is to apply the same honest and fearless critical methods to the study of Muḥammad and his revelation as have been applied to Jesus and the Bible.

The educated Muslims of India are in a better position to make this study than those of any other country. They are better trained in the scientific method; they have had freer contacts with other religions; they are more tolerant; they have better precedents to follow; they can conduct their work with less fear of reactionary opposition. The day for that will surely come, and when it does come another period in the development of Islam will have arrived: a period not less, and possibly even more, significant than that inaugurated by Sir Syed Aḥmad Khān, who was himself the prophet of the New Islam.

Conclusion

The introduction, spread, and development of Islam in India forms one of the most interesting scenes in the whole world drama of Islam. Torn with internal divisions of sect and caste, and modified by the influence of Indian environment, the Muslim community is none the less conscious of its underlying unifying principle. An account of the processes which contributed to the formation of this diversity in unity has been sketched. With this picture before us, and in spite of all the weakness that division and communalism breed, one cannot help concluding that Islam in India to-day is better organized, better educated, more progressive, more reasonable and tolerant in its attitude toward its neighbours than ever before in its history. But the future glory of Islam in India will consist in the extent to which it truly exemplifies the spirit of toleration, peace, brotherhood, and the uplift of woman, which, its apologists of the present day assert, represent the true Islam.

APPENDIX

I. HISTORICAL OUTLINE[1]

A.D.

711 The Arab conquest of Sind under Muḥammad bin Qāsim.
1001–1030 The invasions by Maḥmūd of Ghaznī.
1193 Delhi became the capital of the Muslim Empire of the north under the Afghān dynasties: Ghūrīs, Khaljīs, Tughluqs, Sayyids, and Lodīs.
1195 Gujarat annexed by Quṭb-ud-Dīn Aybak.
1202 Bengal conquered by Bakhtyār Khaljī.
1241 Mongol invasion.
1294 The Deccan invaded by ʻAlā-ud-Dīn.
1306 Mālik Kāfūr conquered central and south India.
1327 Muḥammad Tughluq transfers his capital to the Deccan.
1347–1518 Spread of Islam in south by Shīʻah Bahmanī kings.
1347 The Deccan independent under ʻAlā-ud-Dīn Bahman Shāh.
1352 Bengal united and independent under Ilyās.
1382 Foundation of Kingdom of Khandesh.
1394 The Sharqī (eastern) Kingdom of Jaunpur founded.
1396 Gujarat Kingdom founded.
1398 Invasion of Tīmūr.
1392 Malwa Kingdom founded.
1484–92 Foundation of Deccan Kingdoms of Berar, Bijapur, Aḥmadnagar, and Bidar.
1512 Golkonda Kingdom founded.
1526 Bābur annexes Delhi and begins the establishment of the Mughul Empire.
1540 Battle of Kanauj: Sher Shāh defeats Humāyūn, who flees to Persia.

1. The Greatest of the Mughuls

1556–1605 Akbar.
1628–1658 Shāh Jahān.
1659–1707 Aurangzīb, greatest extent of Muslim power ever attained.

2. Period of Disintegration

1708 Revolt of the Sikhs.
1738 The Marāthas advance to Delhi.
1748 Afghān invasion under Aḥmad Shāh.

[1] *The Cambridge History of India*, III, ed. Sir Wolseley Haig, 664 ff., and *R.M.M. Annuaire*, 1925.

1820 The Wahhābī revival under Sayyid Aḥmad.
1857 The last of the Mughul emperors, Bahādūr Shāh, deposed.

3. The Modern Revival

1875 Founding of the Muḥammadan Anglo-Oriental College, Aligarh, by Sir Syed Aḥmad Khān.
1906 The All-India Muslim League organized.
1920 The Khilāfat Committee organized, Mr. Gandhi supports Khilāfat and secures temporary Hindu-Muslim Unity.
1924 Abolition of the Turkish caliphate—Indian Muslims greatly disturbed.
1924–27 Serious Hindu-Muslim Riots. Hindu-Muslim Unity recognized as a political necessity.
1926 Indian delegates participate in the abortive Caliphate Conference at Cairo, and also in the Muslim World Congress at Mecca.

4. The British Period

I. Period of Adjustment: *up to 1864*, marked by:
1. Suppression of Persian as the official language.
2. The final putting down of the last political ambitions of the Mughuls, by the deposition of Bahādūr Shāh in 1857.
3. The suspension of the appointment of *qāḍīs* as officials of the Government in 1864.

II. Period of Progress: *since 1864:*
1. Founding of the M.A.-O. College at Aligarh, 1875.
2. Development of various associations, like the All-India Muslim League in 1906.
3. The Waqf Validating Act, 1913.
4. The Muslim University Act (Aligarh), passed 1920.

II. GENERAL FACTS ABOUT ISLAM IN INDIA[1]

1. Population

(a) General Comparison

India has 68,735,233 Muslims out of a total population of 316,128,721, or 21 per cent. The populations of the other communities are as follows:

Muslims	68,735,233
Hindus	216,734,586
Untouchables (about)	60,000,000
Sikhs	3,238,803
Christians	4,754,079
Buddhists (Burma mostly)	11,571,268
Jains	1,178,596
Jews	21,778
Parsis	101,778

[1] *R.M.M. Annuaire*, 1925, and *C.I.R.*, 1921.

(*b*) *Detailed Figures of Muslim Population for India and Burma*

Province, Etc.	Persons	Males	Females
India	68,735,233	36,003,447	32,731,786
Provinces	59,444,331	31,094,988	28,349,343
1. Ajmīr-Marwara	101,776	59,580	42,196
2. Andamans and Nicobars ...	4,104	3,650	454
3. Assam	2,202,460	1,151,675	1,050,785
4. Baluchistan	367,282	213,240	154,042
5. Bengal	25,210,802	12,957,775	12,253,027
6. Bihar and Orissa	3,690,182	1,802,720	1,887,462
Bihar	3,212,862	1,563,435	1,649,427
Orissa	117,789	54,421	63,368
Chota Nagpur	359,531	184,864	174,667
7. Bombay (Presidency) ...	3,820,153	2,113,720	1,706,433
Aden (*Arabia*)	45,055	...	...
Bombay	1,369,075	735,352	633,723
Sind	2,406,023	1,348,301	1,057,722
8. Burma	500,592	314,527	186,065
9. Central Provinces and Berar ...	563,574	294,928	268,646
10. Coorg	13,021	8,352	4,669
11. Delhi	141,758	81,667	60,091
12. Madras	2,840,488	1,404,000	1,436,488
13. North-West Frontier Province	2,062,786	1,105,265	957,521
14. Punjab	11,444,321	6,195,738	5,248,583
15. United Provinces	6,481,032	3,388,151	3,092,881
States and Agencies	9,290,902	4,908,459	4,382,443
16. Assam State (Manipur) ...	17,487	8,765	8,722
17. Baluchistan States	366,195	198,950	167,245
18. Baroda State	162,328	83,458	78,870
19. Bengal States	275,322	146,532	128,790
20. Bihar and Orissa States ...	16,095	8,371	7,724
21. Bombay States	840,675	427,228	413,447
22. Central India (Agency) ...	331,520	173,327	158,193
23. Central Provinces States ...	18,458	9,184	9,274
24. Gwalior State	176,883	94,692	82,191
25. Hyderabad State	1,298,277	664,022	634,255
26. Kashmir State	2,548,514	1,345,957	1,202,557
27. Madras States	363,992	187,385	176,607
Cochin State	68,717	34,940	33,777
Travancore State ...	270,478	140,396	130,082
Other Madras States ...	24,797	12,049	12,748
28. Mysore State	340,461	181,878	158,583
29. N.-W.F.P. (Agencies and Tribal Areas)	21,337	20,859	478
30. Punjab States	1,369,062	751,819	617,243
31. Rajputana (Agency) ...	900,341	476,632	423,709
32. Sikkim State	20	19	1
33. United Provinces States ...	243,935	129,381	114,554

STATEMENT SHOWING THE INCREASE IN THE NUMBER OF HINDUS AND MUSLIMS IN THE AREAS ENUMERATED IN 1881 AND 1911

Province	Increase per cent since			
	1911		1881	
	Hindu	Muslim	Hindu	Muslim
Assam	+ 13·6	+ 16·7	+ 34·1	+ 67·1
Bengal	− ·6	+ 5·1	+ 17·6	+ 41·1
Bihar and Orissa	− ·4	+ ·6	+ 13·8	+ 1·8
Central Provinces and Berar ...	+ 2·5	− ·5	+ 17·0	+ 21·5
Madras	+ 1·8	+ 3·6	+ 18·1	+ 31·5
Punjab and N.-W.F.P.	+ 4·5	+ 4·7	+ ·1	+ 28·7
United Provinces	− 2·0	− 2·6	+ 2·4	+ 9·1

2. RACIAL ORIGIN[1]

Arabs : About 200,000 Arab immigrants, chiefly in Sind and occasionally elsewhere. They are Qurayshī Sayyids; Ḥaḍramawtīs in Hyderabad, etc. There are a few Somālīs, or Habshīs, in the Bombay Presidency.

Persians : About 300,000.

Turks : About 300,000, known as Mug͟huls.

Afg͟hāns or Pathāns : About 3,500,000, in all the provinces except the Deccan.

Hindu origin : The great majority of the Muslims of India are converts or descendants of converts, and are found chiefly in the two social classes Shayk͟h and Julāhā. The number of the latter is increasing. They come from the Aryo-Dravidian races in the north, and from the Dravidian in the south.

3. SOCIAL CLASSIFICATION

Sayyid	1,657,000
Shayk͟h	33,392,000
Mug͟hul	302,000
Pathān	3,564,000
Others	28,820,000
Total (approx.)	68,735,000

4. DISTRIBUTION OF MUSLIMS ACCORDING TO CASTE, TRIBE, RACE OR NATIONALITY[2]

Caste and Locality	*Persons*
Ahir (Punjab, United Provinces)	2,124
Arab (Bombay, including Aden)	96,168

[1] *R.M.M. Annuaire*, 1925. [2] *C.I.R.*, 1921.

Caste and Locality	*Persons*
Arain (Punjab, Kashmir)	1,117,574
Arora (N.-W.F.P., Punjab)	318
Awan (N.-W.F.P., Punjab)	693,735
Baghban (N.-W.F.P., United Provinces)	24,095
Balai (Central India, Rajputana)	25
Balti (Kashmir)	124,760
Baluch (Baluchistan, Bombay, N.-W.F.P., Punjab)	1,342,053
Baniya	99
Banjara or Lambadi (Bombay, Hyderabad, Punjab, Mysore)	4,302
Barhai (Bihar and Orissa, Central Provinces, United Provinces)	87,690
Barwala (Punjab)	59,475
Bhangi (Bombay, United Provinces, Baroda, Rajputana)	38,920
Bharai (Punjab)	61,489
Bhil (Western and Central India)	4
Bohrah (Bombay, Baroda)	153,363
Brāhman (All India)	230
Brahui (Baluchistan, Bombay)	214,471
Burmese (Andamans, Nicobars, Burma)	8,596
Chakar (Rajputana)	155
Chamar (All India)	2,248
Charan (Rajputana)	25
Chhimba (Punjab, Rajputana)	55,417
Chinese (Burma)	1,517
Chuhra Mussali or Bhangi (N.-W.F.P., Punjab)	391,614
Daroga (Rajputana)	85
Darzada (Baluchistan)	10,707
Darzi (Bombay, Central Provinces, United Provinces, Baroda, Central India, Hyderabad, Mysore, Rajputana)	154,930
Dehwar (Baluchistan)	5,433
Dhakad (Central India, Rajputana)	42
Dhobi (Assam, Bengal, Bihar and Orissa, Bombay, Central Provinces, N.-W.F.P., Punjab, United Provinces, Central India, Hyderabad, Rajputana)	330,604
Dholi (Rajputana)	695
Dhund (N.-W.F.P., Kashmir)	42,908
Dhuniya (Bihar and Orissa, Central Provinces, United Provinces)	558,767
Dogar, Dogra (?) (Punjab)	73,997
Faqir (Punjab, Rajputana, United Provinces)	638,348
Gadaria (All India)	10
Gadra (Baluchistan)	6,958
Ghanchi (Baroda)	4,070
Gujar (Central Provinces, N.-W.F.P., Punjab, United Provinces, Central India, Kashmir, Rajputana)	982,465
Hajjam or Nai (Assam, Bengal, Bihar and Orissa, Bombay, Central Provinces, N.-W.F.P., Punjab, United Provinces, Baroda, Central India Kashmir, Mysore, Rajputana)	560,640
Indo-Burman (Burma)	119,420
Jat (N.-W.F.P., Punjab, United Provinces, Kashmir, Rajputana)	2,782,236
Jatt (Baluchistan)	66,982
Jhinwar (Punjab)	94,028
Jogi or Yogi (Bengal, Punjab, Rajputana)	31,158
Jolaha or Julaha (Bengal, Bihar and Orissa, N.-W.F.P., Punjab, United Provinces, Kashmir)	2,624,873
Jonakan (Madras)	138,073
Kachhi (All India)	27
Kalwar (All India)	3,467

Caste and Locality	*Persons*
Kamboh (Punjab)	81,491
Karal (N.-W.F.P.)	21,823
Kasai or Qassab (N.-W.F.P., Punjab, United Provinces)	286,758
Kashmiri (N.-W.F.P., Punjab, Kashmir)	982,323
Khatri (N.-W.F.P., Punjab, Kashmir)	64
Khojah (Bombay, Punjab)	146,109
Khokhar (Punjab)	69,181
Koli or Dagi (All India)	301
Kuki-Chin (Burma)	84
Kumhar (Assam, Bengal, Bihar and Orissa, Bombay, Central Provinces, Madras, N.-W.F.P., Punjab, United Provinces, Baroda, Central India, Hyderabad, Kashmir, Mysore, Rajputana) ...	447,075
Kunbi (All India)	38
Kunjra (Bihar and Orissa)	164,733
Labbai (Madras)	382,313
Lasi or Panj Raj (Baluchistan)	23,212
Lodha or Lodhi (All India)	102
Lohar (Bombay, Central Province, N.-W.F.P., Punjab, United Provinces, Baroda, Central India, Hyderabad, Kashmir, Rajputana)	377,395
Lori (Baluchistan)	6,890
Machhi (Punjab)	280,524
Mahimal (Assam)	22,443
Mahtam (Punjab)	11,841
Mali (Bombay, Punjab, United Provinces)	89,826
Mallah (Bihar and Orissa, Punjab and United Provinces) ...	69,783
Mappilla (Coorg, Madras)	1,108,385
Mazhabi (Punjab)	23
Memon (Bombay, Baroda)	151,850
Meo or Mewati (Punjab, Rajputana)	270,908
Mina (Central India, Rajputana)	95
Mirasi (Punjab, N.-W.F.P.)	243,279
Mochi (Assam, Bengal, N.-W.F.P., Punjab, Kashmir) ...	480,035
Moghal or Mughul (N.-W.F.P., Punjab, Hyderabad, Kashmir)	189,674
Naik (Bombay, Rajputana)	331
Nakib (Baluchistan)	5,577
Paracha (N.-W.F.P.)	13,560
Pathān (Baluchistan, Bengal, Bihar and Orissa, Bombay, Madras, N.-W.F.P., Punjab, United Provinces, Baroda, Central India, Hyderabad, Kashmir, Mysore, Rajputana)...	3,547,868
Qurayshī or Kureshī (N.-W.F.P., Punjab)	126,197
Rabari	2
Raigar (Rajputana)	25
Rajput or Chhatri (Andamans and Nicobars, Assam, Bengal, Bihar and Orissa, Bombay, Central Provinces, N.-W.F.P., Punjab, United Provinces, Baroda, Central India, Hyderabad, Kashmir, Rajputana)	1,716,679
Ramgarhia (Punjab)	20
Rawat (Rajputana)	11
Saini (Punjab)	1,323
Sayyid (Baluchistan, Bengal, Bihar and Orissa, Bombay, Madras, N.-W.F.P., Punjab, United Provinces, Hyderabad, Kashmir, Mysore, Rajputana	1,601,247
Shaykh (Assam, Bengal, Bihar and Orissa, Bombay, Burma, Madras, N.-W.F.P., Punjab, United Provinces, Baroda, Central India, Hyderabad, Kashmir, Rajputana)	33,387,861

Caste and Locality	*Persons*
Shin (Kashmir)	15,106
Sindhi (Bombay, Rajputana)	858,018
Sonar or Sunar (Bihar and Orissa, Bombay, Central Provinces, N.-W.F.P., Punjab, United Provinces, Central India, Hyderabad, Rajputana)	174,154
Sudhan (Kashmir)	63,992
Sutradhar (All India)	12
Swathi (N.-W.F.P.)	56,904
Tanaoli (N.-W.F.P.)	69,560
Tarkhan (N.-W.F.P., Punjab, Kashmir)	373,562
Telī (Bengal, Bihar and Orissa, Bombay, Punjab, United Provinces, Hyderabad, Kashmir, Rajputana)	647,506
Vadda (Bombay, Hyderabad, Mysore)	870
Yashkun (Kashmir)	44,087

5. The Peaceful Spread of Islam[1]

Aside from the effect of militant Islam for the conversion of Hindus, the lower castes have been won to Islam chiefly from two causes so far as preaching is concerned:

(1) *The Sunnī preachers*, belonging chiefly to the mystic *darwīsh* orders, their leading representatives being: Mālik bin Dīnār, Malabar Coast, A.D. 750 (?); Shaykh Ismā'īl, Lahore, A.D. 1005; Sayyid Nathar Shāh, Trichinopoly, A.D. 1020; Mu'īn-ud-Dīn Chishtī, Ajmīr, A.D. 1195; Sayyid Jalāl-ud-Dīn, Uch, Sind, A.D. 1244; Shaykh Jalāl-ud-Dīn Tabrīzī, Bengal (d. 1244); Pīr Mahābīr Khamdāyat, Bijapur, A.D. 1304; Yūsuf Sindhī (Memons), Cutch, A.D. 1350; Sayyid 'Alī Hamadānī, Kashmir, A.D. 1388. The movement has been greatly extended with the rise of Muslim congregations around the tombs of the saints of Ajmīr, Delhi, Pāk Pattan, Panipat, Uch, Gulbarga, and Sylhet.

(2) *The Ismā'īlian preachers*, of the two sects, Nizārite (Khojahs) and Musta'lite (Bohrahs), who adopted the method of syncretism in preparing their teachings for their disciples, and using chiefly the Hindu theology and terminology as a basis for approach. They made headway chiefly in Sind from the ninth to the fifteenth centuries; and in Gujarat in the twelfth and fifteenth centuries; Qarmaṭian preachers in Sind, ninth century on; 'Abd Allāh (Bohrahs), Gujarat, A.D. 1067; Nūr Satāgar (Khojahs), Gujarat, A.D. 1140 (?); Ṣadr-ud-Dīn (Khojahs), Sind, A.D. fifteenth century.

6. Muslim Sects in India[2]

(1) *Sunnīs*: About 63,235,000, may be classified as follows:

(*a*) Ḥanafīs: About 48,000,000.

(*b*) Shāfi'īs: About 1,000,000, the Mappillas, Malabar, Madras Presidency.

[1] *R.M.M. Annuaire*, 1925. [2] *R.M.M. Annuaire*, 1925.

(*c*) Sunnīs with Wahhābī tendencies: About 10,000,000 (Salafīyah; Ahl-i-Ḥadīth; Farā'iḍīyah; Ghayr-Muqallid; Ahl-i-Qur'ān), in the United Provinces, Bengal and the north-west.

(*d*) Sunnīs with modern tendencies: Neo-Mu'tazilites or Necharīs. First and chief leader, Sir Syed Aḥmad Khāṇ. He established the Muḥammadan Anglo-Oriental College, Aligarh, 1875. Other important leaders are the late Rt. Hon. Syed Amir 'Alī, a Shī'ah; Sir Shaikh Muḥammad Iqbāl, Prof. S. Khudā Bakhsh and H.H. the Aghā Khāṇ, head of the Āghā Khāṇī Khojahs.

(*e*) Irregular Sunnīs: Memons of Cutch, about 200,000; Mahdawīs of Gujarat and the Dhikrīs (Zikrīs) of Baluchistan, about 300,000; the Aḥmadīs (Aḥmadīyah sect), founded by Mīrzā Ghulām Aḥmad, of Qadian, Punjab: two branches, Qadianī and Lāhorī, about 60,000 (?).

(2) *Shī'ahs*: About 5,500,000:

(*a*) Ithnā 'Asharīyah, or 'Twelvers' (Imāmīs), found chiefly in Oudh and certain Indian States, as Rampur, Hyderabad, etc. Their chief centre is Lucknow. Number, about 5,000,000 (?).

(*b*) Ismā'īlians: About 500,000 (?).

Bohrahs, in the Bombay Presidency, Bombay and Gujarat. Number, 153,363.

Khojahs, in Bombay, Baroda, Sind, Punjab. Number, 146,109. Two sections. One section, known as the Āghā Khāṇī, has the Āghā Khāṇ as its head; the other the Punjab Khojahs.

RELATIVE STRENGTH OF SUNNĪS AND SHĪ'AHS[1]

PROVINCE, ETC.	TOTAL MUSLIMS	SUNNĪS	SHĪ'AHS	PERCENTAGE OF	
				SUNNĪS	SHĪ'AHS
Assam	2,219,947	2,219,513	434	100	...
Baluchistan	733,477	706,355	3,739	96	1
Bengal and Sikkim ...	25,486,144	25,483,564	2,580	99	1
Bihar and Orissa ...	3,706,277	3,689,277	17,000	99	1
Bombay	4,660,828	4,107,221	144,427	88	3
C.P. and Berar ...	582,032	570,392	11,640	98	2
Madras	2,865,285	2,681,945	54,114	94	2
N.-W.F. Province ...	2,084,123	1,994,898	80,200	95	4
Punjab and Delhi ...	12,955,141	12,605,472	259,351	97	2
Baroda	162,328	142,863	15,897	88	10
Kashmir	2,548,514	2,421,089	127,425	95	5
Rajputana and Ajmīr	1,002,117	980,141	20,291	98	2

'An attempt has been made in most provinces to obtain approximate figures of these two communities; . . . but complete figures for the whole of India are not available.'—*Census of India Report*, 1921, I, pt. I, para. 98, 119, Calcutta, 1924.

[1] *C.I.R.*, 1921.

7. Indo-Muslim Sects[1]

Certain Indo-Muslim sects have also been developed which attempted to reconcile the antagonistic cultures of Islam and Hinduism on a mystic basis. The chief groups are the Kabīrpanthīs and the Sikhs. Other similar groups are the Ḥusaynī Brāhmans, the Satnāmīs and the Pīrzādas. Prince Dārā Shikūh, in the middle of the seventeenth century, attempted a most remarkable synthesis of Hindu-Muslim culture and religion; but both his and Akbar's efforts remained isolated examples of attempts to bridge the gap.

8. The Religious Orders

(1) *The Regular or Ba-Shar' Orders, Sunnite.*
- (*a*) Chishtīyah, Mu'īn-ud-Dīn Chishtī, Ajmīr, A.D. 1195. Chief branches:
  - Niẓāmī (Niẓām-ud-Dīn Awliyā, Delhi).
  - Ṣābirī ('Alī Aḥmad Ṣābir, Piran Kalir, Rurki).
- (*b*) Suhrawardīyah, Bahā-ud-Dīn Zakarīyā, Multan, A.D. 1250.
- (*c*) Shaṭṭārīyah, 'Abd Allāh Shaṭṭārī, Malwa (d. A.D. 1406).
- (*d*) Qadirīyah, Sayyid Bandagī Muḥammad Ghawth, Uch (A.D. 1482–d. 1517).
- (*e*) Naqshbandīyah, Khwājah Muḥammad Baqī Bi'llāh Berang, died, Delhi, A.D. 1603.

(2) *The Irregular or Be-Shar' Orders, Sunnite.*
- (*a*) Qalandarīyah, Abū (Bū) 'Alī Qalandar, d., Panipat, A.D. 1323.
- (*b*) Benawā.
- (*c*) Naushāhī, Ḥājī Pīr Muḥammad Sachiar, Naushahra, Punjab.
- (*d*) Jalālī, Punjab.
- (*e*) Madārī, Zinda Shāh Madār, d. A.D. 1436, Makanpur, Oudh.
- (*f*) Rafā'ī (Gurzmār).
- (*g*) Miscellaneous: Mūsā Sohāgī, Malang, Shamsī, Alif Shāhī, Dafalī, Mawlāī.

9. Languages Used by Indian Muslims

While there are at least seventeen important languages used by the Muslims of India, yet most of these have only local or provincial significance compared with Urdū. Urdū is the Muslim lingua franca of India. It is used to a greater or less extent in every province in India, as will be seen from the accompanying table. Though as a mother-tongue it is claimed by a smaller number than Bengālī, which would head the list from this point of view, yet it must be remembered that there are millions, whose mother-tongue is another vernacular, who also use Urdū, or

[1] *R.M.M. Annuaire*, 1925.

Western Hindī as it is designated in the census report. For these reasons Urdū easily can claim first place as the Muslim language of India.

Persian is used largely as a literary language of the educated classes. Arabic, as a theological language, is still used in all the principal *madrasahs*. English is extensively used by those of modern education.

The following tables, compiled from the *Census of India Report for 1921*, are an attempt to give *approximately* the distribution of the Muslim population of India according to language:

(1) *Languages used in India by Muslims in order of Importance.*

Language	Number
Urdū (Western Hindī)	20,791,000
Bengālī	23,995,000
Punjābī	7,700,000
Sindhī	2,912,000
Kashmīrī (and allied languages)	1,500,000
Pushtū	1,460,000
Gujarātī	1,400,000
Tamil	1,250,000
Mālayālam	1,107,000
Telugū	750,000
Oriyā	400,000
Balūchī	224,000
Brāhūī	122,000
Arabic	42,000
Persian	22,000
Other	5,060,000
Total ...	68,735,000

English is used by 315,348 persons.

Hindī is used to a limited extent, and the number would be included in the figure given for Urdū.

All of the above languages used by Muslims have been greatly modified by contact with Islam, through the large infusion of Arabic and Persian words in the vocabulary. Urdū may be described as Musulmānī Hindī, just as the language used by the Muslims of Bengal is called Musulmānī Bengālī. Tamil, Punjābī and Kashmīrī have undergone a similar change. Many of the Indo-Muslim languages, too, have adopted the use of the Arabic character. The chief of these are Urdū, Sindhī, Punjābī, Tamil, and Kashmīrī.

(2) *Language Distribution by Provinces*

(*a*) URDŪ

Province	Number
Andamans ...	4,000
Assam	450,000
Baluchistan ...	16,000
Baroda	62,000
Bengal	1,780,000
Bihar and Orissa	3,216,000
Bombay	1,200,000
Burma	100,000
Central India ...	800,000

Coorg	6,000
Delhi	141,000
Gwalior	175,000
Hyderabad ...	1,000,000
Kashmir	500,000
Madras	300,000
N.-W.F.P.	
Punjab	3,400,000
Rajputana ...	1 001,000
United Provinces ...	6,640,000
Total ...	20,791,000

(*b*) Bengālī

Assam	1,750,000
Bengal	22,245,000
Total ...	23,995,000

(*c*) Punjābī

N.-W.F.P.	800,000
Punjab	6,900,000
Total ...	7,700,000

(*d*) Sindhī

Baroda...	12,000
Sind	2,400,000
Bombay States ...	500,000
Total ...	2,912,000

(*e*) Kashmīrī

Kashmir	1,500,000

(*f*) Pushtū

Baluchistan ...	200,000
N.-W.F.P.	1,200,000
Punjab	60,000
Total ...	1,460,000

(*g*) Gujarātī

Baroda	1,000,000
Bombay	400,000
Total ...	1,400,000

(*h*) Tamil

Burma	50,000
Madras	1,200,000
Total ...	1,250,000

(*i*) Mālayālam

Coorg	7,000
Madras	1,100,000
Total ...	1,107,000

(*j*) Telugū

Burma	50,000
Hyderabad ...	200,000
Madras	500,000
Total ...	750,000

(*k*) Oriyā

Bihar and Orissa	400,000

(*l*) Balūchī

Baluchistan ...	224,000

(*m*) Brāhūī

Baluchistan ...	122,000

(*n*) Arabic

Aden (Bombay) ...	32,000
All India	10,000
Total ...	42,000

(*o*) Persian

Baluchistan ...	9,000
Bombay ...	3,000
N.-W.F.P. ...	2,000
Punjab	1,500
Other Provinces...	7,000
Total ...	22,000

10. Education.[1]

(1) In 1920 there were 230,836 private *Primary Muslim Schools* out of 644,638. In all the schools there were 1,824,364 Muslim students, of whom 284,661 were girls. This number represented 23 per cent of all the pupils of India.

(2) *Secondary and High Schools* (teaching English, Urdū, Persian and Arabic): The more important ones are found as follows—six in Madras Presidency, four in Bombay Presidency, four very important ones in Bengal (Decca, Calcutta, Hooghly and Chittagong), ten in the United Provinces, and twelve in the Punjab and N.-W.F. Province.

[1] *R.M.M. Annuaire*, 1925.

(3) *Higher Educational Institutions*, and centres of Islamic culture:

Aligarh: Muslim University, founded 1875.
Ambala: Central Jamī'yat-i-Tablīgh-ul-Islām.
Aurangabad: Anjuman-i-Taraqqī-i-Urdū.
Azamgarh: Shiblī Academy, publishers of the *Ma'ārif*.
Bankipore (Patna): The Khudā Bakhsh Library, the leading Oriental (Arabic and Persian) library in India.
Calcutta: The Calcutta Madrasah.
Dacca: Dacca University.
Delhi: National Muslim University; Yunānī Medical School, founded by Hakīm Ajmal Khān.
Deoband: Dār-ul-'Ulūm, the 'al-Azhar of India'.
Hyderabad: Osmānia University (teaching for degrees in Urdū), Niẓām College; the Osmānia University Press.
Lahore: The Islāmīyah College. The Lahore Aḥmadīyah headquarters—Anjuman-i-Ishā'at-i-Islām.
Lucknow: The Shī'ah Intermediate College; Shī'ah, Madrasat-ul-Wā'iẓīn; Firinghī Mahal Madrasah, Niẓāmī, Sunnī; Nadwat-ul-'Ulamā.
Peshawar: Islāmīyah College.
Ponani (Malabar): Chief *madrasah* of the Mappillas.
Poona: Jamī'yat-i-Da'wat-o-Tablīgh-i-Islām, with 13 branches.
Qadian: Aḥmadīyah H.S., headquarters of the Qādiānī Aḥmadīs, and all their propaganda work.
Rampur: Rampur State Library (one of the best Oriental collections in India), and art collection.

(4) There are *High Schools for girls* at Aligarh, Bhopal, Hyderabad, Lahore, Lucknow and other places. Also an Intermediate College for girls at Aligarh.

(5) *Educational Associations*:
(*a*) The Muḥammadan Educational Conference, founded in 1886, with headquarters at Aligarh.
(*b*) The Muḥammadan Educational Nadwat-ul-'Ulamā, Lucknow, founded in 1890.
(*c*) The Muḥammadan Educational All-India Shī'ah Conference, started in 1909.

11. Indian Muslims' Literacy[1]

(1) *General*

Total Persons	68,670,717	*Total Illiterate*	65,508,172
Males	35,967,380	Males	33,046,931
Females	32,703,337	Females	32,461,248
Total Literate	3,162,545	*Literate in English*	315,341
Males	2,920,449	Males	306,275
Females	242,096	Females	9,073

[1] *C.I.R.*, 1921.

(2) *Number per 1,000 who are Literate*

PROVINCE, ETC.	MALES	FEMALES
INDIA	93	9
PROVINCES	93	8
Ajmīr-Marwara	187	18
Andamans and Nicobars	214	55
Assam	85	5
Baluchistan	149	43
Bengal	109	6
Bihar and Orissa	99	8
Bombay	114	15
Burma	302	87
C.P. and Berar	225	27
Coorg	204	24
Delhi	182	31
Madras	201	18
N.-W.F.P.	33	2
Punjab	37	4
United Provinces	73	8
STATES AND AGENCIES	103	15
Baroda State	309	48
Central India Agency	169	19
Cochin State	178	18
Gwalior State	142	26
Hyderabad State	140	35
Kashmir State	20	1
Mysore State	238	62
Rajputana Agency	66	9
Sikkim State	833	...
Travancore State	238	50

N.B.—The figures in this table are for persons five years of age and over only.

III. THE MUSLIM PRESS IN INDIA

N.B.—Abbreviations: D.—Daily; W.—Weekly; M.—Monthly; Q.—Quarterly; S.—Sunnī; Sh.—Shīʻah; Wh.—Wahhābī; Is.—Ismāʻīlī; Sf.—Ṣūfī; L.—Literary; Sc.—Scientific; Wm.—Woman's; Ch.—Children's; Pr.—Propaganda. Where NO language is indicated the language used is Urdū.

1. GENERAL.

The Muslim Press publishes 238 periodicals, in 10 languages, from presses in 67 different places. Most of the periodicals are in Urdū, to the number of 165. There are 18 in English, but only 1 each in Persian and Arabic. There are several bi-lingual papers.

There is a Qur'ān Publishing Society in Bombay. The Qur'ān has been translated into Urdū, Persian, Bengālī, Hindī, Tamil and English. Many of the translations are inter-linear; there is one translation which has both Urdū and Persian translations interlined between the original. An Urdū metrical version of the Qur'ān has just been published.

Besides the Muslim books published in India, there is a considerable number in Arabic regularly imported from Cairo and Beirut, by dealers in Bombay, Surat, Calcutta, and other places.

2. List of Periodicals Alphabetically Arranged by Places

AGRA, U.P.
Agra Akhbār
Darbār
Purdah Nishīn (Wm.)
Surman-i-Rozgār
Tablīgh (Pr.)

AHMADABAD, Bombay
Fayḍ-i-'Āmm (Gujarātī)

ALIGARH, U.P.
Aligarh Gazette
Urdū-i-Mualla

ALLAHABAD, U.P.
Chānd (Hindi, Urdū)
Hindustan Review, (Eng. M.)

AMRITSAR, Pnujab
Ahl-i-Ḥadīth (Wh.)
al-Faqīh
al-Mailij
al-Quraysh
Angora
Ittiḥād-ul-Islam
Muslim Rajput
Political Rahnumā
Riyāḍ-i-Hind
Tawhīd (Wh.)

AMROHA, U.P.
Ittiḥād

ASANSOL TOWN, Bengal
Ratnukar (Bengali)

AZAMGARH, U.P.
Ma'ārif (M., L.)

BANGALORE, Madras
Qāsim-ul-Akhbār (2 W.)

BANKIPORE, B.O.
Bihārī (Eng.-Hindī) (D., W.)

BAREILLY, U.P.
Rohilkhand Gazette
Rozānah Akhbār

BATALA, Punjab
al-'Azīz
Punjābī Khiyālāt
Rafīq-i-Ṣādiq
Silk-i-Marwārid
Ustānī (Wm.)

BIJNOR
al-Khalīl
Manṣūr
Madīnah
Najāt

BOMBAY
Akhbār (Gujarātī)
Akhbār-i-Saudāgar aur Hindustan (D., 2 W.)
Akhbār-i-Islām (Gujarātī)
al-Islām aur Mominmitra (Gujarātī)
al-Kamāl (Gujarātī)
Bohre Majlis (Gujarātī, Is.)
Insāf (Gujarātī)
'Irfān
Ishā'at-i-Islām (Gujarātī, Pr.)
Ismā'īlī (Eng.-Gujarātī, Khojah)
Khilāfat (Gujarātī)
Khilāfat Bulletin (Eng.)
Manhar (Gujarātī)
Memon Mitra (Gujarātī)
Muslim Herald
Roznāmah-i-Khilāfat
Sulṭān-ul-Akhbār

BUDAUN, U.P.
Mushā'ar (L.)
Nāqib
Dhū'l-Qurnayn

BULANDSHAHR, U.P.
Nawad

BURHANPUR, C.P.
al-Burhān

CALCUTTA, Bengal
Ahl-i-Ḥadīth (Bengālī, Wh.)
al-Jāmi'ah (Arabic), Editor, Abū'l-Kalām Azād (M.)
al-Kamāl
ar-Rafīq
Bahādūr (Bengālī)
Bangiya Muslim Sahitya Patrika (Bengālī)
Dhumketū (Bengālī)
Ḥabl-ul-Matīn (Persian), Editor, Jalāl-ud-Dīn Ḥusaynī

Hunter Phatkar
Inqilāb Zamānah
Islām Darshan (Bengālī)
Muḥammadī (Bengālī)
Mussalmān (Eng., W.)
Payghām (M., Wh.)
Rayat Bandhū (Bengālī)
Sonār Bhārat (Eng.-Bengālī)

CALICUT, Madras
Muslim Sahakārī (Mālayālam)

CAWNPORE, U.P.
al-Bārid
Hamdard
Indian World (Eng.)
Niẓām-i-'Ālam

COLOMBO, Ceylon
Muslim Friend (Tamil, M.)
Crescent (Eng.-Tamil, M.)

DACCA, Bengal
Ā'īn-Islām (Bengālī)
Jādū
Peace (Eng., M.)

DELHI
Comrade (Eng., W.), Editor, Muḥammad 'Alī
Darwīsh (2 W., Pr.), Editor, Ḥasan Niẓāmī
Hurriyat
Niẓām-ul-Mashā'ikh (M.), Editor, Ḥasan Niẓāmī
Ustānī (M., Wm.)

FATHPUR, U.P.
Dilchasp Akhbār

FYZABAD, U.P.
Payghām-i-Ṣubḥ

GORAKHPUR, U.P.
Mashriq

HYDERABAD, Deccan
Islamic Culture (Eng., Q., L.)
Rahbar-i-Deccan
Risālah-i-Atāliq
Risālah-i-Maḥbūb-un-Naẓā'ir
Risālah-i-Nau Nihāl
Risālah-i-Wā'iẓ (Religious)
Risālah-un-Nisā (Wm.)
Ṣaḥīfah

HYDERABAD, Sind
Ta'līm (Sindhī)

JAUNPUR, U.P.
Jādū

JODIYA, Bombay
al-'Azīz (Gujarātī)

JUBBULPORE, C.P.
Tāj

JULLUNDUR, Punjab
al-Falāh
Muzārah

KARACHI, Sind
al-Wāḥid (Arabic-Sindhī)
Bahāī News (Pers.-Eng., Pr.)
Memon Samachar
Tawḥīd (Sindhī)

KARUNAGAPALLI, Madras
Shams-ul-Islām (Mālayālam)

KAYAMKULAM, Madras
Islām Dootan (Mālayālam)
Munīr-ul-Islām (Mālayālam)

KHAMAGAON, C.P.
Gulzār-i-Ḥākimī (Gujarātī)

LAHORE, Punjab.
Akhbār-i-'Āmm (D., W.)
Akhtar
al-Burhān
al-Ḥākim
al-Islām
al-Kamāl
al-Munīr
Anwār as-Ṣūfīyah
Bachchon kā Akhbār (M., Ch.)
Dāktar (Medical)
Ḍiyāfat Punch
Dhū'l-Fiqār
Hamdard
Hazār Dastān
Humāyūn
Hurriyat
Indian Architect
Indian Cases and Statutes (Eng.)
Intikhāb lā-Jawāb (W., L.)
Inqilāb
Ishā'at-ul-Islām (Pr., Aḥmadīyah)
Ishā'at ul-Qur'ān (Pr., Ahl-i-Qur'ān)
Islāmic Review (Urdu, M., Pr., Aḥmadīyah)
Islāmic World (Eng., M., L.)
Kakkazāī National Magazine
Khāksār
Light (Eng.,2 W., Pr., Ahmadīyah)
Manẓar
Mushīr al-Aṭibbah
Mister Gazette

Mitra Vilasa (W.)
Muḥabbat
Muslim Outlook (Eng., D.)
Nuṣrat
Paisa Akhbār (D., W.)
Payyām-i-Muḥabbat
Phūl (Ch.)
Political Rahnumā (Eng.)
Rafīq-ut-Ta'līm
Rahnumā-i-Ṣiḥḥat (Health)
Risālah-i-Anjuman-i-Ḥimāyat-i-Islām (Communal)
Ṣanā'at (Industrial)
Shihāb-i-Urdū
Sharīf Bībī (Wm.)
Siyāsat
Ṭabīb (Medical)
Tablīgh
Tafrīḥ
Tahrīk
Tahdhīb-un-Niswān
Urdū Bulletin
Wafadār
Waṭan (W., D.)
Zamindār (D.)
Zamzamah
Zarā'at (Agricultural)

LARKANA, Bombay
al-Ḥaqīqat (Gujarātī)
al-Kāshif (Sindhī)

LIMBDI, Bombay
Muḥibb (Gujarātī)

LUCKNOW, U.P.
Bayān (Arabic-Urdu)
Ḥaqīqat
Hamdam
Inqilāb
Nazr
Oudh Akhbār
Oudh Punch (W.)
Sayyārah
Suhayl-i-Yaman (M., Sh.)
Wā'iẓ (Shī'ah College News, M.)

LUDHIANA, Punjab
Iṣlāḥ
Risālah Sutlej

LYALLPUR, Punjab
Risālah Shaykh Qānūngoyān

MADRAS
Anjuman Bulletin (Eng., M.)
Ḥakīm and Vythian (Eng.)
Qāsim-ul-Akhbār (Eng., Urdū, Tamil)
Mukhbīr-i-Deccan
Qawmī Riport
Dār-ul-Islām (Tamil)
Sayf-ul-Islām (Tamil)
Sugathara Bodhīnī (Tamil)
Mohammedan (Eng., W.)
Muslim Herald (Eng., W.)
Islamic Review (Tamil, Aḥmadīyah)

MADURA, Madras
Dakhshina Mitran (Tamil)

MEERUT, U.P.
Millat

MIANA, Punjab
Ḥubb-i-Waṭan

MORADABAD, U.P.
Iqdam
Makka-Madīnah
Mukhbīr-i-'Ālam
Nayyar-i-'Āzam
Rahnumā

MUZAFFARNAGAR, U.P.
Imdād

NARSINGHPUR, C.P.
Sasimī-i-Sahā (Urdū-Gujarātī)

NATOR, Bengal
Bengal Presidency Gazette (Eng.-Bengālī)

NAVSARI, Baroda
Wafadār (Eng.-Gujarātī, Urdū)

PANIPAT, Punjab
Istiqlāl

PINDI-BAHAUDDIN, Punjab
Ṣūfī (Sf.)

POONA, Bombay
Gulzār-i-Sukhan

QADIAN, Punjab
Aḥmadīyah Gazette (M.)
al-Bushrah (Eng.)
al-Faḍl (2 W., Aḥmadīyah)
al-Farūq (W., Pr., Aḥmadīyah)
al-Ḥakam
Miṣbāḥ (2 W., Wm., Aḥmadīyah)
Nūr (2 M., Pr., Aḥmadīyah)
Review of Religions (M., Eng., Urdū, Pr., Aḥmadīyah)

RAGHUNATHPUR, Bihar
Iṣlāḥ

RAJKOT PARA, Bombay
Āftāb-i-Islām

RAMPUR, U.P.
Dabdabah-i-Sikandarī

RANGOON, Burma
Universal Peace (Eng., Q.)

RAWALPINDI, Punjab
Ismā'īlī Ṣadāqat

SAHARANPUR, U.P.
Ẓarīf

SHAHDARA, Punjab
Tabṣīrat-ul-Āṭibbah

SIALKOT, Punjab
Durr-i-Najaf

SODHRA, Punjab
Musalmān

SUKKUR, Bombay
Ḥaqq (Eng.-Sindhī, W.)
Sind Zamindār (Eng.-Sindhī)

TRAVANCORE, Madras
Muslim Akhiam (Mālayālam)
Keralachandrika (Eng.-Mālayālam)

TRIPLICANE, Madras
Āzād Hind

UPLETA, Bombay
Kathiawār (Gujarātī)

Note.—This list was prepared from information supplied by the Rev. Wm. Paton, formerly Secretary of the National Christian Council of India, who secured it from the Department of Public Information of the Government of India. Certain additions and emendations have been made. I am also indebted to the *Revue du Monde Musulman*, *Annuaire*, Paris, 1925, for the suggestion as to the method of arrangement.

IV. THE PRINCIPAL MUSLIM FESTIVALS

1. SUNNĪ

1. *Those officially recognized by the Mughul Emperors :*
    (1) Muḥarram 10th ('Ashurah).
    (2) Ṣafar 13th (by decree of Jahāngīr), Akhirī Chār Shambah, the last convalescence of the Prophet.
    (3) Sha'bān 14th, Shab-i-Barāt—the Night of the Book or Record. It is thought that this is the night on which God records all actions of mankind which will be performed during the year to come, and the names of those who will be born and die. It is celebrated with fireworks.
    (4) Ramaḍān 21st—Death of 'Alī.
    (5) Shawwāl 1st, 'Īd-ul-Fiṭr—the Breaking of the Fast of Ramaḍān.
    (6) Dhī'l-Ḥijjah 18th, 'Īd-uḍ-Ḍuḥā, or Baqarah 'Īd—the Feast of the Sacrifice of the Cow (*Baqarah*).

2. *Others commonly observed :*
    (1) Rajab 27th, Mi'rāj—the Miraculous Night-journey of the Prophet.
    (2) Ramaḍān 27th, Laylat-ul-Qadr—the Night of the Revelation of the Qur'ān.

(3) Rabī'-ul-Awwal, 12th—Bārāh Wafāt commemorates the death of the Prophet (in India), though it is also observed throughout the Muslim world as the day of his birth, and, as such, is known as the *Mawlid.*

3. *Anniversaries of the Saints'* '*Urs* (the date of death is observed):

(1) Sālār Mas'ūd Ghaznawī, Muḥarram 11th, d. A.D. 1033, Bahraich, Oudh, U.P.

(2) Mu'īn-ud-Dīn Chishtī, Rajab 6th, A.D. b. 1236, Ajmīr, Rajputana.

(3) Quṭb-ud-Dīn Bakhtyār Kākī Chishtī, Rabī' I 14th, A.D. 1236, Old Delhi.

(4) Bābā Farīd-ud-Dīn Shakarganj Chishtī, Muḥarram 5th, A.D. 1265, Pāk Pattan, Punjab.

(5) Niẓām-ud-Dīn Awliyā, Chishtī . . . , A.D. 1325, Delhi.

(6) 'Alī Aḥmad Ṣābir, Chishtī, Rabī' I 13th, A.D. 1291, Piran Kalir, Rurki.

(7) Gīsū Darāz, Chishtī, Dhī'l-Qa'dah 16th, A.D. 1325 (?), Gulbarga.

(8) Abū (Bū) 'Alī Qalandar, Ramaḍān 13th, A.D. 1323, Panipat, Punjab.

(9) Zinda Shāh Madār, Jumādā I 17th, A.D. 1436, Makanpur, Oudh.

(10) Khwājah Khiḍr.

2. Shī'ah

Imāmite (as in Persia).[1]

In addition to the two 'Īds which are required of all Muslims ('Īd-ul-Fiṭr and 'Īd-uḍ-Ḍuḥā), the Shī'ahs have officially recognized a certain number of festivals connected with the history of their Twelve Imāms.

1.	Muḥarram	1—10.	Ceremonies connected with the martyrdom of Ḥusayn. 'Ashurah, or the 10th, being the climax.
2.	,,	22.	Death of Mūsā Kāẓim.
3.	,,	26.	Death of Zayn-ul-'Ābdīn.
4.	Ṣafar	1.	Between 'Alī and Mu'āwiyah at Siffin.
5.	,,	3.	Birth of Bāqir.
6.	,,	7.	Birth of Mūsā Kāẓim.
7.	,,	17.	Death of 'Alī Riḍā (2nd festival: Ramaḍān 24th).
8.	,,	20.	Ziyārat-ul-Arba'īn.
9.	Rabī' I	5.	Birth of Ḥusayn (2nd festival: Sha'bān 3rd).
10.	,,	8.	Death of Ḥasan 'Askarī.
11.	,,	12.	Mawlid, birth of the Prophet.

[1] *R.M.M. Annuaire*, 1925.

12. Rabī‘ I	14.	Usurpation of Abū Bakr.
13. ,,	15.	Death of Yazīd, who had caused the death of Ḥusayn.
14. Rabī‘ II	4.	Birth of Ḥasan ‘Askarī.
15. Jumādā I	4.	Death of Ḥasan.
16. ,,	15.	Birth of Zayn-ul-‘Abdīn.
17. Jumādā II	3.	Death of Fāṭimah (2nd festival: Ramaḍān 2nd).
18. ,,	20.	Birth of Fāṭimah (2nd festival: Sha‘bān 15th).
19. Rajab I	2.	Birth of ‘Alī Naqī.
20. ,,	13.	Birth of ‘Alī.
21. ,,	27.	Mi‘rāj of the Prophet.
22. Sha‘bān	15.	Birth of Mahdī.
23. Ramaḍān	1.	Rūyā.
24. ,,	15.	Birth of Ḥasan, and Muḥammad Taqī.
25. ,,	21.	Death of ‘Alī.
26. ,,	27.	Execution of his assassin, Ibn Muljam.
27. Shawwāl	4.	Disappearance of the XIIth Imām, Mahdī in A.H. 265, A.D. 879.
28. ,,	12.	Miracle of Shaqq-ul-Qamar (Splitting of the Moon).
29. ,,	25.	Death of Ja‘far as-Ṣiddīq.
30. Dhū'l-Qa‘dah	11.	Birth of ‘Alī Riḍā.
31. Dhū'l-Ḥijjah	13.	Accession of ‘Alī to the caliphate.
32. ,,	18.	Investiture of ‘Alī by the Prophet.
33. ,,	25.	Festival of Khātm Bakhsh.
34. ,,	26.	Death of the usurper ‘Umar.

V. NOTES ON THE PROVINCES[1]

AJMĪR-MARWARA.—101,776 Muslims out of 495,271 inhabitants, or 20·5 per cent. They are mostly from the Rājputs, Jāts and Gūjars. The tomb of Mu‘īn-ud-Dīn Chishtī (d. A.D. 1236) is found at Ajmīr. He founded the Chishtī order in India.

ANDAMANS AND NICOBARS.—4,104 out of 27,086 inhabitants are Muslims.

ASSAM.—(1) Province—2,202,460 Muslims out of 7,606,230 inhabitants, or 27·78 per cent. (2) State of Manipur—17,487 Muslims out of 384,016 inhabitants. Muslims chiefly around Sylhet, where Jalāl-ud-Dīn preached and was buried, A.D. 1384. The low caste of Muslims is called *Matias*.

BALUCHISTAN. — (1) Province — 367,282 Muslims out of 420,648 inhabitants, or 91·7 per cent. (2) States—366,195 Muslims

[1] *R.M.M. Annuaire*, 1925.

out of 378,977 inhabitants, or 91·7 per cent. The total number of Sunnīs is about 600,000; heterodox (*Dhikrīs*, or *Mahdawīs*, and *Ismā'īlians*), about 133,000 Muslims are chiefly Brāhūīs by race.

BARODA.—State; 162,328 Muslims out of 2,126,522 inhabitants, or 7·5 per cent.

BENGAL.—(1) Province—25,210,802 Muslims out of 46,695,536 inhabitants, or 53·5 per cent. (2) States—275,322 Muslims out of 896,926 inhabitants. The Islamization of Bengal was due to the governors from A.D. 1202, after the Ghūrid conquest, who had their headquarters at Gaur (Lakhnauti). Jatmall, son of Rājā Kans, accepted Islam and mounted the throne in A.D. 1414, with the name of Jalāl-ud-Dīn Muḥammad Shāh. Murshid Qulī Khāṇ founded the line of the Nawābs of Murshidabad. He converted many Hindus. The majority of the Muslims, aside from the Pathāns, is composed of Bengālī converts, Shaykhs coming from the low-caste Julāhās and outcastes. The greater part are Sunnīs of the Ḥanafite school. There are a few Shī'ahs at Dacca and Burdwan. The low-castes of the south and east profess an aggressive and fanatical form of Islam, and are termed Wahhābīs; notably the sect of the Farā'iḍīyah, founded by Sharī'at Allāh, and his son, Dūdhū Miyāṇ (d. A.D. 1862), who attacked British forces and rejected saint worship. They are found in the villages, and are often called *Salafīyah*, or *Ghayr-muqallid*. There are very important *waqfs* in Bengal.

BIHAR AND ORISSA.—(1) Province—3,690,182 Muslims out of 34,002,189 inhabitants, or 9·8 per cent. (2) States—16,095 Muslims out of 3,959,669 inhabitants. There is a minority of Muslims around Patna, which is imbued with a fervent and aggressive religious zeal of Wahhābī tendencies. At Gaya are found some Shī'ahs. There is a *khānaqāh*, or monastery, of Shaykh Kabīr Darwīsh, d. A.D. 1717 at Sasaram; and a library of Khudā Bakhsh (d. 1876) at Bankipore. The tomb of Shāh Arzakī (d. A.D. 1623) is venerated. There is a group of some 20,000 Kabīrpanthīs at Sambalpur, Orissa.

BOMBAY and SIND.—(1) Presidency—3,820,153 Muslims out of 19,348,219 inhabitants, or 19·7 per cent. (2) States—840,675 Muslims out of 7,409,429 inhabitants. Sind has a majority of Muslims, 73 per cent, many of whose ancestors came from Arabia. The centre of the old Muslim province was Thatta. Site not known. Besides Sunnīs there are found Bohrahs, Khojahs and Mahdawīs or Dhikrīs.

In Cutch the Muslims form 23 per cent of the population, and are mostly a semi-Muslim sect called the *Memons*, converted about the fourteenth century.

Gujarat was a Muslim state from the fourteenth to the seventeenth centuries. The chief Muslim city is Aḥmadabad. The *Bohrahs*, *Khojahs* and *Mahdawīs* are found here, in addition to orthodox Sunnīs.

On the coast of the Konkan are found Sunnī descendants and converts of Arab immigrants of the early centuries. They are called *Konkanīs*. In Bombay there are 89 mosques, 77 for Sunnīs, 8 for Bohrahs, 2 for Khojahs, and 1 for Mughuls.

The Āghā Khān, who is the head of a branch of the Ismā'īlian Khojahs, makes his headquarters in Bombay. He was the first president of the All-India Muslim League in 1906.

BURMA.—500,592 Muslims out of 13,169,099 inhabitants, or 3·84 per cent. They speak Burmese and Urdū, and are largely Shaykhs from Bengal, and *Zerbādīs*, that is, Muslims born of Burman mothers.

CENTRAL INDIA.—331,520 out of 5,997,023 inhabitants. The principal state is Bhopal, founded in 1707 by an Afghān Nawāb.

CENTRAL PROVINCES AND BERAR.—(1) Province—563,574 Muslims out of 13,912,760, or 3·66 per cent. (2) States—18,458 Muslims out of 2,066,900.

COORG.—13,021 Muslims out of 163,838 inhabitants, or 7·9 per cent. Two thirds of these Muslims are Mappillas and Shāfi'is, while the remainder are Ḥanafī Shaykhs.

DELHI.—141,758 Muslims out of 488,188 inhabitants, or 29·03 per cent.

GWALIOR STATE.—176,883 Muslims out of 3,186,075 inhabitants.

HYDERABAD STATE.—1,298,277 Muslims out of 12,471,770 inhabitants, or 10·5 per cent. The Muslim dynasty of the Niẓām was founded by Subadār Āṣaf Jāh (d. 1748). 83 per cent of the madrasahs, 45 per cent of the secondary schools, and 42 per cent of the primary schools are Muslim. The important Osmānia University, with its 20 professors, gives instruction in Urdū and makes special attempts to diffuse Arabic culture. It is producing a distinct literature in Urdū through its translation and publication of western scientific and literary texts. There is an important colony of Ḥaḍramawtī Arabs here, who are *Shāfi'īs*. The majority are *Sunnī Ḥanafī*. There are some *Shī'ites* and *Mahdawīs*.

KASHMIR STATE.—2,548,514 Muslims out of 3,320,518 inhabitants, or 76·8 per cent. The country was Islamized about the twelfth century by Ismā'īlian missionaries, and in the fourteenth by Sunnī mystics, the most noted being Sayyid 'Alī Hamadānī, who converted the dynasty in A.D. 1326 (Shams-ud-Dīn Shāh). The king, Sikandar, nicknamed Butshikān, or Idol-breaker (d. A.D. 1417), destroyed many temples. Kashmir was a famous summer resort for the Mughul emperors.

In Jammu are found Rājput Muslims. To the north-east the people of Baltistan are Ismā'īlians.

It is in Srinagar that the tomb of one, Yūs Āṣaf, is found, which was located by Mīrzā Ghulām Aḥmad of Qadian, in Khān Yār Street. It is this tomb which he and the adherents of the Aḥmadīyah sect declare is the real tomb of Jesus Christ.

There are many places of pilgrimage for Muslims in Kashmir, which are termed *ziyārat*. Part are the tombs or sacred sites of indigenous Hindu or Buddhistic origin. Others are tombs of foreigners called, *Sayyid*, *pīrzāda*. There is also a local religious order of jugglers, called *Sayyid Makkār*.

MADRAS AND THE COAST OF MALABAR. — (1) Presidency — 2,840,488 Muslims out of 42,318,985 inhabitants, or 6·7 per cent. (2) States — 363,992 Muslims out of 5,460,312 inhabitants, or 6·6 per cent.

The Laccadive Islands are entirely Muslim, with 10,600 inhabitants, Mappillas.

The Muslims of south India are of the Dravidian race. The Shaykh, Sayyid and Pathān classes, numbering about 1,000,000, speak Urdū.

Tamil is written in the Arabic characters. The Mappillas of Malabar speak Mālayālam. They are a mixed people, part Arab, and follow the law of ash-Shāfi'ī. Their chief religious heads are at Kondatti and Ponani. At the latter place there is a well-known school for the training of missionaries and converts.

N.-W.F. PROVINCE.—(1) Province—2,062,786 Muslims out of 2,251,340 inhabitants, or 91 per cent. (2) Agencies—21,337 Muslims out of 54,470 inhabitants, or 39·1 per cent.

The people are largely warlike tribes of Pathāns from Afghānistān: Bannūchīs, Dards, Marwats, Yūsufzāīs, Niāzīs, Wazīrīs, Ghilzāīs, Mohmands, Afrīdīs, Orakzāīs. Some of the tribes are Sunnīs: Bannūchīs, Marwats; some are Wahhābīs, as the Yūsufzāīs and Bonairs of Dir, and were connected with the *jihād* which was carried on against the Sikhs by Sayyid Aḥmad, of Rae Bareli, in 1826. The rest are neo-Ismā'īlians, having been converted since the twelfth century. They are found in Baltistan (Mughuls), Chitral, Panyal, Ludkho, Wakhan, Hunza, and Hazara. The Afrīdīs, who made a *jihād* against Great Britain in 1897, are of the Roshanīyah sect, which was founded in the sixteenth century by Miyān Bāyazīd, or Pīr Roshan. The Qādirī order of the Sunnīs has adherents in Dera Ghazi Khān.

PUNJAB.—(1) Province—11,444,321 Muslims out of 20,685,024 inhabitants, or 50·6 per cent. (2) States—1,369,062 Muslims out of 4,416,036 inhabitants, or 31 per cent.

Of the Sikhs, there are 2,294,207 in the province and 813,080 in the states.

The Punjab was invaded as far as Multan by the Arab general, Muḥammad bin Qāsim, about A.D. 711. At the end of the ninth century a sect of Muslims, known as Qarmaṭians, from al-Aḥsa, in Baḥrain, Arabia, founded a principality at Multan. This continued till the invasion of Maḥmūd of Ghaznī, in the eleventh century, when an attempt was made to put an end to the heresy of the Qarmaṭians and Ismā'īlians and establish the orthodox Sunnī religion. Through the efforts of some of the conquerors and the Ṣūfī preachers of Uch and Pāk Pattan, most of the converts became Sunnīs.

The work of the Ṣūfīs, or mystics, in attempting to bring about a reconciliation of Hinduism and Islam, resulted in the creation of the curious syncretism of the Sikhs, founded by Gurū Nānak, who died in A.D. 1539.

Many low castes have been converted in mass to Sunnī Islam.

The tombs of the saints of Uch, Jalāl Surkhposh (d. A.D. 1291) and Muḥammad Ghawth (d. A.D. 1517), together with that at Pāk Pattan of Bābā Farīd Shakarganj (d. A.D. 1265), are greatly venerated.

The states having Muslim rulers are Bahawalpur, Firozpore, Laharu, Malerkotla, Chamba and Patawdi.

RAJPUTANA STATE.—900,341 Muslims out of 9,844,384 inhabitants, or 9·1 per cent.

In Malwa there were two Muslim dynasties between A.D. 1401–1530: the Ghūrīs and Khaljīs, which have left their monuments at Mandu. The Bohrahs are found at Ujjain.

The semi-Muslim sect of the Dādūpanthīs was founded in the sixteenth century.

The only Muslim ruler is the Rājā of Tonk, of the Rājput Chauhān caste. Only 10 per cent of his subjects are Muslims.

SIKKIM STATE.—20 Muslims out of 81,721 inhabitants.

UNITED PROVINCES OF AGRA AND OUDH.—(1) Province—6,481,032 Muslims out of 45,375,787 inhabitants, or 14·8 per cent. (2) States—243,935 Muslims out of 1,134,881 inhabitants, or 21·4 per cent.

The percentage of Muslims is only 14 per cent, in spite of continuous Muslim administration from the fall of the kingdom of Kanauj in the twelfth century: the sovereigns of Delhi, the Sharqī kings of Jaunpur (A.D. 1394–1500), Mughul governors, Nawābs of Oudh. Part of the family of the latter have been refugees in Baghdad since 1857.

Agra has 60,000 Muslims out of 285,000 people; Lucknow 95,000 out of 240,000, and Benares 50,000 out of 198,000. The Muslims are Sunnī Ḥanafites, Wahhābīs (5 per cent at Benares) and Shī'ahs (Twelvers), which are found chiefly in Lucknow, where they number 16 per cent of the Muslim population.

Lucknow is the centre of Indian Shī'ahs, because of the ancient Nawabs of Oudh, who erected the chief buildings there.

The Muslims of the province by origin are indicated as follows—Arab: Shaykh, Qurayshī, Siddīqī, Farūqī, 'Uthmānī and Anṣārī; Afghāns: Yūsufzāīs, Afrīdīs, Ghūrīs, Lodīs, and Sherwānīs; Mughuls or Qizilbāsh, and Hindu converts: Julāhās.

The semi-Muslim sect of the *Kabīrpanthīs* has a centre at Benares, and the *Satnāmīs* are found in Oudh.

There are four great educational centres for the Muslims: Aligarh, which is the modern reform centre where the Muslim university, founded by Sir Syed Aḥmad Khān, is located; Deoband, in the Saharanpur district, where the orthodox Sunnī *madrasah*, Dār-ul-'Ulūm, is found; Azamgarh, centre of the moderate Sunnī reform movement; and Lucknow, with its Shī'ah Intermediate College, affiliated with the Lucknow University and the seminary, *Madrasat-ul-Wā'iẓīn*.

Agra was the capital of Akbar (d. A.D. 1605). Here are found his tomb (at Sikandra) and the Taj Mahal. At Bahraich is found the tomb of the Ghaznawī martyr prince, Sālār Mas'ūd (d. A.D. 1033), which was uncovered in the fifteenth century. He is greatly venerated under the name of Ghāzī Miyān.

There is one Muslim state at Rampur, in Rohilkhand, which was founded by Pathāns. The present Nawāb is a Shī'ah. A well-known Arabic *madrasah* is found here, and also one of the best Arabic, Persian and Urdū libraries of India. The Nawāb is a great patron of Indo-Muslim music.

BIBLIOGRAPHY

N.B.—This list is arranged chapter-wise, and includes not only the references cited, but other books which have been found useful as collateral material.

Chapter I. The Religious Objectives of the Muslim Conquerors

'Abbās Khān ... *Ta'rīkh-i-Sher Shāhī*, E.D., IV.

Aghnides, Nicholas P. *Mohammedan Theories of Finance.* New York, 1916.

Aitken, E. A. ... *The Gazetteer of Sind.* Karachi, 1907.

Aiyangar, S. K. ... *South India and Her Muhammadan Invaders.* Oxford, 1921.

Al-Balādhurī ... *Kitāb Futūḥ-ul-Buldān*, ed. M. J. de Goeje. Leyden, 1866. (Arabic.)

— — tr. F. C. Murgotten, *Origins of the Islamic State*, pt. II. New York, 1924.

— — tr. E.D., I.

Al-'Utbī ... *Ta'rīkh-i-Yamīnī*, E.D., I.

Amīr Khusrū ... *Ta'rīkh-i-'Alā'ī*, E.D., III.

Bābur ... *Wāqi'āt-i-Bāburī*, E.D.

Elphinstone, Monstuart ... *The History of India*, 6th ed. London, 1874.

Firishtah ... *Ta'rīkh-i-Firishtah*, tr. Briggs, 4 vols. London, 1829.

Fīrūz Shāh, Emperor *Futūḥāt-i-Fīrūz Shāhī*, E.D., III.

Gribble, J. D. B. ... *A History of the Deccan*, 2 vols. London, 1896.

Ḥasan Niẓāmī ... *Tāj-ul-Ma'āthir*, E.D., II.

Horovitz, Josef ... *Epigraphia Indo-Moslemica.* Calcutta.

Lane-Poole, S. ... *Mediæval India Under Moslem Rule*, 12th ed. Fisher Unwin. London, 1917.

Mīrzā Muḥammad Kāẓim ... *Ta'rīkh-i-Kachh-o-Makrān.* Moradabad, 1905.

Muir, Sir Wm. ... *The Annals of the Early Caliphate.* London, 1883.

— *The Caliphate, Its Rise, Decline and Fall.* Edinburgh, 1915.

O'Leary, De Lacy ... *Arabia Before Muhammad.* Kegan Paul, London, 1927.

Unknown Author ... *Chach-nāmah*, E.D., I.

Chapter II. The Methods of the Conquerors

'Abd-ul-Ḥamīd Lāhorī ... *Bādshāh-nāmah*, E.D., VII.

— — ed. W. N. Lees, Kabīr Ahmad and 'Abd-ur-Raḥīm, 2 vols. Calcutta, 1867–68. (Persian.)

Abū'l-Faḍl 'Allāmī ... *Akbar-nāmah*, E.D., VI.

— ed. Aḥmad 'Alī and 'Abd-ur-Raḥmān, 3 vols. Calcutta, 1877–86.

Aghnides, Nicholas P. *Mohammedan Theories of Finance.* New York, 1916.

Aitken, E. A. ... *The Gazetteer of Sind.* Karachi, 1907.

AIYANGAR, S. K. ... *South India and Her Muhammadan Invaders.* Oxford, 1921.
AL-BALĀDHURĪ ... *Kitāb Futūḥ-ul-Buldān*, tr. Murgotten. See above Ch. I.
AL-'UTBĪ ... *Ta'rīkh-i-Yamīnī*, E.D., I.
AMĪR KHUSRŪ ... *Ta'rīkh-i-'Alā'ī*, E.D., III.
ARNOLD, SIR THOMAS W. ... *The Preaching of Islam.* Westminster, 1896.
BĀBUR ... *Wāqi'āt-i-Bāburī*, E.D.
BAKHTĀWAR KHĀN ... *Mir'āt-i-'Ālam*, E.D., VII.
BANNINGA, J. J. ... 'The Moplah Rebellion of 1921', the *Moslem World*, Vol. XIII, 379. New York, 1923.
COUSENS, H. ... *Bījāpūr and Its Antiquities.* Bombay, 1916.
ḌIYĀ-UD-DĪN BARANĪ *Ta'rīkh-i-Fīrūz Shāhī*, E.D., III.
ELLIOT, SIR H. M. and DOWSON, J. ... *The History of India as Told by Its Own Historians*, 8 vols. London, 1867–77.
FANSHAWE, H. C. ... *Delhi, Past and Present.* London, 1902.
FIRISHTAH ... *Ta'rīkh-i-Firishtah*, tr. Briggs, 4 vols. London, 1829.
FĪRŪZ SHĀH, EMPEROR *Futūḥāt-i-Fīrūz Shāhī*, E.D., III.
GAIT, E. A. ... *A History of Assam.* Calcutta, 1906.
GRIBBLE, J. D. B. ... *A History of the Deccan*, 2 vols. London, 1896.
GUL BADAN BEGAM ... *Humāyūn-nāmah (A History of Humāyūn)*, tr. A. S. Beveridge. London, 1902.
ḤASAN NIẒĀMĪ ... *Tāj-ul-Ma'āthir*, E.D., II.
KEENE, HENRY G. ... *The Turks in India.* London, 1879.
MĀLIK MUḤAMMAD DĪN ... *The Gazetteer of the Bahawalpur State.* Lahore 1904.
MINHĀJ AS-SIRĀJ JUZJĀNĪ ... *Ṭabaqāt-i-Nāṣirī*, E.D., II.
MUḤAMMAD ASLAM ... — E.D., VIII.
MUḤAMMAD SĀQĪ MUSTA'IDD KHĀN ... *Ma'āthir-i-'Ālamgīrī*, E.D., VII.
SHAMS-I-SIRĀJ 'AFĪF ... *Ta'rīkh-i-Fīrūz Shāhī*, E.D., III.

CHAPTER III. PEACEFUL PENETRATION

'ABD-UR-RAZZĀQ ... 'Narrative of a Voyage to India,' tr. from the French, by R. H. Major, in *India in the Fifteenth Century.* London, 1857.
ARNOLD, SIR THOS. W. *The Preaching of Islam.* Westminster, 1896.
DUNCAN, J. ... 'The Coast of Malabar,' in the *Asiatic Review*, V.
GAIT, E. A. ... *A History of Assam.* Calcutta, 1906.
IBN BAṬŪṬAH ... *Travels in Bengal and China*, tr. H. Yule, *Cathay and the Way Thither*, 4 vols. London, 1915.
NAJM-UL-GHANĪ KHĀN *Madhāhib-ul-Islām.* Newul Kishore Press, Lucknow, 1924.
RISLEY, H. H. ... *The Tribes and Castes of Bengal*, 2 vols. Calcutta, 1891.
SHAYKH ZAYN-UD-DĪN *Tuḥfat-ul-Mujāhidīn*, tr. Rowlandson (part only).
TASSY, J. H. GARCIN DE *Histoire de la littérature hindoue et hindoustanie*, 3 vols., 2nd ed. Paris, 1870.
THURSTON, E. ... *The Castes and Tribes of Southern India.* Madras, 1909.
Census of India Report, 1911; *Punjab*, pt. I; *Madras*, 1891, XVI.
The Bombay Gazetteer, V and XVI, Bombay, 1877-1904.
Madras District Gazetteers, *Trichinopoly*, 1907, I.

Chapter IV. Organization of the Sunnī Community

'Abd-ul-Qādir Budāyūnī ... *Muntakhab-ut-Tawārīkh*, E.D., V. Also ed. Maulvī Aḥmad 'Alī, 3 vols. Calcutta, 1865–69. (Persian.)

'Abdur Raḥīm, Sir ... *The Principles of Muḥammadan Jurisprudence.* London, 1911.

Arnold, Sir Thos. W. *The Caliphate.* Oxford, 1924.

Bakhtāwar Khāṇ ... *Mir'āt-i-'Ālam*, E.D., VII.

Bernier, F. ... *Travels in the Mogul Empire*, tr. Constable, 2nd ed. by V. A. Smith. Oxford, 1914.

Blochmann, H. ... *Introduction to the Ā'īn-i-Akbarī.* Calcutta, 1872–77.

Buckler, F. W. ... 'A New Interpretation of Akbar's Infallibility Decree of 1579,' *Journal of the Royal Asiatic Society*, 1924, 590 f.

Ḍiyā-ud-Dīn Baranī *Ta'rīkh-i-Fīrūz Shāhī*, E.D., III.

Fīrūz Shāh, Emperor *Futūḥāt-i-Fīrūz Shāhī*, E.D., III.

Hamilton, Charles ... *The Hedaya*, tr. from the Arabic, 2nd ed. London, 1870.

Hammer, J. de ... 'Memoir on the Diplomatic Relations between the Courts of Delhi and Constantinople in the Sixteenth and Seventeenth Centuries,' *Transactions of the Royal Asiatic Society*, II, 462 f.

Ḥasan Niẓāmī ... *Tāj-ul-Ma'āthir*, E.D., II.

Jadunath Sarkar ... *Mughal Administration.*

Keene, Henry G. ... *The Turks in India.* London, 1879.

Law, N. N. ... *The Promotion of Learning during Mohammedan Rule.* London, 1916.

Manucci, N. ... *Storia do Mogor*, ed. and tr. Wm. Irvine. Abridged. London, 1913.

Minhāj as-Sirāj Juzjānī ... *Ṭabaqāt-i-Nāṣirī*, E.D., II.

Ni'mat Allāh ... *Ta'rīkh-i-Jahān Lodī*, E.D., V.

Niẓām-ud-Dīn Aḥmad *Ṭabaqāt-i-Akbarī*, E.D., V.

Raḥmān 'Alī ... *Tadhkirah-i-'Ulamā-i-Hind*, 2nd ed. Lucknow, 1914.

Roy, Sripati C. ... *Customs and Customary Law in British India.* Calcutta, 1911.

Sayyid 'Asghar Ḥusayn ... *Ḥayāt-i-Shaykh-ul-Hind.* Deoband, no date.

Shihāb-ud-Dīn Abū'l-'Abbās Ḥamīd ... *Masālik-ul-Abṣār fī Mamālik-ul-Amṣār*, E.D., III.

Sell, E. ... *The Khalifate Agitation in India.* C.L.S., Madras, 1922.

Williams, L. F. Rushbrook ... *India in 1920.* Government of India Press, Calcutta, 1921.

The Indian Khilāfat Delegation Publications. Nos. I–VII. London, 1920.

Chapter V. Shī'ahs and Mahdawīs

'Abd-Allāh ... *Ta'rīkh-i-Dā'ūdī*, E.D., IV.

'Abd-ul-Qādir Budāyūnī ... *Muntakhab-ut-Tawārīkh*, E.D., V.

Abū Ṭālib ... *History of Āṣaf-ud-Dawlah.*

'Alī Muḥammad Khāṇ *Mir'āt-i-Aḥmadī*, tr. James Bird, *The History of Gujarat.* London, 1835.

Baillie, N. B. E. ... *A Digest of Moohummudan Law, Hanifeea and Imameea*, 2 vols. London, 1875.

BLOCHMANN, H. ... *Introduction to the Ā'īn-i-Akbarī*. Calcutta, 1872–77.

BROWNE, E G. ... *Persian Literature in Modern Times*. Cambridge, 1924.

BUCKLER, F. W. ... 'A New Interpretation of Akbar's Infallibility Decree of 1579,' *J.R.A.S.*, 1924.

CHATELIER, A. LE ... 'The Agā Khān,' *R.M.M.*, 1, 48.

DUMASIA, N. M. ... *A Brief History of the Āghā Khān*. Bombay, 1903.

ELLIOT, SIR H. M. and DOWSON, J. ... *The History of India as Told by Its Own Historians*, I. See Ch. II.

ELPHINSTONE, M. ... *History of India*.

FĪRŪZ SHĀH, EMPEROR *Futūḥāt-i-Fīrūz Shāhī*, E.D., III.

GOLDZIHER, I. ... *Vorlesungen über den Islam, Heidelberg*, 1910; and tr. by K. C. Seelye. New Haven, 1917.

HAIG, SIR W. ... 'The Religion of Aḥmad Shāh Bahmanī,' *J.R.A.S.*, 1924, 73 f.

HOROVITZ, JOSEF ... *Monograph on the Dā'irewāle Sect*.

IBN ATHĪR ... *Kāmil-ut-Tawārīkh*, E.D., II.

JAWHAR ... *Tadhkirat-ul-Wāqi'āt, Private Memoirs of the Emperor Humāyūn*, tr. Major Chas. Stewart. London, 1832.

KARĪM GHULĀM 'ALĪ *An Open Letter to H.H. the Āghā Khāṇ*. Karachi, 1927.

KHĀFĪ KHĀṆ ... *Muntakhab-ul-Lubāb*, E.D., VII.

LEYDEN, J. ... 'The Rosheniah Sect,' *A.R.*, XI.

MEER HASSAN ALI, MRS. ... *Observations on the Mussulmauns of India*, ed. W. Crooke. Oxford, 1917.

MENANT, D. ... 'Les Bohoras du Guzarate,' *R.M.M.*, X, 465 ff.

— 'Les Khodjas du Guzarate,' *R.M.M.*, XII, 21 ff.

MĪRZĀ MUḤAMMAD HĀDĪ ... *Nūr Allāh Shūstarī, Shahīd-i-Thālith*. Lucknow, 1925. (Urdū, Compiled.)

NAJM-UL-GHANĪ KHĀṆ *Madhāhib-ul-Islām*. Newul Kishore Press, Lucknow, 1924.

— *Dā'ūdī Bohron kī Ta'rīkh*. Moradabad, 1914. (Urdū.)

NŪR ALLĀH BIN SHARĪF AL ḤUSAYNĪ AL MAR'ASHĪ SHŪSTARĪ *Majālis-ul-Mu'minīn*, MS. in the Asiatic Society of Bengal Library. Calcutta. (Arabic.)

ROSE, H. A. ... *A Glossary of Tribes and Castes of the Punjab and North-West Frontier Province*, 3 vols. Lahore, 1911–19. I.

SPRENGER, A. ... *Catalogue of the King of Oudh MSS*. Calcutta, 1854.

SULṬĀN MUḤAMMAD SHĀH, H. H. THE ĀGHĀ KHĀṆ ... *India in Transition*. London, 1918.

Census of India Report, 1911, N.-W.F.P., 1921, I, pt. i.

Revue du Monde Musulman, X. Paris.

CHAPTER VI. RELIGIOUS ORDERS

ABD-UL-QĀDIR BUDĀYŪNĪ ... *Muntakhab-ut-Tawārīkh*, III. (Persian.) See Chap. IV.

ABŪ'L-FAḌL 'ALLĀMĪ *Ā'īn-i-Akbarī*, III. (Persian); and tr. H. S. Jarrett. Calcutta, 1894.

DOUGLAS, J. ... *Bombay and Western India*, 2 vols. London, 1893.
FIRISHTAH ... *Ta'rīkh Firishtah*, Maqālah 12. (Persian.)
GHULĀM AḤMAD KHĀN *Majmū'ah-i-Malfūẓāt-i-Khwājagān-i-Chisht*. Delhi, A.H. 1324.
HAR BILĀS SĀRDĀ ... *Ajmer, Historical and Descriptive*. Ajmīr.
ḤASAN NIẒĀMĪ ... *Hindūstān ke do paigambar Rām-o-Krishan*. Lahore, A.H. 1325.
HERKLOTS, G. A. ... *Islam in India*, ed. W. Crooke. Oxford, 1921.
HUGHES, T. P. ... *A Dictionary of Islam*. London, 1885.
KHĀJA KHĀN ... *Studies in Taṣawwuf*. Madras, 1923.
MĀLIK MUḤAMMAD DĪN *The Gazetteer of the Bahawalpur State*. Lahore, 1904.
MUḤAMMAD ḤĀFIẒ ALLĀH AS-SORONĪ ... *Guldastah-i-Gulshan-i-Faqīrī*, pt. i, A.H. 1309.
MUḤAMMAD YĀSĪN ... *Ḥālāt-i-Ṣābir*. Moradabad, 1910.
NICHOLSON, R. A. ... *The Mystics of Islam*. London, 1914.
— *Studies in Islamic Mysticism*. Cambridge, 1921.
ROSE, H. A. ... *A Glossary of the Tribes and Castes of the Punjab etc.*, 3 vols. Lahore, 1911–19.
SELL, E. ... *The Religious Orders of Islam*. C.L.S., Madras, 1908.
TASSY, J. H. GARCIN DE *Memoire sur les Particularites de la Religion musulmane dans l'Inde*. Paris, 1831.

CHAPTER VII. SAINT-WORSHIP

ABŪ'L-ANWĀR ... *The Moslem Festivities*. Calcutta, 1892.
AMĪR KHUSRŪ ... *Ta'rīkh-i-'Alā'ī*, E.D., III.
BERNIER, F. ... *Travels in the Mogul Empire*, tr. Constable, 2nd ed. by V. A. Smith. Oxford, 1914.
CROOKE, W. ... *An Introduction to the Popular Religion and Folklore of Northern India*. Allahabad, 1894.
— *Popular Religion and Folklore of North India*, 2 vols. Westminster, 1896.
FĪRŪZ SHĀH, EMPEROR *Futūḥāt-i-Fīrūz Shāhī*, E.D., III.
HAR BILĀS SĀRDĀ ... *Ajmer, Historical and Descriptive*. Ajmīr.
HERKLOTS, G. A. ... *Islam in India*, ed. W. Crooke. Oxford, 1921.
ROSE, H. A. ... *G.T.C.P.*, I.
SHAMS-I-SIRĀJ 'AFĪF ... *Ta'rīkh-i-Fīrūz Shāhī*, E.D., III.
ZWEMER, S. M. ... *Animism in Islam*. Macmillan, New York, 1920.

CHAPTER VIII. ISLAM IN ITS HINDU ENVIRONMENT

'ABD-UL-QĀDIR BUDĀYŪNĪ ... *Muntakhab-ut-Tawārīkh*, E.D., V.
'ABD-UL-WALĪ ... *The Mohammedan Castes of Bengal*.
AL-BĪRŪNĪ ... *India*, tr. E. C. Sachau, 2 vols. London, 1888.
— E.D.
BĀBUR ... *Wāqi'āt-i-Bāburī*, E.D.
BAINS, SIR A. ... *Ethnography: The Castes and Tribes of India*. Strassburg, 1912.
BAKHTĀWAR KHĀN ... *Mir'āt-i-'Ālam*, E.D., VII.
BERNIER, F. ... *Travels in the Mogul Empire*, tr. Constable, 2nd ed. V. A. Smith. Oxford, 1914.

BLOCHMANN, H. ... *Introduction to the Ā'īn-i-Akbarī*. Calcutta, 1872–77.

BOER, T. J. DE ... *The History of the Philosophy of Islam*. London, 1903.

CROOKE, W. ... *Tribes and Castes of the North-West Provinces and Oudh*, 4 vols. Calcutta, 1896.

— *P.R.F.L.*, I.

— *Natives of Northern India*. London, 1907.

DĀRĀ SHIKŪH ... *Majma'-ul-Baḥrayn*, tr. and pub. Asiatic Society of Bengal. Calcutta, 1929.

ELLIOT, SIR H. M. ... *Races of the North-West Provinces of India*, 2 vols. London, 1869.

FARQUHAR, J. N. ... *An Outline of the Religious Literature of India*. Oxford, 1920.

GOLDZIHER, I. ... *Vorlesungen über den Islam*. Heidelberg, 1910. Tr. by K. C. Seelye. New Haven, 1917.

ḤASAN NIẒĀMĪ ... *Tāj-ul-Ma'āthir*, E.D., II.

HERKLOTS, G. A. ... *Islam in India*, ed. W. Crooke. Oxford, 1921.

HORTEN, DR. M. ... *Indische Strömungen in der islamischen Mystik. I. Zur Geschichte und Kritik*. Heidelberg, 1927.

IBBETSON, SIR D. ... *Outlines of Punjab Ethnography*.

JAHĀNGĪR, EMPEROR... *Wāqi'āt-i-Jahāngīrī*, E.D., VI.

KHONDKĀR FAḌL-I-RABBĪ ... *The Origin of the Musulmans of Bengal*. Calcutta, 1895.

MACAULIFFE, M.A. ... *The Sikh Religion*, 6 vols. Oxford, 1909.

MINHĀJ AS-SIRĀJ JUZJĀNĪ ... *Ṭabaqāt-i-Nāṣirī*, E.D., II.

MUḤAMMAD KĀẒIM ... *'Ālamgīr-nāmah*, E.D., VII.

NICHOLSON, R. A. ... *The Mystics of Islam*. London, 1914.

O'LEARY, DE LACY ... *Arabia Before Muhammad*. See Ch. I.

RISLEY, SIR H. H. ... *T.C.B.*, I (*Tribes and Castes of Bengal*). Calcutta, 1891–92.

SEN, D. C. ... *History of Bengali Language and Literature*. Calcutta, 1911.

UNKNOWN AUTHOR ... *Chach-nāmah*, E.D., I.

Census of India Report, 1911, I, pt. i; VII, Baroda; XV, United Provinces.

CHAPTER IX. MODERN MOVEMENTS: REACTIONARY AND PROGRESSIVE

'ABD ALLĀH CHAKRĀLAWĪ ... *Ishā'at-ul-Qur'ān*. Lahore, A.H. 1320 (Urdū.)

— *Radd-un-Naskh al-Mashhūr fī Kalām Allāh al-Ghafūr*. Lahore, 1909. (Urdū.)

— *Rūḥ-ul-Insān kamā bayyana al-Qur'ān*. Lahore, 1907. (Urdū.)

ABŪ'L-WAFĀ THANĀ ALLĀH *Risālah Ahl-i-Ḥadīth*. Amritsar. No date.

CHIRĀGH 'ALĪ, MAULVĪ *Reforms Under Muslim Rule*. Bombay, 1883.

FARQUHAR, J. N. ... *Modern Religious Movements in India*. New York, 1915.

GRAHAM, LIEUT.-COL. G. *The Life and Work of Syed Ahmad Khan*. Edinburgh, 1885.

HUNTER, W. W. ... *The Indian Musulmans*. London, 1871.

MUḤAMMAD 'ALĪ, MAULĀNĀ ... *A Scheme of Studies for the National Muslim Educational Institutions in India*, Bombay, 1921.

MUḤAMMAD ISMĀ'ĪL ... *Ṣirāṭ-ul-Mustaqīm.* Delhi. No date. (Urdū.)
— *Taqwīyat-ul-Īmān.* Delhi. No date. (Urdū.)
MORRISON, THEODORE *The History of the M.A.-O. College, Aligarh.* Allahabad, 1903.
SULṬĀN MUḤAMMAD SHĀH, H. H. THE ĀGHĀ KHĀN ... *India in Transition.* London, 1918.
SYED AḤMAD KHĀN, SIR ... *Essays on the Life of Mohammad.* London, 1869.
— *The Mohammedan Commentary on the Holy Bible.* I, Ghazipur, 1862. II, Aligarh, 1865. (Incomplete, Urdu-English.)
SYED MAḤMŪD ... *A History of English Education in India.* Aligarh, 1895.
TASSY, J. H. GARCIN DE *Histoire de la littérature hindoue et hindoustanie*, 3 vols., second edition. Paris, 1870.
Prospectus of the Osmānia University. Hyderabad, 1919.
Prospectus of the Jām'ia Millīa Islamīa. Aligarh, 1923.
The Indian Year Book, 1918, 1927. Times of India Press, Bombay.

CHAPTER X. THE NEW MUSLIM APOLOGETIC AND POLEMIC

AḤMAD ḤUSAIN, SIR ... *Notes on Islam.* Hyderabad.
FARQUHAR, J. N. ... *Modern Religious Movements in India.* New York, 1915.
KAMĀL-UD-DĪN, KHWĀJAH ... *The Sources of Christianity.* Unwin Bros., London, 1924.
MĪRZĀ GHULĀM AḤMAD ... *The Teachings of Islam.* London, 1910.
MUḤAMMAD 'INĀYAT ALLĀH KHĀN ... *Tadhkirah*, Vol. I. Amritsar, 1924.
MUḤAMMAD 'ALĪ, MAULVĪ ... *Translation and Commentary : The Holy Qur'ān*, 2nd ed. Lahore, 1920.
— *Muhammad or Christ.* Madras.
SHAIKH MUḤAMMAD IQBĀL, SIR ... *Asrār-i-Khudī*, tr. R. A. Nicholson. London, 1920.
SYED AḤMAD KHĀN, SIR ... *Essays on the Life of Mohammed.* London, 1869.
— *The Mohammedan Commentary on the Holy Bible.* As in chap. IX.
SYED AMĪR 'ALĪ, THE RT. HON. ... *The Spirit of Islam*, or *The Life and Teachings of Muhammad.* London, 1891.
WALTER, H. A. ... *The Aḥmadīya Movement.* Association Press, Calcutta, 1918.
ZULFIQĀR 'ALĪ KHĀN, SIR ... *The Poetry of Iqbal.* Lahore, 1922.
Qur'ān Majīd, pt. I, with English tr. and notes. Qadian, 1915.
The Islamic Review. (Monthly.) Woking, England.
The Review of Religions. (Monthly.) Qadian (Urdū). London (English).

GENERAL

HAIG, SIR WOLSELEY ... *The Cambridge History of India*, III. *Turks and Afghans*. Cambridge, 1928.

HUGHES, T. P. ... *A Dictionary of Islam*, London, 1885.

IVANOW, WLADMIR ... *Descriptive Catalogue of the Persian Manuscripts in the Collection of the Asiatic Society of Bengal*, 3 vols. Calcutta, 1924–27.

The Bombay Gazetteer. Bombay, 1877–1904.

The Census of India Reports, 1891, 1901, 1911, 1921.

The Encyclopædia of Islam, 3 vols. Luzac, London. Since 1913, in progress.

The Indian Year Book. Times of India Press, Bombay. Since 1914.

GLOSSARY OF ISLAMIC TERMS

'Abbāsid. The name of a dynasty of *khalīfahs* (caliphs), descended from al-'Abbās, paternal uncle of the Prophet, which succeeded the Ummayad dynasty of Damascus, and ruled at Baghdad from A.D. 749 to A.D. 1258. This dynasty was overthrown by the Mongols under Hūlāgū.

Adhān. The call to public prayer (*ṣalāt* or *namāz*) proclaimed by the Mu'adhdhin (crier) from the mosque.

'Ādil. *Lit.* 'one who dispenses justice'. A title for a common law judge.

Āghā Khāṇ. The title of the head of an extensive and scattered branch of the Ismā'īlians, which in India is known as the Khojahs. He is a resident of Bombay.

Aḥādīth. Plural form of *ḥadīth* (tradition), *q.v.*

Ahl-i-Ḥadīth. See *Wahhābī.*

Ahl-i-Khidmat. *Lit.* 'the people of service'. A class of inmates in a *khānaqāh* (monastery) of *darwīshes.*

Ahl-i-Khilwat. *Lit.* 'the people of retirement or privacy', i.e. the recluses, the most advanced class of inmates of a *khānaqāh* (monastery).

Ahl-i-Qur'ān. A sect with extreme Wahhābite tendencies, founded in the Punjab in 1902 by 'Abd Allāh Chakrālawī.

Ahl-i-Ṣuḥbat. *Lit.* 'the people of society', a class of *darwīshes* among the inmates of a *khānaqāh* (monastery).

Ahl-ul-Kitāb. *Lit.* 'people of the book', i.e. those to whom a divine revelation by means of Scripture has been given: Jews, Christians, and Sabeans.

Aḥmadīyah. The name of a modern Indian sect, founded in the year 1889, at Qadian, in the Punjab, by Mīrzā Ghulām Aḥmad.

Ajlāf zāt (dhāt). The technical term meaning low caste.

Akhbār. Plural of *khabar* (news). The common term for newspaper.

Akhlāq. Morals, ethics.

Amrīyah. The title given to the commander-in-chief of the pre-Mughul Muslim army of the Delhi government.

Anjuman. A society or association.

'Aqīdah. Plural, *'aqā'id.* A creed or belief.

'Aqīqah. A custom observed by Muslims after the birth of a child (in India any time up to seven years of age or more), when the hair is shaved and goats or sheep are sacrificed; in some parts, two animals for a boy and one for a girl.

Āzād. Free. A term applied to those *darwīshes* or *faqīrs*

who are anti-nomians, and do not regard themselves as bound to observe the Law (*Sharī'at*) of Islam.

BAQĀ. Continuance, i.e. of the personality in or with Allāh. A Ṣūfī doctrine connected with that of *fanā* (absorption) *fī Allāh* (in God).

BA-SHAR'. According to or with the Law (*Sharī'at*) of Islam. A term applied to those *darwīshes* who regulate their lives according to the *Sharī'at* (Law) of Islam.

BĀṬINĪ. Esoteric, having an *inner* or hidden meaning.

BERĀ. A raft. The name of the festival of Khwājah Khiḍr, celebrated in India by setting little rafts afloat on a stream in the name of Khwājah Khiḍr, on which have been placed lights, flowers, fruits, sweetmeats, and other eatables.

BE-SHAR'. Without the Law (*Sharī'at*) of Islam. A term applied to those *darwīshes* who are anti-nomians, and who regard themselves as not bound to follow the *Sharī'at* (Law) of Islam.

BIHISHTĪ. *Lit.* 'a heavenly one'. A euphemistic term applied to the Muslim water-carrier of India.

BOHRAH. Also spelled Bohorā. The name of an Ismā'īlī Shī'ah sect, found chiefly in Bombay and Baroda.

BURŪZ. A coming forth, appearance, or manifestation. The term used by Mīrzā Ghulām Aḥmad, of Qadian, to describe his relation to Muḥammad the Prophet.

CHAMĀR. The name of an outcaste group of Hindus who work in leather (*chamrā*).

CHAUKĪDĀR. A watchman. The name or title of a petty police officer of an Indian village.

CHELĀ. A disciple of a Hindu ascetic.

CHERŪMAN. An agricultural labouring caste on the Malabar coast.

CHIRĀGH. A lamp or light.

CHISHTĪYAH. The name of the *darwīsh* order which was introduced into India by Mu'in-ud-Dīn Chishtī, the saint of Ajmīr.

DĀBIR. 'A secretary.' An officer who supervised the arrangements for travellers, ambassadors, and men of letters at the Court at Delhi in pre-Mughul days.

DĀ'Ī. This title literally means 'one who calls', i.e. to the true faith, hence a 'missionary'. It is used in this sense by the Ismā'īlian sects, notably the Bohrahs, Khojahs, and Qarmaṭians.

DĀ'IRAH. A circle or circuit.

DARGĀH. A shrine or tomb of a saint which usually is an object of worship and pilgrimage.

DĀR-UL-ḤĀRB. 'The Abode of War.' A term used by Muslims with reference to a country belonging to infidels which has not been brought under the rule of Islam.

DĀR-UL-ISLĀM. 'The Abode of Islam.' A country where the Law (*Sharī'at*) of Islam is in full force.

DĀR-UL-KHILĀFAT. The seat of the caliphate.

DĀR-UL-'ULŪM. 'The Abode of the Sciences.' A name applied to an Arabic *madrasah* where the Islamic 'sciences' are taught.

DARWĪSH. A religious mendicant. *Lit.* 'one who goes from door to door'. The *darwīsh* is also called a *faqīr*.

DHĀT. The essence of a thing; in theology it is used of the essence of Allāh. In India it is used to mean 'caste', and is pronounced '*zāt*', which see.

DHIKR. *Lit.* 'remembering', i.e. remembering Allāh. It is the religious ceremony which is practised by the various religious orders of *faqīrs* or *darwīshes*.

DHIMMĪ. A non-Muslim subject of a Muslim government who, for the payment of a poll-tax (*jizyah*), is guaranteed the security of his person and property in a Muslim country.

DHOBĪ. An Indian washerman.

DĪN. The Islamic word for 'Religion', particularly for the religion of the prophets.

DIWĀLĪ. *Lit.* 'a row of lamps'. A Hindu festival at which the houses and streets are illuminated, and the night is spent in gambling.

DĪWĀN. The chancellor of the exchequer of the Mughuls.

DRŪZES. An heretical sect of Muslims which arose, about the beginning of the eleventh century A.D., in the Syrian mountains. They are still found in the Lebanon mountains and near Damascus.

FANĀ. Extinction, or absorption of the personality of the mystic in Allāh. It is the final stage in the journey of the Ṣūfī.

FAQĪR. *Lit.* 'poor', in the sense of being poor in spirit, or in need of the mercy of Allāh. The term is used of those who are members of religious (*darwīsh*) orders.

FARḌ. That which is obligatory. A term used of those rules and ordinances of Islam which are held to have been established by Allāh Himself, as distinguished from those which are based on the precept or example of the Prophet, and which are called *sunnah*.

FĀTIḤAH. The name of the first Sūrah of the Qur'ān.

FĀṬIMIDS. The dynasty of caliphs (*khalīfahs*) which ruled over Egypt and North Africa (A.D. 908–1171), and which claimed descent from Fāṭimah, the daughter of the Prophet and 'Alī.

FATWĀ. A legal decision in Islam based on the *Sharī'at*, given by the Khalīfah, a muftī or a qāḍī.

FIKR. The religious meditation of a Muslim mystic.

FIQH. The branch of Muslim knowledge or 'science' which deals with Muslim law (*Sharī'at*).

G͟HĀZĪ. A hero, a warrior. One who fights in the cause of Islam.

ḤADĪT͟H. Plural *Aḥādīt͟h*. *Lit.* 'a saying'. The technical term used by Muslims to indicate the authoritative collections of Traditions. They are records of what Muḥammad did, what Muḥammad enjoined, and that which was done in his presence which he did not forbid. Sunnīs and Shī'ahs have separate collections of Ḥadīt͟h. The best known are the *Ṣiḥāḥ-us-Sittah* (The Six Correct Collections) of the Sunnīs. These are the collections of:

1. Muḥammad Ismā'īl *al-Buk͟hārī*, A.H. 256.
2. *Muslim* Ibn-ul-Ḥajjāj, A.H. 261.
3. Abū 'Īsā Muḥammad *at-Tirmid͟hī*, A.H. 279.
4. *Abū Dā'ūd* as-Sajistānī, A.H. 275.
5. Abū 'Abd-ir-Raḥmān *an-Nasā'ī*, A.H. 303.
6. Abū 'Abd-Allāh Muḥammad *Ibn Mājah*, A.H. 273.

ḤAḌRAT. *Lit.* 'presence'. A title of respect which is the equivalent of 'your honour', or 'his honour'; when applied to holy persons it may be said to have the meaning 'your reverence', or 'his reverence'.

ḤĀJĪ. A person who has performed the pilgrimage (*ḥajj*) to Mecca. It is also used as an honorific title for one who has performed the *ḥajj*.

ḤAJJ. The pilgrimage to Mecca, which occurs annually in the month of D͟hī'l-Ḥijjah, the twelfth month of the Muslim calendar.

ḤĀL. *Lit.* 'state or condition'. A term used among *darwīshes* to indicate the 'state', or ecstasy, attained by the mystic who induces it by the auto-hypnotic process of *d͟hikr*.

ḤALQAH. A circle or circuit. It refers to the circuit of villages to which the member of a *darwīsh* brotherhood is appointed for the purpose of collection of gifts for the *k͟hānaqāh* (monastery) with which he is connected.

ḤANAFĪ. A follower of the Sunnite legal school, founded by Abū Ḥanīfah, (d. A.H. 150).

ḤAQĪQAH. The final knowledge of things, as they are in Allāh, to which the *Ṣūfī* attains in the last stage of the mystic journey.

ḤARBĪ. From *ḥarb*, meaning 'war'. A person of an infidel country who has not been subjected to a Muslim government, and who does not pay the poll-tax (*jizyah*), which those who have been conquered (*d͟himmīs*) pay.

HIBAH. A legal term used for a gift of property.

HIDDEN IMĀM. The twelfth *imām* of the It͟hnā 'Asharīyah Shī'ahs, Muḥammad, son of Ḥasan al-'Askarī, who is so called because the Shī'ahs believe that he is still alive but has been divinely 'hidden' for a time, and will appear again in the last days as the *Mahdī*.

HIJRAH, or HIJRAT. *Lit.* 'migration'. It has three common

usages: (1) The departure of Muḥammad from Mecca to Medina; (2) The Muslim era; (3) the act of a Muslim leaving a country under infidel rule where it is impossible for the provisions of the *Sharī'at* in respect to religious duties to be carried out.

ḤIMĀYAT. Support, assistance, protection, e.g. Anjuman-i-Ḥimāyat-i-Islam (the society for the protection or assistance of Islam).

'IBĀDAT. *Lit.* 'service'. A term used for 'worship' in Islam, which connotes the 'service' of the *'abd* (slave) rendered as a thing due to Allāh, his Master.

'ĪD. Festival. There are two *'Īds* in Islam of universal importance: the 'Īd-ul-Fiṭr, celebrated at the close of the Fast of Ramaḍān, and the 'Īd-uḍ-Ḍuḥā, or Baqarah 'Īd, celebrated on the tenth day of Dhī'l-Ḥijjah, and is a part of the rites of the Mecca pilgrimage also. Outside every Muslim town or city one will find an *'Īd-gāh* (*lit.* festival-place), where the *'Īd* prayers are said at the time of these festivals.

IJMĀ'. One of the four foundations (*uṣūl*) of Islam. It signifies the collective or unanimous agreement of the learned doctors of the Muslim community, in any matter of the interpretation of Islamic principles.

IJTIHĀD. *Lit.* 'exertion'. The opposite of *ijmā'*, as it expresses the idea of a 'logical deduction' on a legal or theological question by a single learned Islamic doctor or divine.

ILĀHĪ. Divine. Pertaining to Allāh (God).

ILHĀM. Divine inspiration or revelation in the subjective sense.

'ILM. Knowledge.

'ILM-UL-GHAYB. Knowledge of the hidden things, or mysteries.

'ILM-UR-RAML. *Lit.* 'knowledge of the sand'. The art of geomancy, a form of magic.

IMĀM. *Lit.* 'one who goes before'. One whose leadership or example is to be followed. (1) The prayer- (*namāz*, *ṣalāt*) leader of a mosque. (2) The *Imām*, or *Khalīfah* (Caliph) of the Muslim people. (3) The leader of any system of theology or law, e.g. Imām Abū Ḥanīfah, or Imām Al-Ghazālī. (4) The Shī'ahs also apply the term to the leaders of their sect.

IMĀM-BĀRAH. *Lit.* 'the enclosure of the Imāms'. A building in which the festival of the Muḥarram is celebrated, and in which is held the service in commemoration of the deaths of 'Alī and his sons, Ḥasan and Ḥusayn. The most noted one in India is that of Āṣaf-ud-Daulah, at Lucknow.

IMĀMĪ. *Lit.* 'a follower of the Imām'. A follower of the chief sect of the Shī'ahs, i.e. those who follow the twelve Imāms, hence called the *Ithnā 'Asharīyah* (the Twelvers).

IMĀM-UZ-ZAMĀN. *Lit.* 'the leader of the time'. A term

applied by the Bohrahs and Khojahs to those whom they have recognized as their leaders since the concealment of their seventh Imām. Hence the Āghā Khāṇ is the present *Imām-uz-Zamān* of the Khojahs.

Īmān. Faith. The doctrines held by Muslims expressed in the six articles of the Muslim creed or belief: (1) in Allāh; (2) in Angels; (3) in Books revealed by God; (4) in the Prophets of God; (5) in the Day of Judgment; (6) in Predestination of man to good or evil.

Insān-ul-Kāmil. The perfect or ideal man. A term which Ṣūfīs use for one who combines in himself all the attributes of divinity and humanity.

Ishā'at. Spread or propagation, as of Islam.

Islām. 'Resignation or submission' to the will of Allāh. For the 'Faith' (*Īmān*) of Islam, see Īmān. On the practical side Islam consists of five duties, which constitute *Dīn*: (1) Bearing witness (*shahādat*) by the use of the *kalimah* (Lā ilāha illa Allāh, wa Muḥammad-ur-Rasūl Allāh), 'There is no god but Allāh, and Muḥammad is His Apostle'; (2) Reciting the five daily prayers (*ṣalāt* or *namāz*); (3) Giving the legal alms (*zakāt*); (4) Keeping the month's fast (*ṣawm* or *rozah*) of Ramaḍān; (5) Making the pilgrimage (*ḥajj*) to Mecca once in a lifetime.

Ismā'īlī. A follower of the Ismā'īlīyah sect.

Ismā'īlīyah. A Shī'ah sect known as the *Sab'īyah* (Seveners), who hold that the Imāmate closed with Ismā'īl, the son of the sixth Imām, Ja'far-as-Ṣiddīq. They are variously subdivided. The two branches in India which belong to this sect are the Bohrahs and Khojahs.

Ithnā 'Asharīyah. *Lit.* 'Twelvers'. The chief division of the Shī'ahs, which recognizes twelve Imāms, beginning with 'Alī, as successors of the Prophet. They regard the twelfth Imām, Muḥammad, son of Ḥasan al-'Askarī, as the concealed or hidden Imām, who will ultimately appear in the last days as the *Mahdī*.

Jabarūt. One of the mystic stages of the Ṣūfīs, which signifies possession of power.

Jalī. Perceptible, evident, clear. The opposite of *khafī*. A term used to describe a form of the *dhikr*, or ritual, practised by the *darwīsh* orders.

Jamā'at. A congregation or collection of people.

Jamā'at-khānah. An assembly hall or meeting house.

Jāmi' Masjid. The large mosque of a city where the Muslim population is supposed to congregate to say the Friday prayers and hear the Friday sermon (*khuṭbah*), delivered by the preacher (*khaṭīb*). It is also called the Jum'ah (Friday) mosque.

Jam'īyat. An association or conference, as the *Jamī'yat* (conference) *-ul-'Ulamā* (of the learned men) *-i-Hind* (of India).

JAZĪRAT-UL-'ARAB. The peninsula of Arabia.

JIHĀD. 'An effort, or striving', i.e. in the interest of the spread of Islam. A religious or 'holy' war waged by a Muslim ruler or any group of Muslims against unbelievers.

JINN. Commonly known as 'genii'. A species of creature believed in by Muḥammad, which occupies a position between men and angels. Whereas angels were created of light, and men of earth, *jinn* were created of 'smokeless fire'.

JIZYAH. The head or poll-tax, levied upon conquered peoples by a Muslim government to whom the protection of government has been extended.

JUZ. One of the thirty sections into which the Qur'ān is divided, to enable the pious Muslim to recite the whole of the book in the month of Ramaḍān. It is also known as *sīpārah*.

KALIMAH. *Lit.* 'a word', i.e. the shortened form of the Muslim creed: *Lā ilāha illa Allāh, wa Muḥammad Rasūl Allāh* ('There is no God but Allāh, and Muḥammad is the Apostle of God').

KARĀMAT. *Lit.* 'generosity, liberality'. A term used to refer to a miracle performed by a *pīr* (saint) through the 'favour' or 'generosity' of Allāh. The plural is *karāmāt*.

KHAFĪ. Imperceptible, hidden. The opposite of *jalī*; which see.

KHALĪFAH. A successor, viceregent or deputy. The Caliph of Sunnī Islam.

KHĀNAQĀH. A monastery of the *darwīsh* orders. Also called *takyah*.

KHĀNDĀN. 'A family'. A term used to signify a *darwīsh* order, as the *Chishtī khāndān*.

KHAN-I-SĀMĀN. *Lit.* 'ruler of the property'. The title of the lord high steward of government property.

KHARĀJ. The land-tax due to a Muslim government.

KHAṬĪB. A preacher. One who delivers the Friday sermon (*khuṭbah*) at the mosque.

KHATM or KHATMAH. A recitation of the whole of the Qur'ān at one sitting.

KHAṬRAH. Plural, *khaṭrāt*. That which occurs to the mind. Used in a technical sense by the Ṣūfīs to indicate divine illumination of the heart.

KHILĀFAT. The office of the *Khalīfah* (Caliph). The Caliphate.

KHIL'AT. A robe of honour presented by a ruler to an inferior, as a mark of favour and distinction.

KHOJAHS. One of the Ismā'īlian sects of India, the leader of the chief branch of which is His Highness the Āghā Khān.

KHUṬBAH. *Lit.* 'an address'. The sermon delivered on Fridays at the mosque at the time of the *ẓuhr*, or mid-day prayer.

KHWĀJAH. A gentleman; a respectable man. A title of honour or reverence prefixed to the name of a *pīr* (saint), as Khwājah Mu'īn-ud-Dīn Chishtī.

LĀHŪT. 'Divine nature.' A term used for the last stage of the mystic journey of the Ṣūfī, which is absorption of individuality in Allāh.

LAYLAT-UL-QADR. 'The night of power or decree.' A night of the month of Ramaḍān the date of which is not now known. See *Sūrat-ul-Qadr* (xcvii) of the Qur'ān.

MADHHAB. 'A way, path.' Hence a religion. Plural, *madhāhib*.

MADRASAH. 'A place where teaching is done.' A school, particularly a school where the Islamic 'sciences' (*'ulūm*) are taught.

MAHDAWĪ. A follower of the Mahdī.

MAHDĪ. *Lit.* 'The directed or guided one'. The eschatological belief of Muslims regarding the mighty one who will appear in the last days.

MAKTAB. 'A place where writing is taught.' The name given to the primary school commonly held in a mosque.

MALAKŪT. 'The nature of angels.' A stage of progress in the way of the Ṣūfī where one is said to attain to the nature of angels.

MANSŪKH. 'The cancelled one.' A term used for a verse or sentence of the Qur'ān or Ḥadīth which has been cancelled or abrogated by a later one.

MAQĀMĀT. *Lit.* 'stages'. The stages of the mystic journey of the Ṣūfī.

MARHAM-I-'ĪSĀ. The ointment of Jesus. The ointment which the Aḥmadīs of Qadian assert was used by the disciples to restore Jesus to life after he was taken down from the cross. An ointment by this name is prepared and sold by the followers of Mīrzā Ghulām Aḥmad of Qadian.

MA'RIFAH. 'Knowledge', especially the *gnosis* of the Ṣūfī when in a state of ecstasy.

MASJID. *Lit.* 'a place of prostration', i.e. before Allāh. Hence a place of worship, a mosque.

MAULVĪ or MAWLAWĪ. A learned man, a graduate in theology.

MINĀR. A tower, as of a mosque, e.g. the Quṭb Minār of Delhi.

MUFTĪ. *Lit.* 'one who gives a legal decision', i.e. on the Muslim *Sharī'at* (canon law). The title of a subordinate law officer who assists the *qāḍī* (judge).

MUGHUL. The Arabic form of the word 'Mongol'. The term is erroneously applied to the Turkish dynasty founded at Delhi by Bābur, A.D. 1526, to distinguish it from the dynasty of the Ottoman Turks. It is a term also applied to one of the four chief social divisions of the Muslims of India. See *Sharīf Zāt*.

MUḤARRAM. *Lit.* 'that which is forbidden', hence anything sacred. (1) It is the name of the first month of the Muslim calendar. (2) It is the name of a festival observed particularly by Shī'ahs (though by many Sunnīs as well in India) during the first ten days of the month of Muḥarram, in commemoration of the martyrdom of Ḥusayn, who was the second son of Fāṭimah, the Prophet's daughter, by 'Alī.

MUḤTASIB. The public censor appointed by a Muslim ruler to hunt out and punish Muslims for neglecting the rites and prohibitions of their religion.

MUJADDID. *Lit.* 'a renewer'. There is a Muslim belief that in every century Allāh sends a person specially endowed with grace for the 'renewal' of the true faith, whose duty it is to sweep away the un-Islamic accretions, and initiate a widespread revival of true religion.

MUJTAHID. *Lit.* 'one who strives', i.e. to attain a high position of scholarship and learning. It is the highest degree conferred on Muslim divines.

MUKKUVĀN. A fisherman caste of the Malabar coast.

MULHID or MULĀHIDAH. *Lit.* 'one who has deviated or turned from the truth' of religion. A heretic.

MULLĀ. A learned man, a scholar.

MUQADDAM. *Lit.* 'the one who is placed first'. The head or chief of a village.

MURĪD. *Lit.* 'one who is desirous'. A disciple of a *pīr*, or *murshid* of a *darwīsh* order.

MURJĪ. *Lit.* 'procrastinator'. One of the sect of Muslims who teach that the judgment of every true believer, who has committed a *gunāh kabīrah* (grievous sin), will be deferred till the Resurrection.

MURSHID. *Lit.* 'one who guides aright'. The title of the spiritual director of a *darwīsh* order. Also called *pīr*.

MUSHĀ'ARAH. An assemblage of poets (*shu'arā*) who meet for a contest of their poetical abilities.

MUSHRIK. *Lit.* 'one who joins' or gives associates to Allāh, hence a polytheist, an idolater.

MUSLIM. *Lit.* 'one who submits' to Allāh, hence a follower of the faith of Islam.

MUSTA'LIAN. A follower of the Ismā'īlian sect which accepts the right of Mustā'lī rather than his brother Niẓār to succeed his father, al-Mustanṣir, the Fāṭimid Caliph of Egypt. The sect in India is represented by the Bohrahs; the Khojahs being the representatives of those who supported the claims of Niẓār.

MU'TAZILAH. *Lit.* 'the separatists'. A rationalistic sect of Muslims, founded by Wāṣil ibn 'Aṭā, who 'separated' from the school of Ḥasan al-Baṣrī (A.H. 110).

NABĪ. A prophet.

NAFL. A voluntary act. A work of supererogation which is not demanded by the teaching of Muḥammad (*farḍ* or *wājib*) nor by his example (*sunnah*).

NAMĀZ. The Persian and common Indian Muslim term for prayer (*ṣalāt*) in its liturgical form.

NAQSHBANDĪYAH. A *darwīsh* (ascetic) order, founded by Khwājah Pīr Muḥammad Naqshband.

NĀSIKH. *Lit.* 'The Canceller'. A term used for a verse or sentence of the Qur'ān or Ḥadīth which cancels or abrogates a previous one.

NĀSŪT. 'Human nature'. A term used by Ṣūfīs to express the natural state of every man before he enters upon the mystic journey.

NAU-GAZĀ PĪR. The tomb or shrine of any legendary person supposed to have been of enormous height. The term signifies 'the nine-yard saint'.

NECHARĪ. 'Naturī', from Nature. The term is applied to Sir Syed Aḥmad and his modernist followers, who emphasized the position that Islam was a religion according to Nature: the nature of man, and Nature in the scientific sense.

NEO-MU'TAZILITE. Another term used to describe the modern Indo-Muslim rationalists, like Sir Syed Aḥmad, who in some ways resemble the Mu'tazilites of former times. See *Mu'tazilah.*

NIẒĀRĪ. A follower of the sect of Ismā'īlians who regard Niẓār as being the rightful successor to his father, al-Mustanṣir, Fāṭimid Caliph of Egypt. Their representatives in India are the Khojahs. See *Musta'lian.*

PURDAH. A curtain or veil. The term applied to the system of seclusion of Muslim women in India.

PATHĀN. *Syn.* AFGHĀN. The name of a tribe inhabiting the mountains north-west of Lahore; the name of a dynasty that ruled at Delhi; the name of one of the four major social divisions of the Muslims of India.

PĪR. An elder. A term used for a *murshid* (spiritual director) of a *darwīsh* order.

PĪR DASTGĪR. 'Guardian saint.' A title especially applied to the saint, 'Abd-ul-Qādir Jīlānī by the Muslims of the Punjab and the north-west, particularly Kashmir.

PĪRĪ-MURĪDĪ. The practice of making disciples (*murīd*) by spiritual preceptors (*pīr* or *murshid*) of *darwīsh* orders.

PĪR-I-PĪRĀN. 'The saint of saints.' The title often given to the famous saint of Baghdad, 'Abd-ul-Qādir Jīlānī.

QADAM SHARĪF, or QADAM RASŪL ALLĀH. A slab of stone bearing an alleged footprint of the Prophet. Such 'relics' are very common in India.

Qāḍī. A judge.

Qādirīyah. A *darwīsh* order founded by 'Abd-ul-Qādir Jīlānī of Baghdad.

Qāḍī-ul-quḍāt. The chief justice.

Qalandar. A common name for a Muslim ascetic. It is also the name of a *darwīsh* order, introduced into India by Abū (Bū) 'Alī Qalandar, whose tomb is at Panipat.

Qalandarīyah. The name of the *darwīsh* order introduced into India by Abū 'Alī Qalandar. See *Qalandar*.

Qarmaṭian, or Qarmaṭī. An heretical sect of Muslims, allied closely to the Ismā'īlis some of whom, after expulsion from Egypt and Iraq, established themselves in Sind in the latter part of the ninth century A.D.

Qur'ān. *Lit.* 'the reading'. The name of the sacred book of the Muslims.

Rak'ah. 'A bowing.' A section of the Muslim prayers.

Ramaḍān. The ninth month of the Muslim calendar, during which a strict fast is observed from dawn until sundown.

Ribā. Usury. The taking of interest on loans, which is forbidden according to the *Sharī'at*.

Roshanīyah. The followers of one, Pīr Roshan, of Jullundur, in the Punjab, who founded an heretical sect on the frontier, beyond Peshawar, in the sixteenth century A.D. They are now almost extinct.

Rozah. This is the Persian word for the Arabic *Ṣawm*, which means fasting.

Sab'īyah. *Lit.* 'Seveners'. See *Ismā'īlīyah*.

Ṣadr-i-Jahān. A title applied to the officer of the court at Delhi who was in charge of the lawyers and learned men (*'ulamā*).

Ṣadr-us-Ṣudūr. The title of an officer of the Muslim government at Delhi who was in charge of religious endowments and trusts (*waqfs*).

Ṣaḥiḥ. *Lit.* 'correct, sound'. A term applied to the six authoritative collections of Traditions (*Aḥādīth*). See *Ḥadīth*.

Sajjādah Nishīn. *Lit.* 'one who sits on the prayer rug'. A title applied to the living head of a *darwīsh* order or sub-order.

Ṣalāt. The term used throughout the Muslim world for the liturgical form of prayer which occurs five times a day. The common Persian term used in India is *Namāz*.

Sālik. *Lit.* 'a traveller'. A term used to describe one who has become a disciple (*murīd*) of a *murshid* (spiritual director) of a *darwīsh* order, and has started the journey on the mystic way of life.

Sarā'ī. A vulgar form of *sarā*. An inn, a temporary home for travellers.

Sayyid. *Lit.* 'lord, chief'. Any descendant of Muḥammad.

Also, one of the four, and chief, of the social divisions into which Indian Muslims are divided. See *Sharīf Zāt*.

SEVENERS. See *Ismā'īlīyah*; and *Sab'īyah*.

SHĀFI'Ī. One of the founders of the four legal sects of Sunnīs, whose whole name was Imām Muḥammad ibn Idrīs ash-Shāfi'ī. Also a follower of the school of ash-Shāfi'ī. In India they are found chiefly among the Mappillas of south India.

SHAHĪD. *Lit.* 'a witness'. One who dies as a martyr for the Muslim faith.

SHARĪ'AT. The canon law of Islam, including that which is based on the Qur'ān and the Traditions (*Ḥadīth*).

SHARĪF ZĀT (DHĀT). The noble, or high, castes in Indian Muslim society. These are four in number, and are stated in order of importance: Sayyid, Shaykh, Mughul, Pathān.

SHARQĪ. Eastern. A term applied to the 'eastern' kings of Jaunpur.

SHAṬṬĀRĪYAH. One of the *darwīsh* orders found in India.

SHAYKH. A term used to denote any one of the following: (1) an old man; (2) a man of authority; (3) a religious teacher; (4) the head of an order of *darwīshes*; (5) one of the four chief social divisions among Indian Muslims. See *Sharīf Zāt*.

SHAYKH-UL-ISLĀM. A title given to an officer of the Muslim government at Delhi who was in charge of the *darwīshes* and *faqīrs*.

SHĪ'AH. *Lit.* 'the followers (of a person), or party'. Particularly the 'followers' of 'Alī, who, as first cousin of the Prophet, and husband of his daughter, Fāṭimah, regard him and his heirs as the rightful successors of the Prophet. See *Ismā'īlīyah* and *Ithnā 'Asharīyah*.

SHIRK. 'Joining, or associating', others with Allāh. Ascribing plurality to the deity. It is a common term for polytheism and idolatry.

SIḤR. Magic. A belief in the magical art.

ṢŪFĪ. A person who professes the mystic doctrines known as *taṣawwuf*, Islamic mysticism. See *Darwīsh*.

ṢŪFĪISM. The mystic doctrines, principles and practices (*taṣawwuf*) of Islamic mystics. A form of pantheism rooting in Hindu-Buddhist doctrines. The *darwīsh* orders are the natural result of the development of Ṣūfīism.

SUHRAWARDĪYAH. A name of one of the *darwīsh* orders found in India.

SUNNAH. *Lit.* 'a path or way; a manner of life'. A term which has become applied to the tradition which records either the sayings or doings of Muḥammad.

SUNNĪ. *Lit.* 'one of the path'. A follower of Tradition. The term usually applied to the major sect of Muslims, who recognize the first four Khalīfahs as the rightful successors of Muḥammad.

TABARRUK. *Lit.* 'that which brings a blessing'. A portion of the offering of food, flowers, or anything else, made to a saint's shrine; sacred relics.

TABLĪGH. Propaganda, particularly of the religious sort.

TAHDHĪB. *Lit.* 'purifying, cleaning'. Hence, reform, e.g. the magazine, *Tahdhīb-ul-Akhlāq* (The Moral Reformer).

TAKBĪR. The expression used by Muslims, *Allāhu Akbar* (God is very great).

TAKYAH. *Lit.* 'a pillow'. A monastery. See *Khānaqāh.*

TANẒĪM. *Lit.* 'ordering, arranging'. A term of modern application used with reference to the movement in India for the economic, educational, and religious improvement of the condition of Indian Muslims. An essentially communal movement.

TAQĪYAH. *Lit.* 'guarding oneself'. A Shī'ah doctrine, whereby a Shī'ah believes he is justified in concealing his religious affiliation in order to avoid religious persecution.

TAQLĪD. *Lit.* 'winding round'. A term used in Muslim law to signify the following of a religious leader blindly or without due inquiry.

TARAQQĪ. *Lit.* 'gradual rising'. Hence, improvement, increase.

TA'RĪKH. Date, history. Plural, *tawārīkh.*

TARĪQAH. *Lit.* 'a path'. A term used by the Ṣūfīs for their special form of the religious life.

TAṢAWWUF. The term used to signify Islamic mysticism, or the doctrines and principles of the Ṣūfī. *Syn.* Ṣūfiism.

TASBĪḤ. A rosary of ninety-nine beads.

TAWBAH. Repentance.

TAWḤĪD. The term used to express the unity of God, which is the great fundamental doctrine of Islam.

TA'WĪDH. *Lit.* 'to flee for refuge'. A charm or amulet used by Muslims.

TA'ZIYAH. *Lit.* 'a consolation'. A representation or model of the tomb of the martyr, Ḥusayn, at Karbala, which is carried in procession at Muḥarram time.

TWELVERS. See *Ithnā 'Asharīyah.*

'ULAMĀ. Plural of '*ālim*,' one who knows'. The learned doctors of Muslim society.

'UMAR. The name of the second Khalīfah.

UMAYYAD. The name of the dynasty of Khalīfahs which succeeded the fourth Khalīfah, 'Alī, and reigned in Damascus from A.D. 661 to A.D. 749.

'URS. Wedding or marriage festivities. It has come to be used as a term for the ceremonies observed at the anniversary of the death of a saint (*pīr* or *murshid*).

USTĀDH. A preceptor, or teacher.

'UTHMĀN. The third Khalīfah.

WAHHĀBĪ. A sect of Muslim puritan revivalists, founded in the eighteenth century in Najd, Arabia, by Muḥammad bin 'Abd-ul-Wahhāb. The sect is found in India under the name *Ahl-i-Ḥadīth*.

WAḤY. Revelation, or divine inspiration. A term used with special reference to the objective revelation of the Qur'ān. See *Ilhām*.

WĀ'IẒ. Plural, *wā'iẓīn*. A preacher. A term of more general application than *khaṭīb*.

WAJD. Ecstasy. A term used by Ṣūfīs to indicate the state of divine illumination achieved by a traveller on the mystic path.

WALĪ. Plural, *awliyā*. One who is very near, i.e. to Allāh. A term used for saints or holy men.

WAQF. *Lit.* 'standing'. An endowment. Property which has been dedicated to charitable uses and the service of God.

WAṢĪ. 'An appointed guardian, executor of a will.' A term applied to 'Alī to indicate his legal right to be the Khalīfah of Muḥammad.

WAṢL. 'Meeting, union.' A Ṣūfī term, describing the stage of the mystic journey to Allāh where the *sālik* (traveller) sees the divine one face to face. It is the stage which immediately precedes *fanā*, or extinction of individuality, in the *dhāt* (essence) of Allāh.

YOGĪ. A Hindu ascetic.

ZAKĀT. The legal alms due from all Muslims who are free, sane, and adults.

ZANĀNAH. Derived from the Persian word *zan* (woman), and so is applied to the household of a Muslim, his wife or wives, and children, and the apartments which they occupy.

ZĀR. A crude, ritualistic service of exorcism, practised extensively in Muslim countries, particularly in Egypt.

ZĀT. See *Dhāt*.

ZIMMĪ. See *Dhimmī*.

ZIYĀRAT, or ZIYĀRAH. 'A visit.' A visit to the grave of the Prophet, or to the tomb of any Muslim saint. In India the term is used to denote the place of visitation, i.e. the tomb or shrine itself. This is true, particularly, in Kashmir.

ZUHD. *Lit.* 'religious devotion, renunciation of the world'. Asceticism.

INDEX